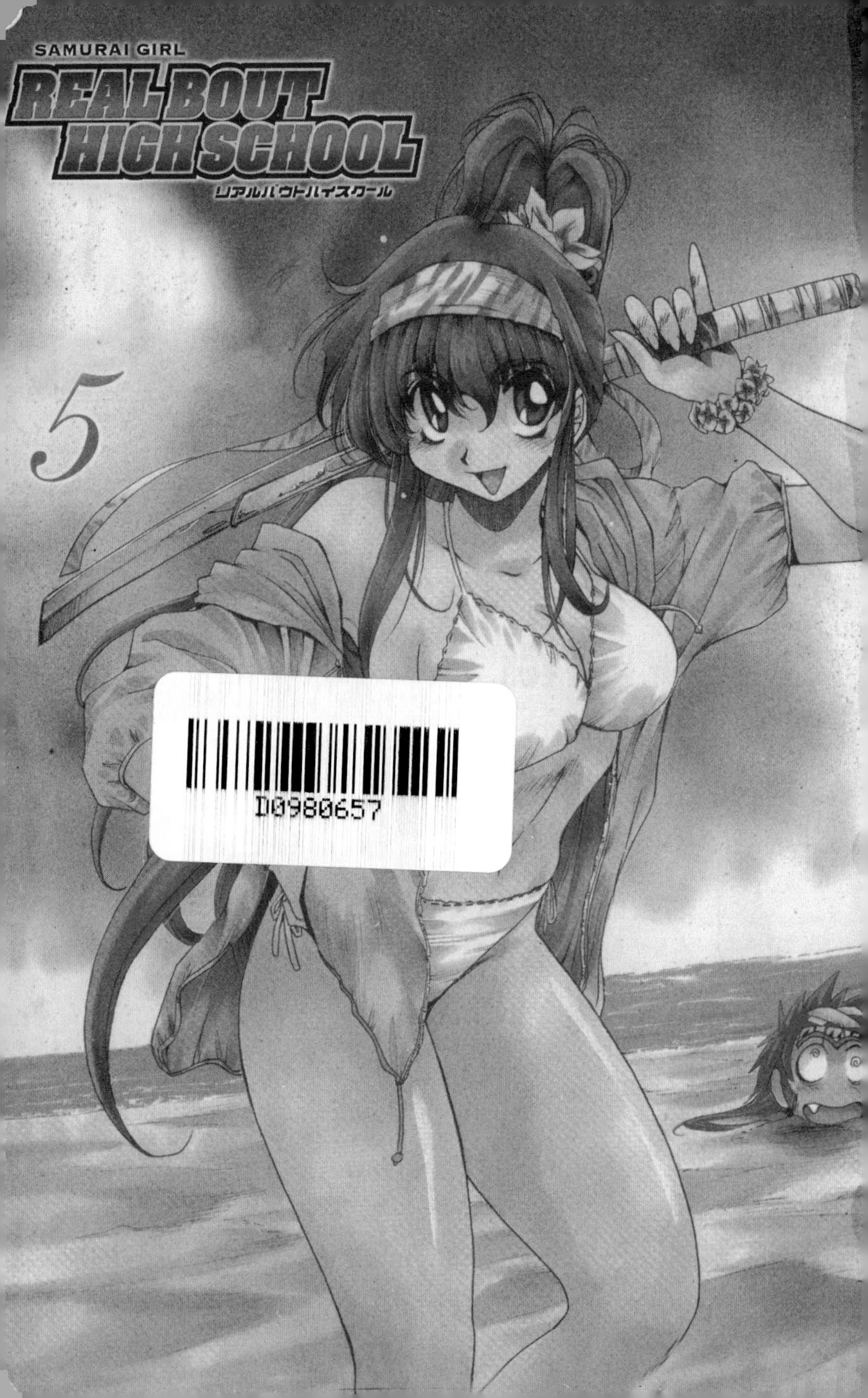
SAMURAI GIRL
REAL BOUT HIGH SCHOOL
リアルバウトハイスクール
5

ALSO AVAILABLE FROM

MANGA

ACTION

ANGELIC LAYER*
CLAMP SCHOOL DETECTIVES* (April 2003)
DIGIMON (March 2003)
DUKLYON: CLAMP SCHOOL DEFENDERS* (September 2003)
GATEKEEPERS* (March 2003)
GTO*
HARLEM BEAT
INITIAL D*
ISLAND
JING: KING OF BANDITS* (June 2003)
JULINE
LUPIN III*
MONSTERS, INC.
PRIEST
RAVE*
REAL BOUT HIGH SCHOOL*
REBOUND* (April 2003)
SAMURAI DEEPER KYO* (June 2003)
SCRYED* (March 2003)
SHAOLIN SISTERS* (February 2003)
THE SKULL MAN*

FANTASY

CHRONICLES OF THE CURSED SWORD (July 2003)
DEMON DIARY (May 2003)
DRAGON HUNTER (June 2003)
DRAGON KNIGHTS*
KING OF HELL (June 2003)
PLANET LADDER*
RAGNAROK
REBIRTH (March 2003)
SHIRAHIME: TALES OF THE SNOW PRINCESS* (December 2003)
SORCERER HUNTERS
WISH*

CINE-MANGA™

AKIRA*
CARDCAPTORS
KIM POSSIBLE (March 2003)
LIZZIE McGUIRE (March 2003)
POWER RANGERS (May 2003)
SPY KIDS 2 (March 2003)

ANIME GUIDES

GUNDAM TECHNICAL MANUALS
COWBOY BEBOP
SAILOR MOON SCOUT GUIDES

ROMANCE

HAPPY MANIA* (April 2003)
I.N.V.U. (February 2003)
LOVE HINA*
KARE KANO*
KODOCHA*
MAN OF MANY FACES* (May 2003)
MARMALADE BOY*
MARS*
PARADISE KISS*
PEACH GIRL
UNDER A GLASS MOON (June 2003)

SCIENCE FICTION

CHOBITS*
CLOVER
COWBOY BEBOP*
COWBOY BEBOP: SHOOTING STAR* (June 2003)
G-GUNDAM*
GUNDAM WING
GUNDAM WING: ENDLESS WALTZ*
GUNDAM: THE LAST OUTPOST*
PARASYTE
REALITY CHECK (March 2003)

MAGICAL GIRLS

CARDCAPTOR SAKURA
CARDCAPTOR SAKURA: MASTER OF THE CLOW*
CORRECTOR YUI
MAGIC KNIGHT RAYEARTH* (August 2003)
MIRACLE GIRLS
SAILOR MOON
SAINT TAIL
TOKYO MEW MEW* (April 2003)

NOVELS

SAILOR MOON
SUSHI SQUAD (April 2003)

ART BOOKS

CARDCAPTOR SAKURA*
MAGIC KNIGHT RAYEARTH*

TOKYOPOP KIDS

DISNEY CLASSICS (June 2003)
STRAY SHEEP (September 2003)

SAMURAI GIRL

REAL BOUT HIGH SCHOOL

リアルバウトハイスクール

Volume 5

Art by Sora Inoue
Story by Reiji Saiga

Los Angeles • Tokyo

Translator - Ai Kennedy
English Adaption - Taliesin Jaffe
Retouch and Lettering - Paul Tanck
Cover Layout - Anna Kernbaum

Senior Editor - Luis Reyes
Managing Editor - Jill Freshney
Production Manager - Jennifer Miller
Art Director - Matthew Alford
VP of Production & Manufacturing - Ron Klamert
President & C.O.O. - John Parker
Publisher - Stuart Levy

Email: editor@TOKYOPOP.com
Come visit us online at www.TOKYOPOP.com

A ⬥TOKYOPOP⬥Manga
TOKYOPOP® is an imprint of Mixx Entertainment, Inc.
5900 Wilshire Blvd. Suite 2000, Los Angeles, CA 90036

ISBN: 1-59182-107-X

First TOKYOPOP® printing: February 2003

10 9 8 7 6 5 4 3 2 1

Printed in the USA

THE STORY THUS FAR . . .

More than anything else, Ryoko Mitsurugi wants to be a great woman, and she has set on achieving this goal in life by taking up the code of the warrior and becoming one of the best Kendo combatants at Daimon High School.

Of course, life at Daimon High School isn't exactly the easiest stretch in a student's academic career. Too many martial arts groups vie for too few training studios, a situation that prompts spontaneous and large-scale battles on campus. Luckily, Principal Todo - a man defined as much by his bloodlust as by his commitment to education - has set up the K-Fight system in which students and teachers can settle disputes, differences of opinion and personal vendettas through sanctioned combat. When do students find time to study? When they're laid up in the hospital licking their wounds.

Ryoko used to bury her insecurities and emotions well beneath her gruff exterior, fettered as she was with a romantic longing for her Kendo sparring partner, Tatsuya. Unfortunately, he has transferred to another school, and left our little samurai girl to find her own emotional strength... which she did in spades fighting Daimon's other female martial arts champion Azumi Kiribayashi, who also had a crush on Tatsuya but was far less physically weakened by his departure.

Now, transformed into a bad-ass, female wrecking machine, she's been approached by student body president Isozaki to head up an all-female team of warriors called Shinsengumi, charged with ridding the schools and the town of hoodlums and thugs. But amongst the undesirables are G, a street smart capitalist who longs to cash in on Shinsengumi fights; Taiho, a street boxer who wants to be more than another fighter in his boxing family; and, of course, Shizuma Kusanagi, a career brawler who hasn't decided on which side of the fence he's going to land - with G and his band of thugs, or with Ryoko and her fighting femmes.

The spectators have gathered at the gates of Dragon Land where Isozaki has set the training of his elite squad... but the girls are nowhere to be found. And after Ryoko's brutal ass-kicking by G at the end of the last volume, perhaps it's time to worry a bit.

CONTENTS

5

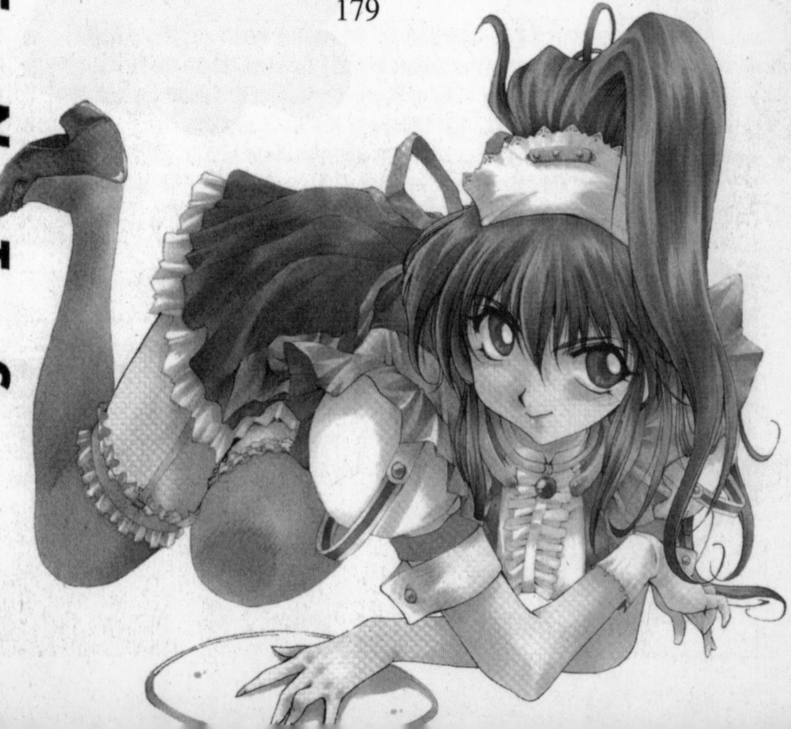

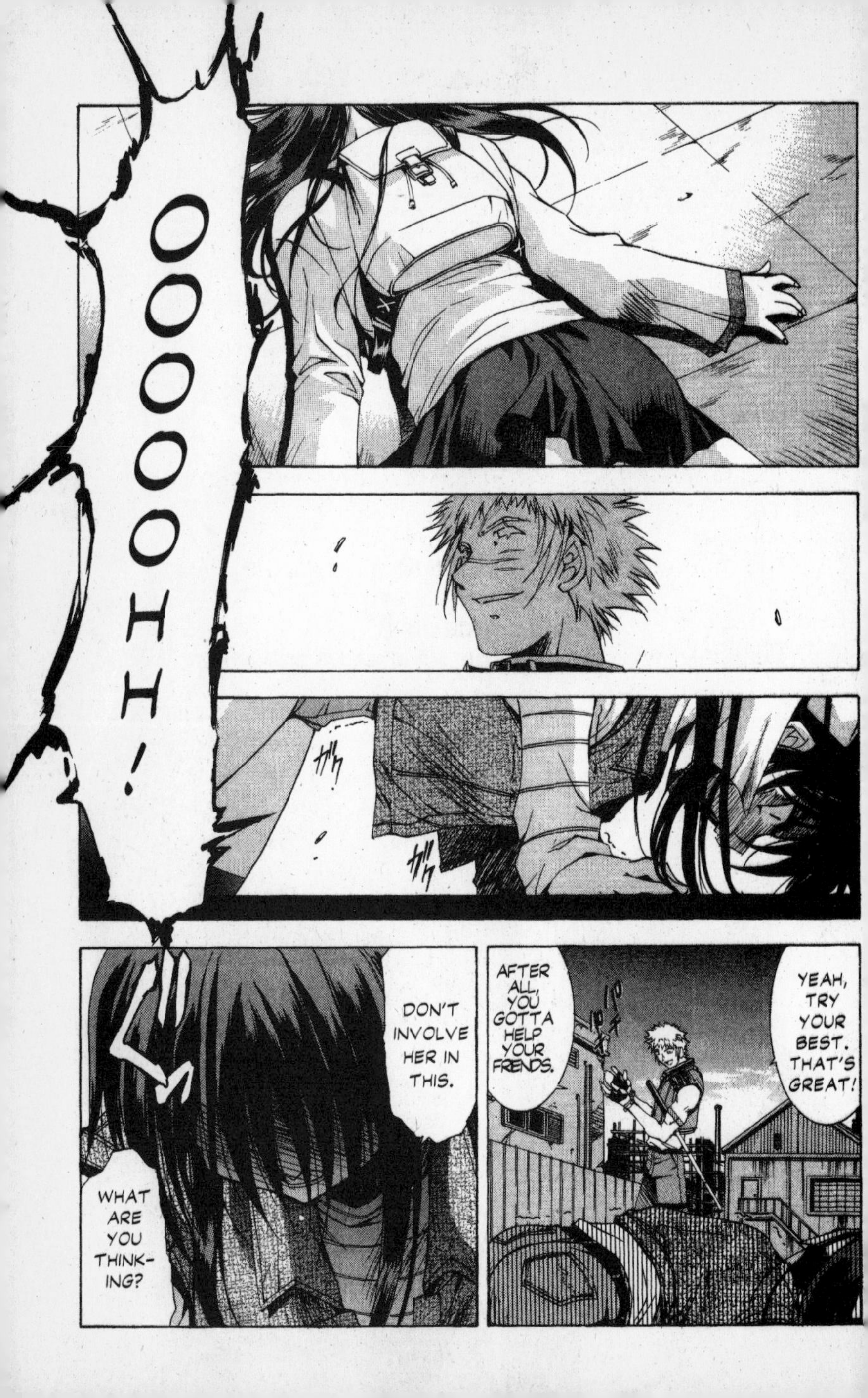

OOOOOHH!
YEAH, TRY YOUR BEST. THAT'S GREAT!
AFTER ALL, YOU GOTTA HELP YOUR FRIENDS.
DON'T INVOLVE HER IN THIS.
WHAT ARE YOU THINKING?

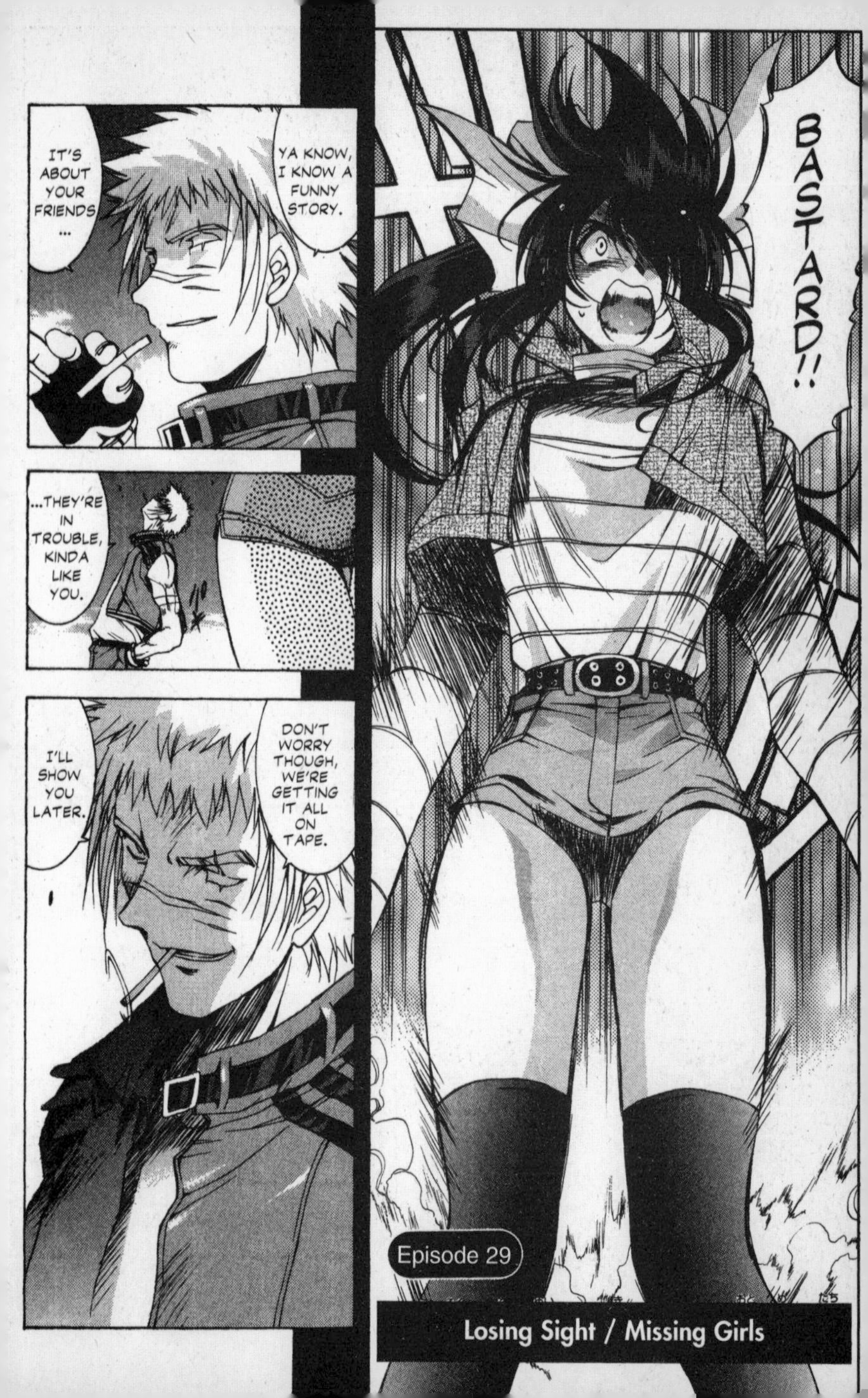
BASTARD!!
Episode 29
Losing Sight / Missing Girls
YA KNOW, I KNOW A FUNNY STORY.
IT'S ABOUT YOUR FRIENDS ...
...THEY'RE IN TROUBLE, KINDA LIKE YOU.
DON'T WORRY THOUGH, WE'RE GETTING IT ALL ON TAPE.
I'LL SHOW YOU LATER.

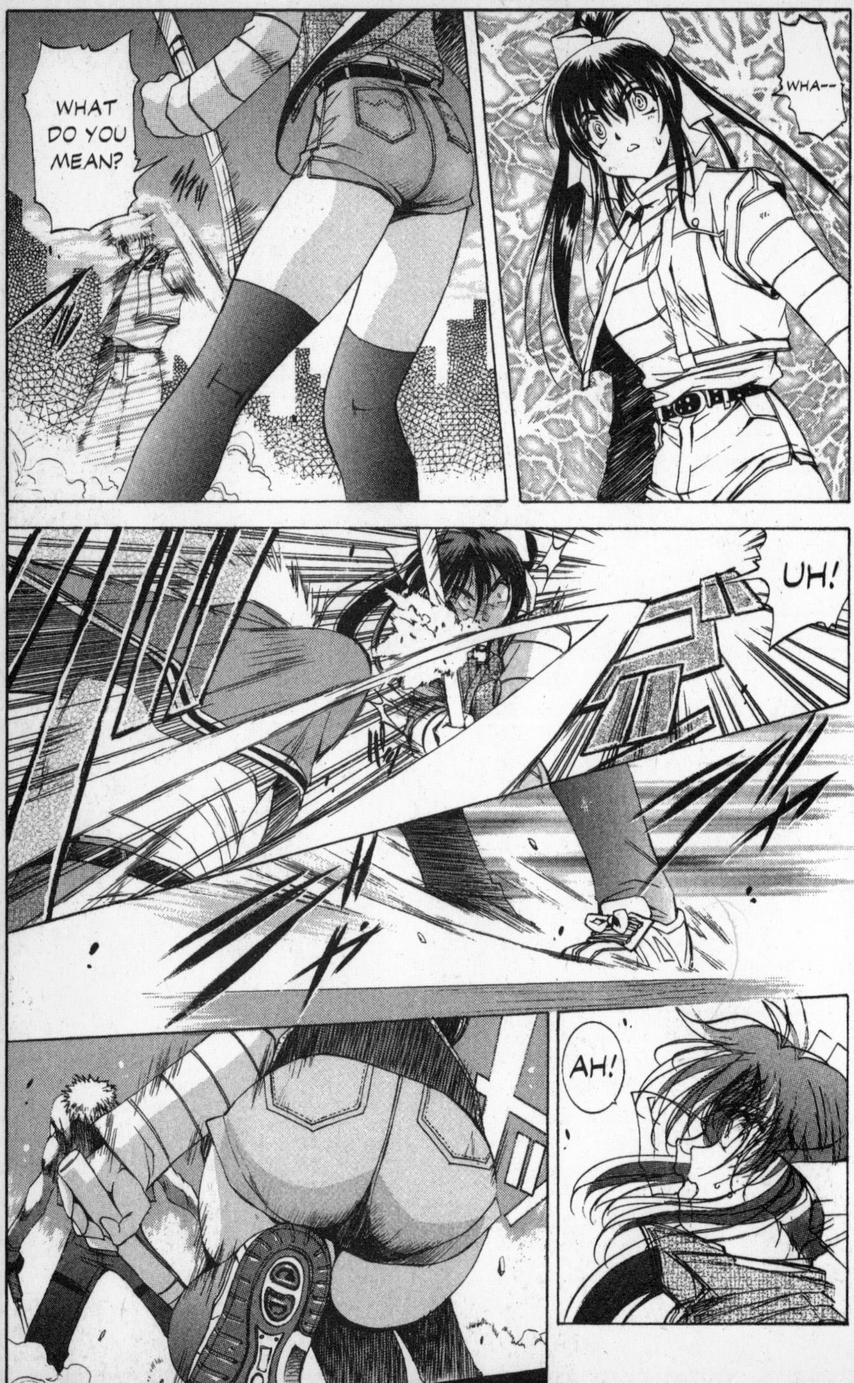
WHA--
WHAT DO YOU MEAN?
UH!
AH!

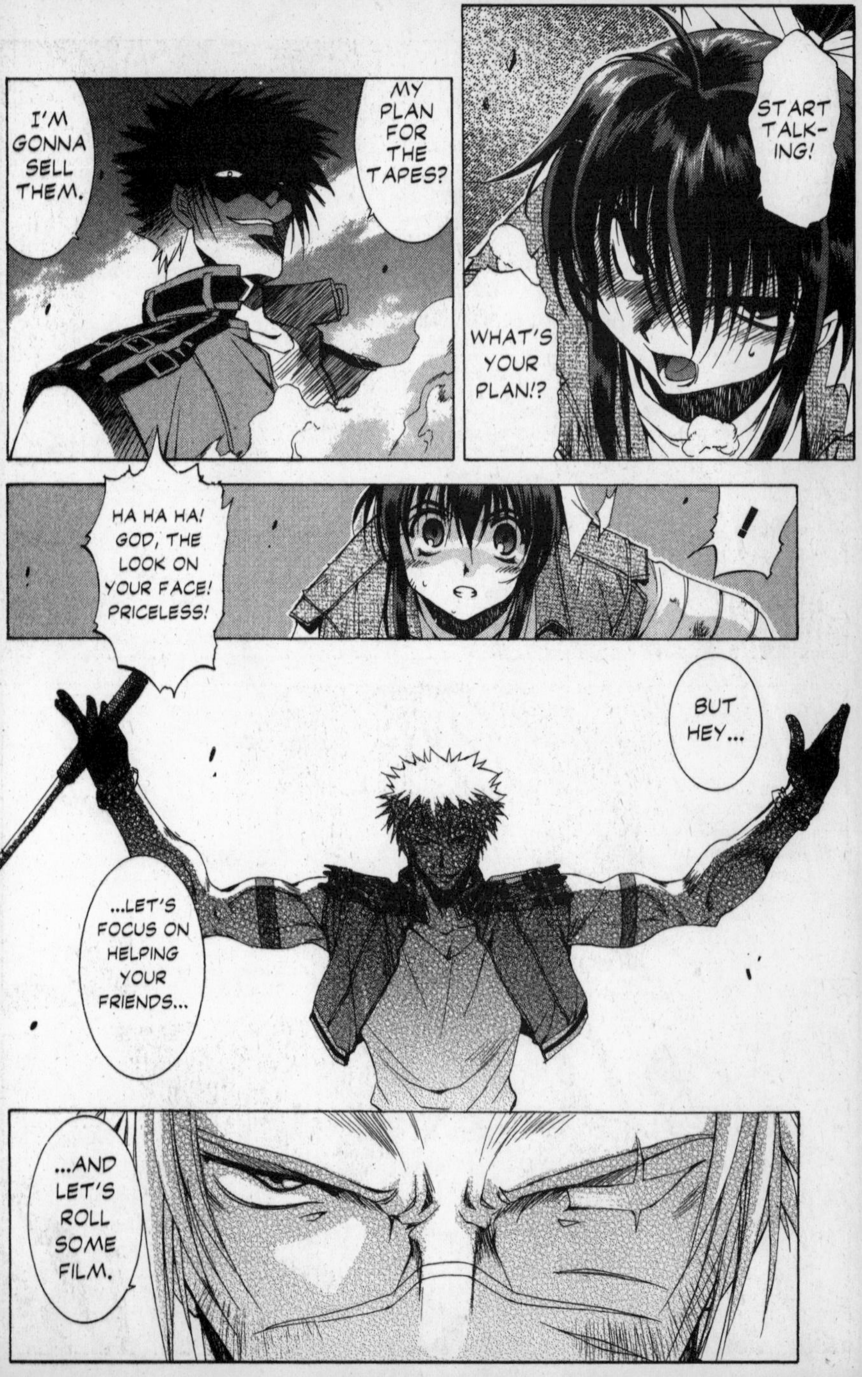

START TALKING!
WHAT'S YOUR PLAN!?
MY PLAN FOR THE TAPES?
I'M GONNA SELL THEM.
!
HA HA HA! GOD, THE LOOK ON YOUR FACE! PRICELESS!
BUT HEY...
...LET'S FOCUS ON HELPING YOUR FRIENDS...
...AND LET'S ROLL SOME FILM.

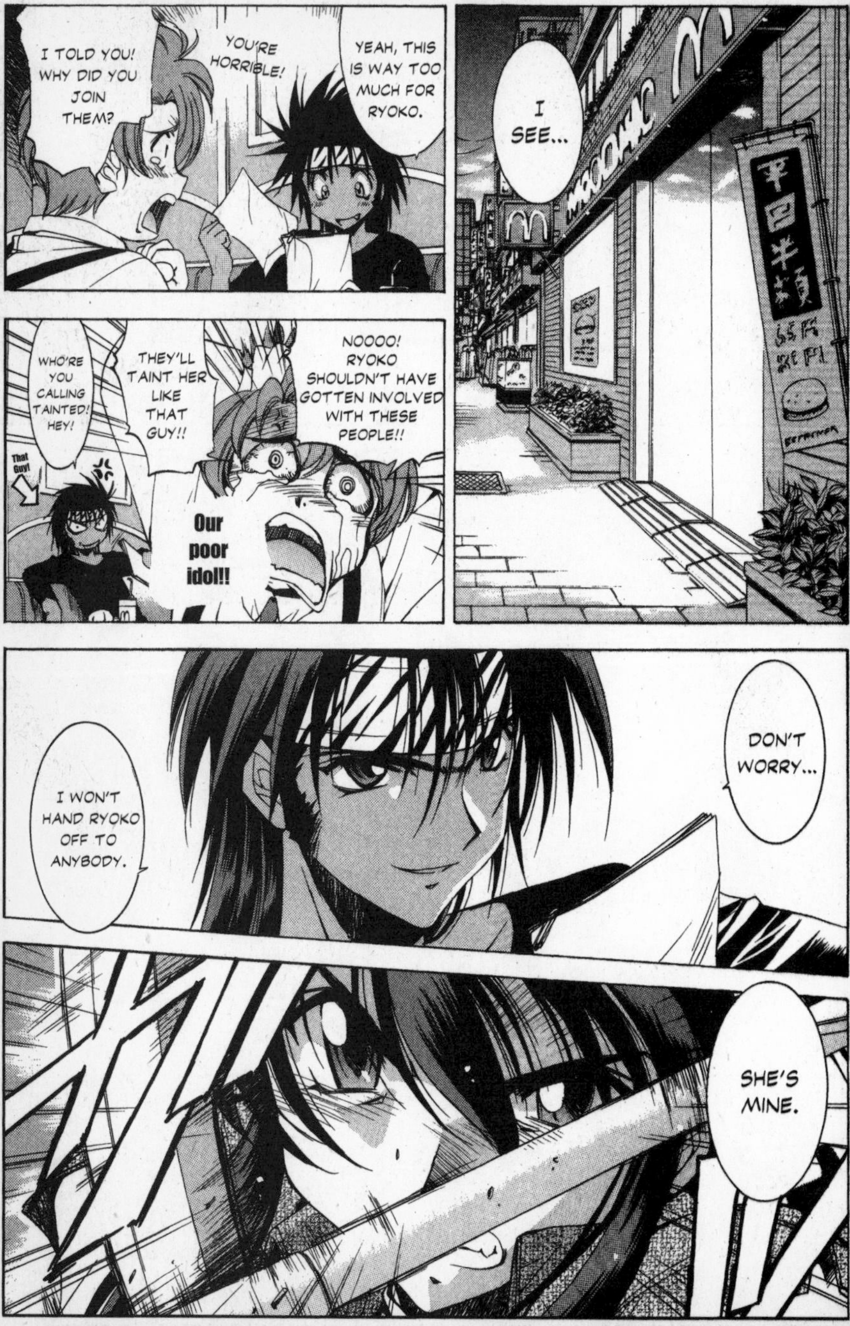
I SEE...
YEAH, THIS IS WAY TOO MUCH FOR RYOKO.
YOU'RE HORRIBLE!
I TOLD YOU! WHY DID YOU JOIN THEM?
NOOOO! RYOKO SHOULDN'T HAVE GOTTEN INVOLVED WITH THESE PEOPLE!!
Our poor idol!!
THEY'LL TAINT HER LIKE THAT GUY!!
WHO'RE YOU CALLING TAINTED! HEY!
That Guy!
DON'T WORRY...
I WON'T HAND RYOKO OFF TO ANYBODY.
SHE'S MINE.

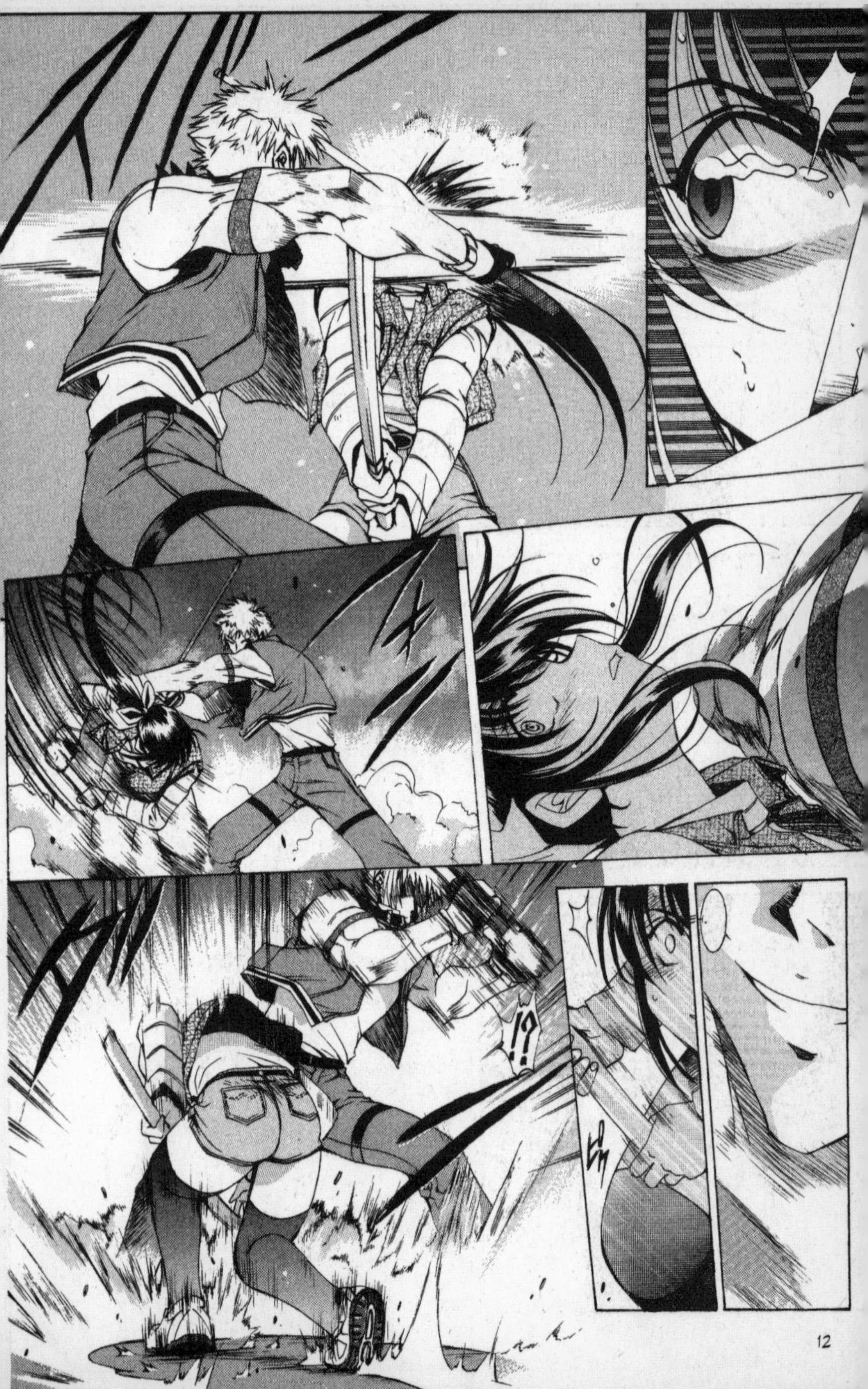
!?

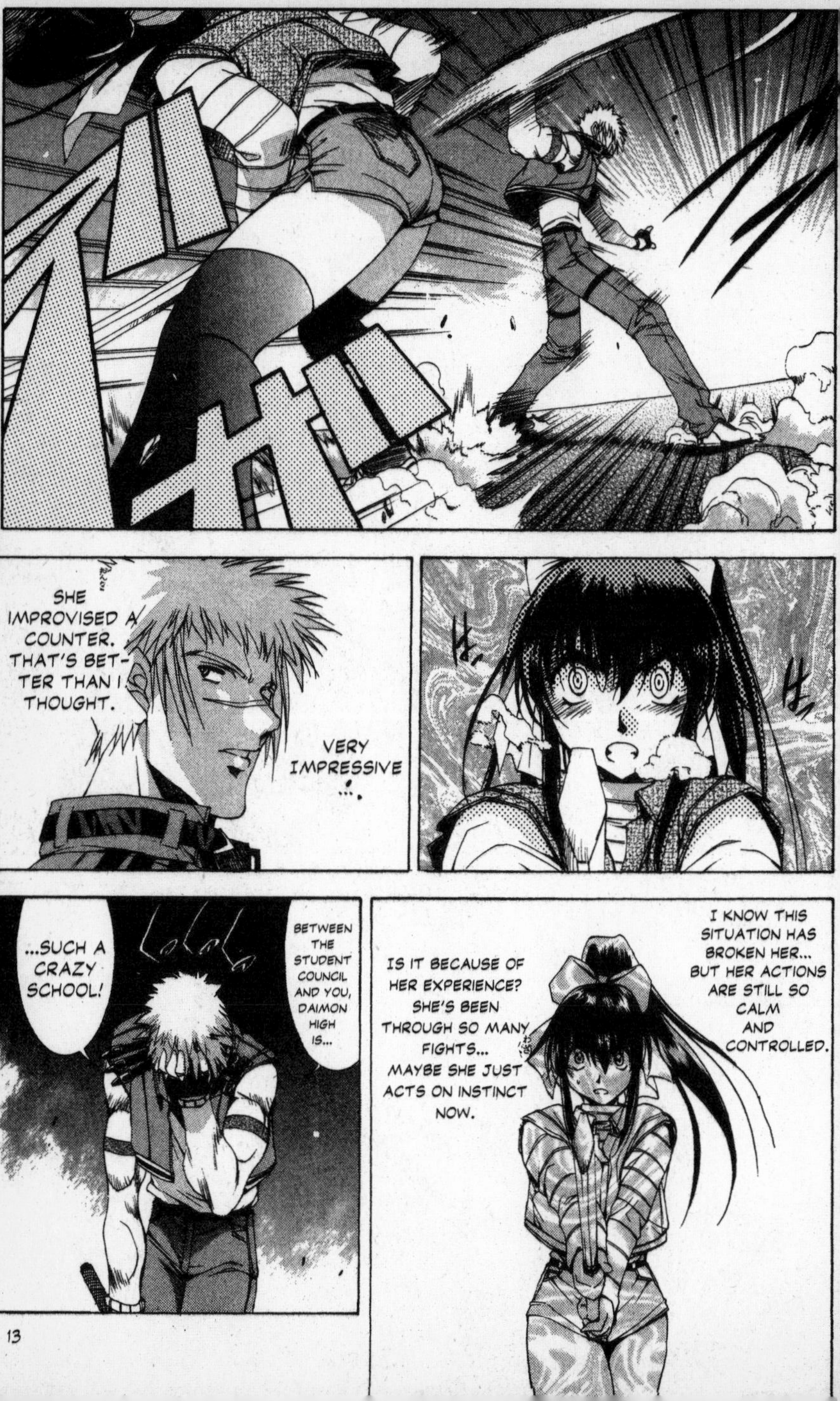
SHE IMPROVISED A COUNTER. THAT'S BET- TER THAN I THOUGHT.
VERY IMPRESSIVE ...
I KNOW THIS SITUATION HAS BROKEN HER... BUT HER ACTIONS ARE STILL SO CALM AND CONTROLLED.
IS IT BECAUSE OF HER EXPERIENCE? SHE'S BEEN THROUGH SO MANY FIGHTS... MAYBE SHE JUST ACTS ON INSTINCT NOW.
BETWEEN THE STUDENT COUNCIL AND YOU, DAIMON HIGH IS...
...SUCH A CRAZY SCHOOL!

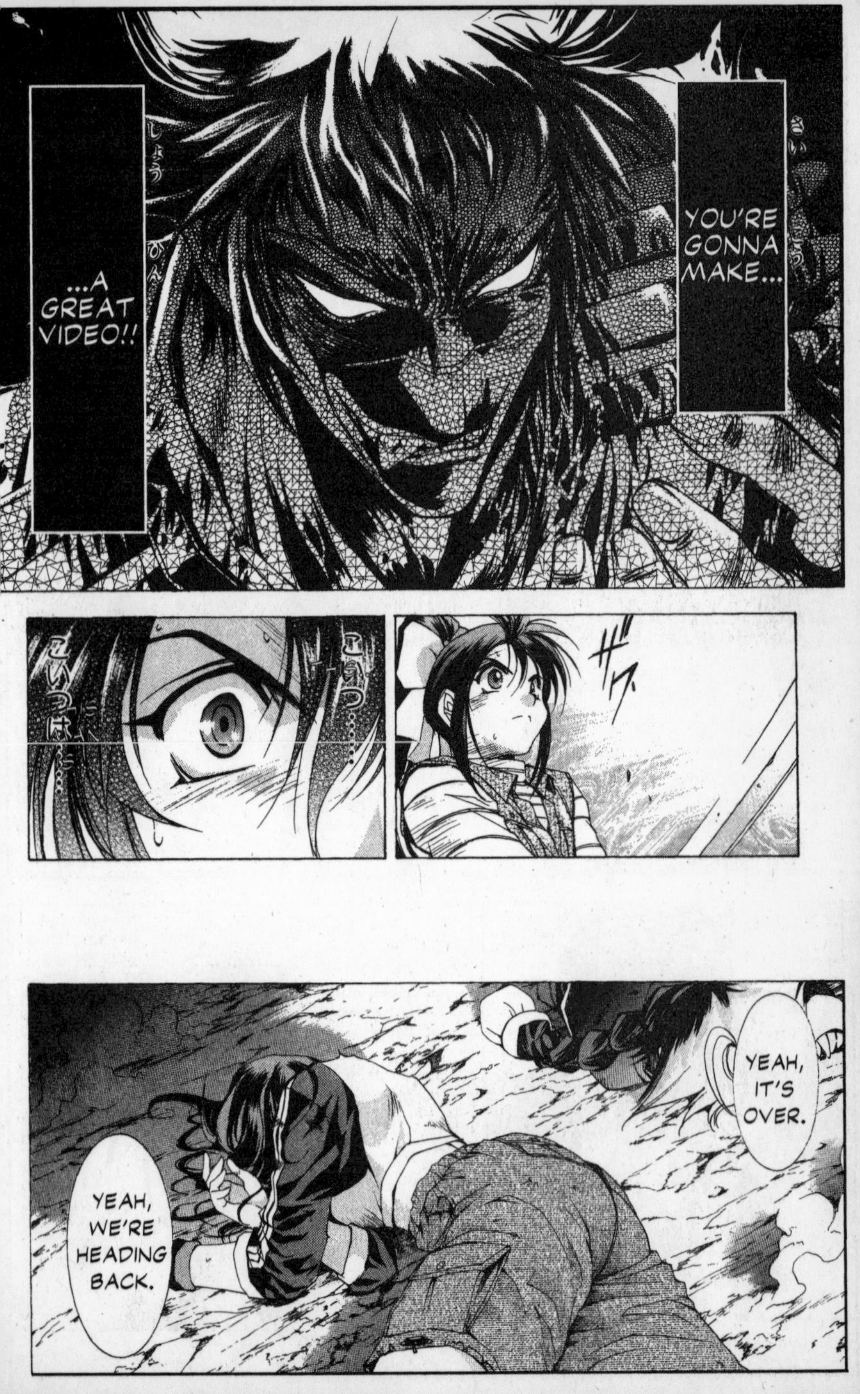
YOU'RE GONNA MAKE...
...A GREAT VIDEO!!
YEAH, IT'S OVER.
YEAH, WE'RE HEADING BACK.

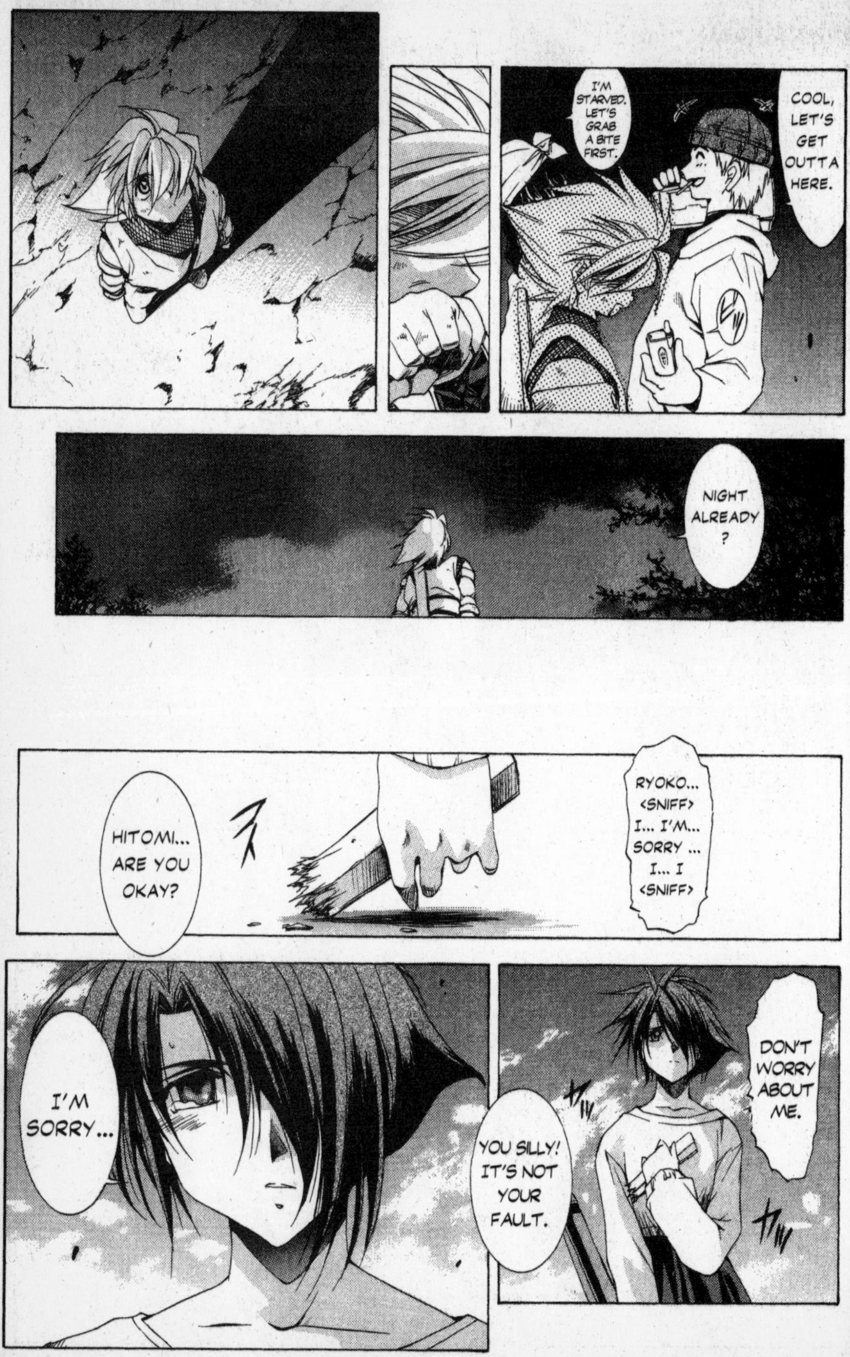
COOL, LET'S GET OUTTA HERE.
I'M STARVED. LET'S GRAB A BITE FIRST.
NIGHT ALREADY?
RYOKO... <SNIFF> I... I'M... SORRY ... I... I <SNIFF>
HITOMI... ARE YOU OKAY?
DON'T WORRY ABOUT ME.
YOU SILLY! IT'S NOT YOUR FAULT.
I'M SORRY...

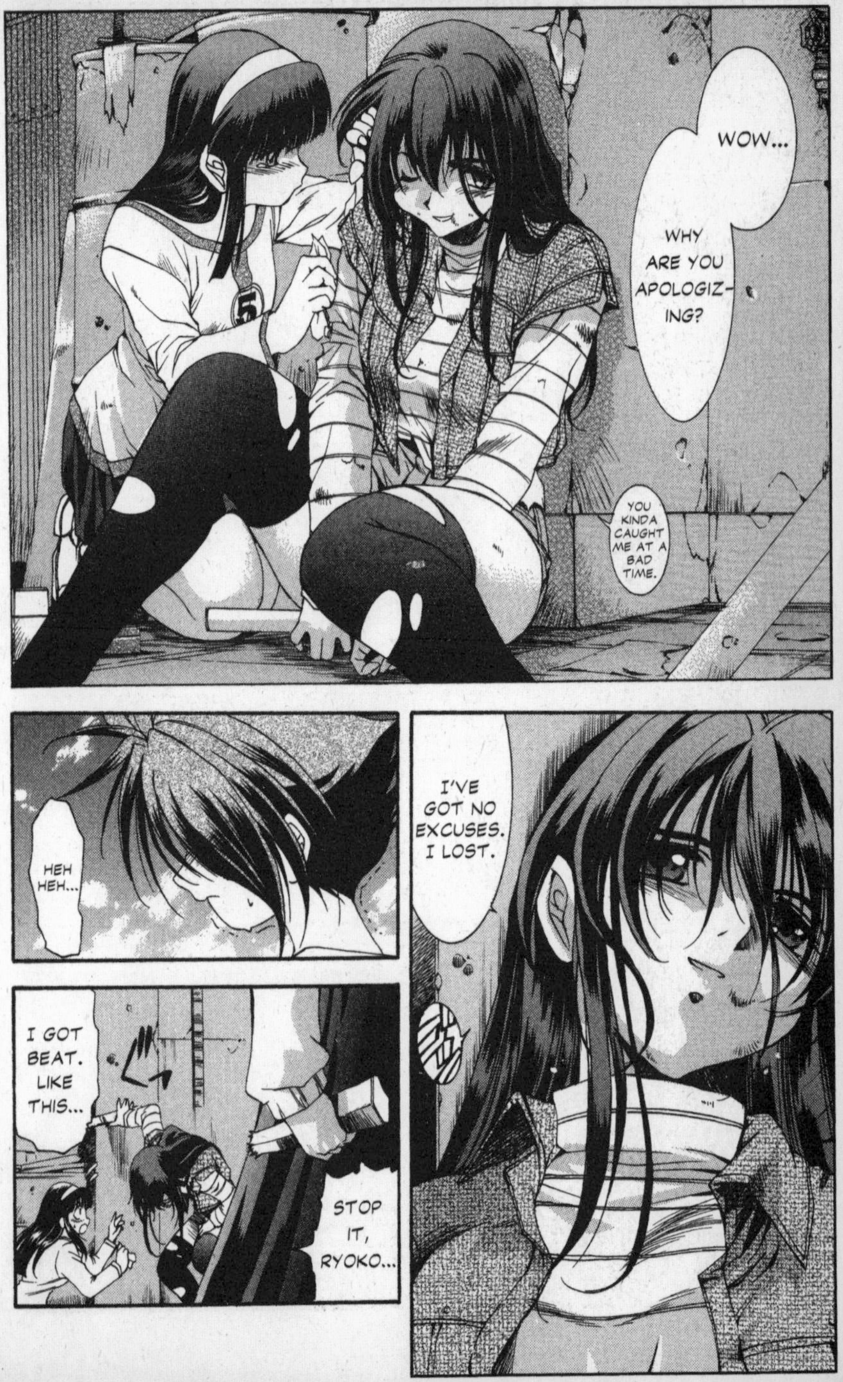

WOW...
WHY ARE YOU APOLOGIZ-ING?
YOU KINDA CAUGHT ME AT A BAD TIME.
I'VE GOT NO EXCUSES. I LOST.
HEH HEH...
I GOT BEAT. LIKE THIS...
STOP IT, RYOKO...

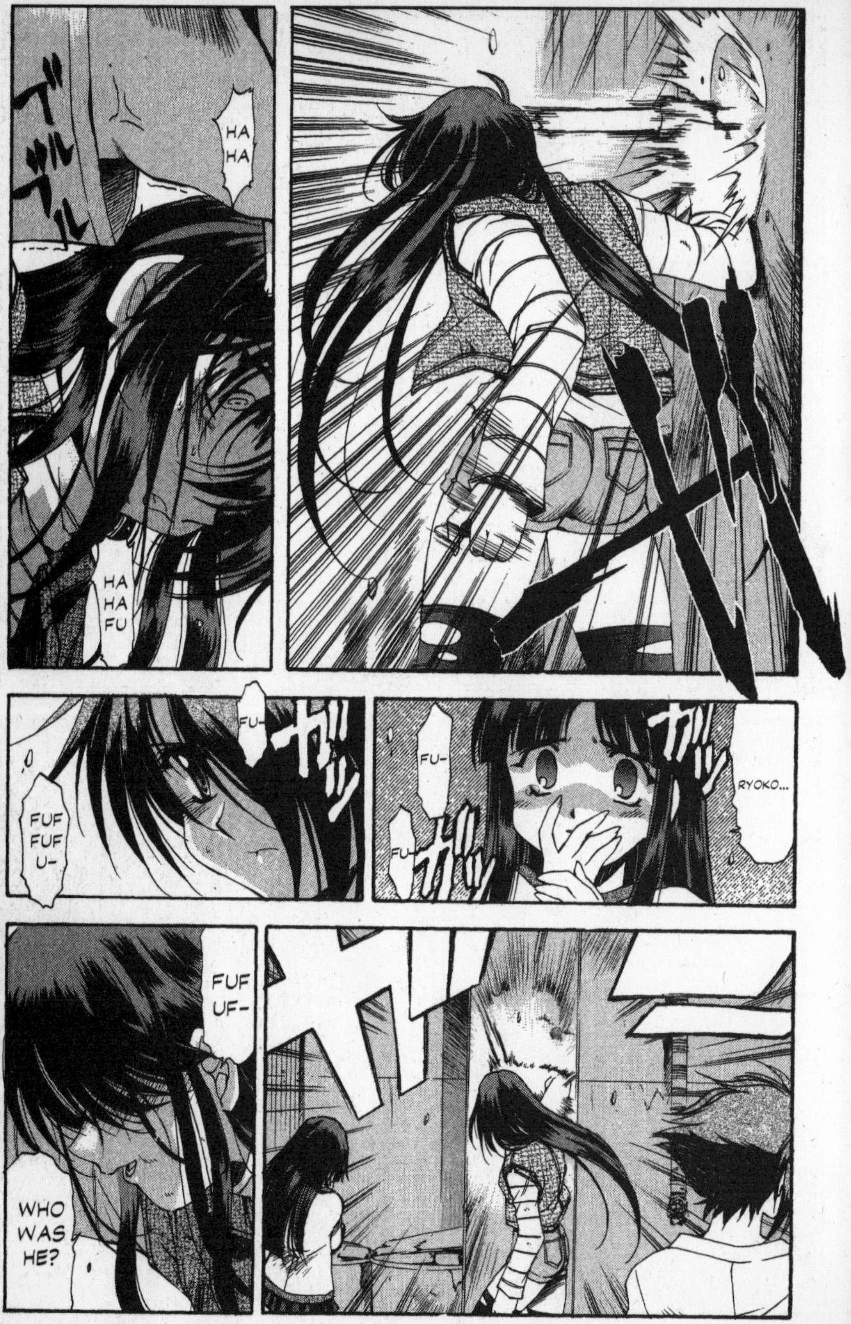
HA HA
HA HA FU
RYOKO...
FU-
FU-
FU-
FUF FUF U-
FUF UF-
WHO WAS HE?

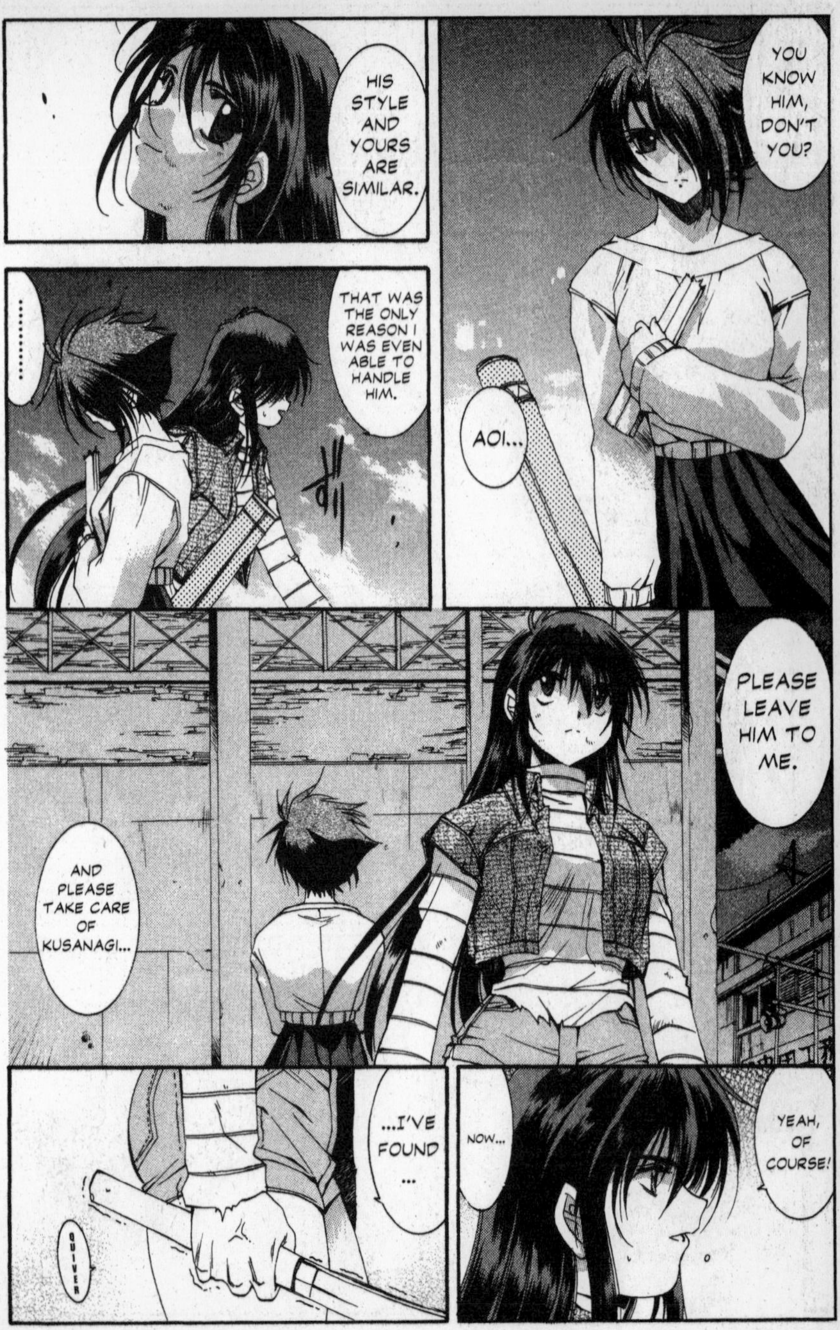
YOU KNOW HIM, DON'T YOU?
HIS STYLE AND YOURS ARE SIMILAR.
AOI...
THAT WAS THE ONLY REASON I WAS EVEN ABLE TO HANDLE HIM.
......
PLEASE LEAVE HIM TO ME.
AND PLEASE TAKE CARE OF KUSANAGI...
YEAH, OF COURSE!
NOW...
...I'VE FOUND ...
QUIVER

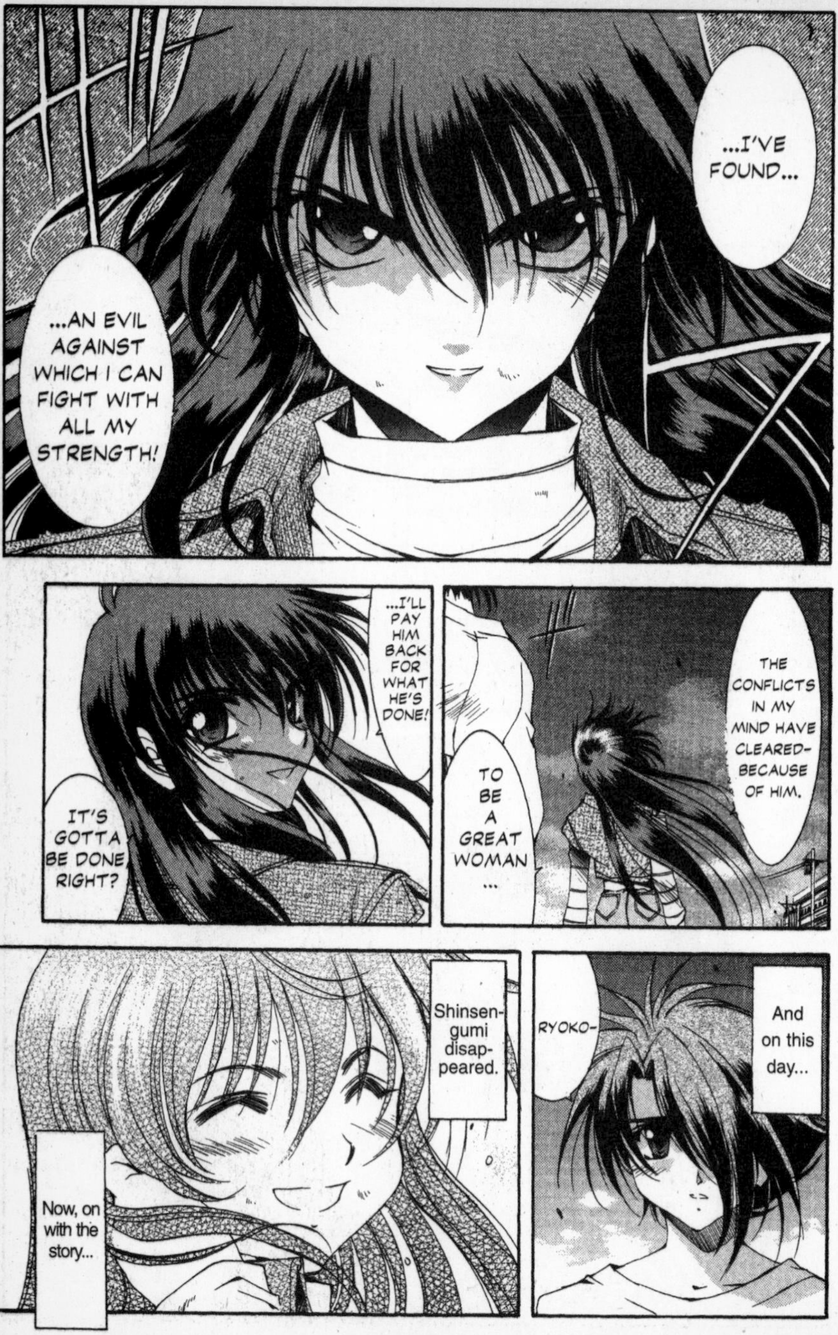
...I'VE FOUND...
...AN EVIL AGAINST WHICH I CAN FIGHT WITH ALL MY STRENGTH!
THE CONFLICTS IN MY MIND HAVE CLEARED- BECAUSE OF HIM.
TO BE A GREAT WOMAN ...
...I'LL PAY HIM BACK FOR WHAT HE'S DONE!
IT'S GOTTA BE DONE RIGHT?
And on this day...
RYOKO-
Shinsen-gumi disap-peared.
Now, on with the story...

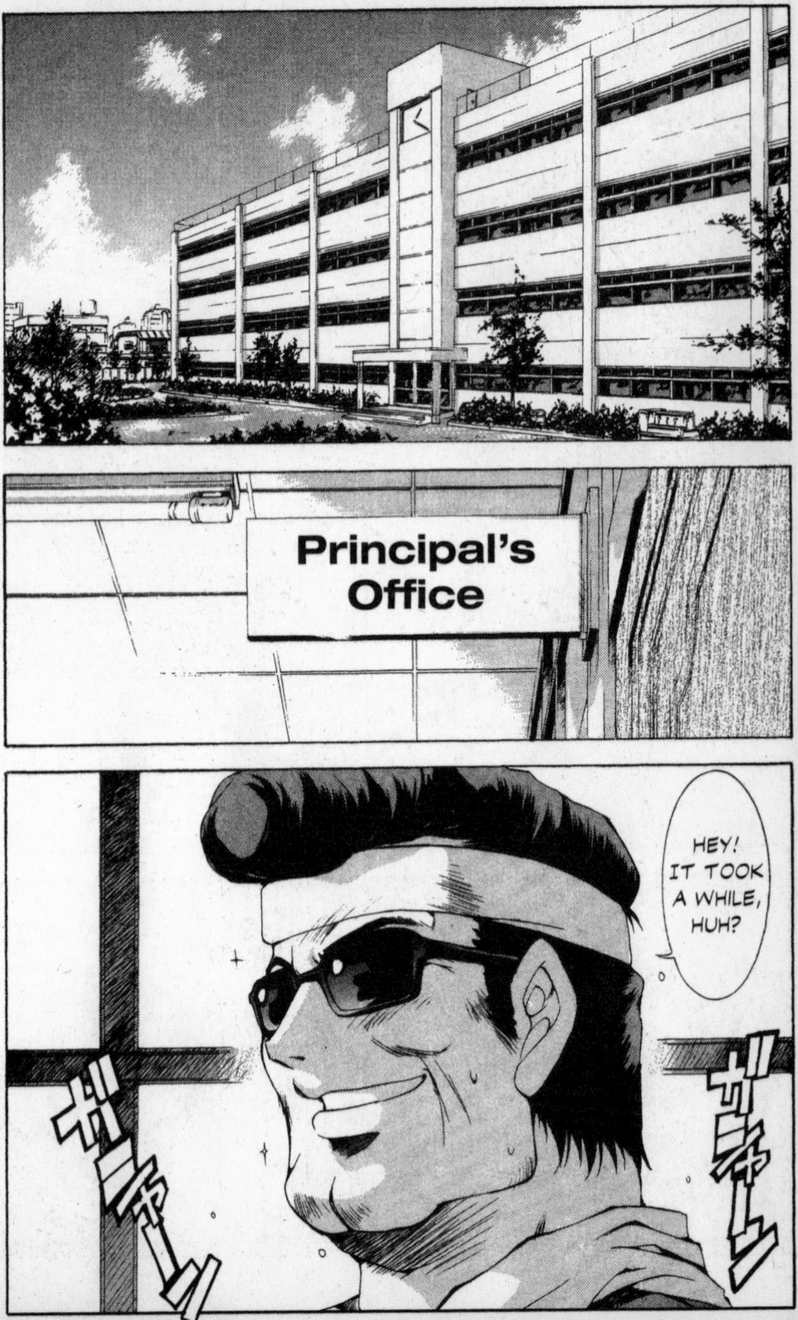
Principal's Office
HEY! IT TOOK A WHILE, HUH?

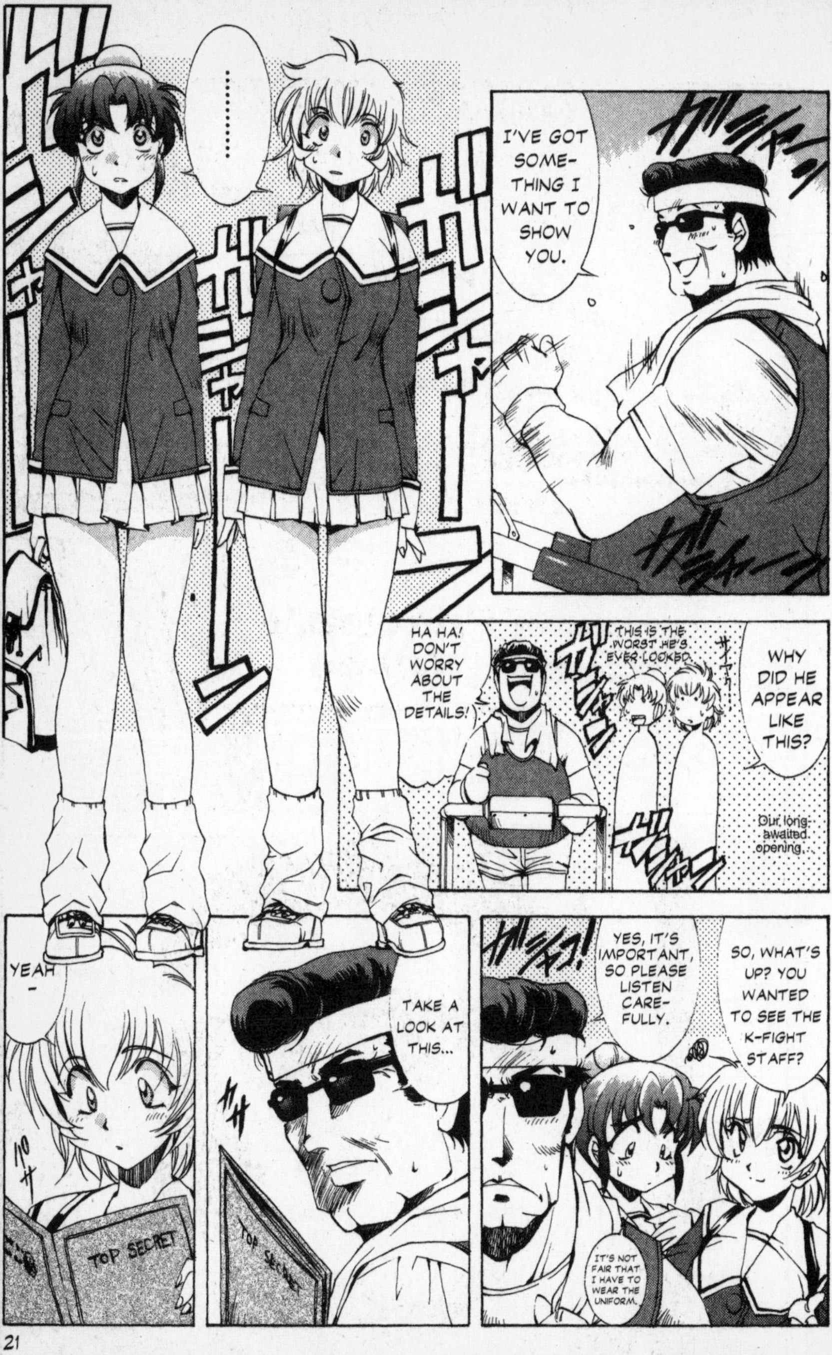
I'VE GOT SOME-THING I WANT TO SHOW YOU.
......
WHY DID HE APPEAR LIKE THIS?
Our long-awaited opening.
THIS IS THE WORST HE'S EVER LOOKED.
HA HA! DON'T WORRY ABOUT THE DETAILS!
SO, WHAT'S UP? YOU WANTED TO SEE THE K-FIGHT STAFF?
YES, IT'S IMPORTANT, SO PLEASE LISTEN CARE-FULLY.
IT'S NOT FAIR THAT I HAVE TO WEAR THE UNIFORM.
TAKE A LOOK AT THIS...
TOP SECRET
YEAH-
TOP SECRET

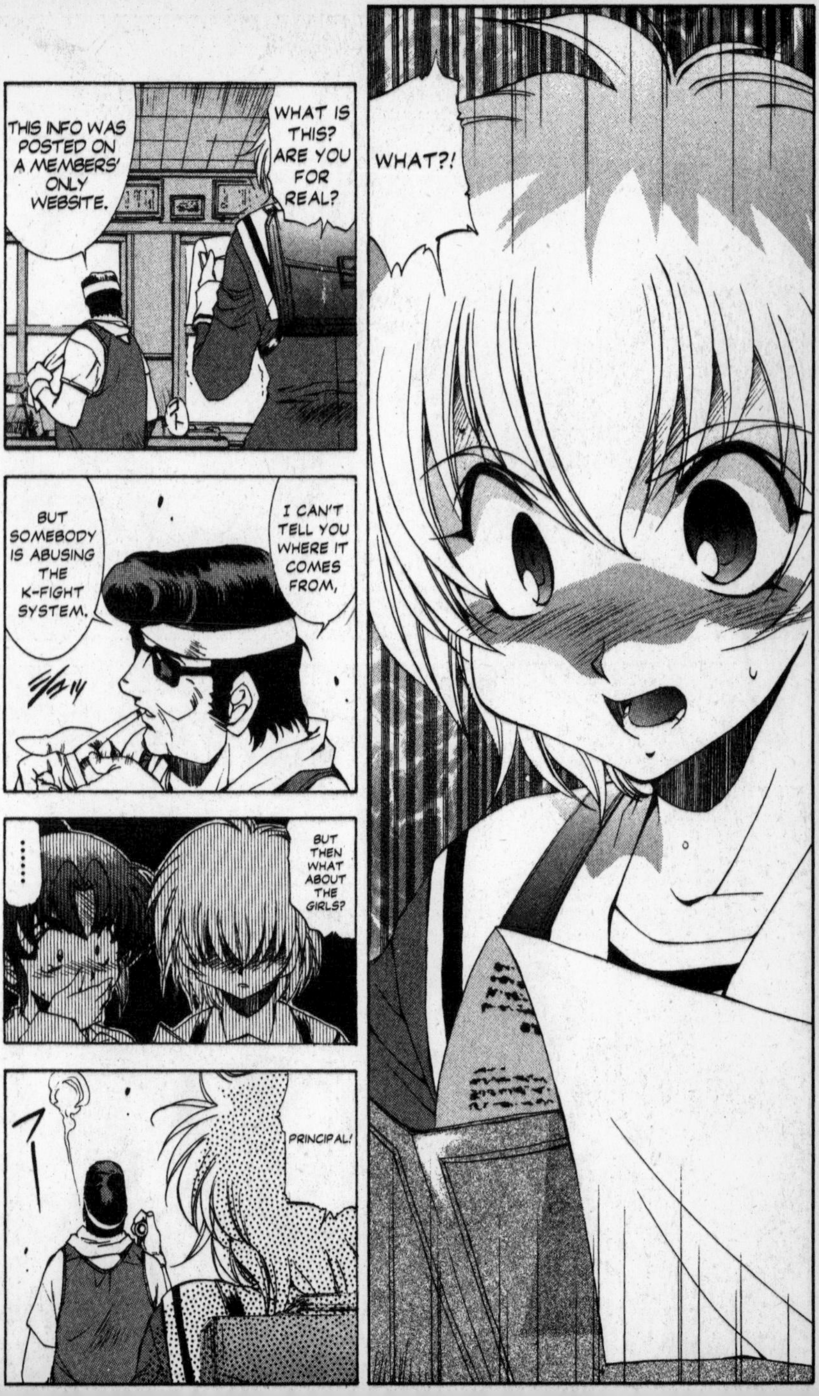
WHAT?!
WHAT IS THIS? ARE YOU FOR REAL?
THIS INFO WAS POSTED ON A MEMBERS' ONLY WEBSITE.
I CAN'T TELL YOU WHERE IT COMES FROM,
BUT SOMEBODY IS ABUSING THE K-FIGHT SYSTEM.
BUT THEN WHAT ABOUT THE GIRLS?
......
PRINCIPAL!

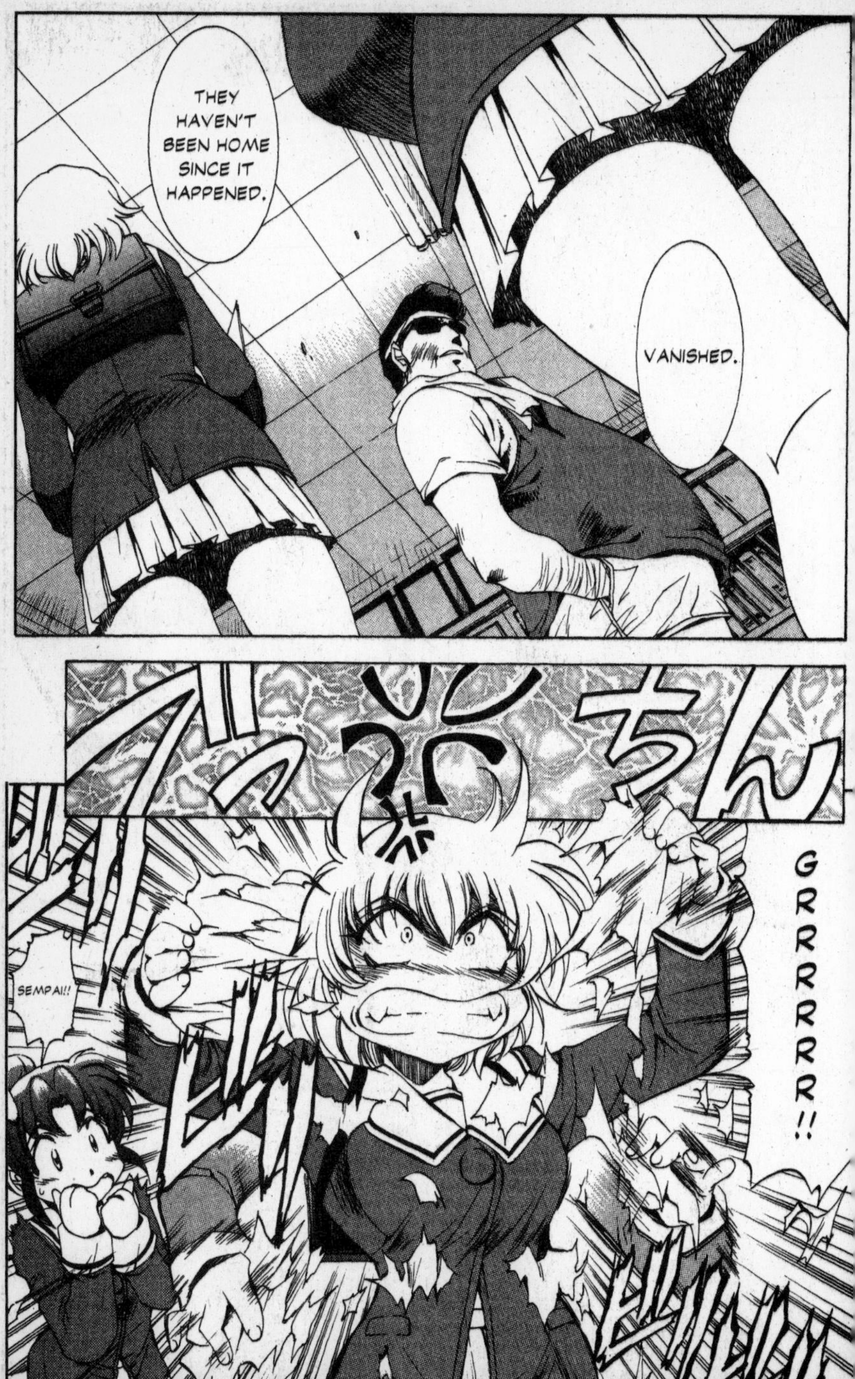
THEY HAVEN'T BEEN HOME SINCE IT HAPPENED.
VANISHED.
GRRRRRRR!!
SEMPAI!!

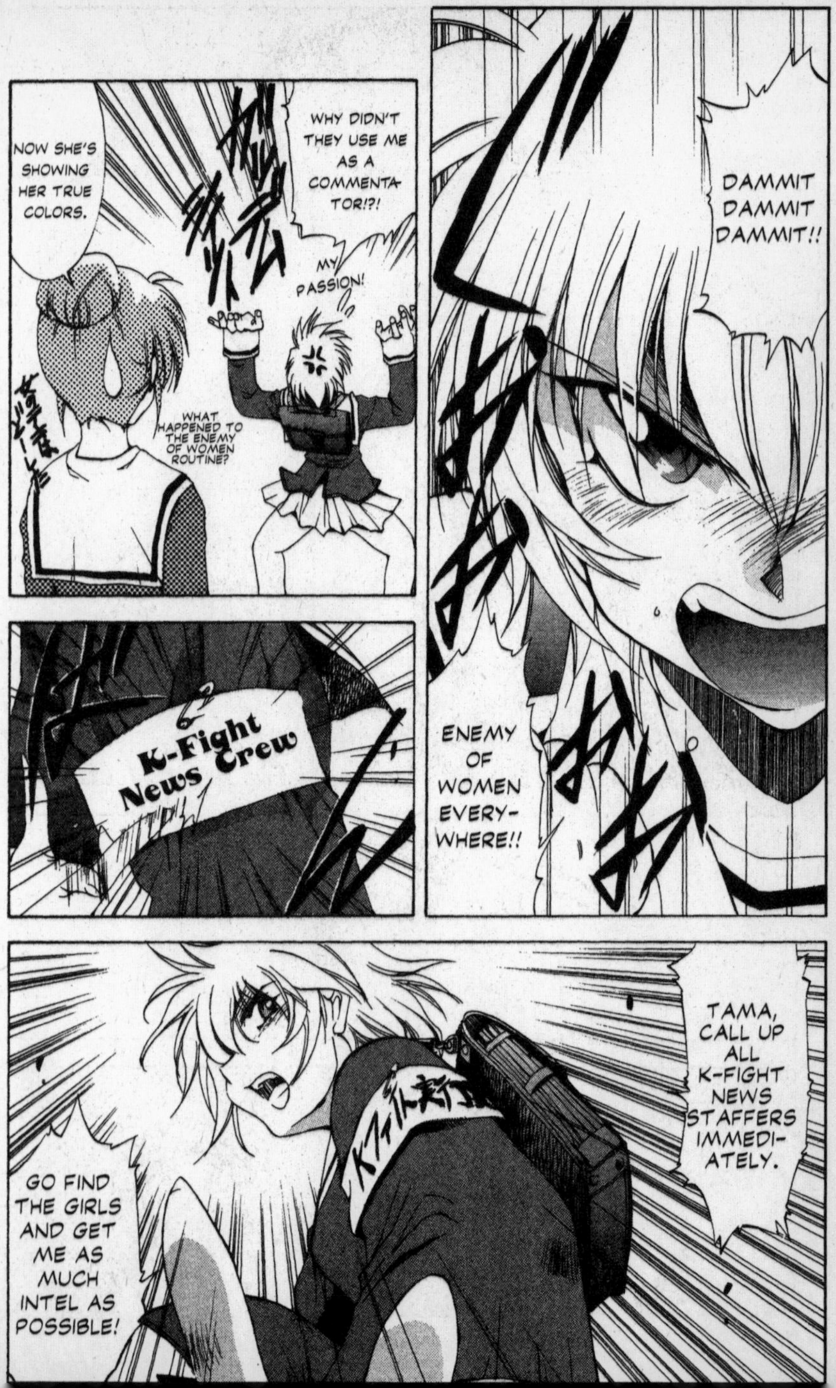
DAMMIT DAMMIT DAMMIT!!
ENEMY OF WOMEN EVERY-WHERE!!
WHY DIDN'T THEY USE ME AS A COMMENTA-TOR!?!
MY PASSION!
NOW SHE'S SHOWING HER TRUE COLORS.
WHAT HAPPENED TO THE ENEMY OF WOMEN ROUTINE?
K-Fight News Crew
TAMA, CALL UP ALL K-FIGHT NEWS STAFFERS IMMEDI-ATELY.
GO FIND THE GIRLS AND GET ME AS MUCH INTEL AS POSSIBLE!

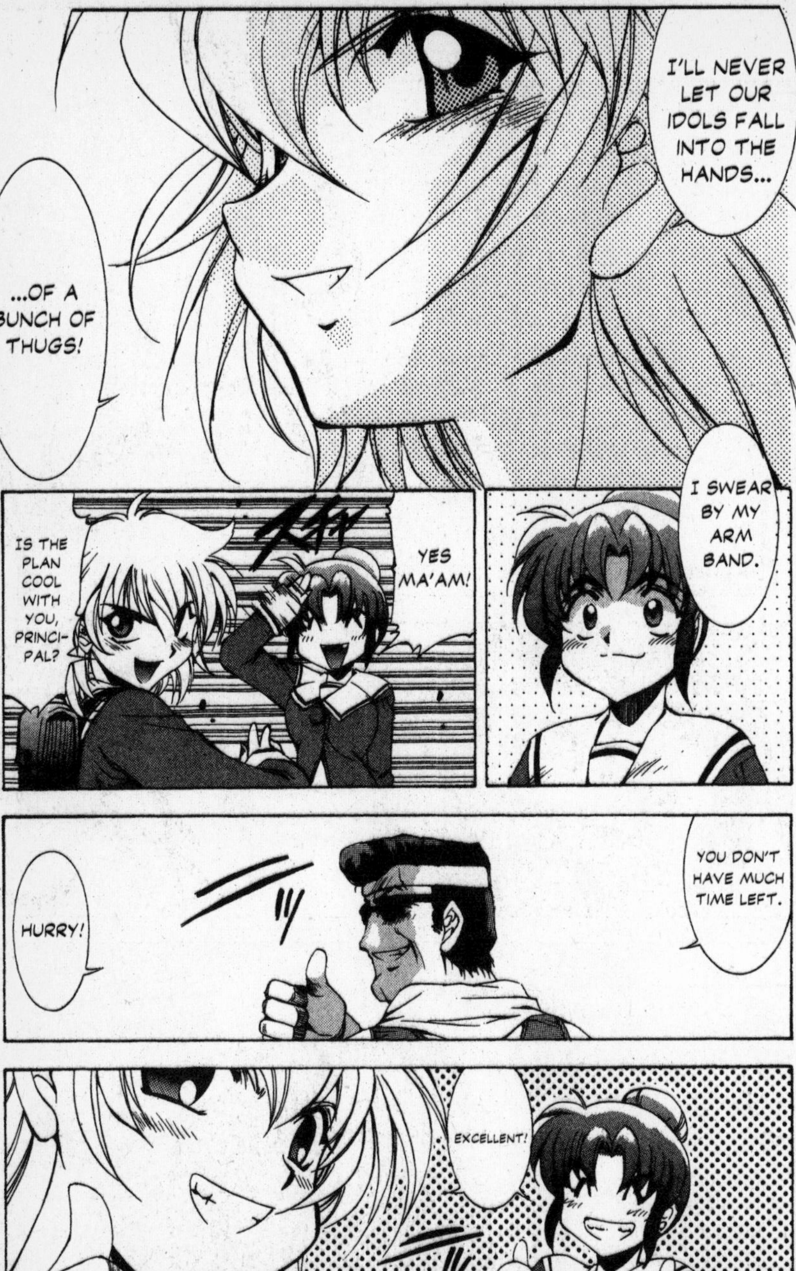

I'LL NEVER LET OUR IDOLS FALL INTO THE HANDS...
...OF A BUNCH OF THUGS!
I SWEAR BY MY ARM BAND.
IS THE PLAN COOL WITH YOU, PRINCIPAL?
YES MA'AM!
YOU DON'T HAVE MUCH TIME LEFT.
HURRY!
EXCELLENT!

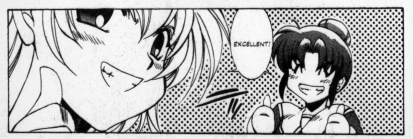

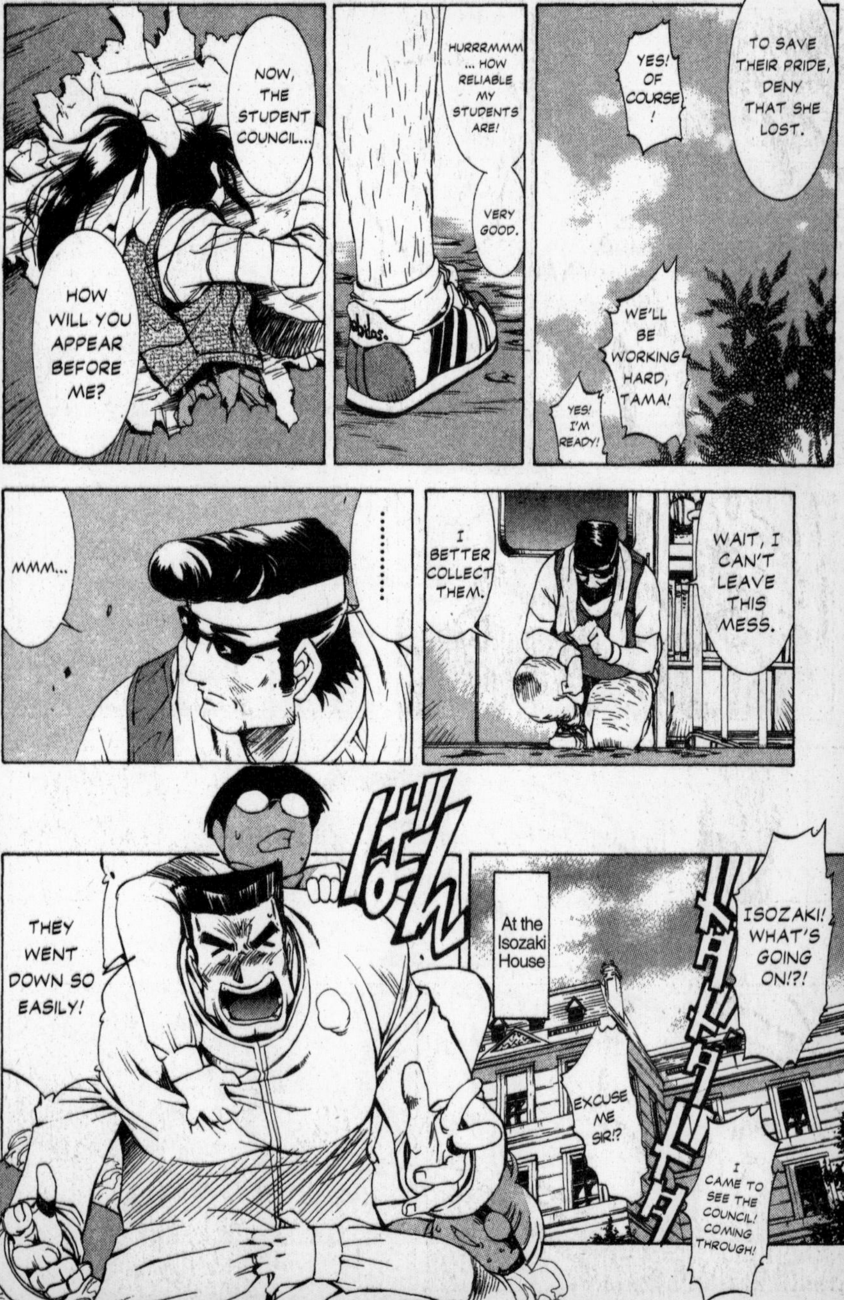
TO SAVE THEIR PRIDE, DENY THAT SHE LOST.
YES! OF COURSE!
WE'LL BE WORKING HARD, TAMA!
YES! I'M READY!
HURRRMMM ... HOW RELIABLE MY STUDENTS ARE!
VERY GOOD.
NOW, THE STUDENT COUNCIL...
HOW WILL YOU APPEAR BEFORE ME?
WAIT, I CAN'T LEAVE THIS MESS.
I BETTER COLLECT THEM.
......
MMM...
At the Isozaki House
ISOZAKI! WHAT'S GOING ON!?!
EXCUSE ME SIR!?
I CAME TO SEE THE COUNCIL! COMING THROUGH!
THEY WENT DOWN SO EASILY!

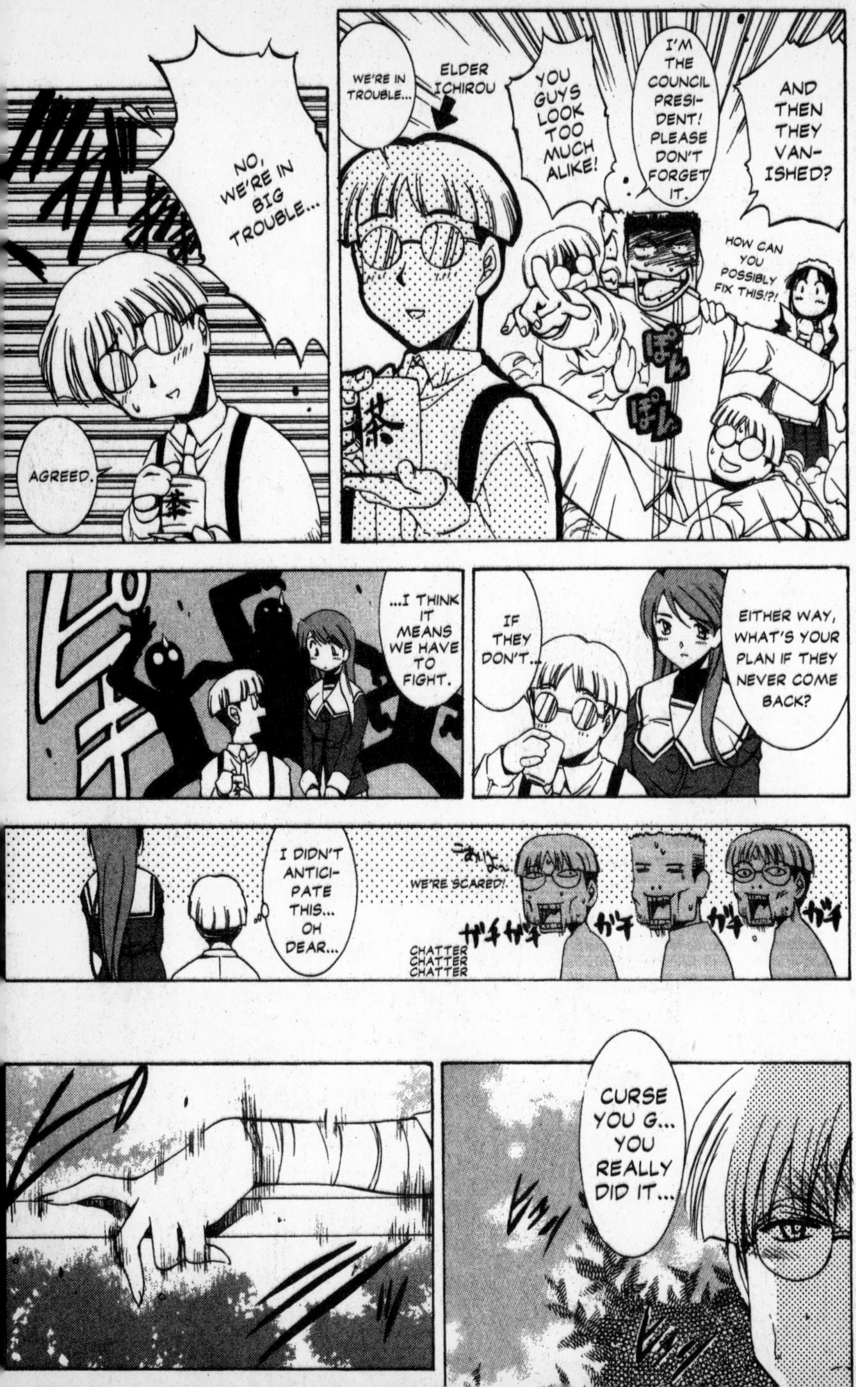
AND THEN THEY VAN-ISHED?
HOW CAN YOU POSSIBLY FIX THIS!?!
I'M THE COUNCIL PRESI-DENT! PLEASE DON'T FORGET IT.
YOU GUYS LOOK TOO MUCH ALIKE!
ぽん ぽん
ELDER ICHIROU
WE'RE IN TROUBLE...
NO, WE'RE IN BIG TROUBLE...
AGREED.
EITHER WAY, WHAT'S YOUR PLAN IF THEY NEVER COME BACK?
IF THEY DON'T...
...I THINK IT MEANS WE HAVE TO FIGHT.
WE'RE SCARED!
ガチ ガチ ガチ ガチ ガチ
CHATTER CHATTER CHATTER
I DIDN'T ANTICI-PATE THIS... OH DEAR...
CURSE YOU G... YOU REALLY DID IT...

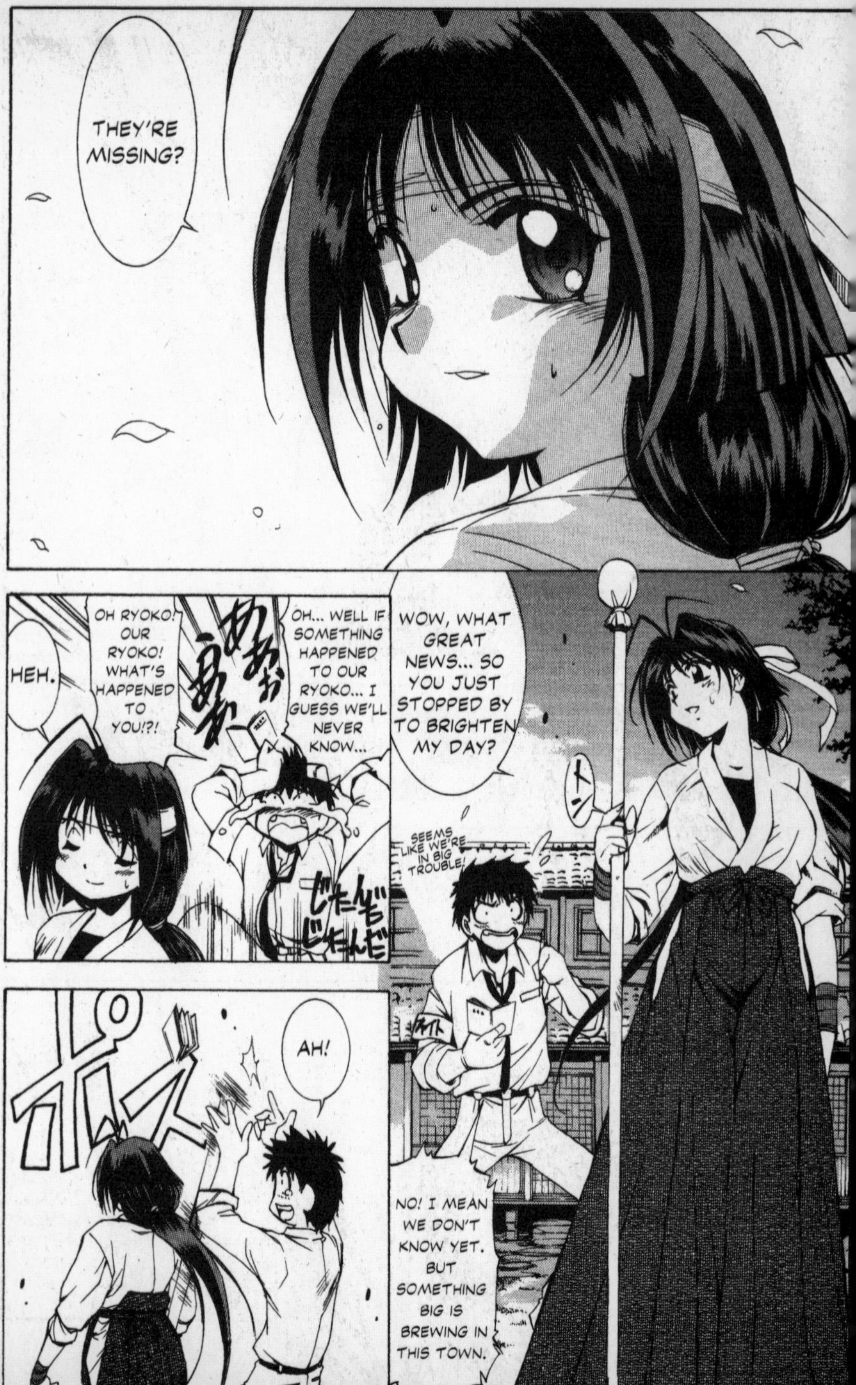
THEY'RE MISSING?
WOW, WHAT GREAT NEWS... SO YOU JUST STOPPED BY TO BRIGHTEN MY DAY?
OH... WELL IF SOMETHING HAPPENED TO OUR RYOKO... I GUESS WE'LL NEVER KNOW...
OH RYOKO! OUR RYOKO! WHAT'S HAPPENED TO YOU!?!
HEH.
SEEMS LIKE WE'RE IN BIG TROUBLE!
NO! I MEAN WE DON'T KNOW YET. BUT SOMETHING BIG IS BREWING IN THIS TOWN.
AH!

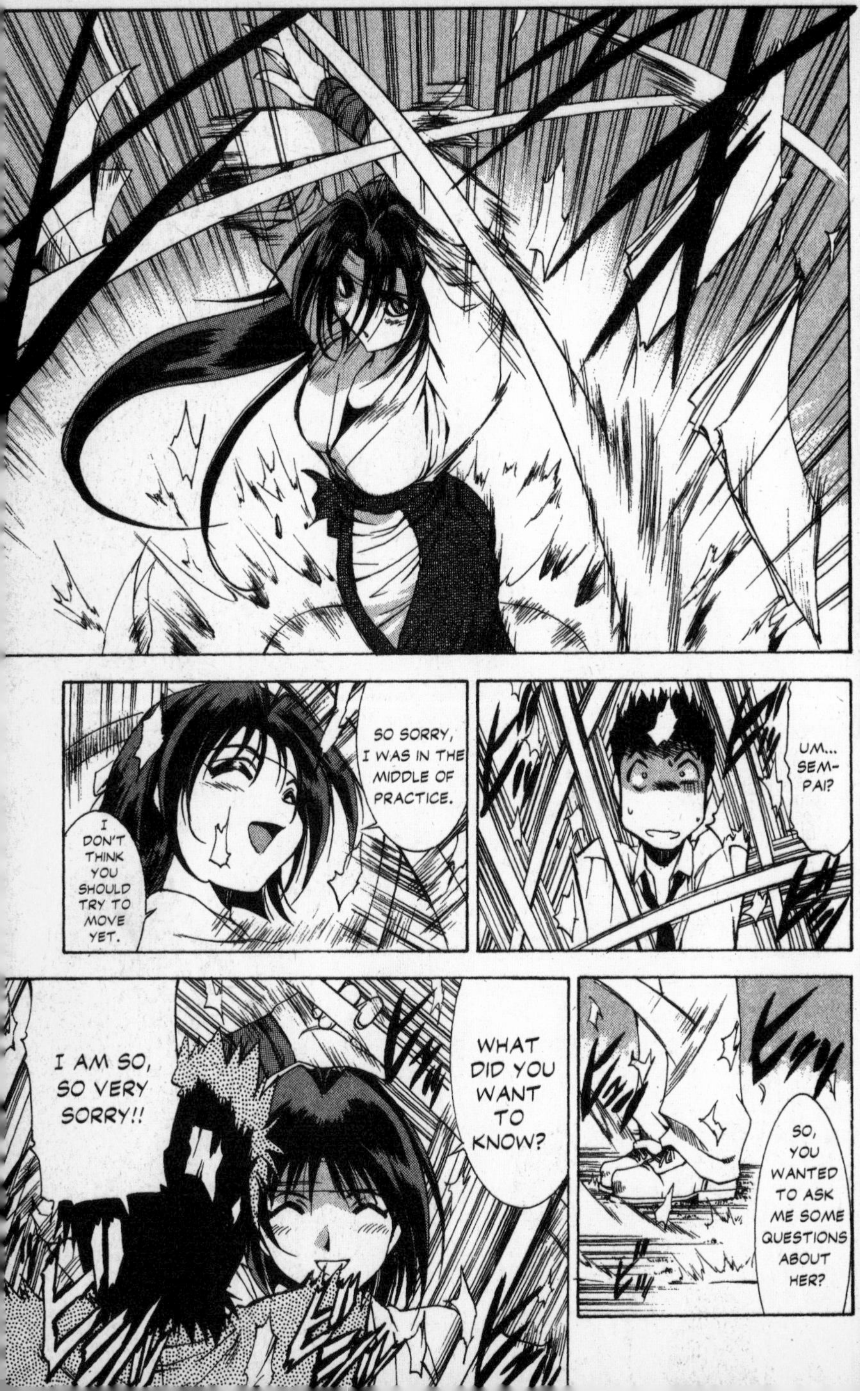
UM... SEMPAI?
SO SORRY, I WAS IN THE MIDDLE OF PRACTICE.
I DON'T THINK YOU SHOULD TRY TO MOVE YET.
SO, YOU WANTED TO ASK ME SOME QUESTIONS ABOUT HER?
WHAT DID YOU WANT TO KNOW?
I AM SO, SO VERY SORRY!!

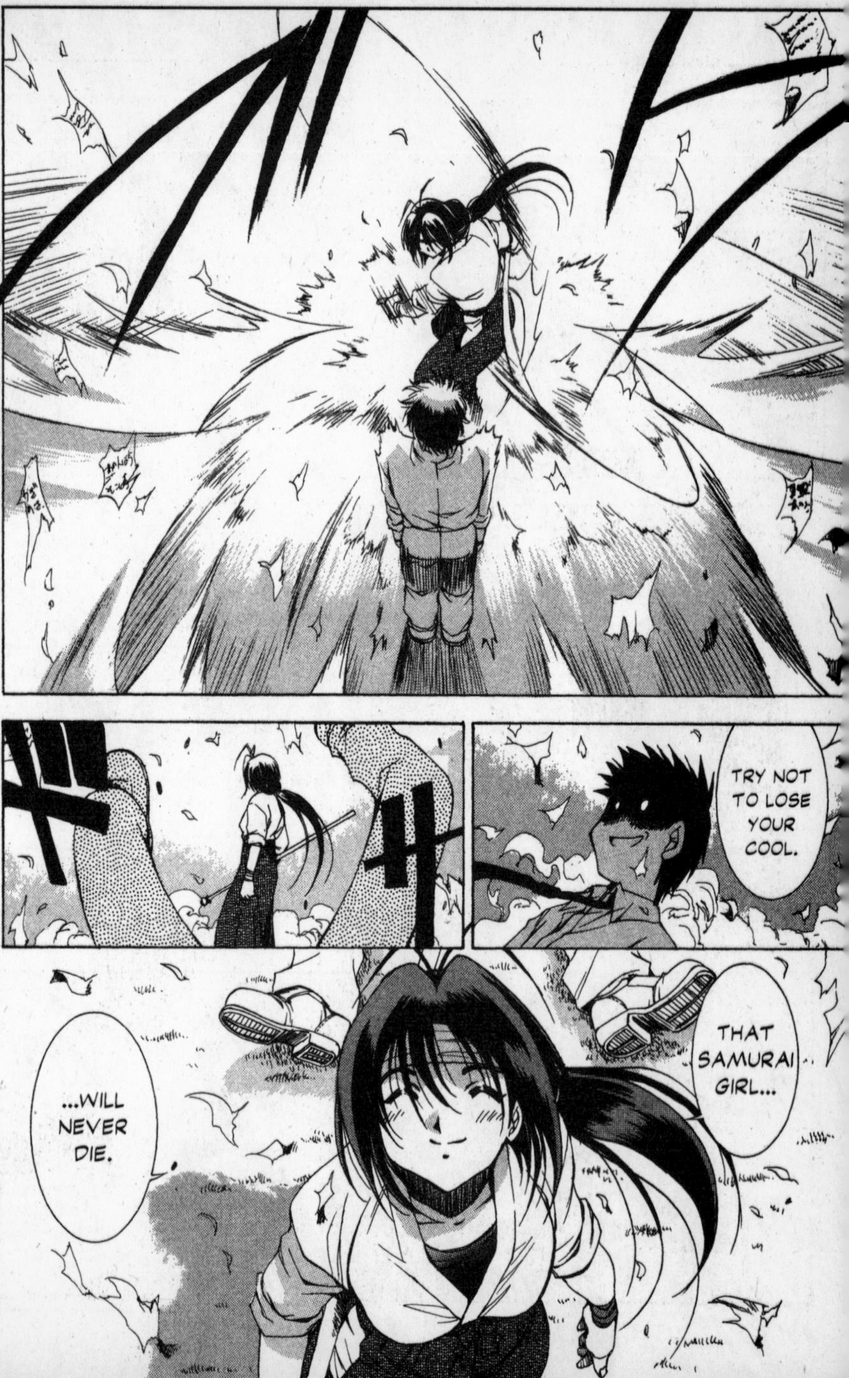
TRY NOT TO LOSE YOUR COOL.
THAT SAMURAI GIRL...
...WILL NEVER DIE.

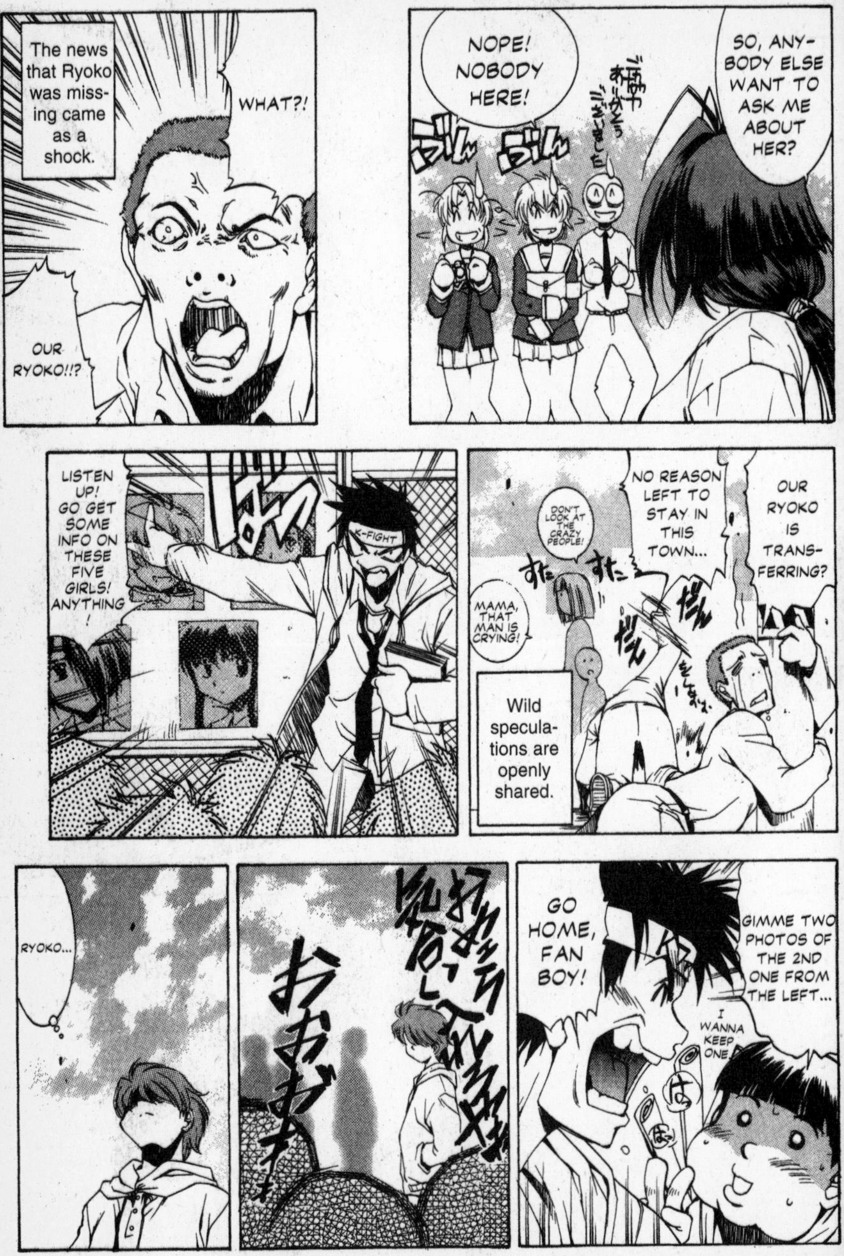
SO, ANY-BODY ELSE WANT TO ASK ME ABOUT HER?
NOPE! NOBODY HERE!
The news that Ryoko was missing came as a shock.
WHAT?!
OUR RYOKO!!?
OUR RYOKO IS TRANSFERRING?
NO REASON LEFT TO STAY IN THIS TOWN...
DON'T LOOK AT THE CRAZY PEOPLE!
MAMA, THAT MAN IS CRYING!
Wild speculations are openly shared.
LISTEN UP! GO GET SOME INFO ON THESE FIVE GIRLS! ANYTHING!
K-FIGHT
GIMME TWO PHOTOS OF THE 2ND ONE FROM THE LEFT...
I WANNA KEEP ONE.
GO HOME, FAN BOY!
RYOKO...

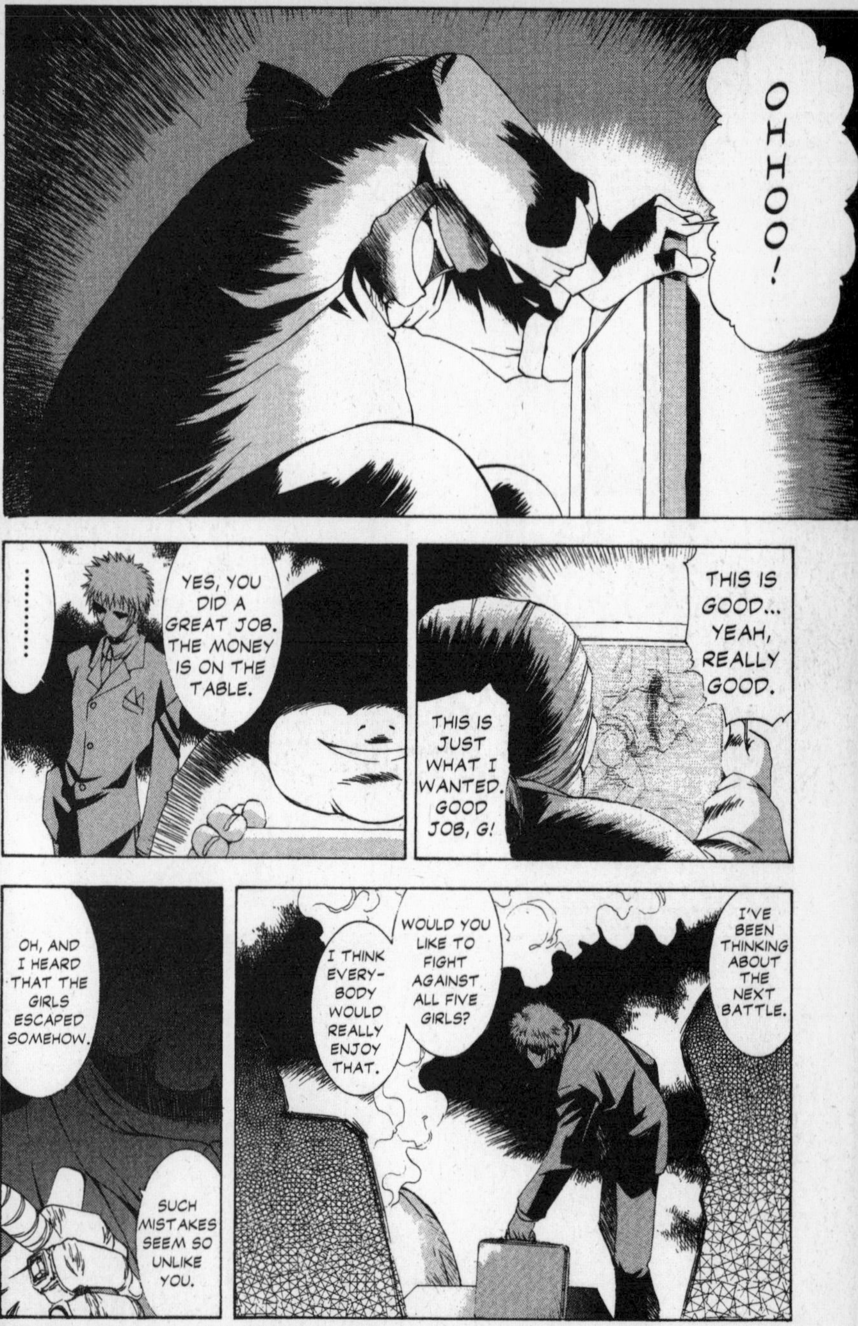
OHHOO!
THIS IS GOOD... YEAH, REALLY GOOD.
THIS IS JUST WHAT I WANTED. GOOD JOB, G!
YES, YOU DID A GREAT JOB. THE MONEY IS ON THE TABLE.
....
I'VE BEEN THINKING ABOUT THE NEXT BATTLE.
WOULD YOU LIKE TO FIGHT AGAINST ALL FIVE GIRLS?
I THINK EVERYBODY WOULD REALLY ENJOY THAT.
OH, AND I HEARD THAT THE GIRLS ESCAPED SOMEHOW.
SUCH MISTAKES SEEM SO UNLIKE YOU.

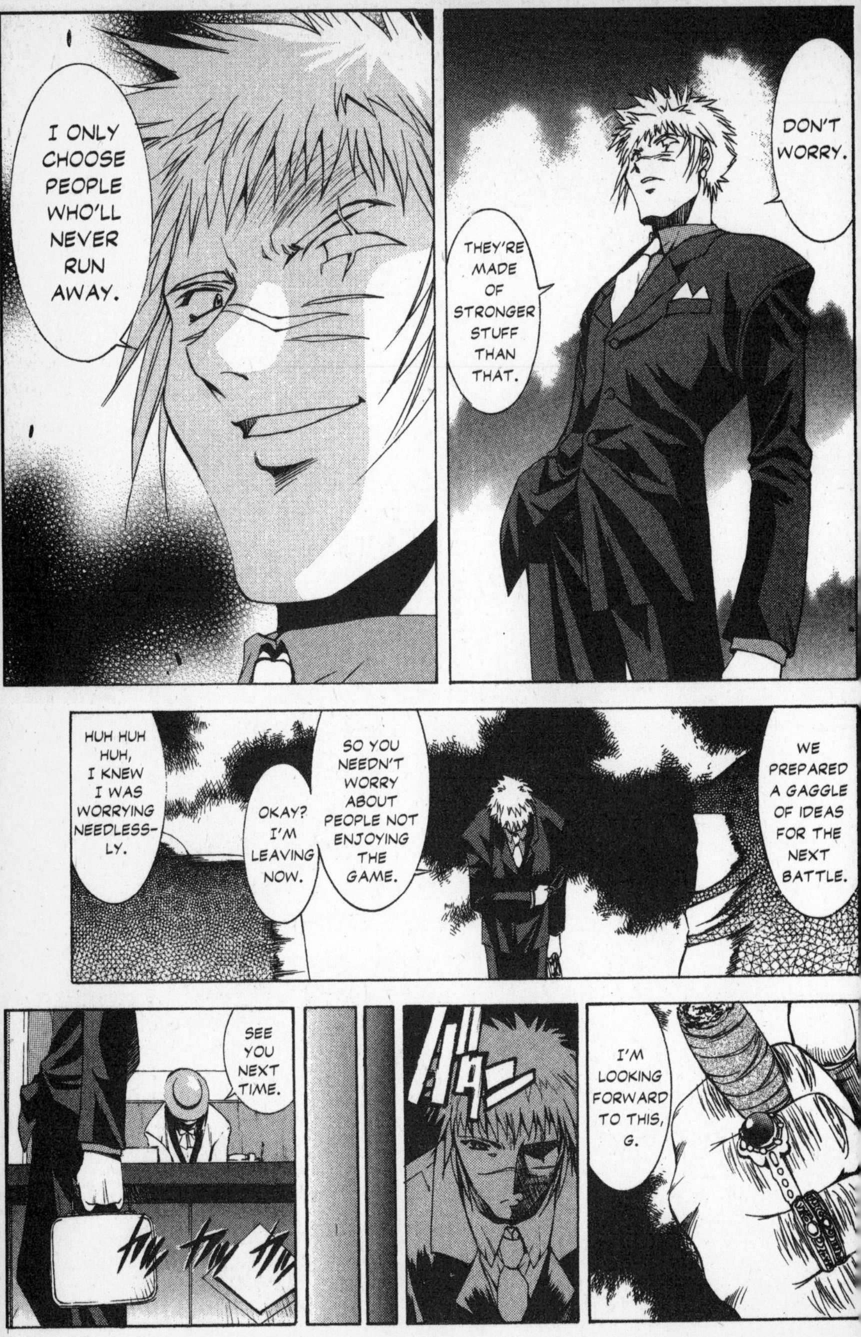
DON'T WORRY.
THEY'RE MADE OF STRONGER STUFF THAN THAT.
I ONLY CHOOSE PEOPLE WHO'LL NEVER RUN AWAY.
WE PREPARED A GAGGLE OF IDEAS FOR THE NEXT BATTLE.
SO YOU NEEDN'T WORRY ABOUT PEOPLE NOT ENJOYING THE GAME.
OKAY? I'M LEAVING NOW.
HUH HUH HUH, I KNEW I WAS WORRYING NEEDLESS-LY.
I'M LOOKING FORWARD TO THIS, G.
SEE YOU NEXT TIME.

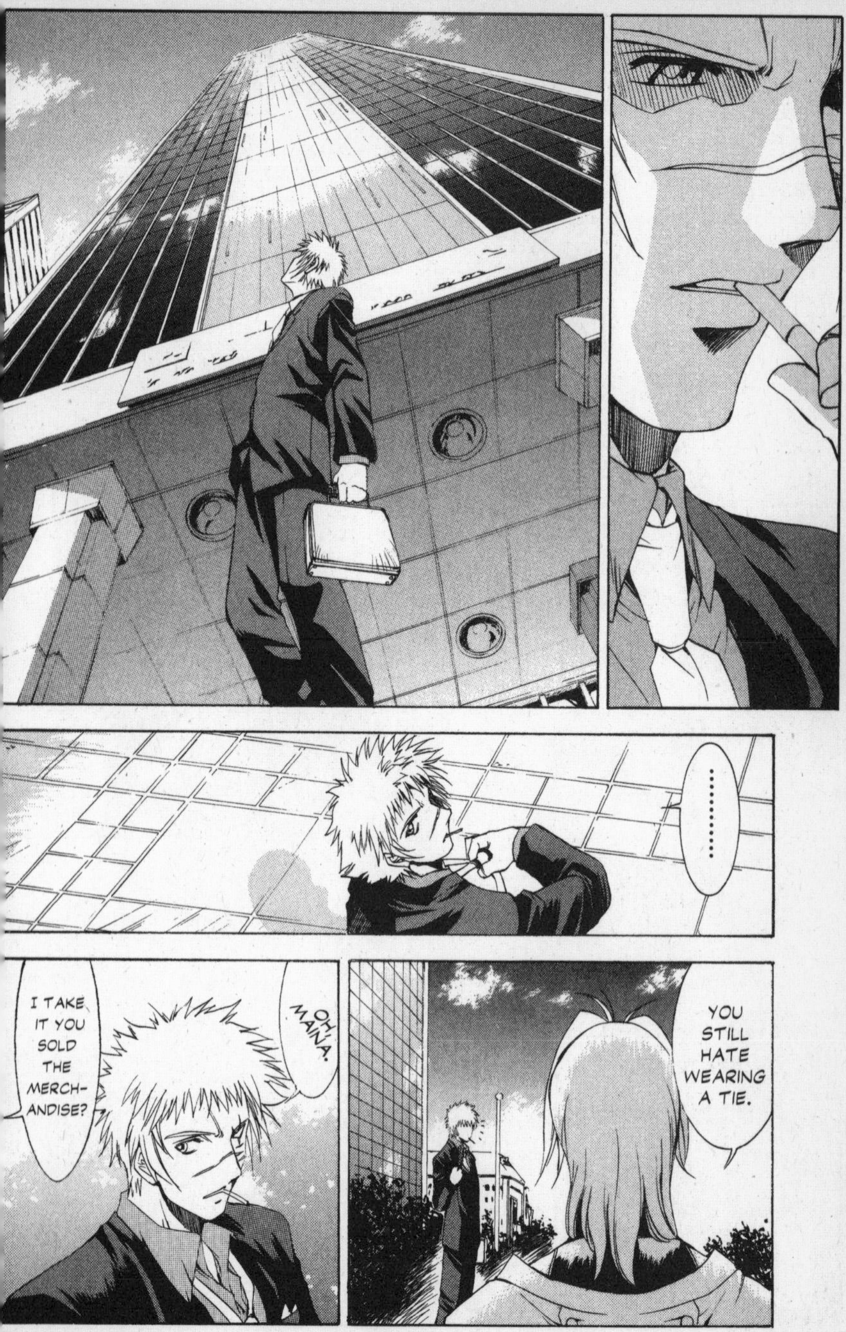
......
YOU STILL HATE WEARING A TIE.
OH, MAINA.
I TAKE IT YOU SOLD THE MERCHANDISE?

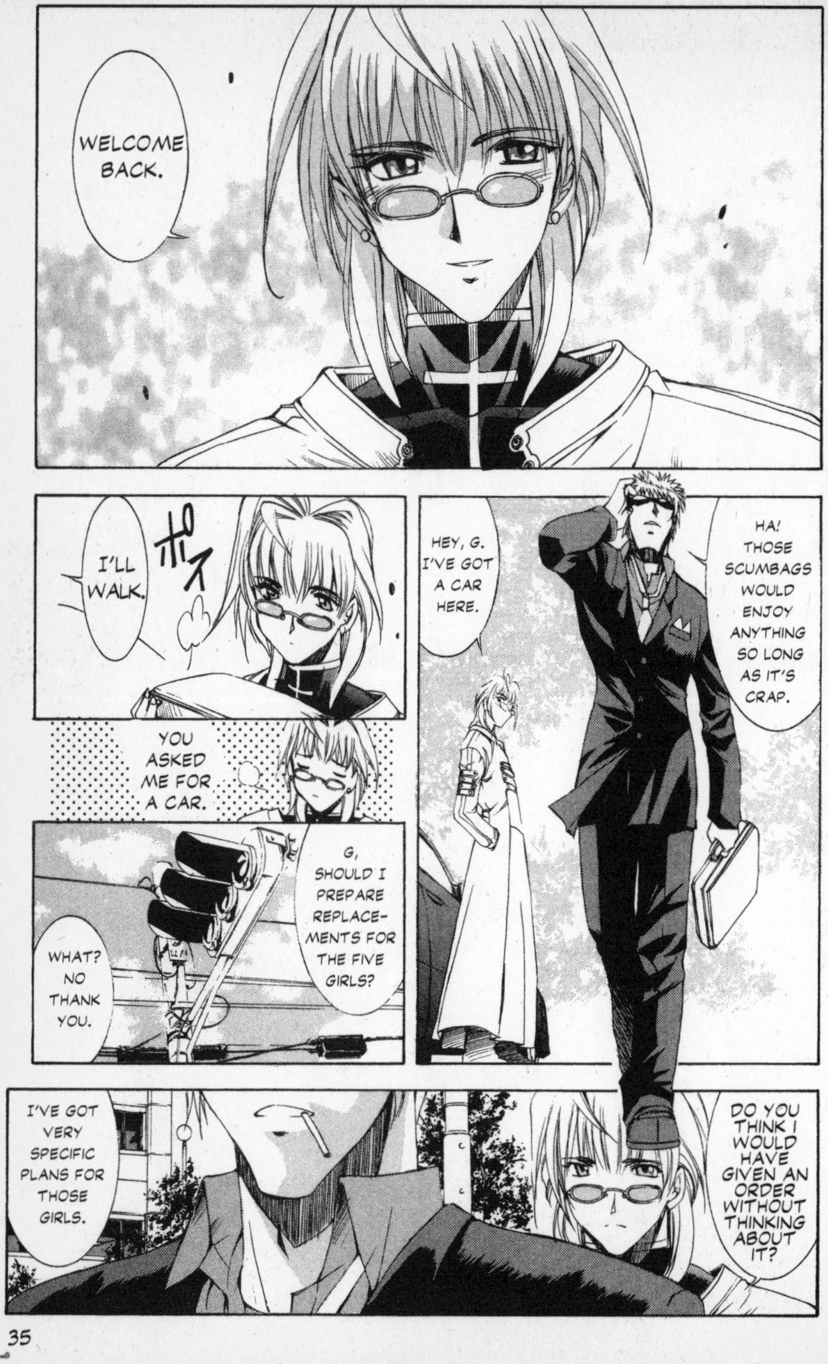
WELCOME BACK.
HA! THOSE SCUMBAGS WOULD ENJOY ANYTHING SO LONG AS IT'S CRAP.
HEY, G. I'VE GOT A CAR HERE.
I'LL WALK.
ポイ
YOU ASKED ME FOR A CAR.
G, SHOULD I PREPARE REPLACE-MENTS FOR THE FIVE GIRLS?
WHAT? NO THANK YOU.
DO YOU THINK I WOULD HAVE GIVEN AN ORDER WITHOUT THINKING ABOUT IT?
I'VE GOT VERY SPECIFIC PLANS FOR THOSE GIRLS.

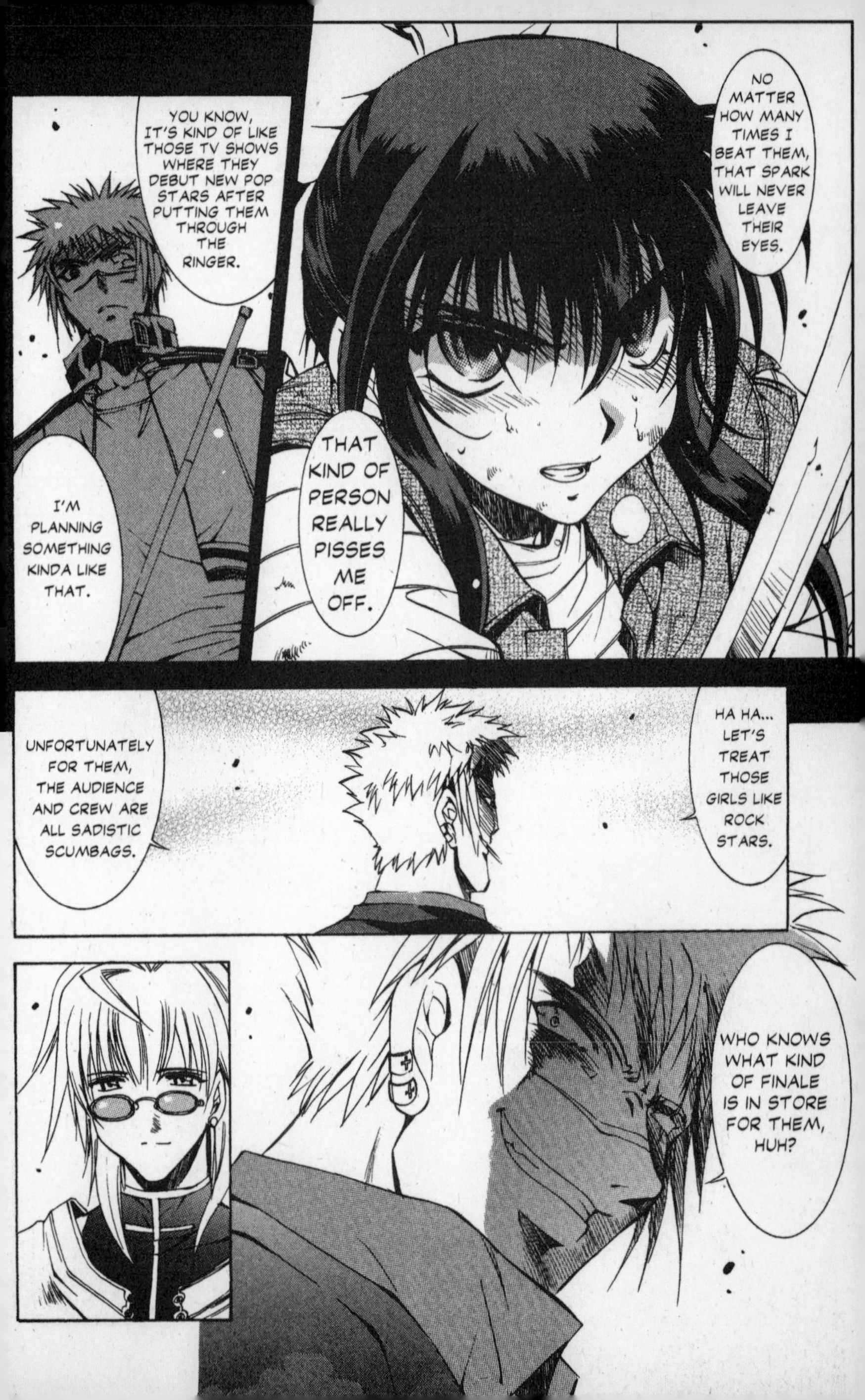
NO MATTER HOW MANY TIMES I BEAT THEM, THAT SPARK WILL NEVER LEAVE THEIR EYES.
THAT KIND OF PERSON REALLY PISSES ME OFF.
YOU KNOW, IT'S KIND OF LIKE THOSE TV SHOWS WHERE THEY DEBUT NEW POP STARS AFTER PUTTING THEM THROUGH THE RINGER.
I'M PLANNING SOMETHING KINDA LIKE THAT.
HA HA... LET'S TREAT THOSE GIRLS LIKE ROCK STARS.
UNFORTUNATELY FOR THEM, THE AUDIENCE AND CREW ARE ALL SADISTIC SCUMBAGS.
WHO KNOWS WHAT KIND OF FINALE IS IN STORE FOR THEM, HUH?

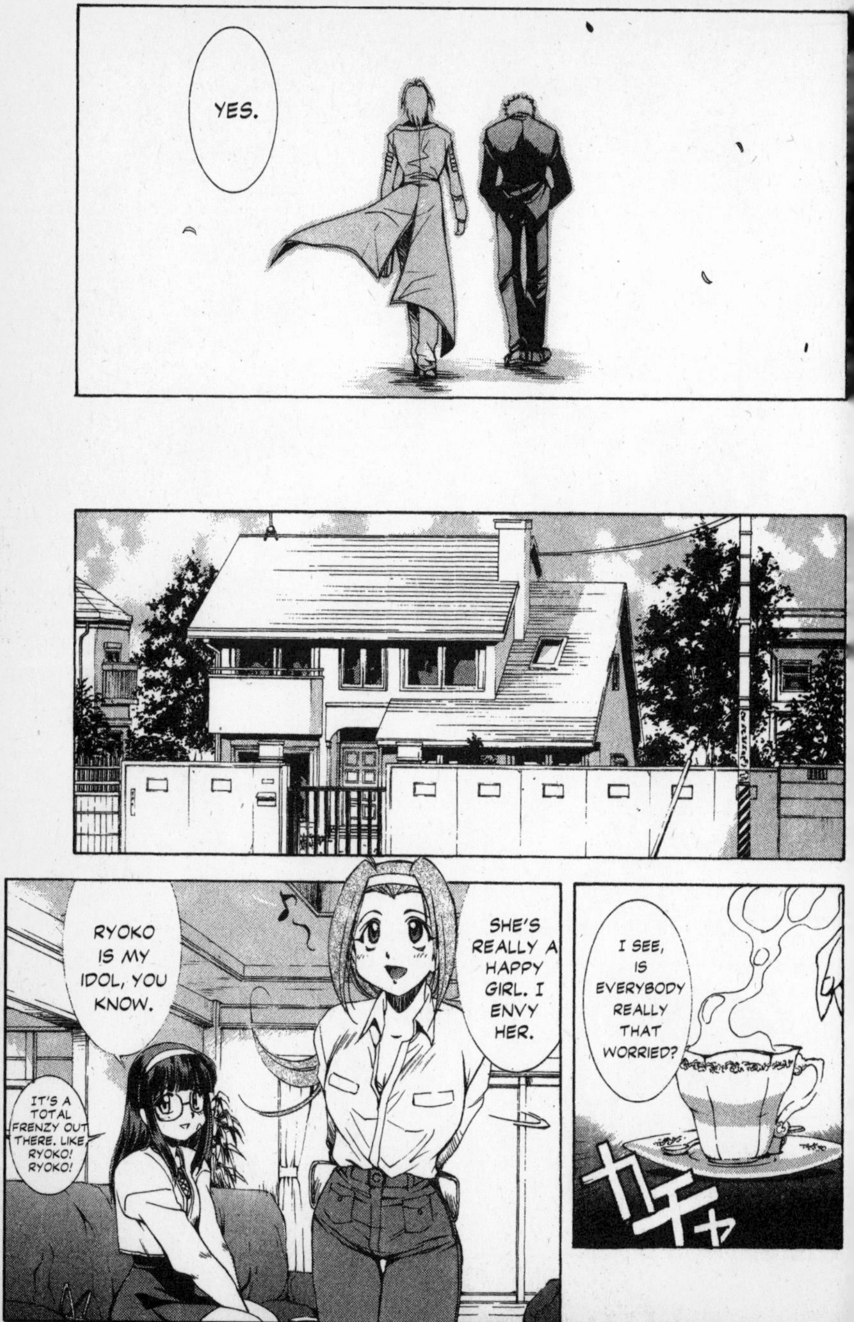
YES.
I SEE, IS EVERYBODY REALLY THAT WORRIED?
カチャ
SHE'S REALLY A HAPPY GIRL. I ENVY HER.
RYOKO IS MY IDOL, YOU KNOW.
IT'S A TOTAL FRENZY OUT THERE. LIKE RYOKO! RYOKO!

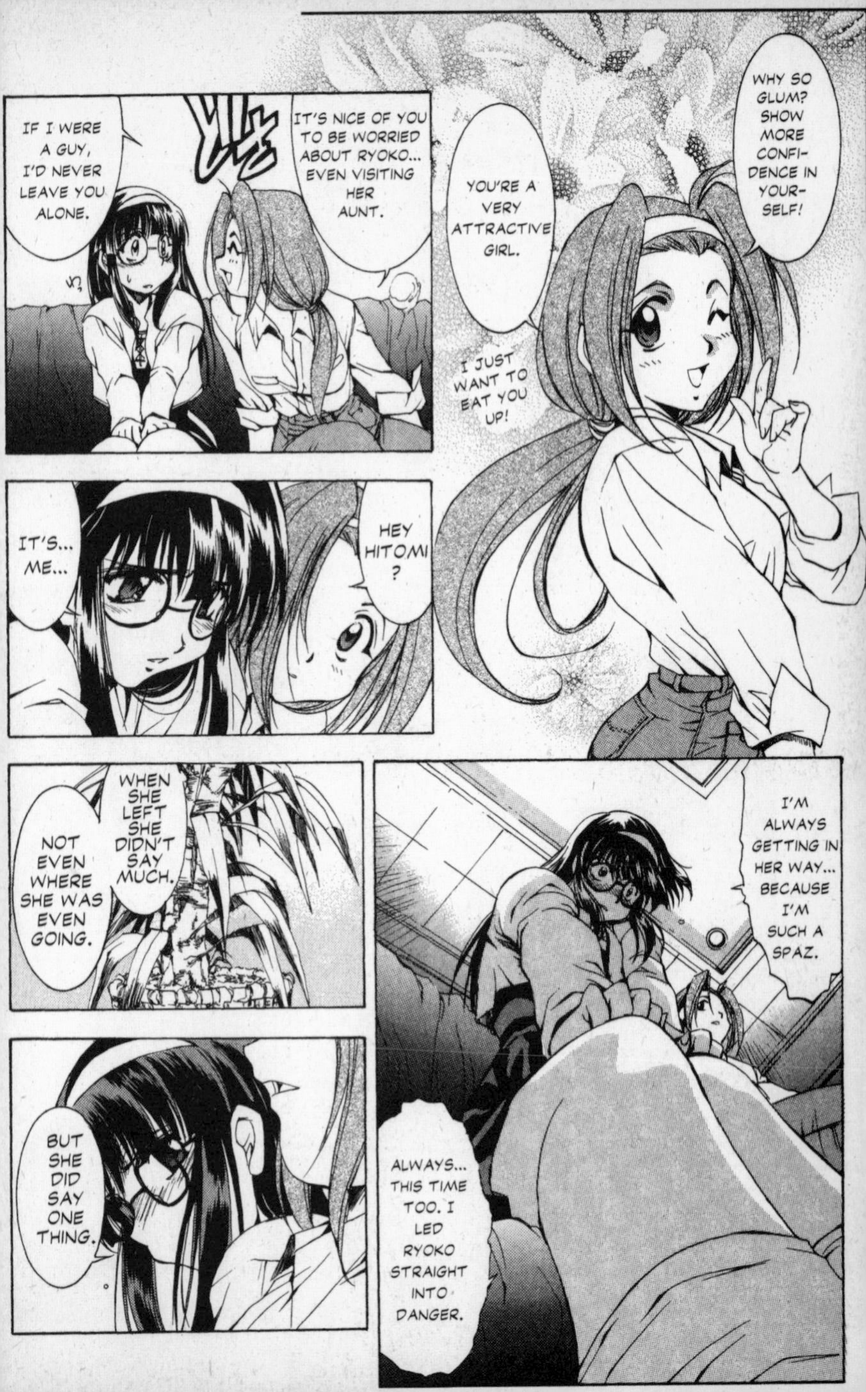

WHY SO GLUM? SHOW MORE CONFIDENCE IN YOURSELF!
YOU'RE A VERY ATTRACTIVE GIRL.
I JUST WANT TO EAT YOU UP!
IT'S NICE OF YOU TO BE WORRIED ABOUT RYOKO... EVEN VISITING HER AUNT.
IF I WERE A GUY, I'D NEVER LEAVE YOU ALONE.
HEY HITOMI?
IT'S... ME...
I'M ALWAYS GETTING IN HER WAY... BECAUSE I'M SUCH A SPAZ.
ALWAYS... THIS TIME TOO. I LED RYOKO STRAIGHT INTO DANGER.
WHEN SHE LEFT SHE DIDN'T SAY MUCH.
NOT EVEN WHERE SHE WAS EVEN GOING.
BUT SHE DID SAY ONE THING.

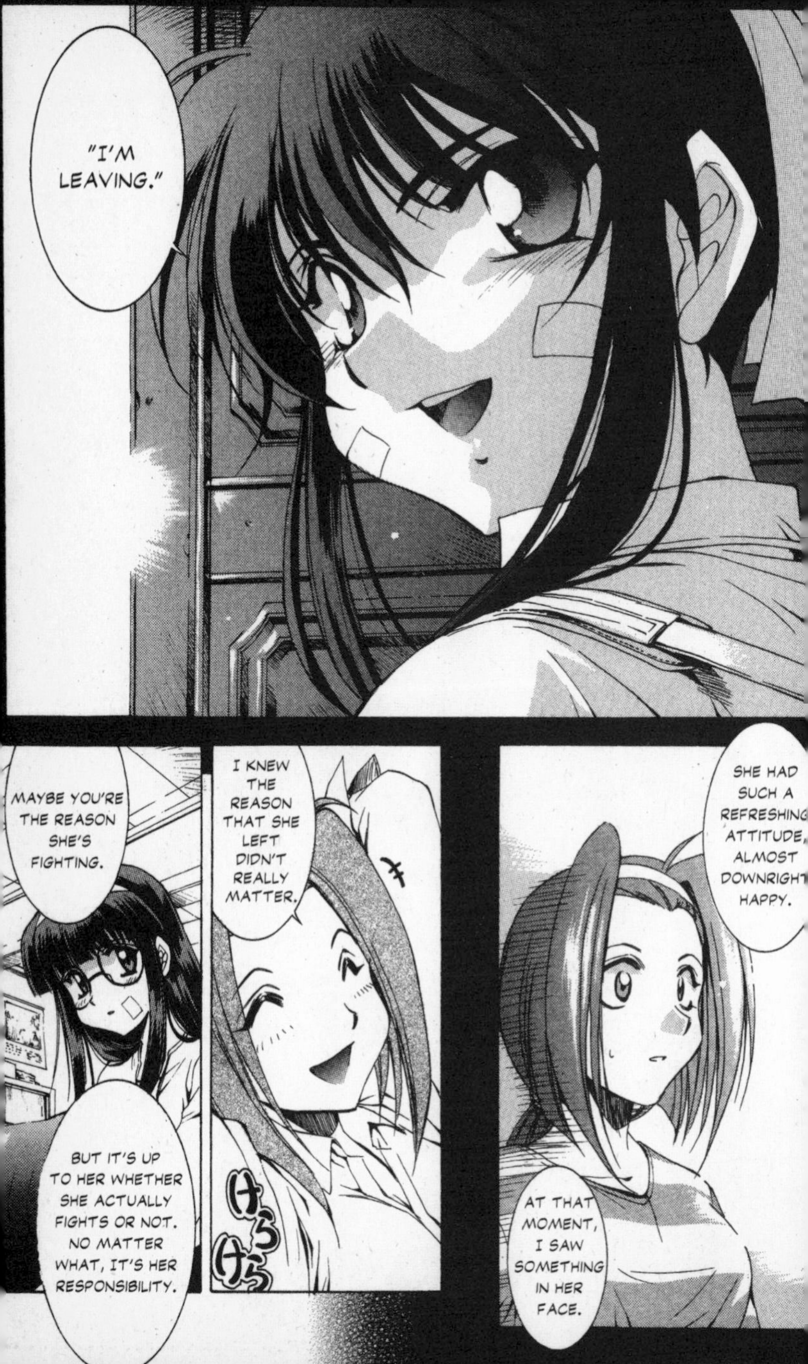
"I'M LEAVING."
SHE HAD SUCH A REFRESHING ATTITUDE, ALMOST DOWNRIGHT HAPPY.
AT THAT MOMENT, I SAW SOMETHING IN HER FACE.
I KNEW THE REASON THAT SHE LEFT DIDN'T REALLY MATTER.
けらけら
MAYBE YOU'RE THE REASON SHE'S FIGHTING.
BUT IT'S UP TO HER WHETHER SHE ACTUALLY FIGHTS OR NOT. NO MATTER WHAT, IT'S HER RESPONSIBILITY.

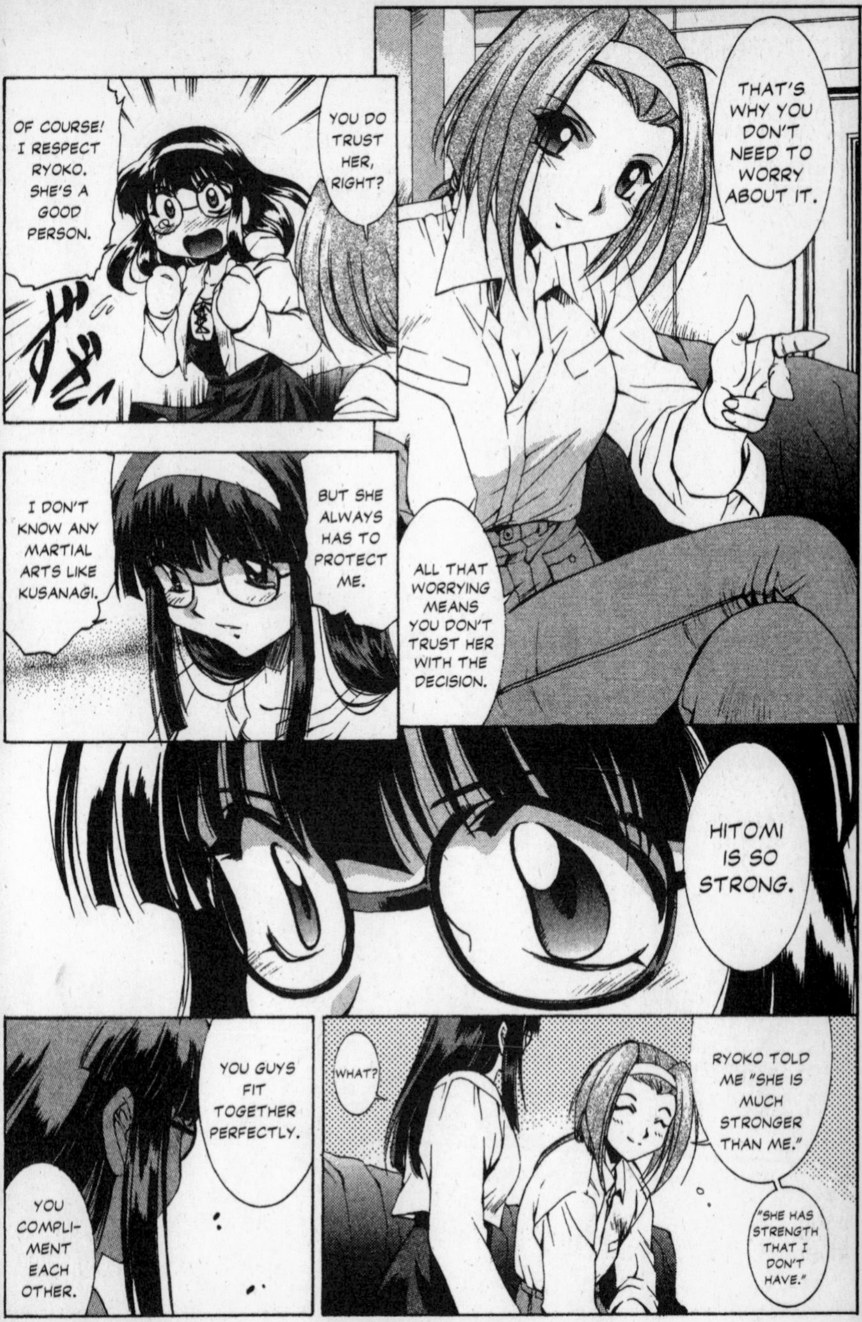
THAT'S WHY YOU DON'T NEED TO WORRY ABOUT IT.
YOU DO TRUST HER, RIGHT?
OF COURSE! I RESPECT RYOKO. SHE'S A GOOD PERSON.
ALL THAT WORRYING MEANS YOU DON'T TRUST HER WITH THE DECISION.
BUT SHE ALWAYS HAS TO PROTECT ME.
I DON'T KNOW ANY MARTIAL ARTS LIKE KUSANAGI.
HITOMI IS SO STRONG.
RYOKO TOLD ME "SHE IS MUCH STRONGER THAN ME."
"SHE HAS STRENGTH THAT I DON'T HAVE."
WHAT?
YOU GUYS FIT TOGETHER PERFECTLY.
YOU COMPLIMENT EACH OTHER.

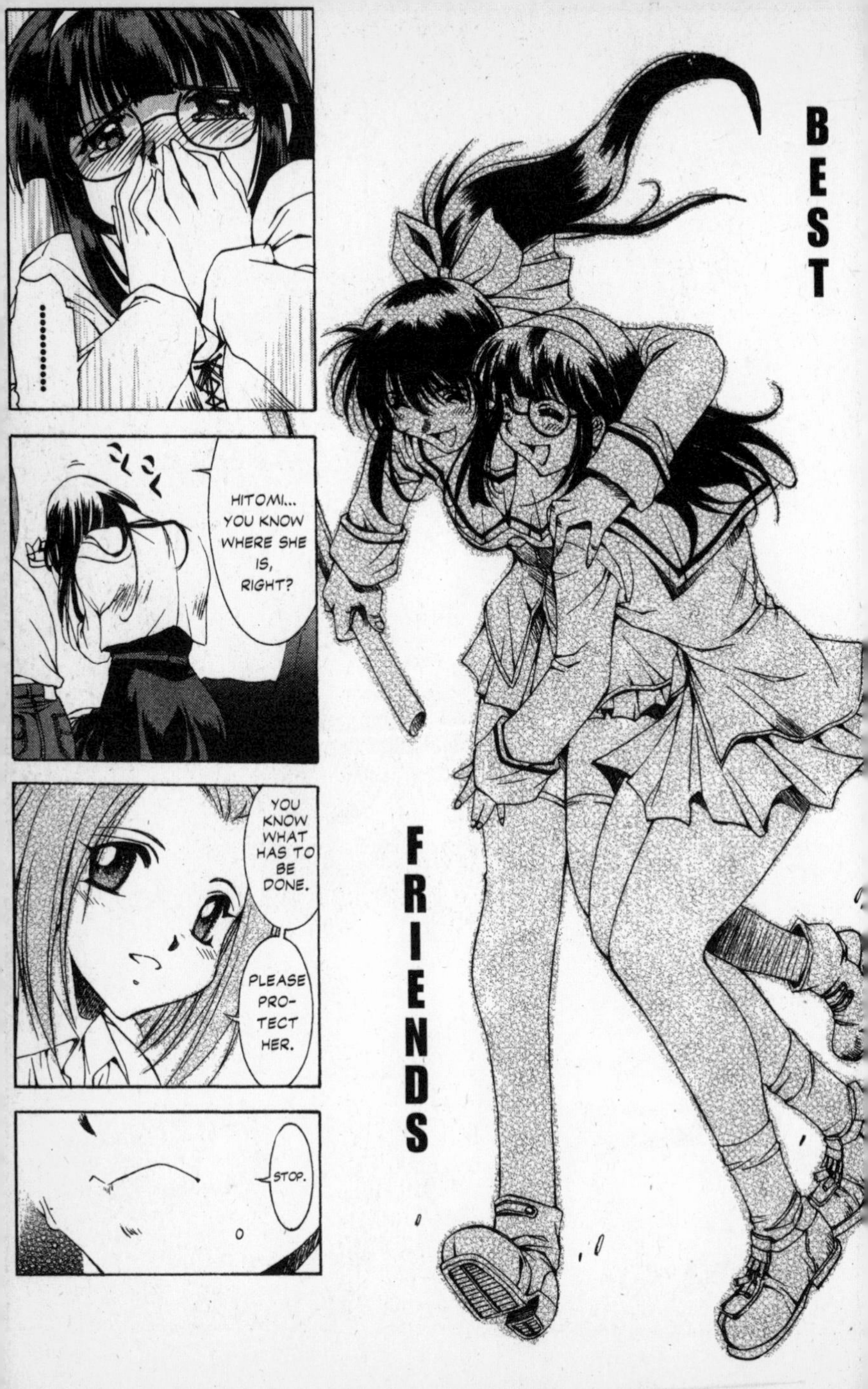
BEST FRIENDS
......
HITOMI... YOU KNOW WHERE SHE IS, RIGHT?
YOU KNOW WHAT HAS TO BE DONE.
PLEASE PRO- TECT HER.
STOP.

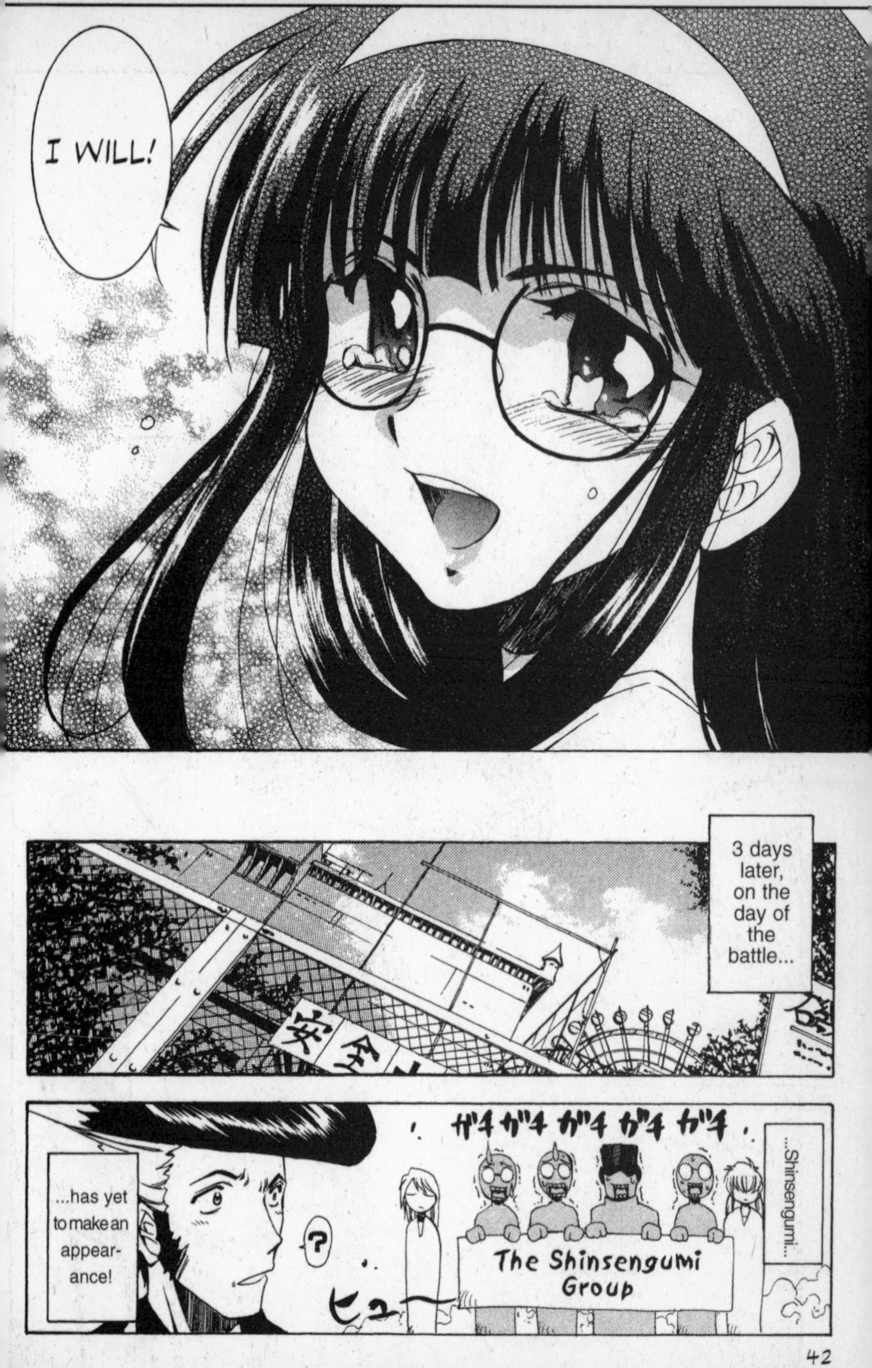
I WILL!
3 days later, on the day of the battle...
安全
...Shinsengumi...
ガチ ガチ ガチ ガチ ガチ
The Shinsengumi Group
?
...has yet to make an appearance!
ヒュー

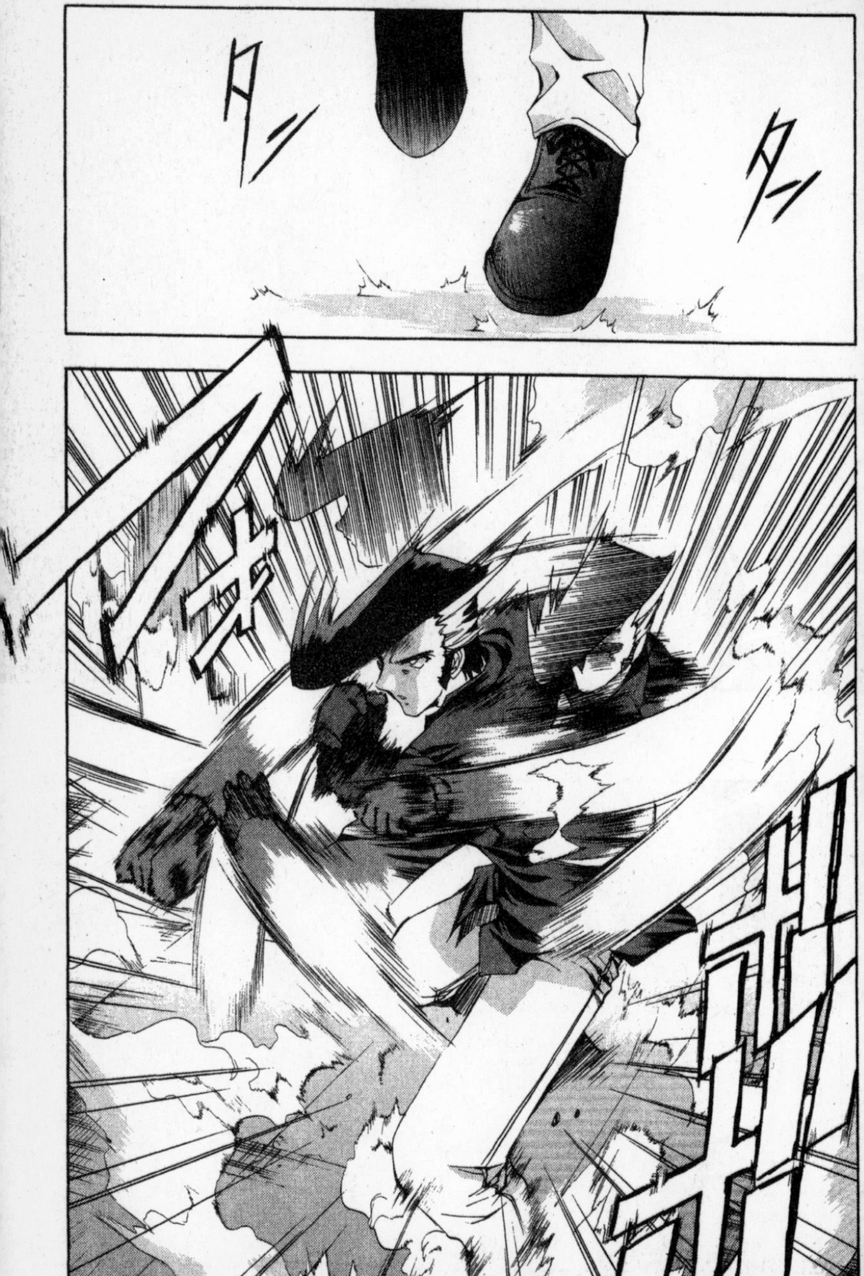
タン
タン

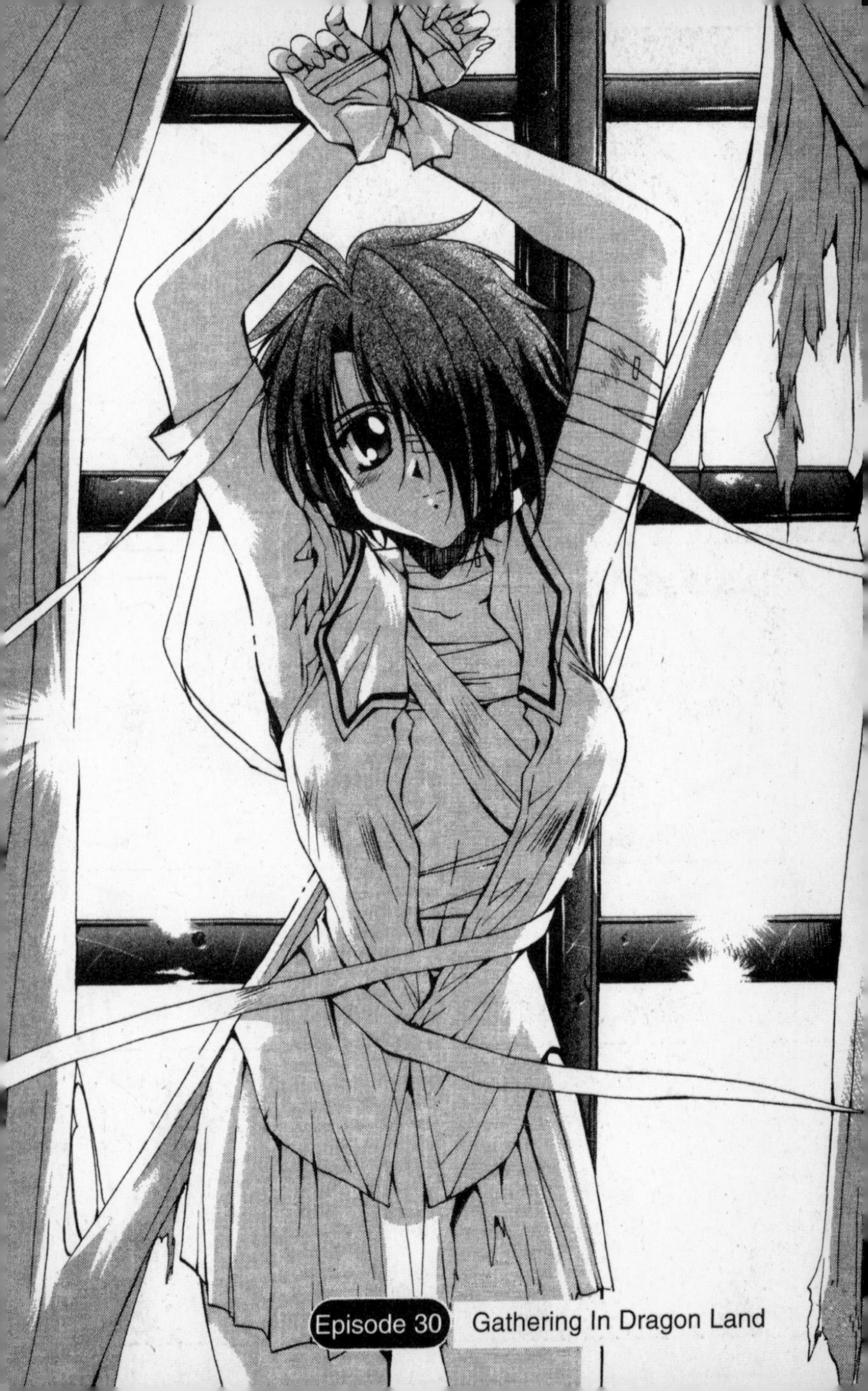
Episode 30
Gathering In Dragon Land

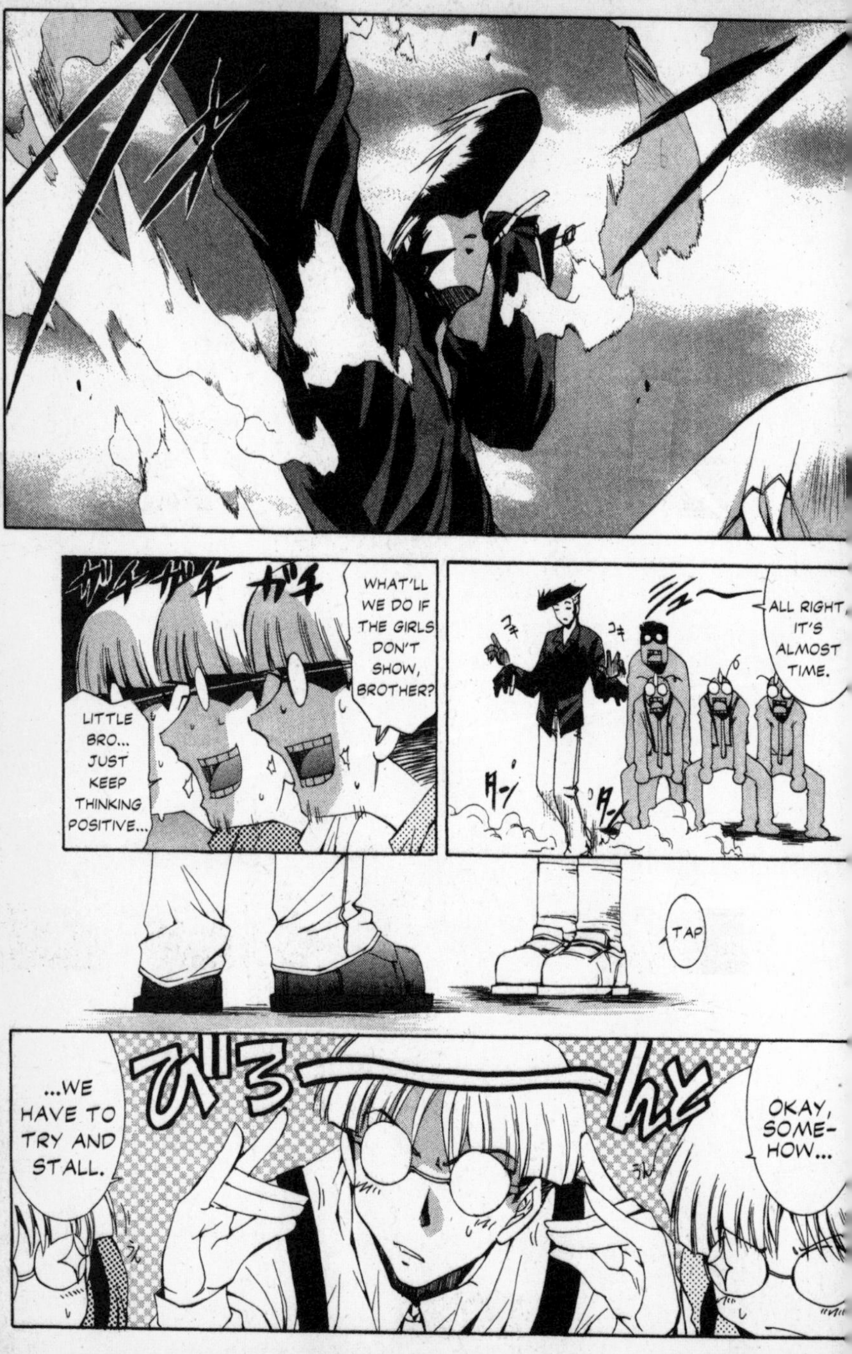
ALL RIGHT, IT'S ALMOST TIME.
WHAT'LL WE DO IF THE GIRLS DON'T SHOW, BROTHER?
LITTLE BRO... JUST KEEP THINKING POSITIVE...
TAP
OKAY, SOME-HOW...
...WE HAVE TO TRY AND STALL.

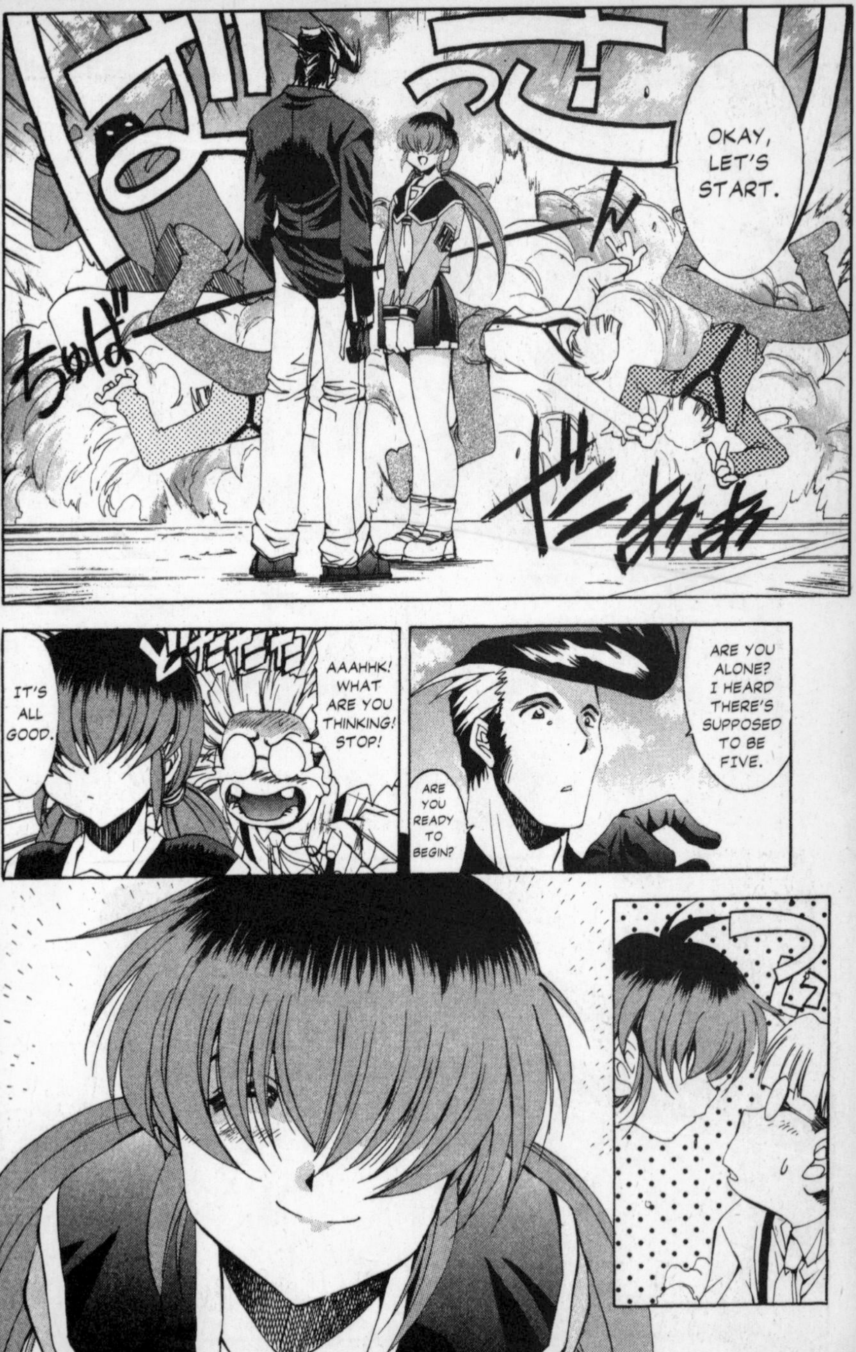
OKAY, LET'S START.
ARE YOU ALONE? I HEARD THERE'S SUPPOSED TO BE FIVE.
ARE YOU READY TO BEGIN?
AAAHHK! WHAT ARE YOU THINKING! STOP!
IT'S ALL GOOD.

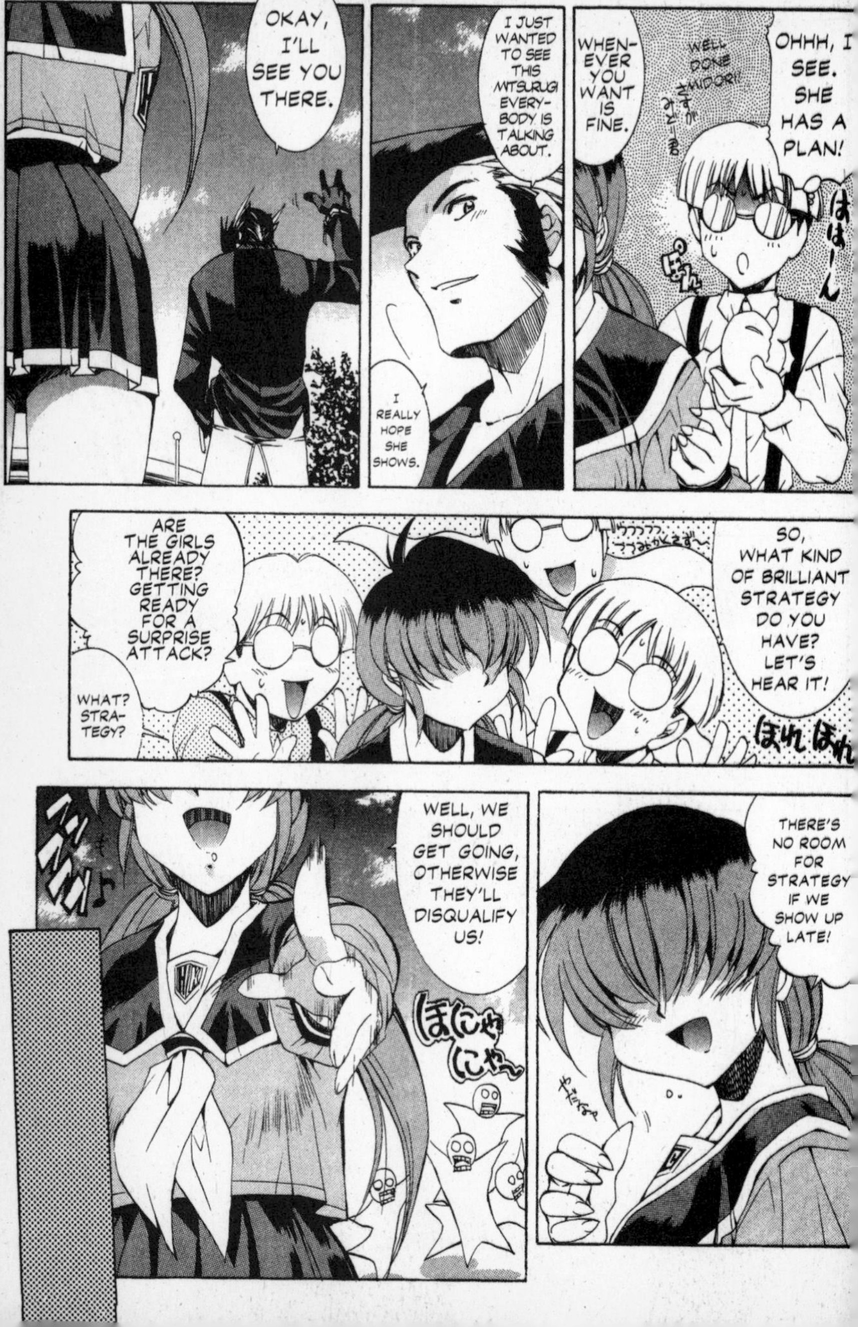
OHHH, I SEE. SHE HAS A PLAN!
WELL DONE MIDORI!!
WHEN-EVER YOU WANT IS FINE.
I JUST WANTED TO SEE THIS MITSURUGI EVERY-BODY IS TALKING ABOUT.
I REALLY HOPE SHE SHOWS.
OKAY, I'LL SEE YOU THERE.
SO, WHAT KIND OF BRILLIANT STRATEGY DO YOU HAVE? LET'S HEAR IT!
ARE THE GIRLS ALREADY THERE? GETTING READY FOR A SURPRISE ATTACK?
WHAT? STRA-TEGY?
THERE'S NO ROOM FOR STRATEGY IF WE SHOW UP LATE!
WELL, WE SHOULD GET GOING, OTHERWISE THEY'LL DISQUALIFY US!

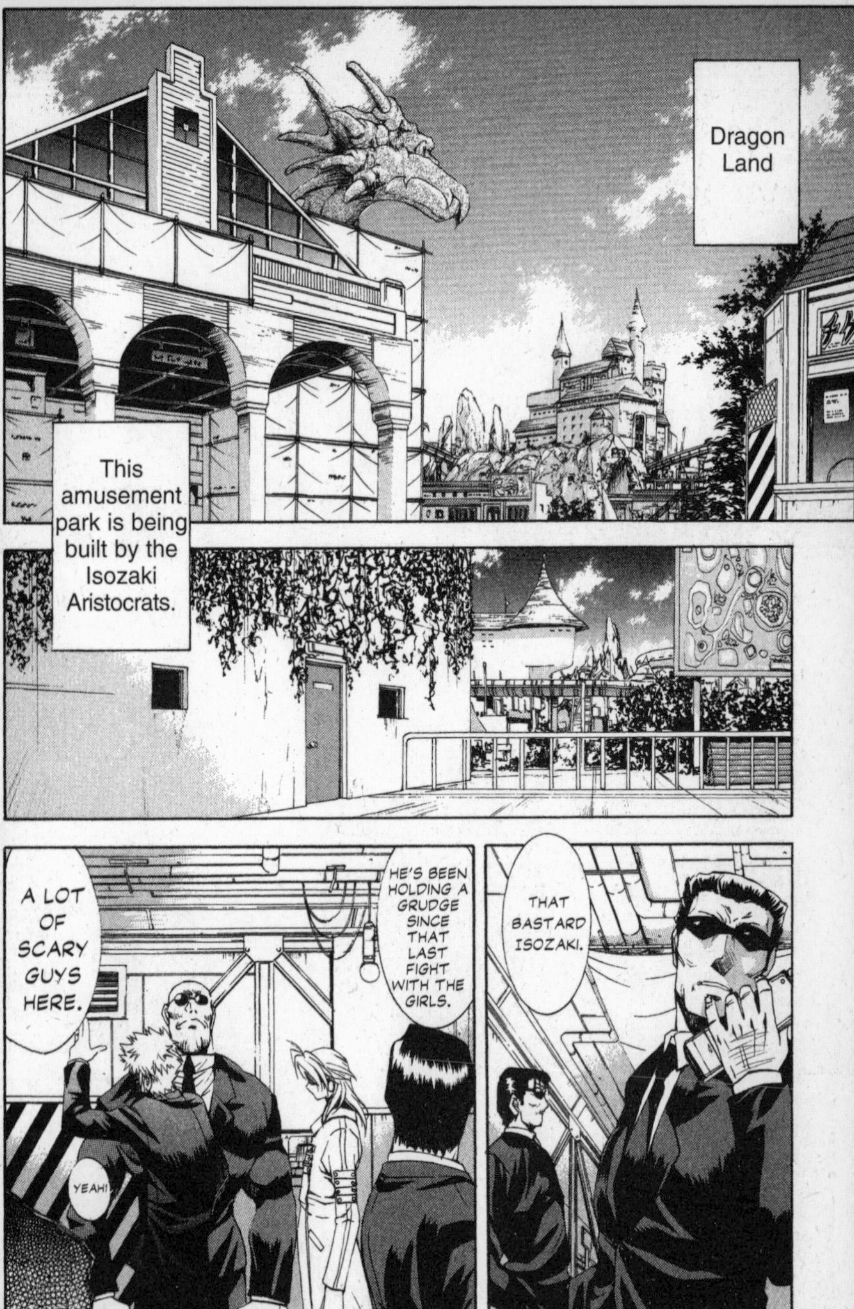
Dragon Land
This amusement park is being built by the Isozaki Aristocrats.
THAT BASTARD ISOZAKI.
HE'S BEEN HOLDING A GRUDGE SINCE THAT LAST FIGHT WITH THE GIRLS.
A LOT OF SCARY GUYS HERE.
YEAH!

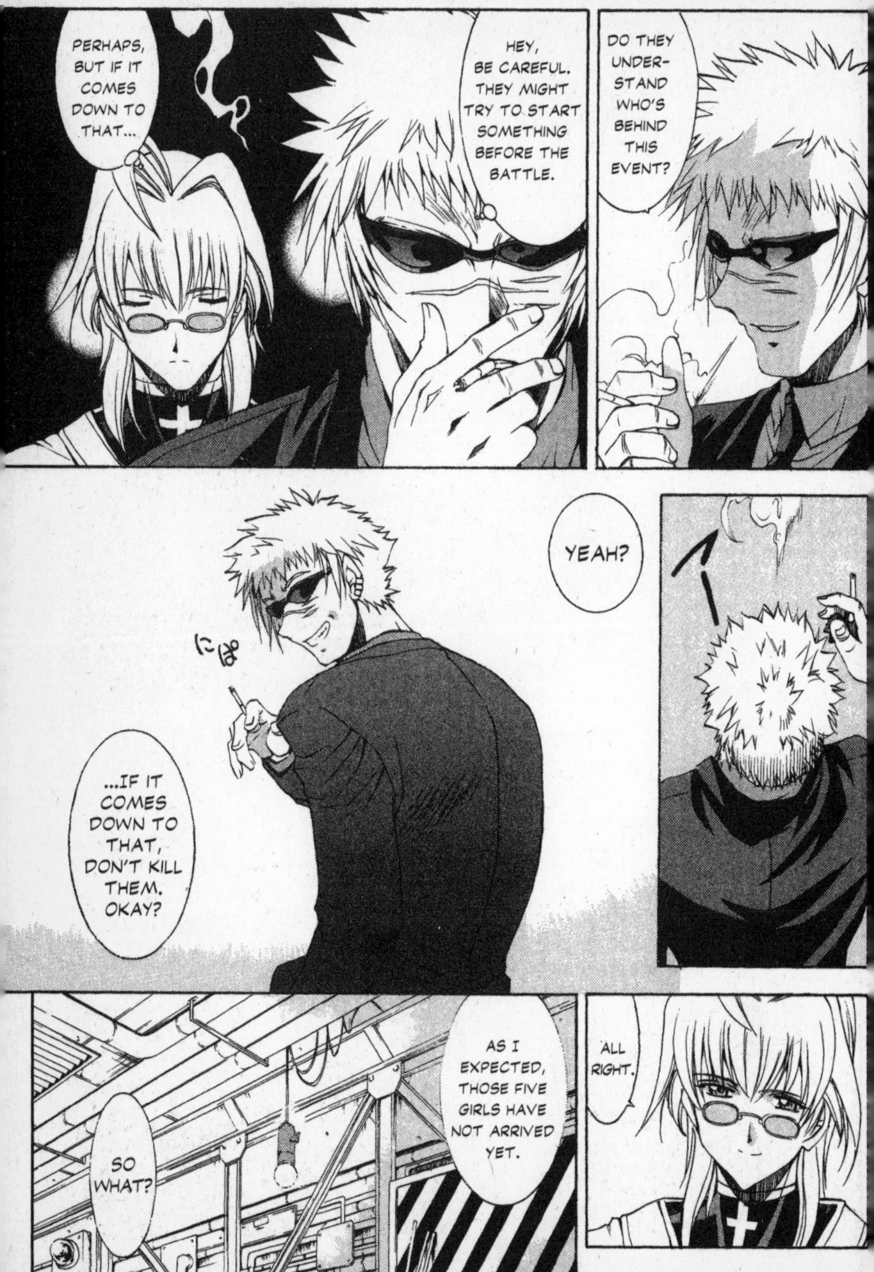
DO THEY UNDER-STAND WHO'S BEHIND THIS EVENT?
HEY, BE CAREFUL. THEY MIGHT TRY TO START SOMETHING BEFORE THE BATTLE.
PERHAPS, BUT IF IT COMES DOWN TO THAT...
YEAH?
にぱ
...IF IT COMES DOWN TO THAT, DON'T KILL THEM. OKAY?
ALL RIGHT.
AS I EXPECTED, THOSE FIVE GIRLS HAVE NOT ARRIVED YET.
SO WHAT?

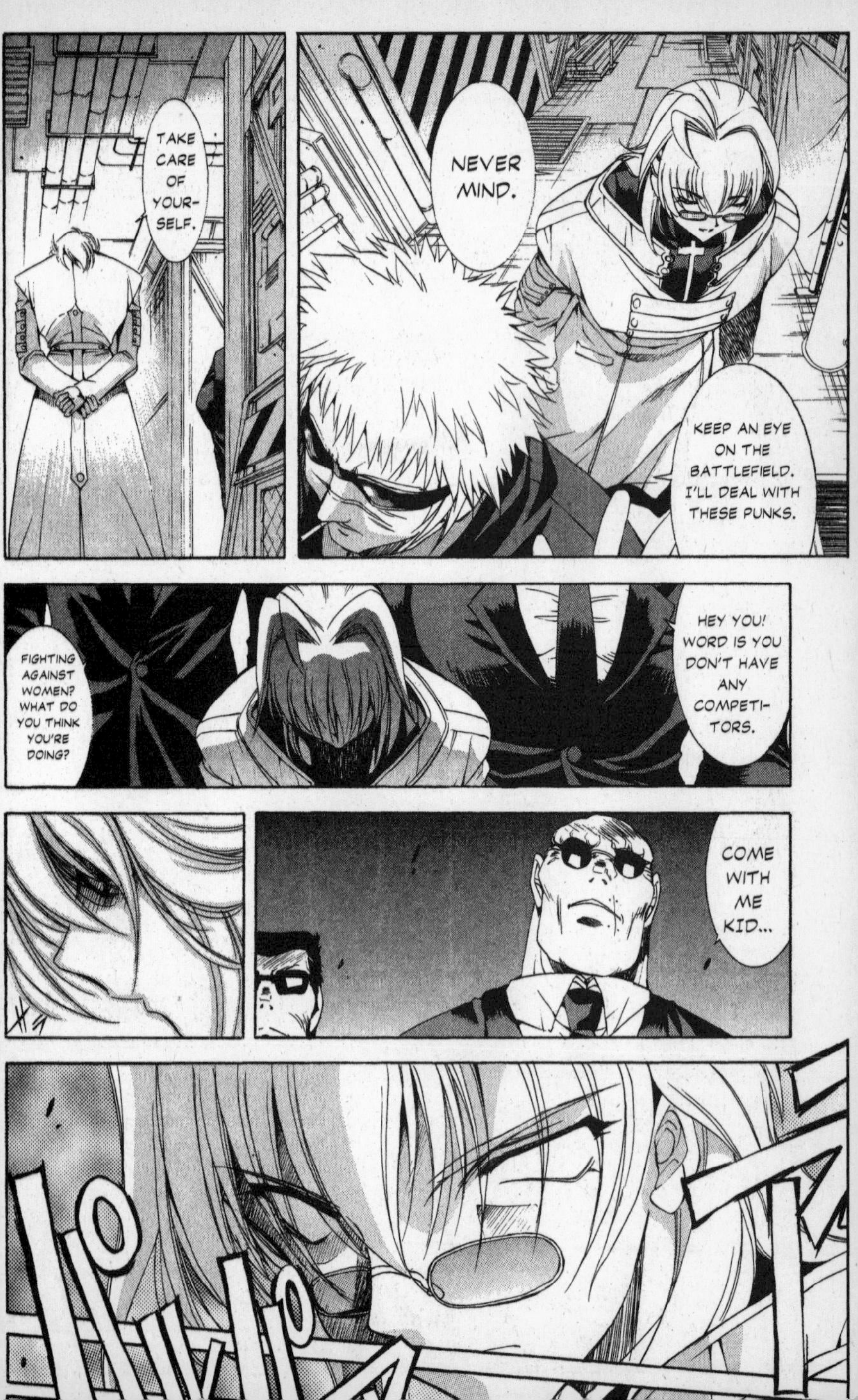
NEVER MIND.
KEEP AN EYE ON THE BATTLEFIELD. I'LL DEAL WITH THESE PUNKS.
TAKE CARE OF YOUR-SELF.
HEY YOU! WORD IS YOU DON'T HAVE ANY COMPETI-TORS.
FIGHTING AGAINST WOMEN? WHAT DO YOU THINK YOU'RE DOING?
COME WITH ME KID...

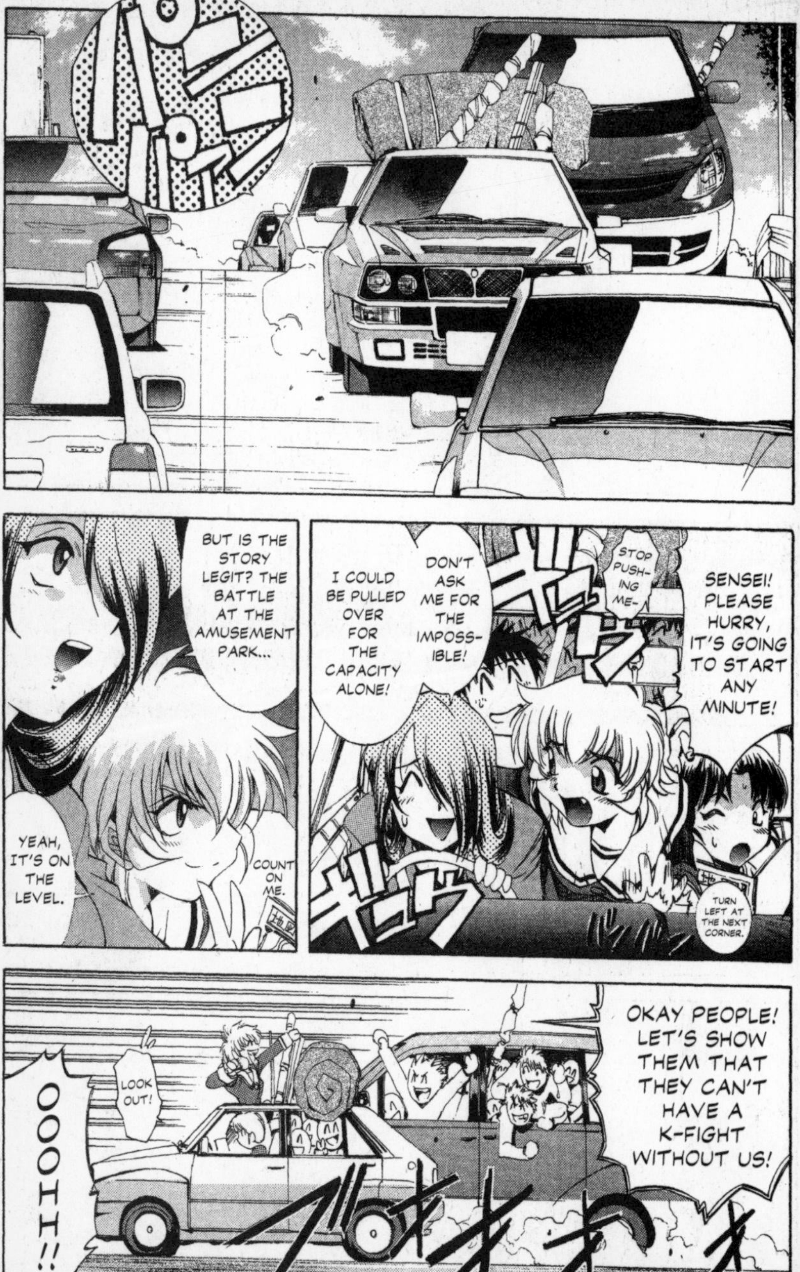
SENSEI! PLEASE HURRY, IT'S GOING TO START ANY MINUTE!
STOP PUSHING ME-
DON'T ASK ME FOR THE IMPOSSIBLE!
I COULD BE PULLED OVER FOR THE CAPACITY ALONE!
TURN LEFT AT THE NEXT CORNER.
BUT IS THE STORY LEGIT? THE BATTLE AT THE AMUSEMENT PARK...
YEAH, IT'S ON THE LEVEL.
COUNT ON ME.
OKAY PEOPLE! LET'S SHOW THEM THAT THEY CAN'T HAVE A K-FIGHT WITHOUT US!
LOOK OUT!
OOOHH!!

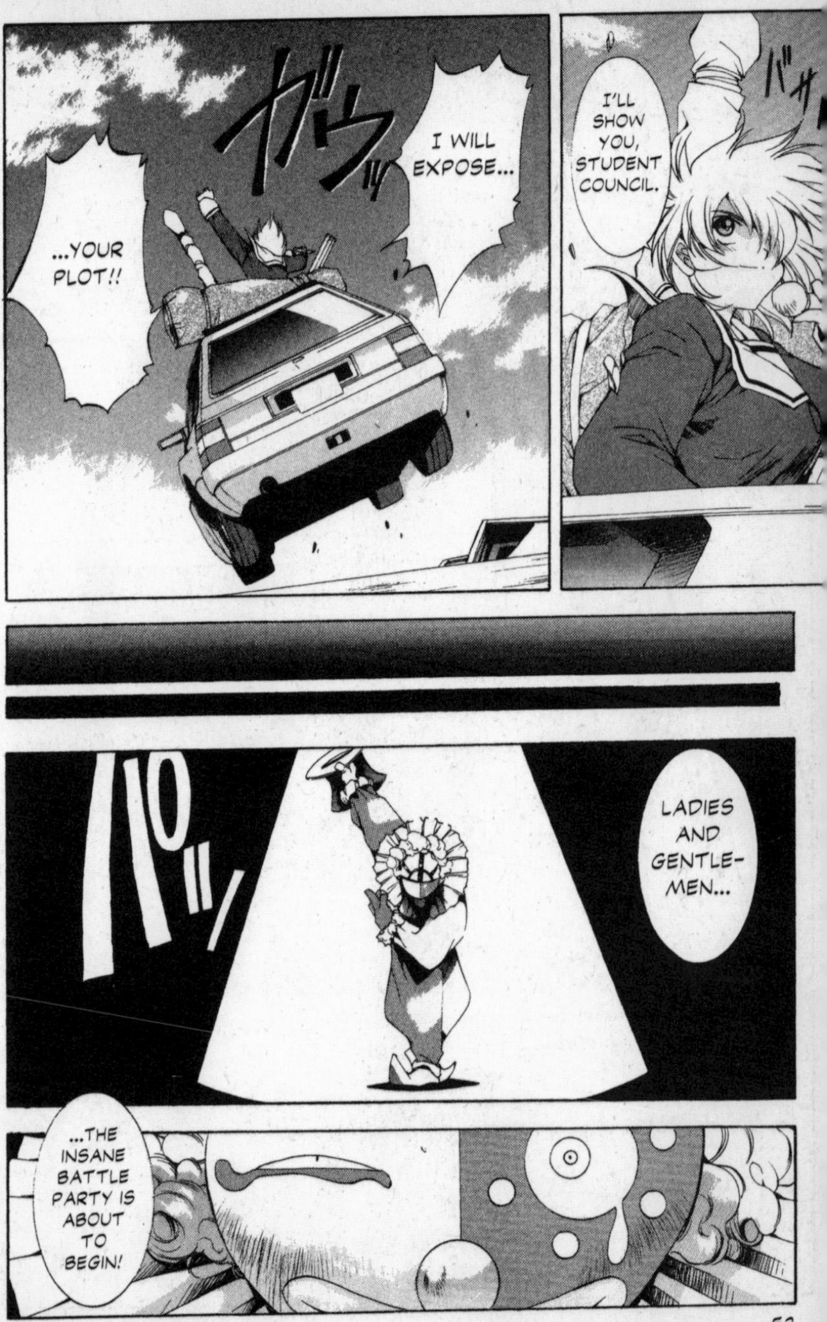
I'LL SHOW YOU, STUDENT COUNCIL.
I WILL EXPOSE...
...YOUR PLOT!!
LADIES AND GENTLE-MEN...
...THE INSANE BATTLE PARTY IS ABOUT TO BEGIN!

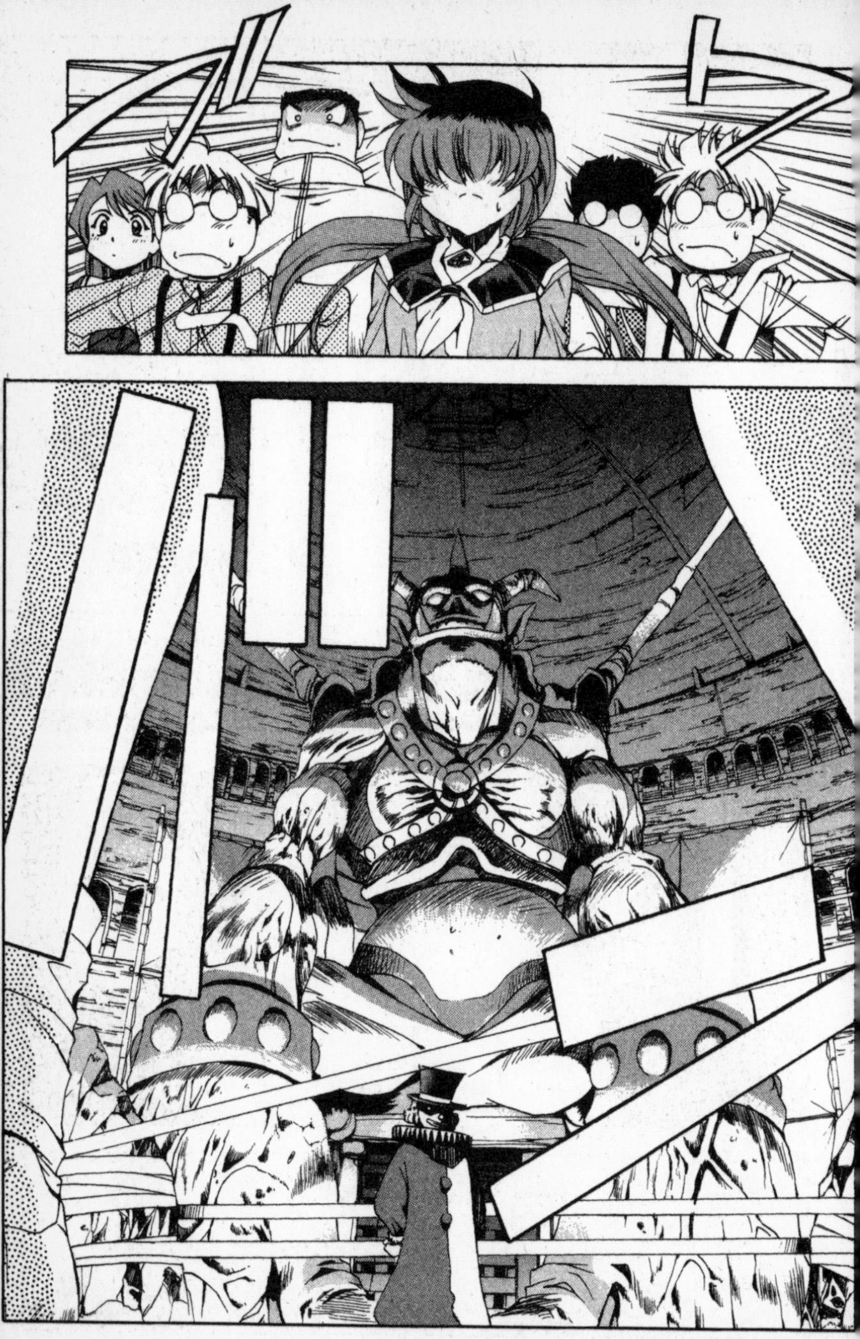

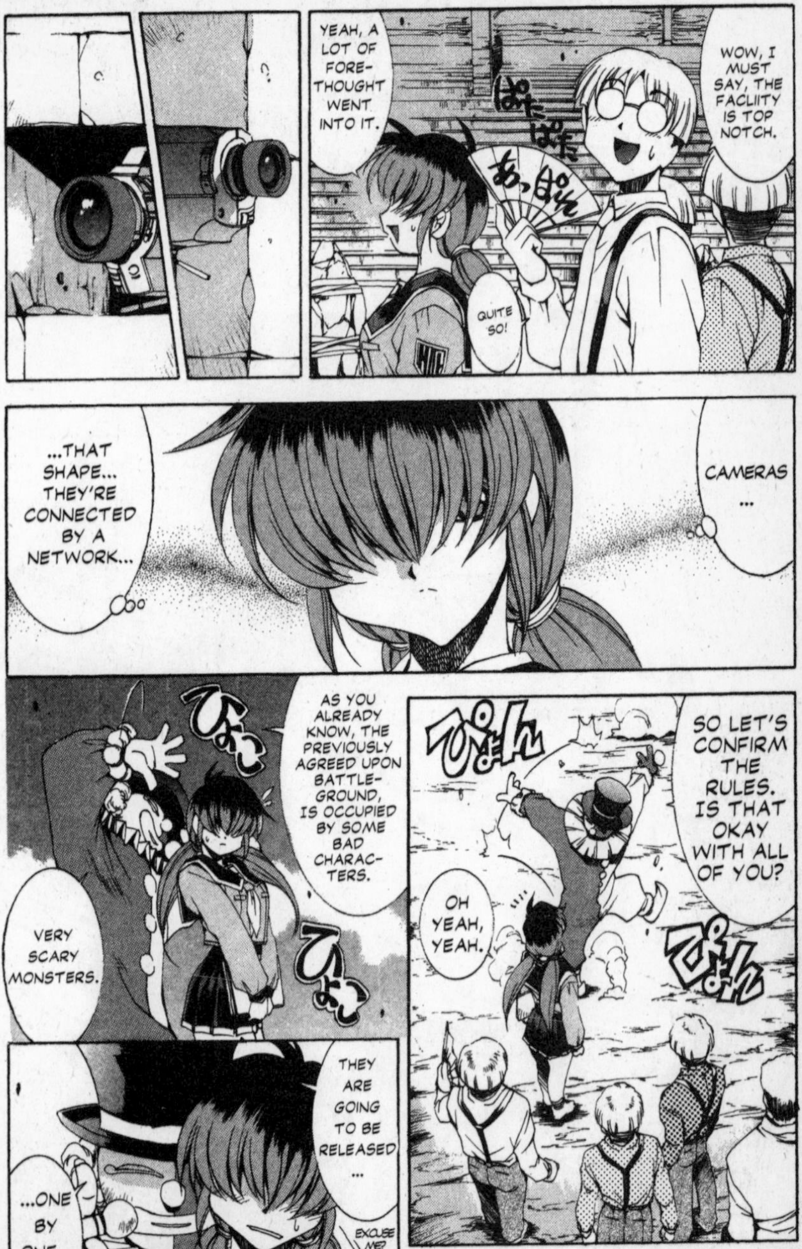
WOW, I MUST SAY, THE FACLIITY IS TOP NOTCH.
ぱたぱた
YEAH, A LOT OF FORE-THOUGHT WENT INTO IT.
QUITE SO!
CAMERAS ...
...THAT SHAPE... THEY'RE CONNECTED BY A NETWORK...
SO LET'S CONFIRM THE RULES. IS THAT OKAY WITH ALL OF YOU?
ぴょん
OH YEAH, YEAH.
ぴょん
AS YOU ALREADY KNOW, THE PREVIOUSLY AGREED UPON BATTLE-GROUND, IS OCCUPIED BY SOME BAD CHARAC-TERS.
ひょこ
VERY SCARY MONSTERS.
ひょこ
THEY ARE GOING TO BE RELEASED ...
...ONE BY ONE...
EXCUSE ME?

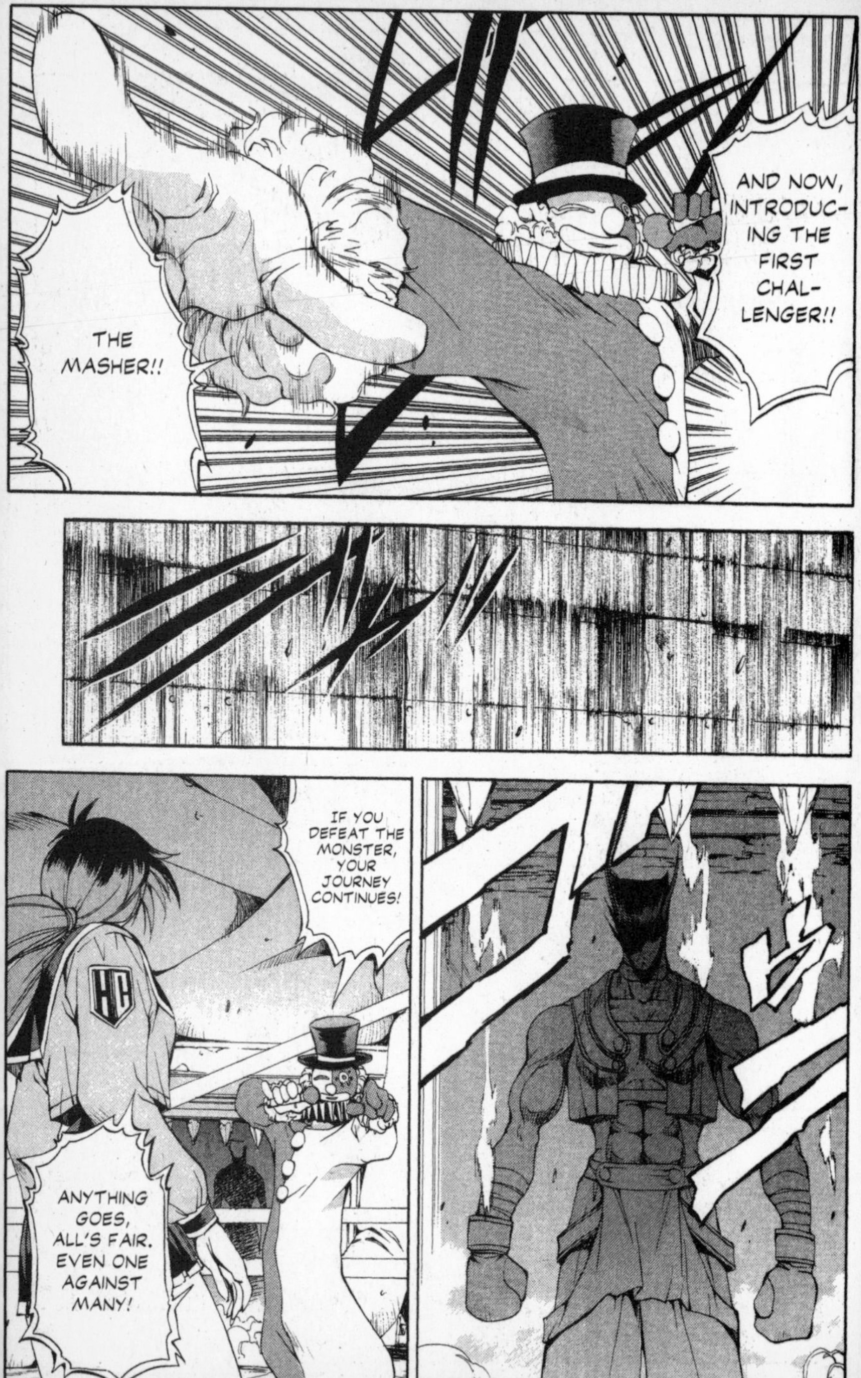
AND NOW, INTRODUCING THE FIRST CHALLENGER!!
THE MASHER!!
IF YOU DEFEAT THE MONSTER, YOUR JOURNEY CONTINUES!
ANYTHING GOES, ALL'S FAIR. EVEN ONE AGAINST MANY!

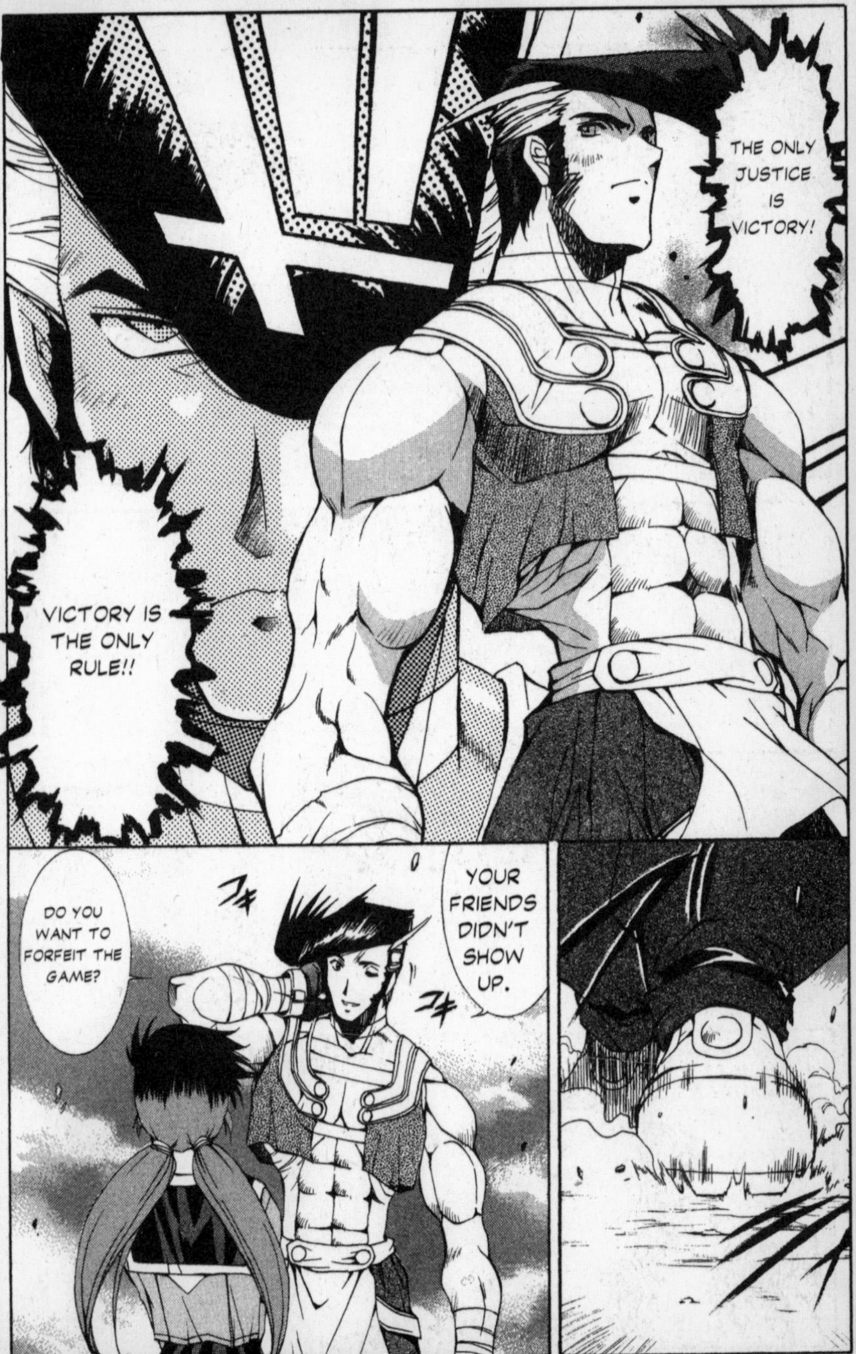
THE ONLY JUSTICE IS VICTORY!
VICTORY IS THE ONLY RULE!!
YOUR FRIENDS DIDN'T SHOW UP.
DO YOU WANT TO FORFEIT THE GAME?

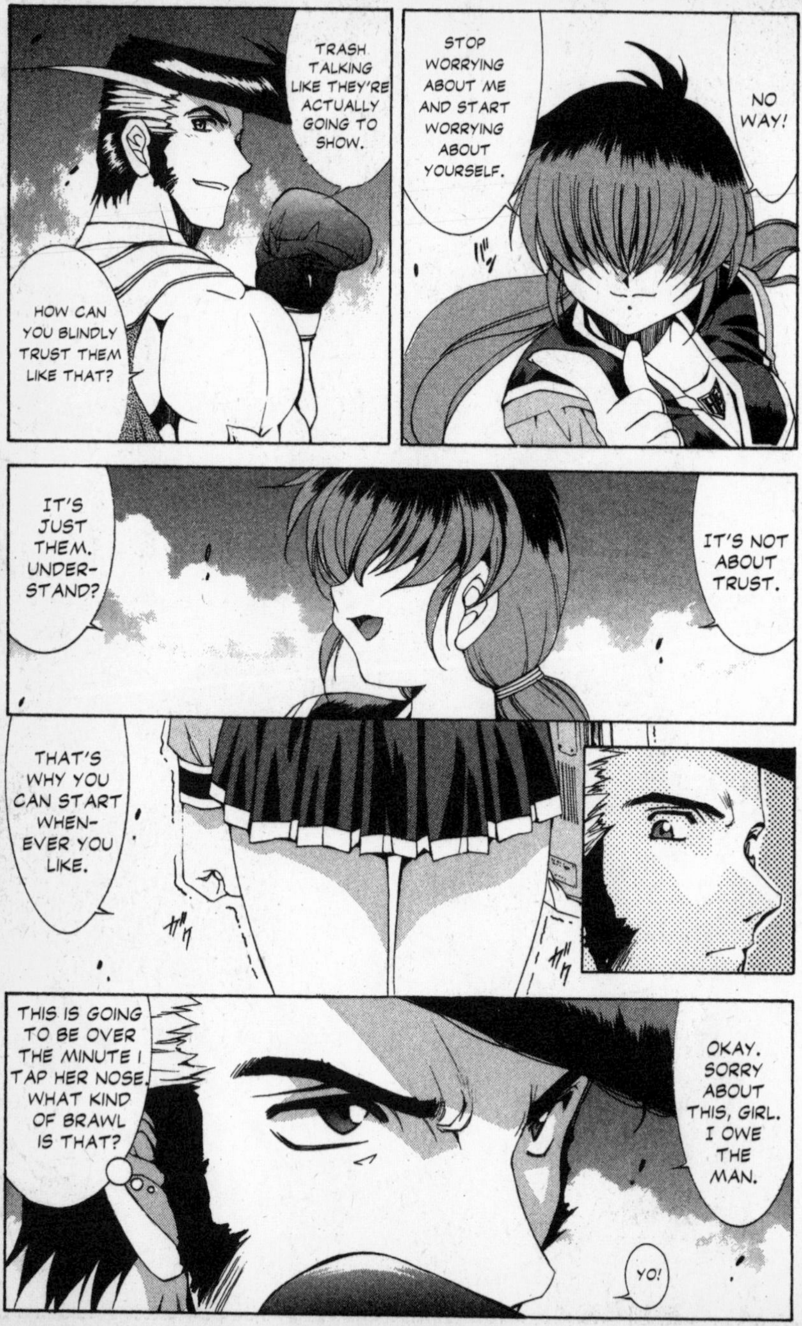
NO WAY!
STOP WORRYING ABOUT ME AND START WORRYING ABOUT YOURSELF.
TRASH TALKING LIKE THEY'RE ACTUALLY GOING TO SHOW.
HOW CAN YOU BLINDLY TRUST THEM LIKE THAT?
IT'S NOT ABOUT TRUST.
IT'S JUST THEM. UNDER-STAND?
THAT'S WHY YOU CAN START WHEN-EVER YOU LIKE.
OKAY. SORRY ABOUT THIS, GIRL. I OWE THE MAN.
THIS IS GOING TO BE OVER THE MINUTE I TAP HER NOSE. WHAT KIND OF BRAWL IS THAT?
YO!

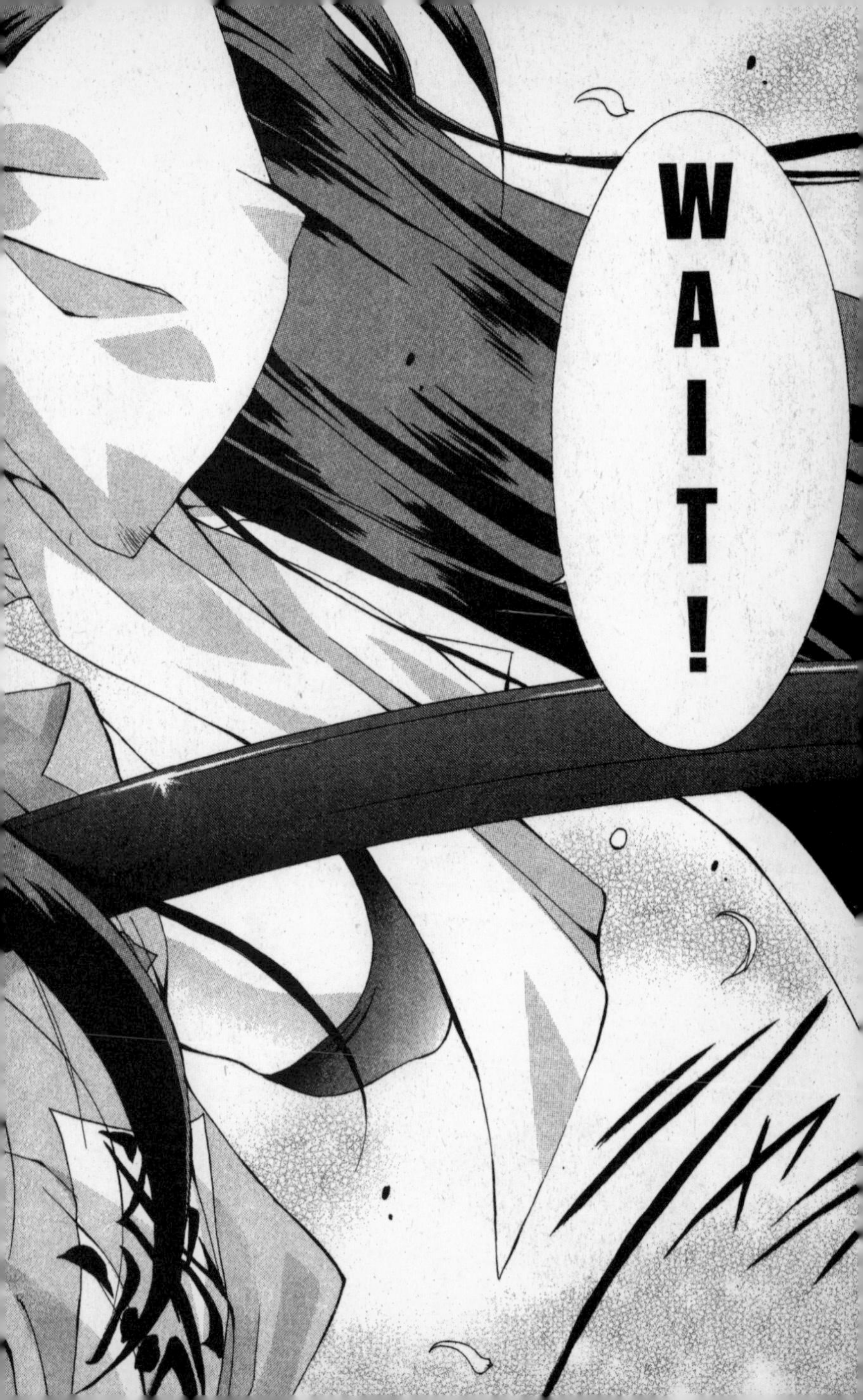
WAIT!

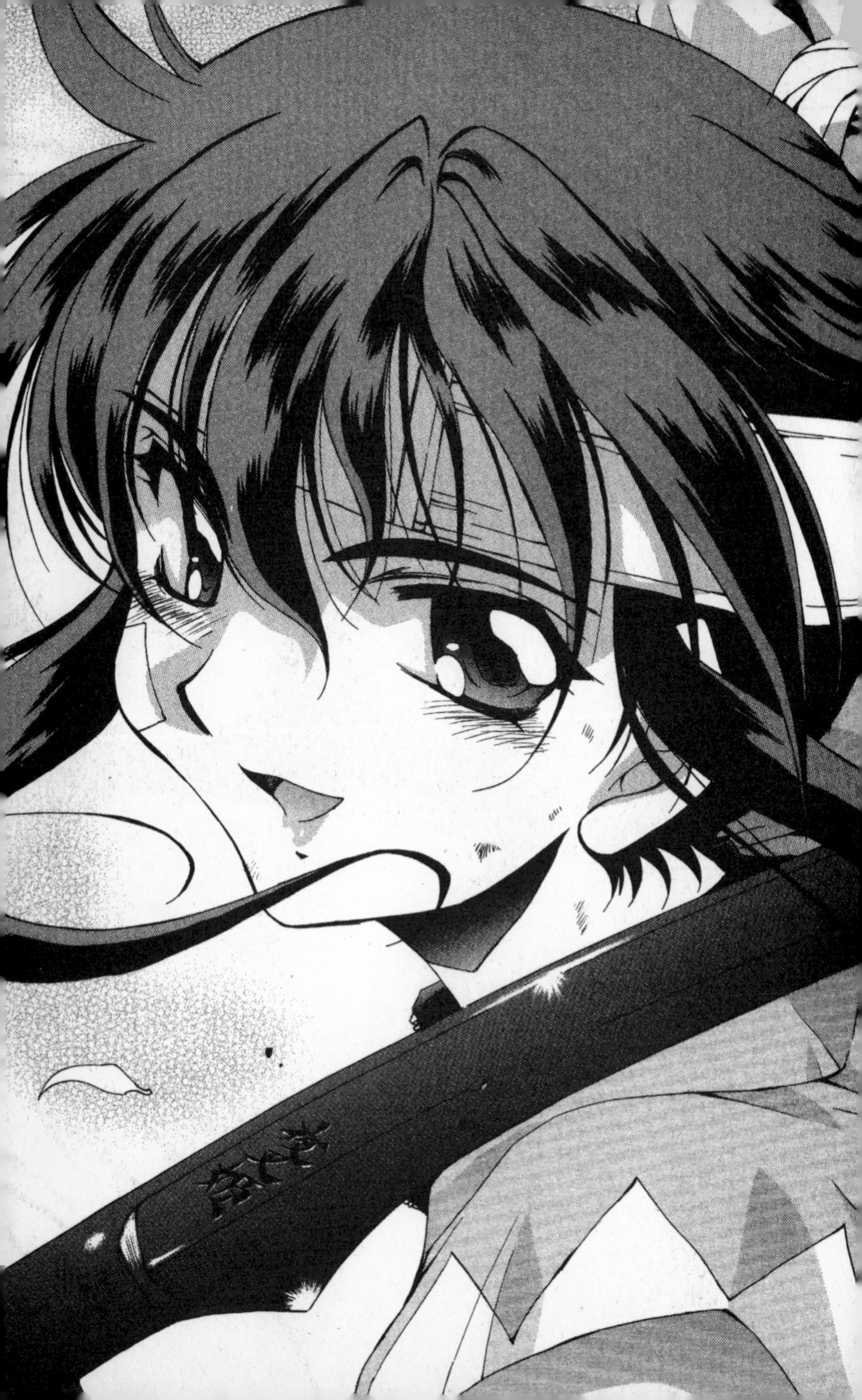

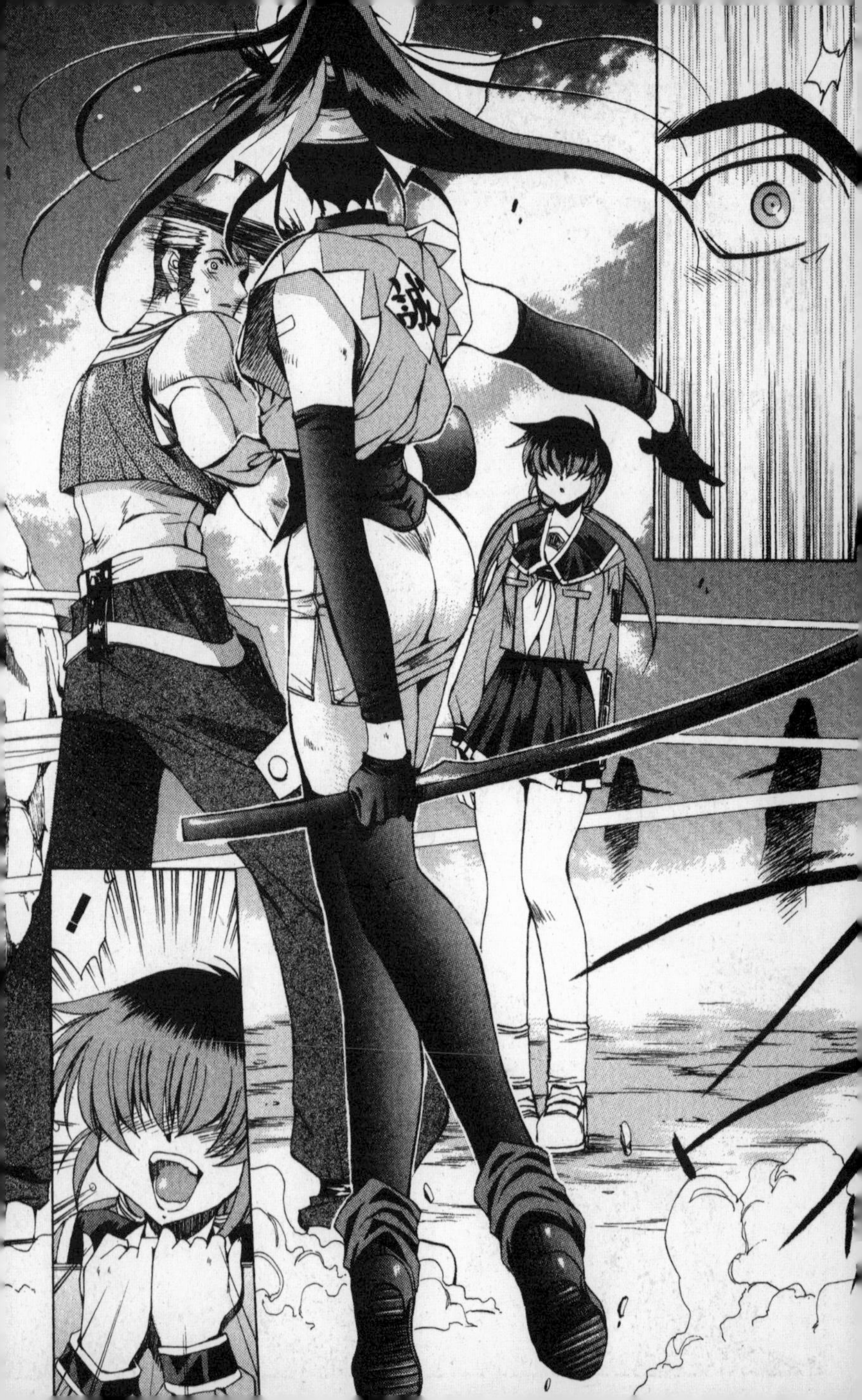
誠
!

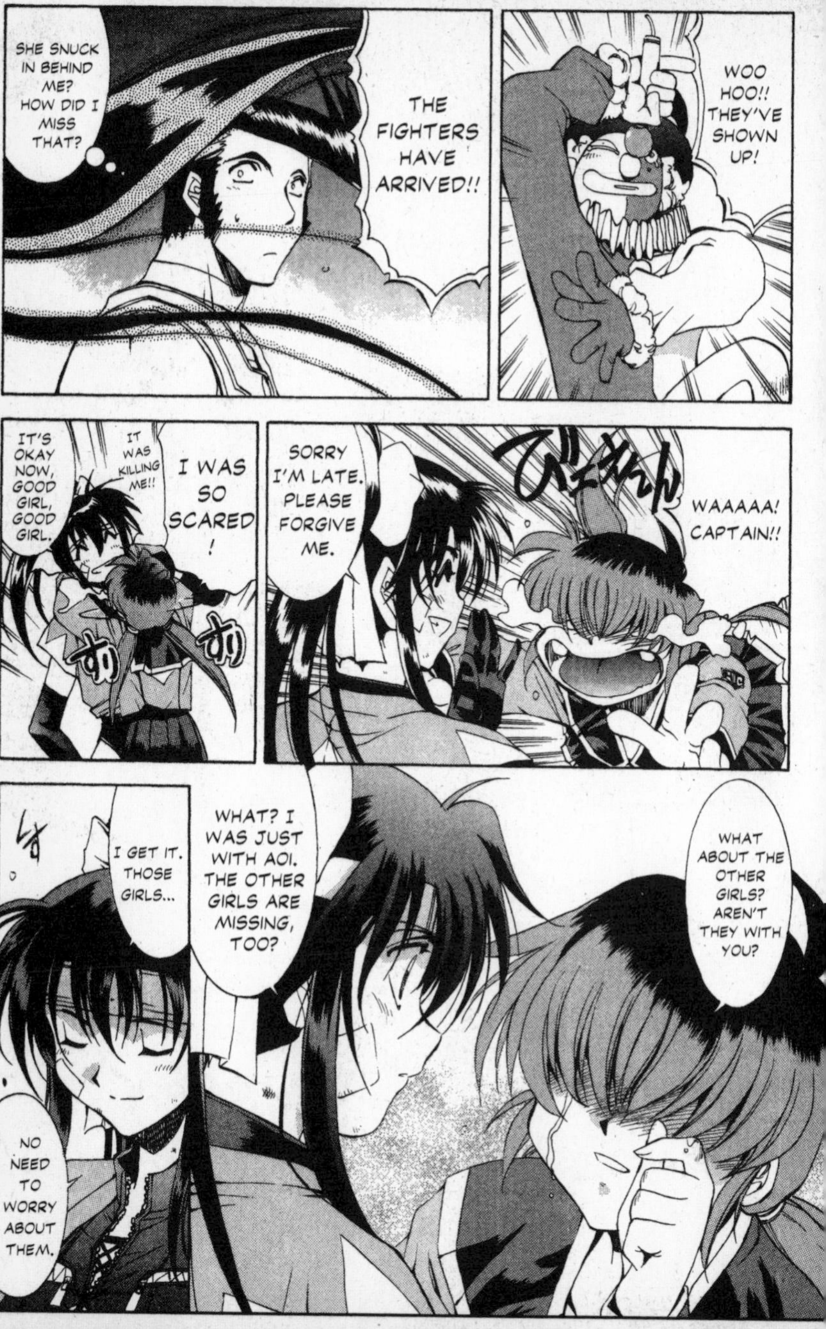
WOO HOO!! THEY'VE SHOWN UP!
THE FIGHTERS HAVE ARRIVED!!
SHE SNUCK IN BEHIND ME? HOW DID I MISS THAT?
WAAAAA! CAPTAIN!!
SORRY I'M LATE. PLEASE FORGIVE ME.
I WAS SO SCARED!
IT WAS KILLING ME!!
IT'S OKAY NOW, GOOD GIRL, GOOD GIRL.
WHAT ABOUT THE OTHER GIRLS? AREN'T THEY WITH YOU?
WHAT? I WAS JUST WITH AOI. THE OTHER GIRLS ARE MISSING, TOO?
I GET IT. THOSE GIRLS...
NO NEED TO WORRY ABOUT THEM.

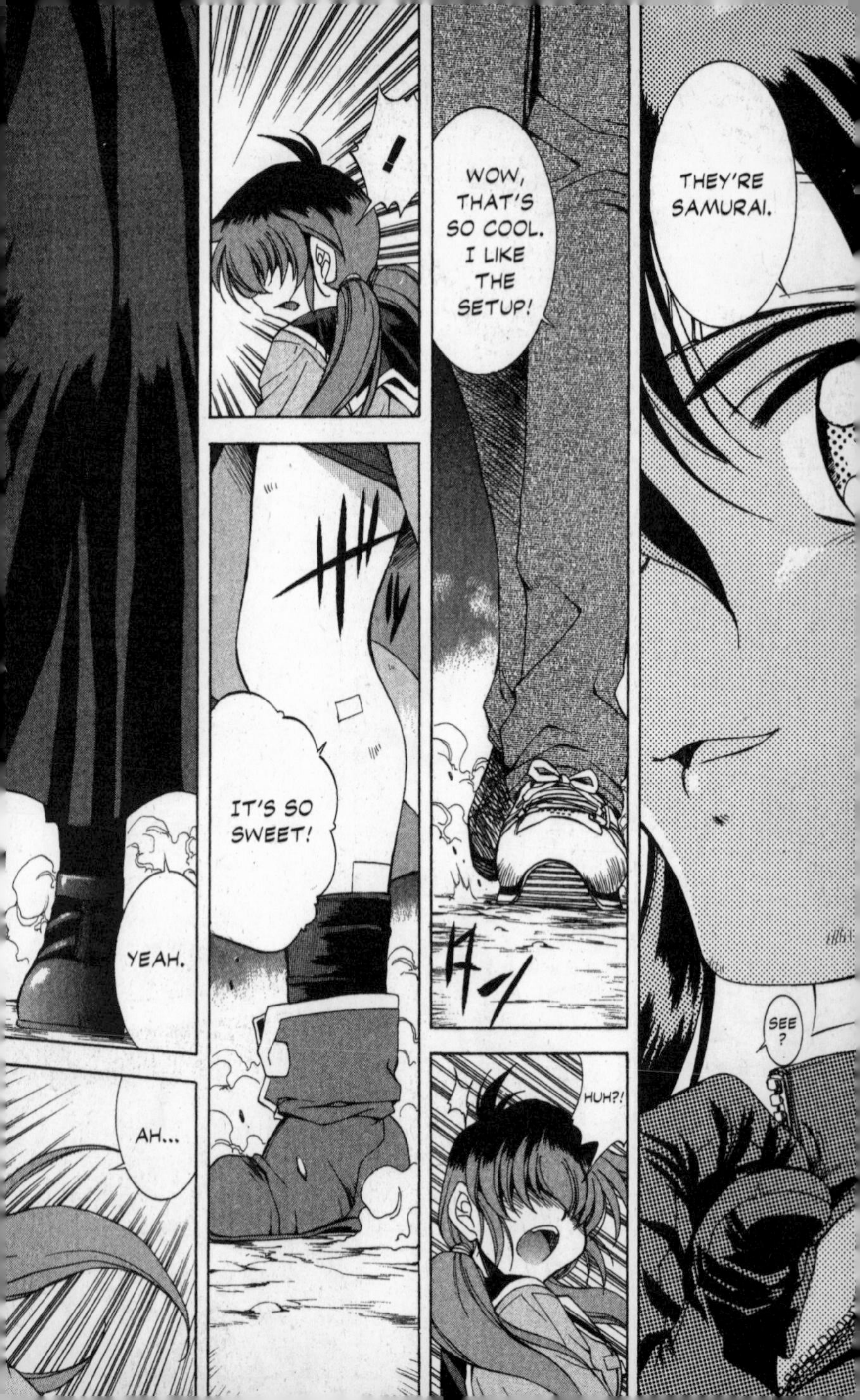
THEY'RE SAMURAI.
SEE?
WOW, THAT'S SO COOL. I LIKE THE SETUP!
!
IT'S SO SWEET!
YEAH.
HUH?!
AH...

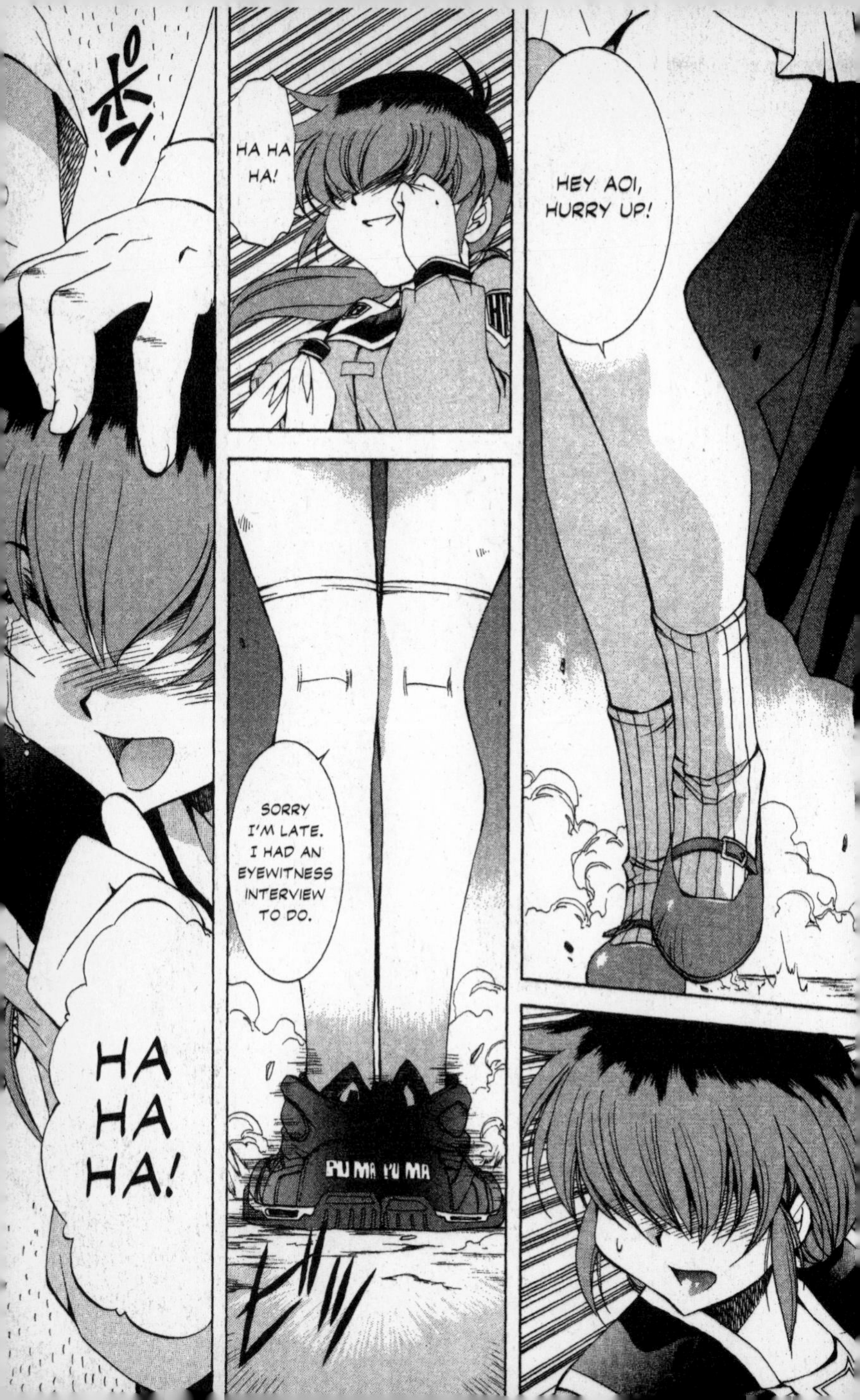
HEY AOI, HURRY UP!
HA HA HA!
SORRY I'M LATE. I HAD AN EYEWITNESS INTERVIEW TO DO.
ポン
HA HA HA!

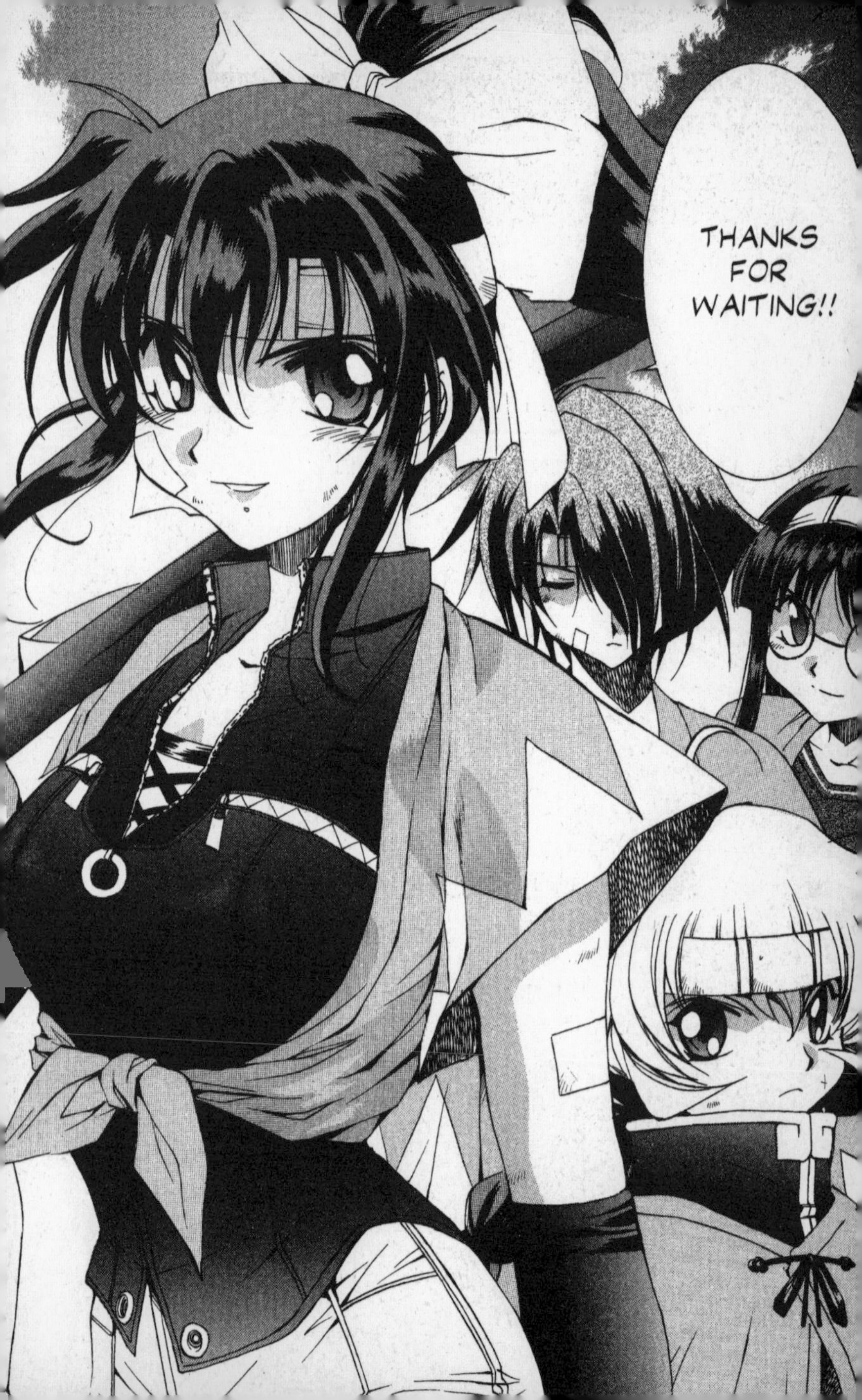
THANKS FOR WAITING!!

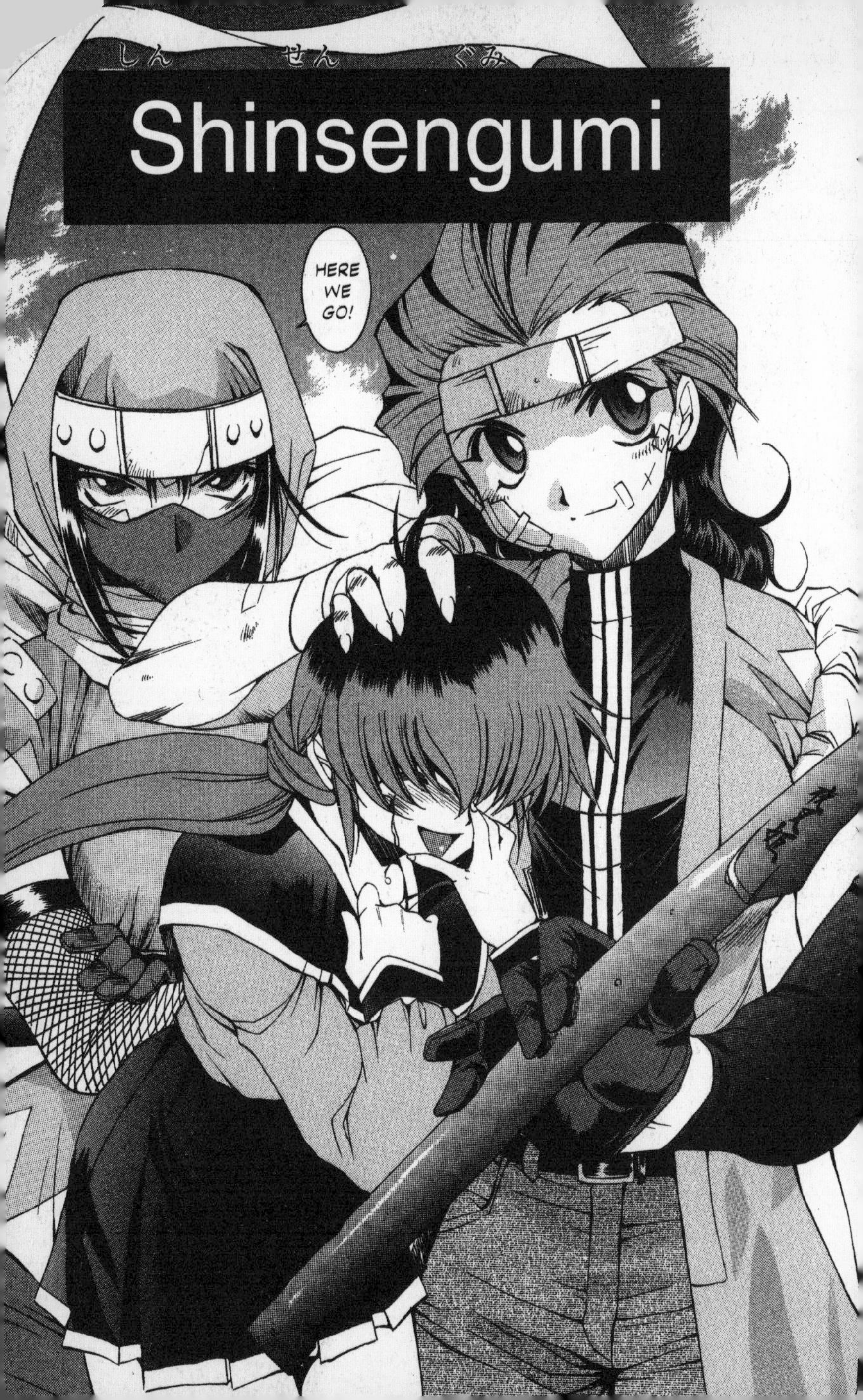
しん せん ぐみ
Shinsengumi
HERE WE GO!

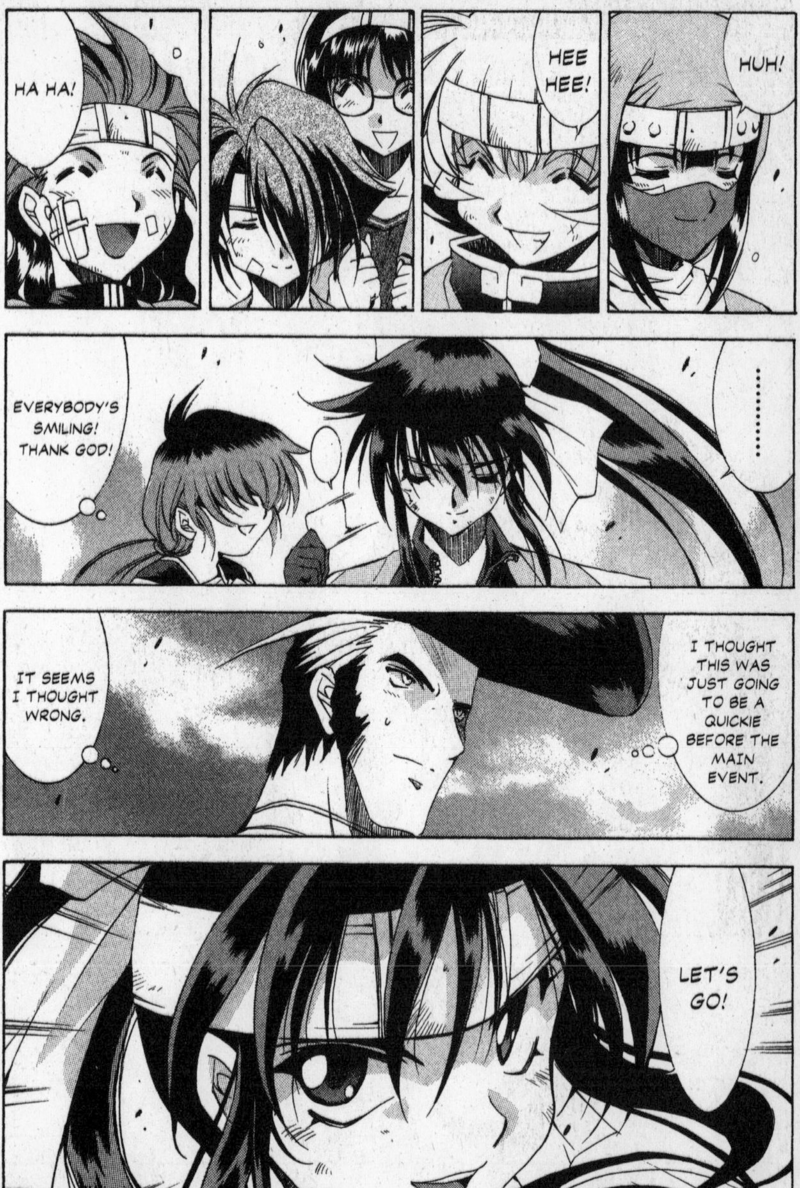
HUH!
HEE HEE!
HA HA!
....
EVERYBODY'S SMILING! THANK GOD!
I THOUGHT THIS WAS JUST GOING TO BE A QUICKIE BEFORE THE MAIN EVENT.
IT SEEMS I THOUGHT WRONG.
LET'S GO!

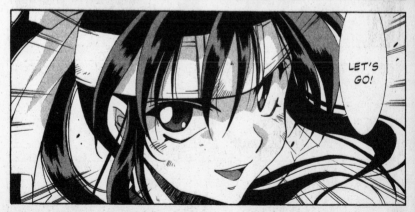

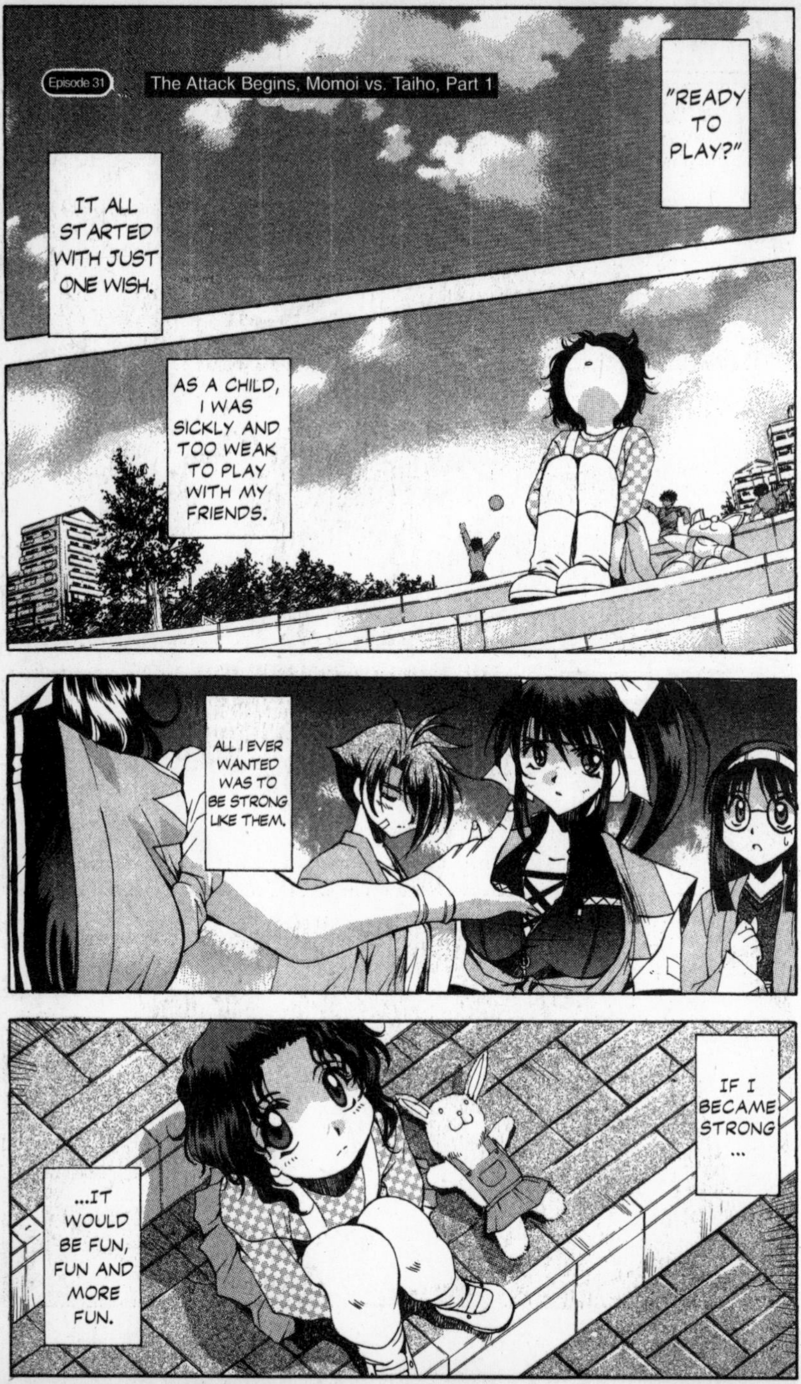
Episode 31
The Attack Begins, Momoi vs. Taiho, Part 1
"READY TO PLAY?"
IT ALL STARTED WITH JUST ONE WISH.
AS A CHILD, I WAS SICKLY AND TOO WEAK TO PLAY WITH MY FRIENDS.
ALL I EVER WANTED WAS TO BE STRONG LIKE THEM.
IF I BECAME STRONG ...
...IT WOULD BE FUN, FUN AND MORE FUN.

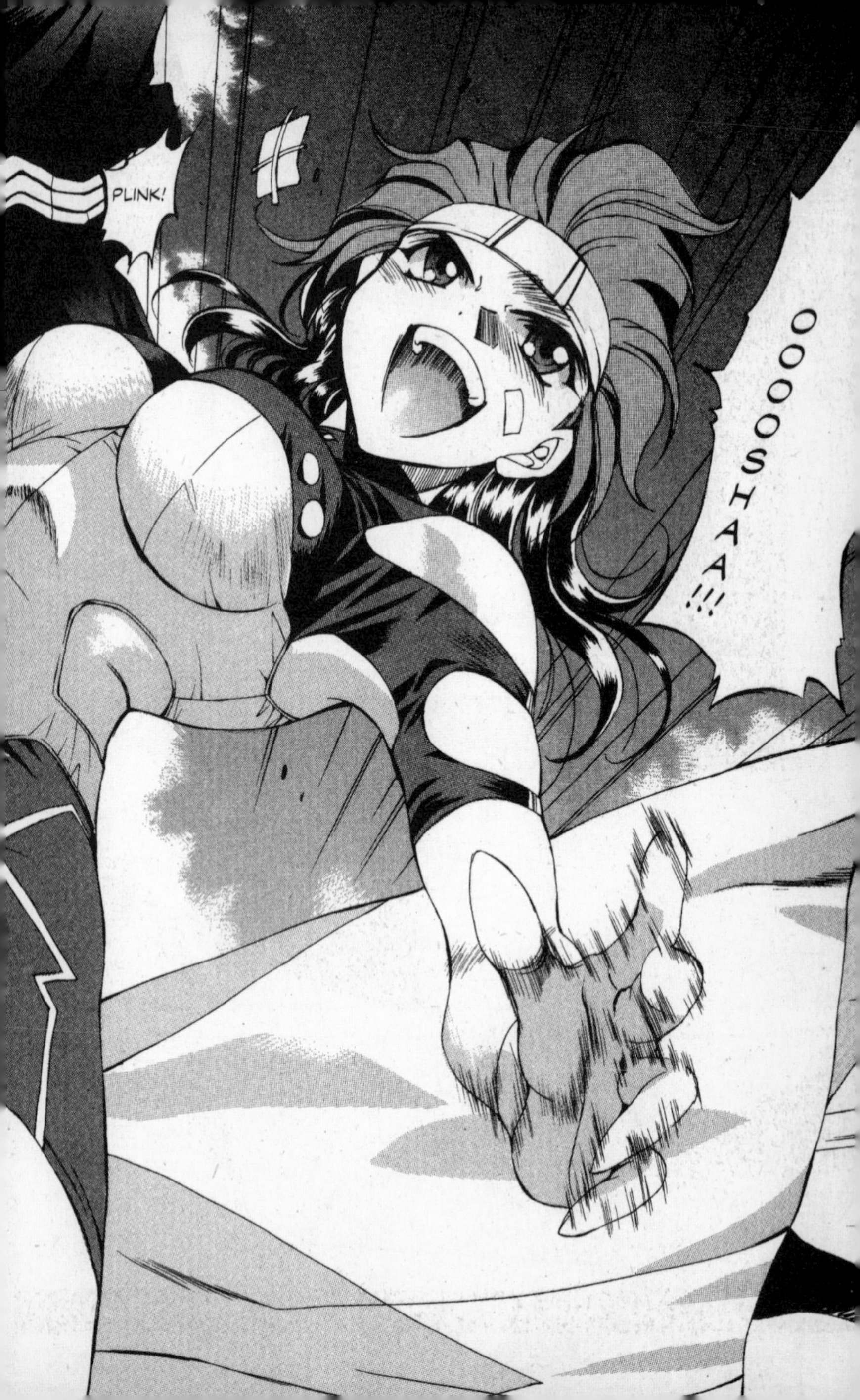
PLINK!
OOOOOSHAA!!!

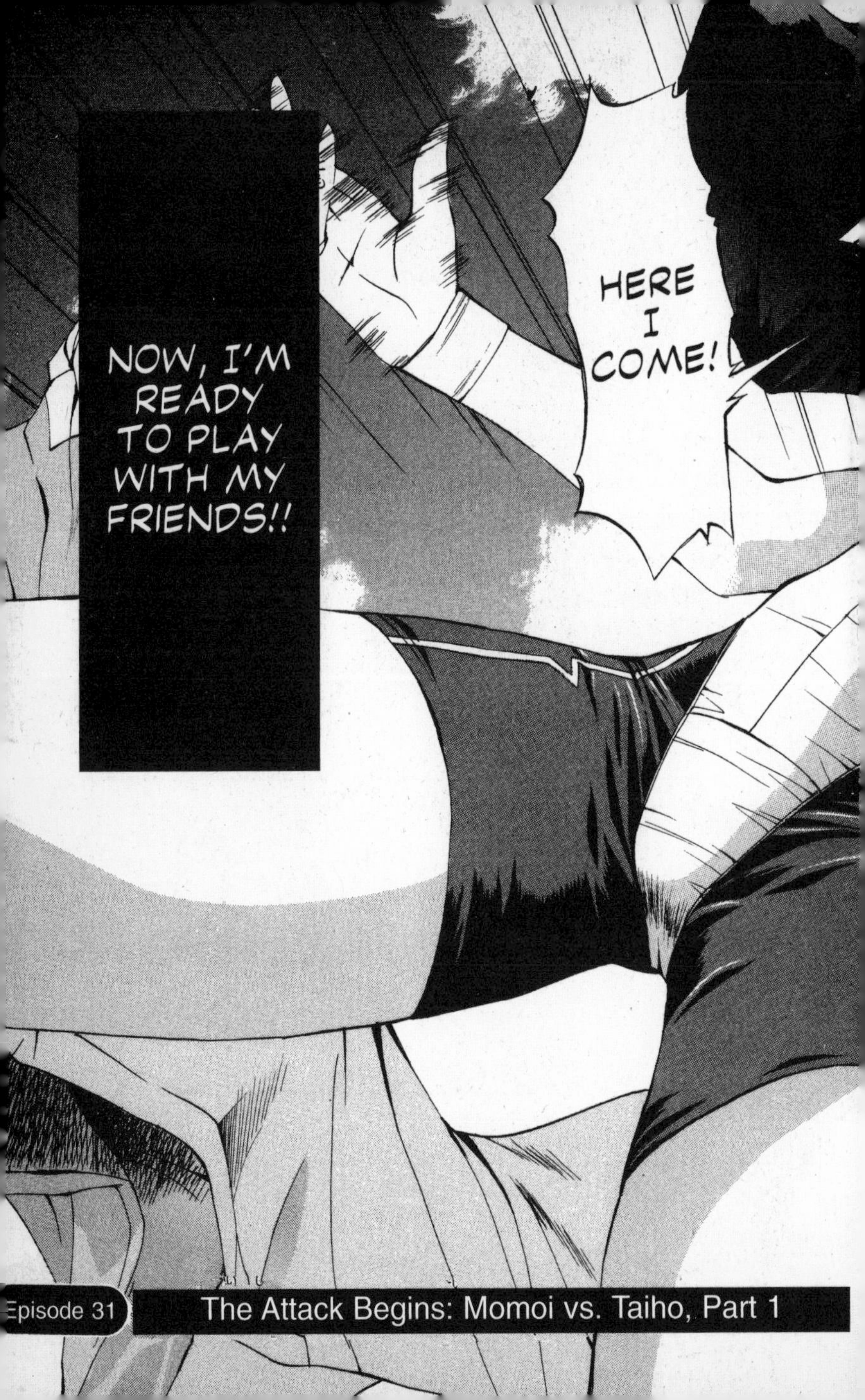
HERE I COME!
NOW, I'M READY TO PLAY WITH MY FRIENDS!!

Episode 31 The Attack Begins: Momoi vs. Taiho, Part 1

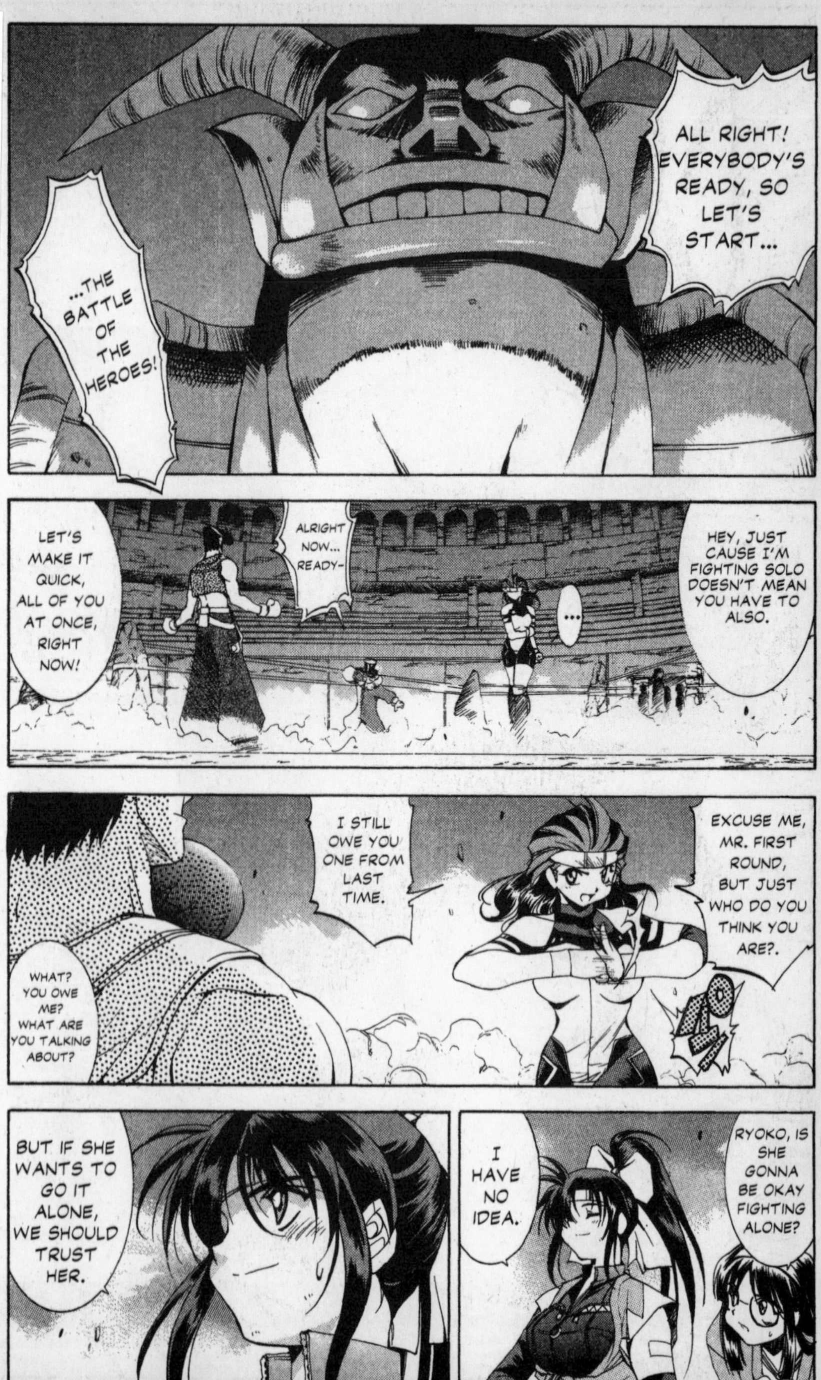
ALL RIGHT! EVERYBODY'S READY, SO LET'S START...
...THE BATTLE OF THE HEROES!
HEY, JUST CAUSE I'M FIGHTING SOLO DOESN'T MEAN YOU HAVE TO ALSO.
...
ALRIGHT NOW... READY-
LET'S MAKE IT QUICK, ALL OF YOU AT ONCE, RIGHT NOW!
EXCUSE ME, MR. FIRST ROUND, BUT JUST WHO DO YOU THINK YOU ARE?.
I STILL OWE YOU ONE FROM LAST TIME.
WHAT? YOU OWE ME? WHAT ARE YOU TALKING ABOUT?
RYOKO, IS SHE GONNA BE OKAY FIGHTING ALONE?
I HAVE NO IDEA.
BUT IF SHE WANTS TO GO IT ALONE, WE SHOULD TRUST HER.

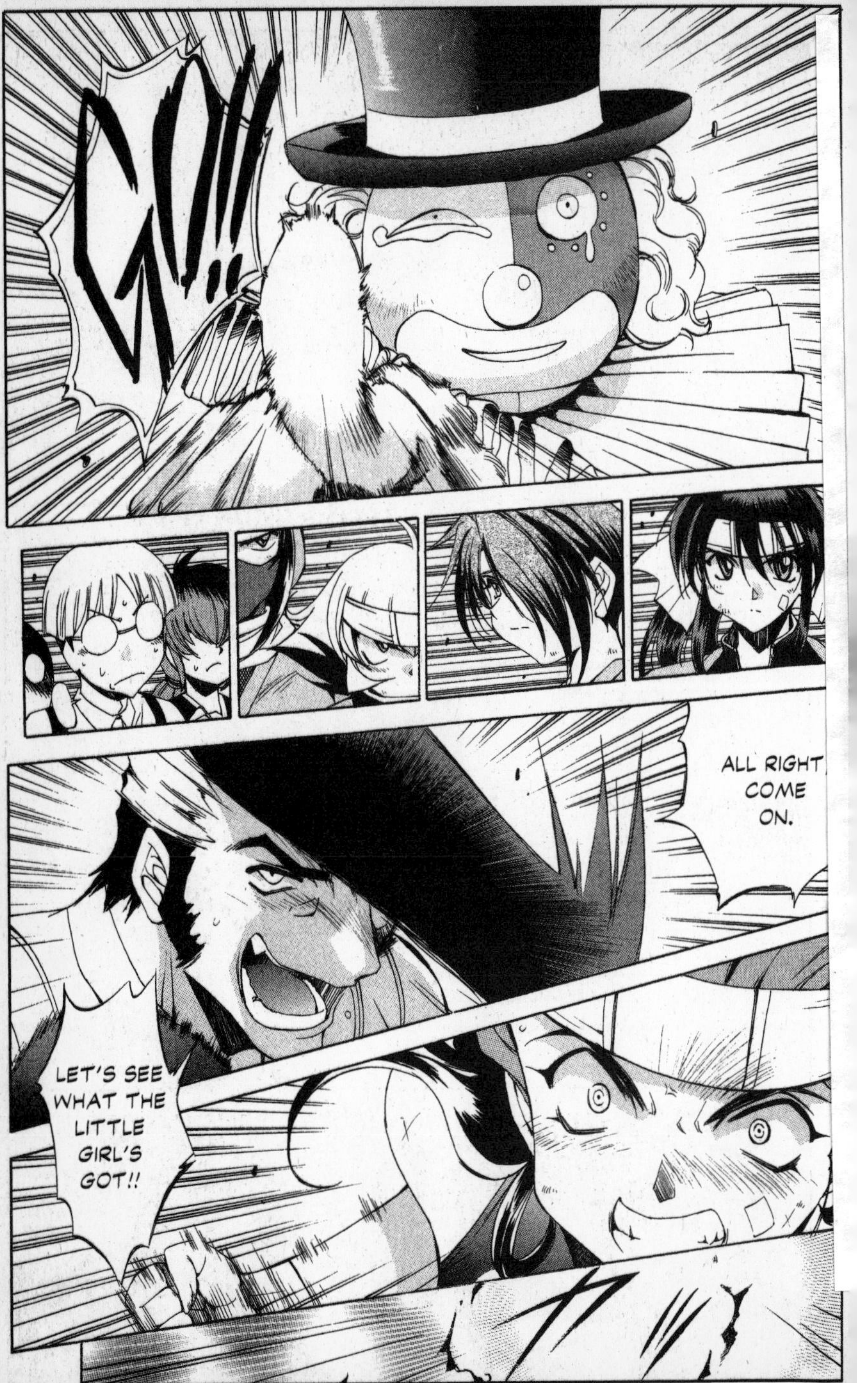
GO!!!
ALL RIGHT, COME ON.
LET'S SEE WHAT THE LITTLE GIRL'S GOT!!

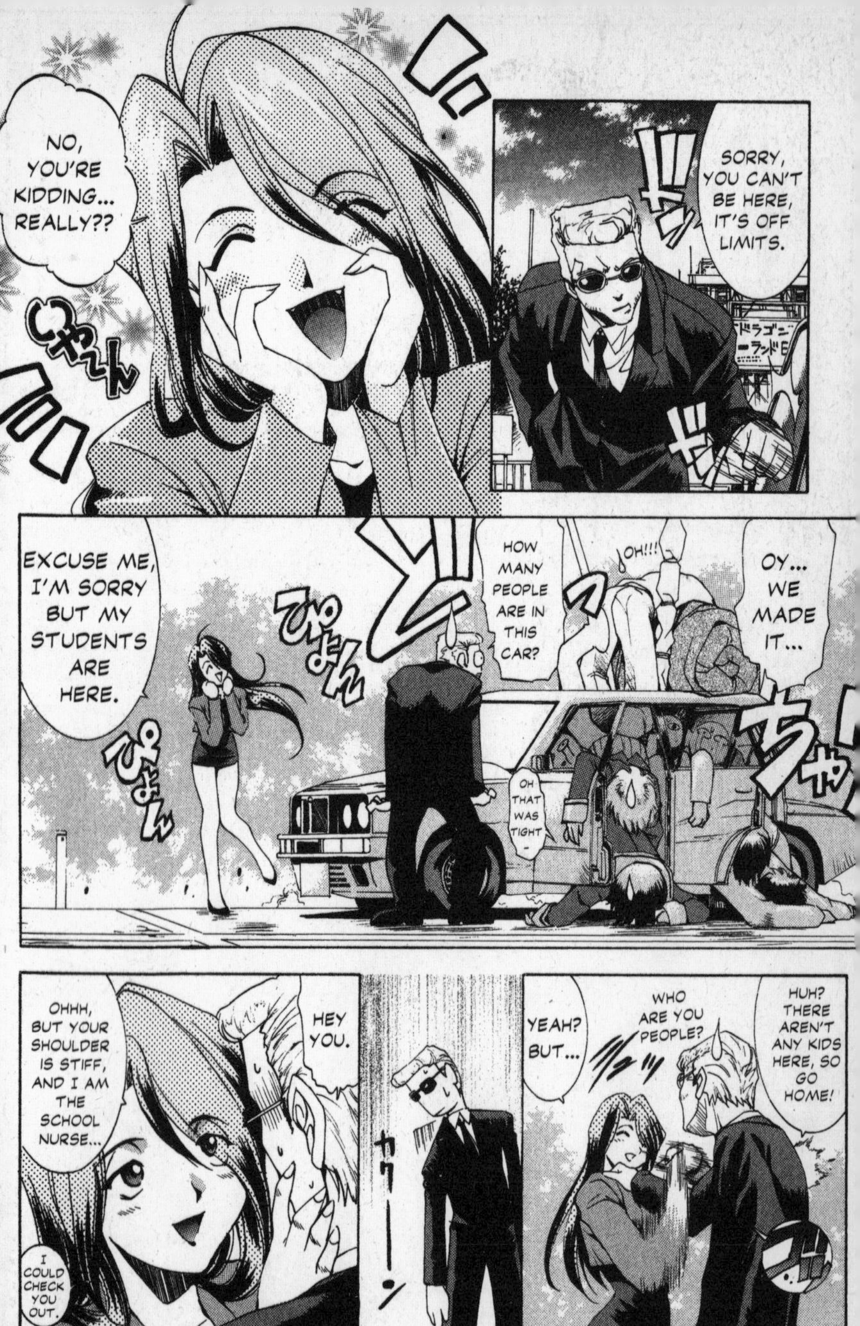
SORRY, YOU CAN'T BE HERE, IT'S OFF LIMITS.
NO, YOU'RE KIDDING... REALLY??
OY... WE MADE IT...
OH!!!
HOW MANY PEOPLE ARE IN THIS CAR?
OH THAT WAS TIGHT
ぴょん
EXCUSE ME, I'M SORRY BUT MY STUDENTS ARE HERE.
ぴょん
HUH? THERE AREN'T ANY KIDS HERE, SO GO HOME!
WHO ARE YOU PEOPLE?
YEAH? BUT...
HEY YOU.
OHHH, BUT YOUR SHOULDER IS STIFF, AND I AM THE SCHOOL NURSE...
I COULD CHECK YOU OUT.

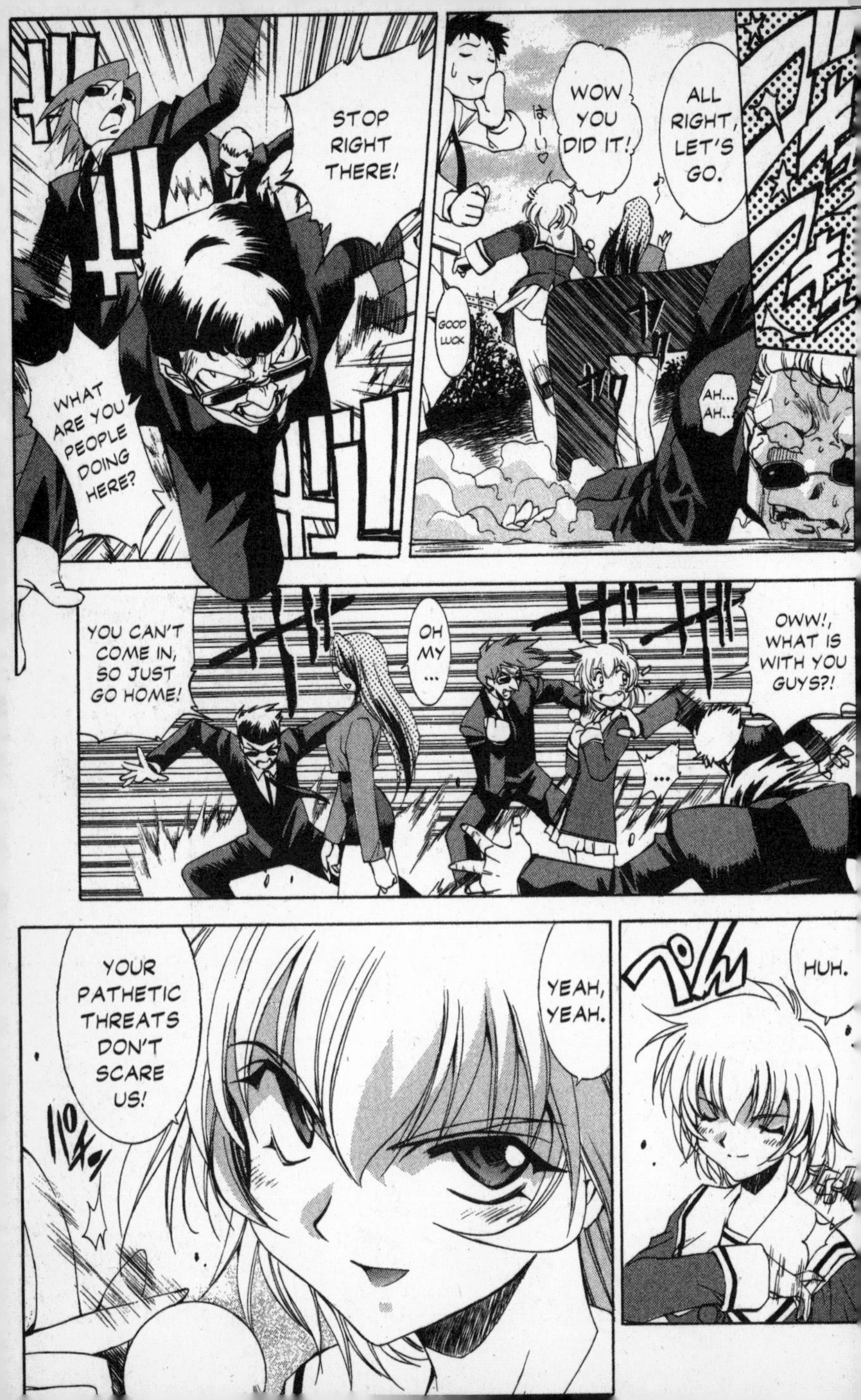
ALL RIGHT, LET'S GO.
WOW YOU DID IT!
はーい♡
GOOD LUCK
AH... AH...
STOP RIGHT THERE!
WHAT ARE YOU PEOPLE DOING HERE?
OWW!, WHAT IS WITH YOU GUYS?!
...
OH MY ...
YOU CAN'T COME IN, SO JUST GO HOME!
HUH.
YEAH, YEAH.
YOUR PATHETIC THREATS DON'T SCARE US!

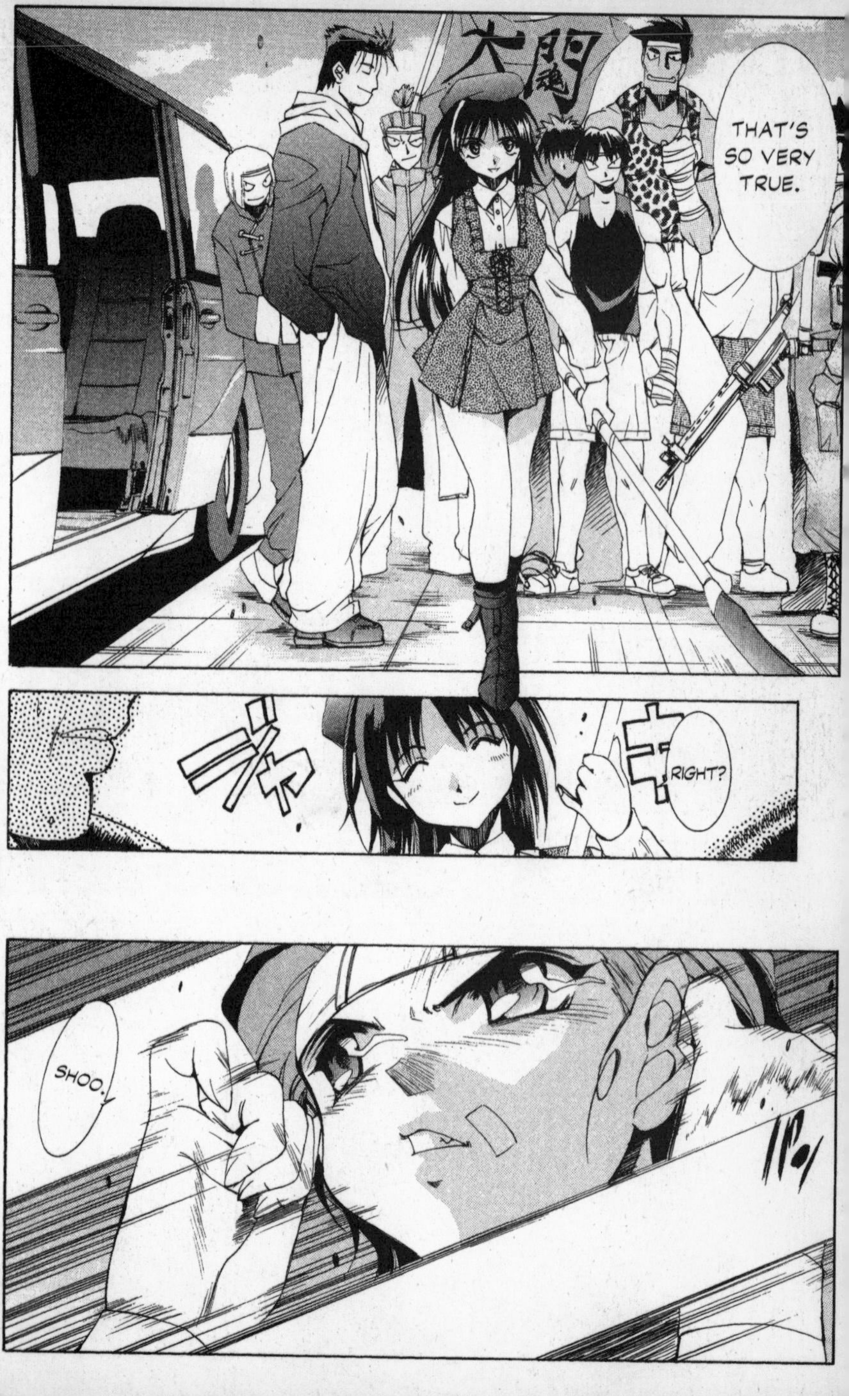
THAT'S SO VERY TRUE.
RIGHT?
SHOO.

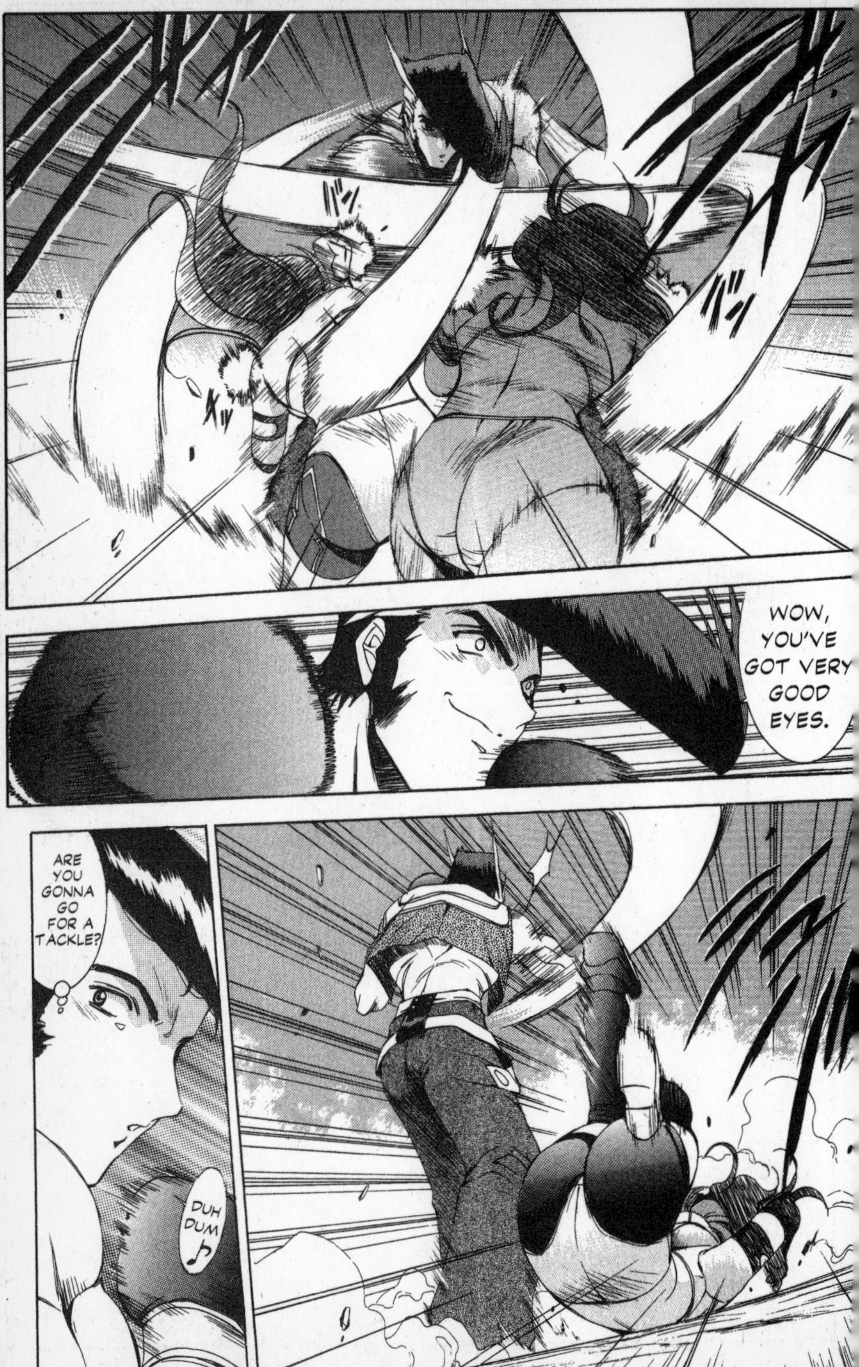
WOW, YOU'VE GOT VERY GOOD EYES.
ARE YOU GONNA GO FOR A TACKLE?
DUH DUM ♪

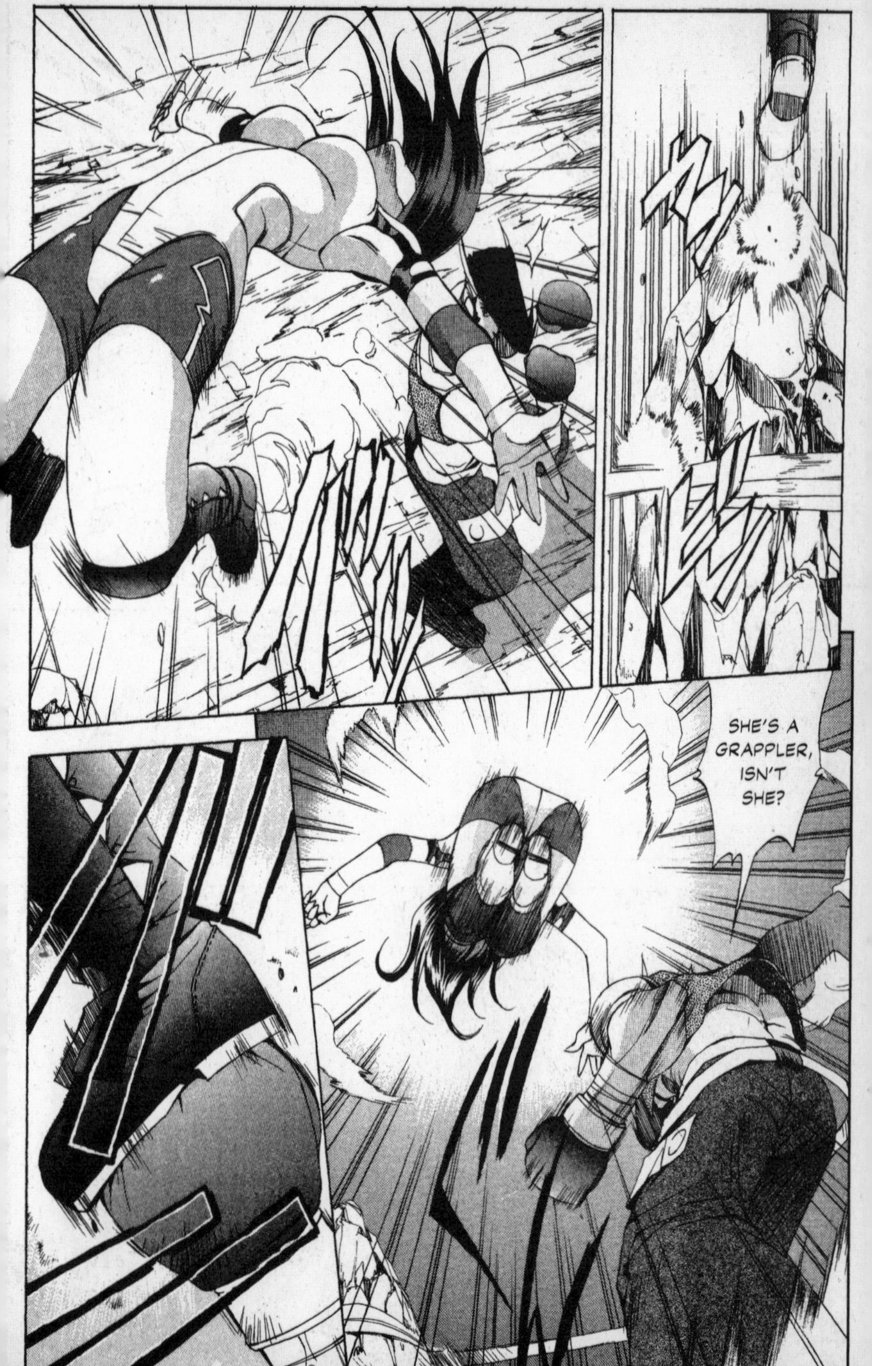
SHE'S A GRAPPLER, ISN'T SHE?

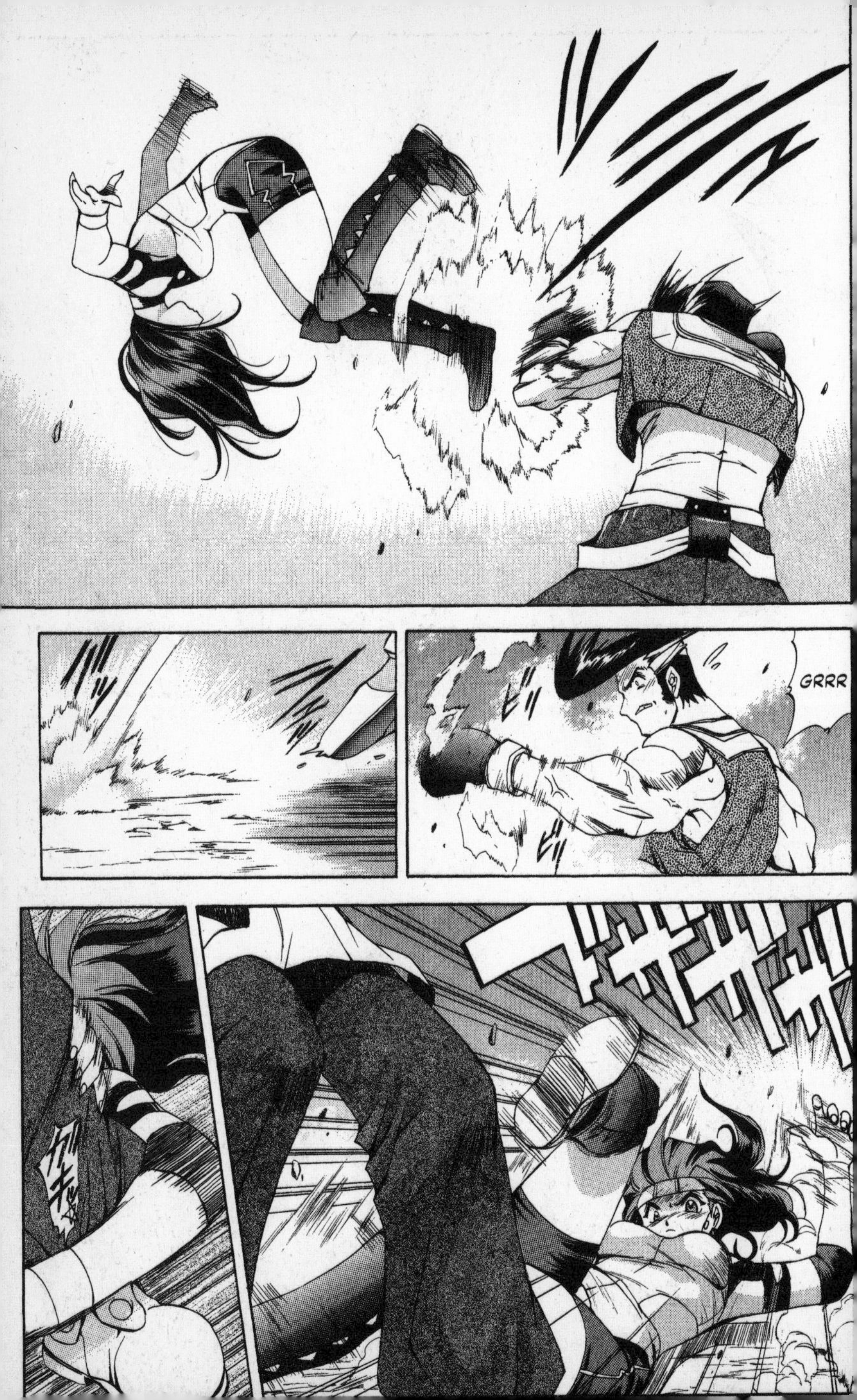
GRRR

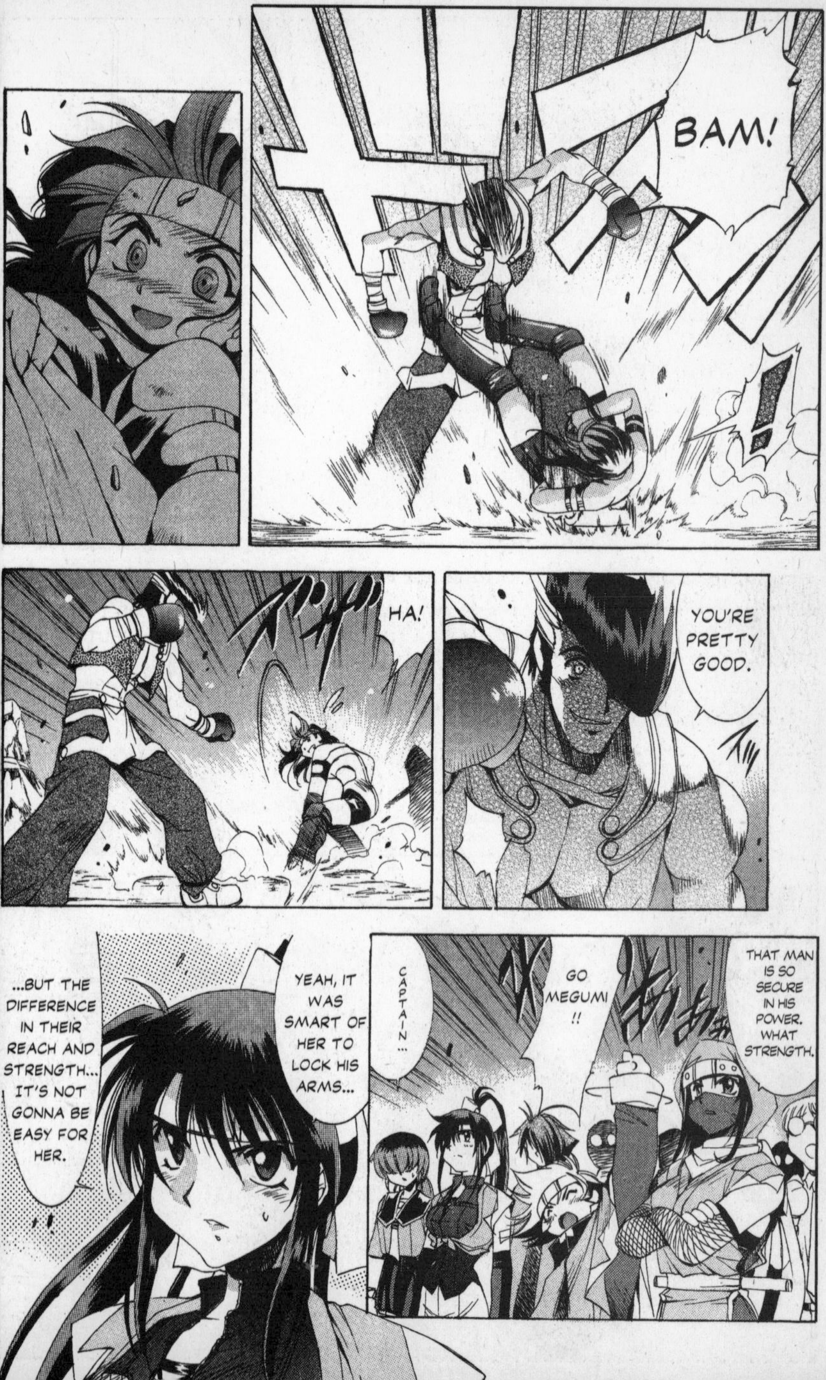
BAM!
!
YOU'RE PRETTY GOOD.
HA!
THAT MAN IS SO SECURE IN HIS POWER. WHAT STRENGTH.
GO MEGUMI !!
CAPTAIN...
YEAH, IT WAS SMART OF HER TO LOCK HIS ARMS...
...BUT THE DIFFERENCE IN THEIR REACH AND STRENGTH... IT'S NOT GONNA BE EASY FOR HER.

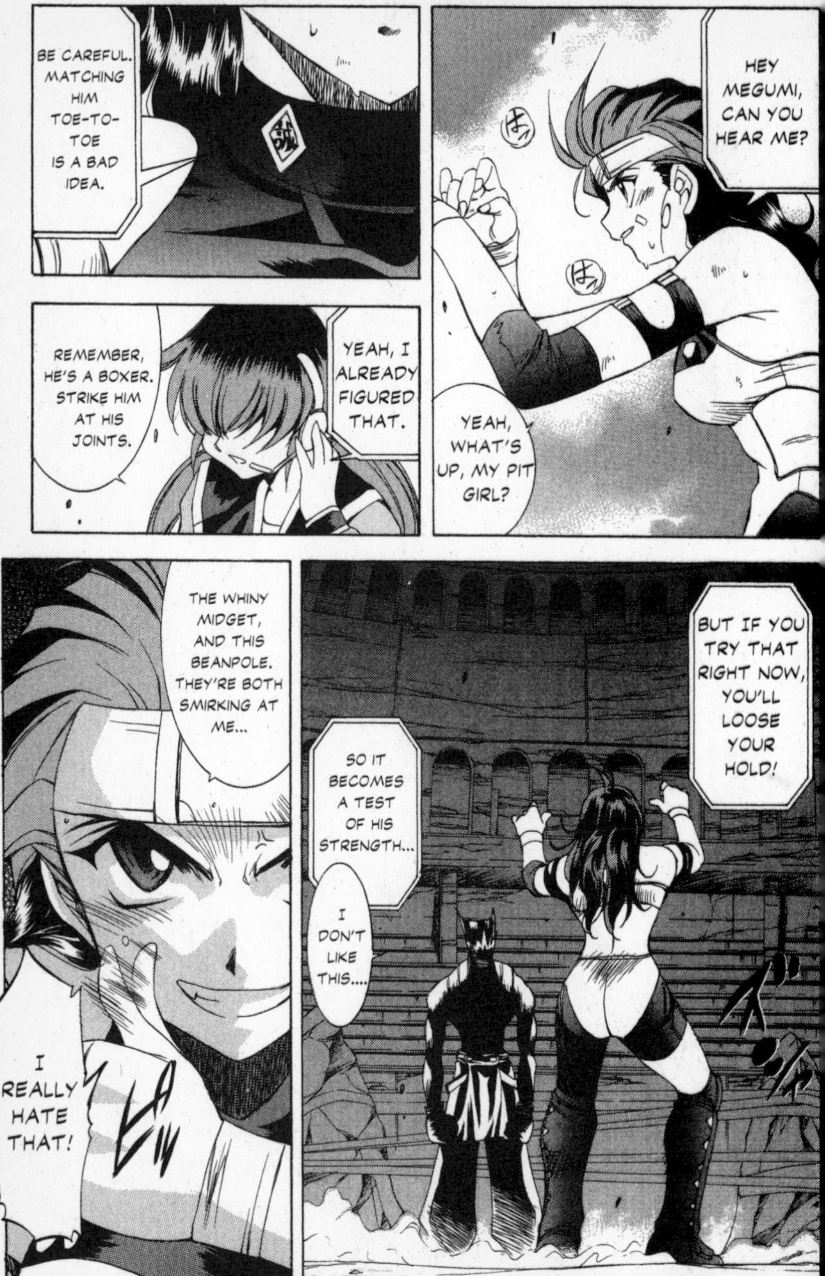
HEY MEGUMI, CAN YOU HEAR ME?
YEAH, WHAT'S UP, MY PIT GIRL?
BE CAREFUL. MATCHING HIM TOE-TO-TOE IS A BAD IDEA.
YEAH, I ALREADY FIGURED THAT.
REMEMBER, HE'S A BOXER. STRIKE HIM AT HIS JOINTS.
BUT IF YOU TRY THAT RIGHT NOW, YOU'LL LOOSE YOUR HOLD!
SO IT BECOMES A TEST OF HIS STRENGTH...
I DON'T LIKE THIS....
THE WHINY MIDGET, AND THIS BEANPOLE. THEY'RE BOTH SMIRKING AT ME...
I REALLY HATE THAT!

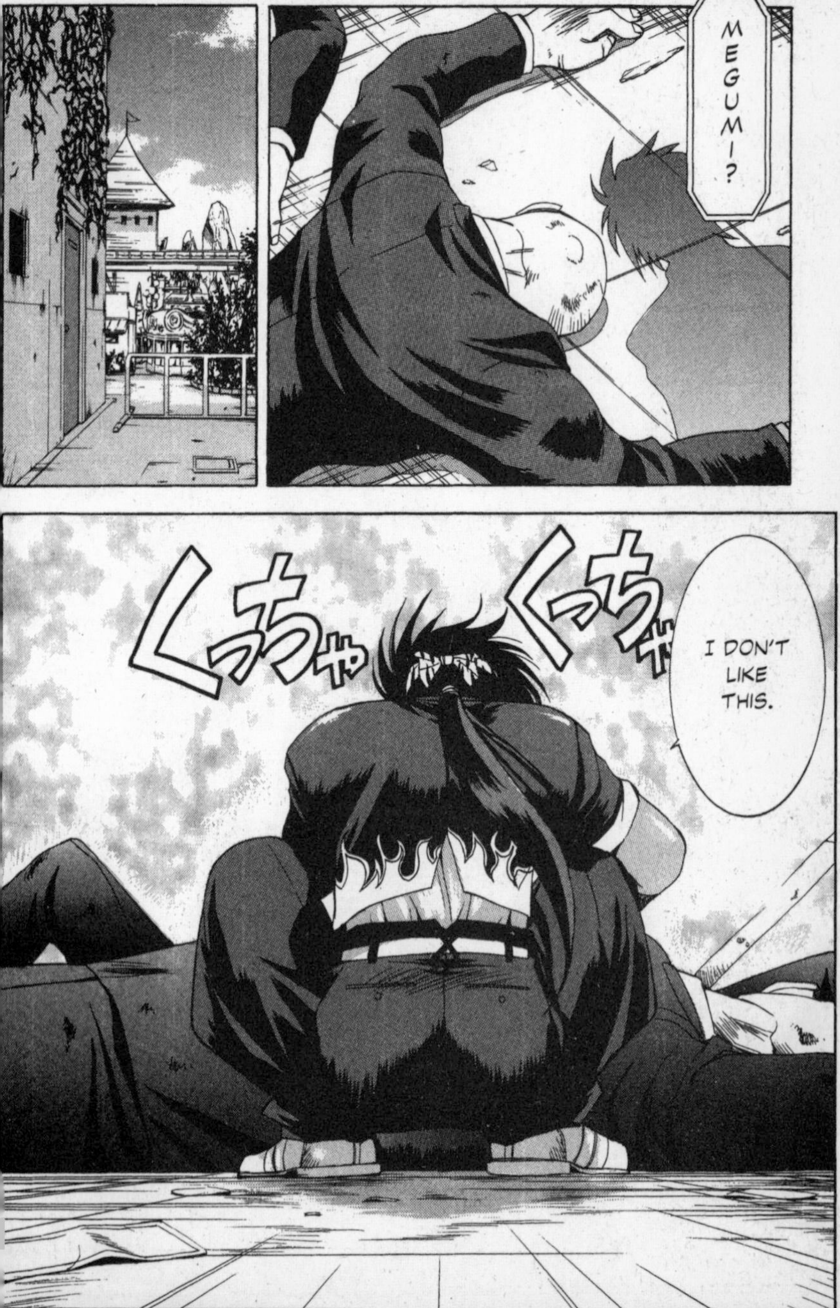
MEGUMI?
くっちゃ くっちゃ
I DON'T LIKE THIS.

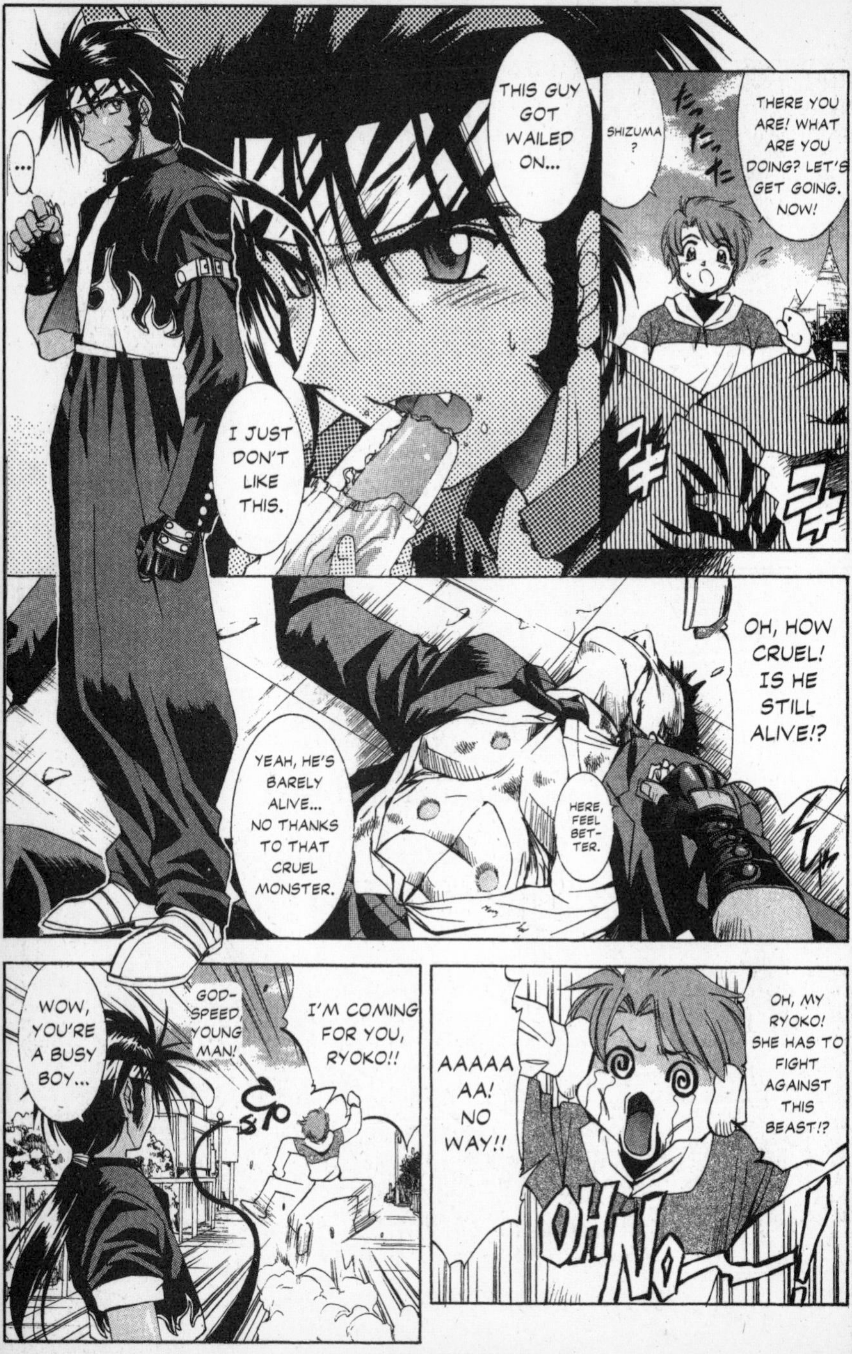
THERE YOU ARE! WHAT ARE YOU DOING? LET'S GET GOING. NOW!
SHIZUMA?
THIS GUY GOT WAILED ON...
I JUST DON'T LIKE THIS.
...
OH, HOW CRUEL! IS HE STILL ALIVE!?
HERE, FEEL BET-TER.
YEAH, HE'S BARELY ALIVE... NO THANKS TO THAT CRUEL MONSTER.
OH, MY RYOKO! SHE HAS TO FIGHT AGAINST THIS BEAST!?
AAAAAAA! NO WAY!!
OH NO—!
I'M COMING FOR YOU, RYOKO!!
GOD-SPEED, YOUNG MAN!
WOW, YOU'RE A BUSY BOY...

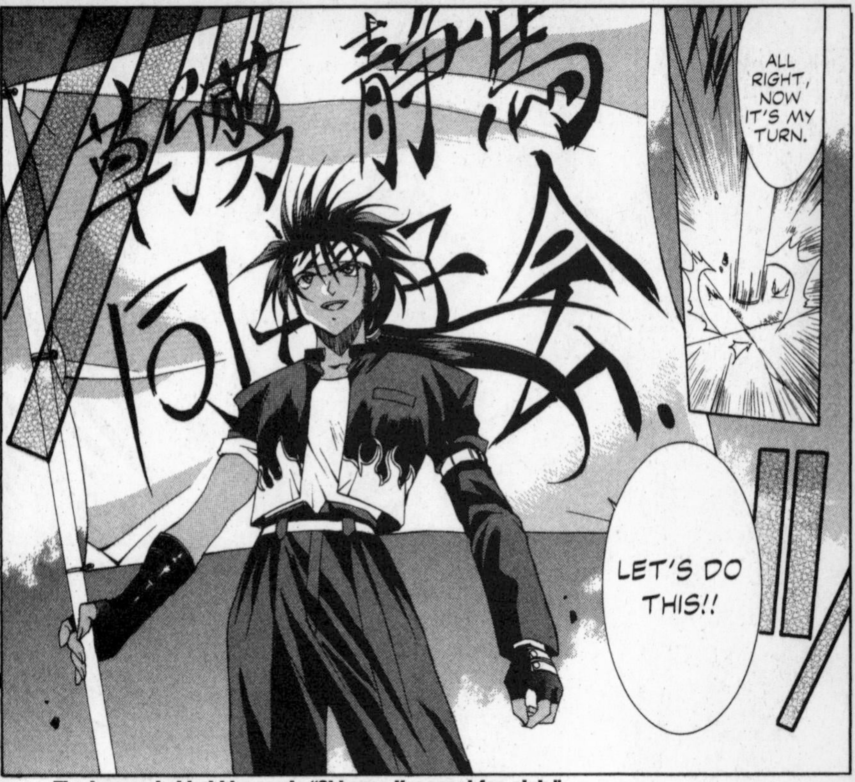
ALL RIGHT, NOW IT'S MY TURN.
LET'S DO THIS!!

The banner behind him reads "Shizuma Kusanagi fan club."

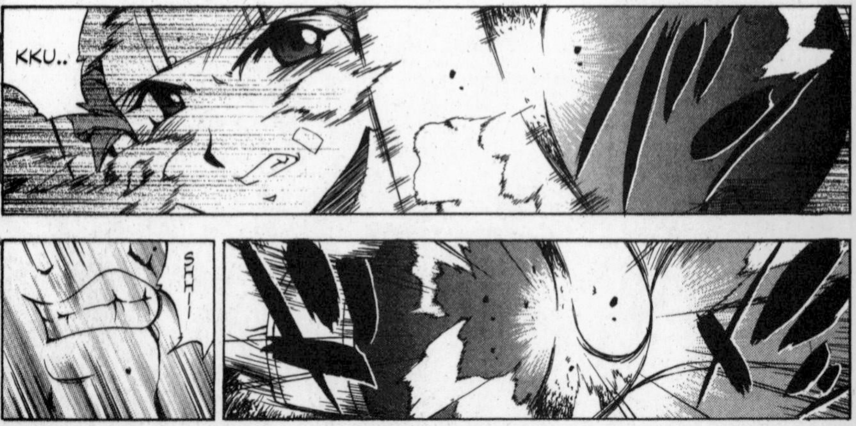
KKU..
SHI-

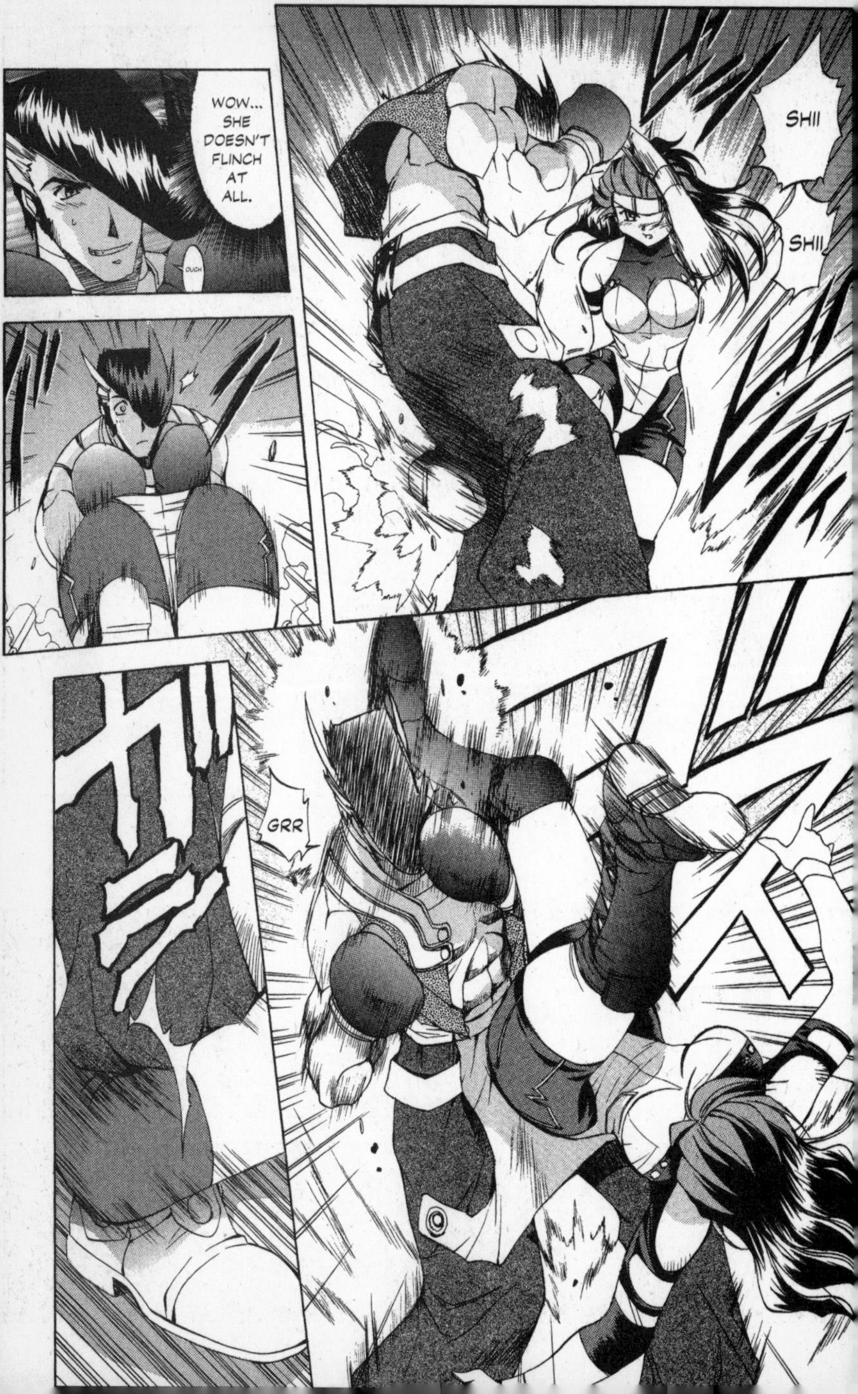
SHII
SHII
WOW... SHE DOESN'T FLINCH AT ALL.
OUCH
GRR

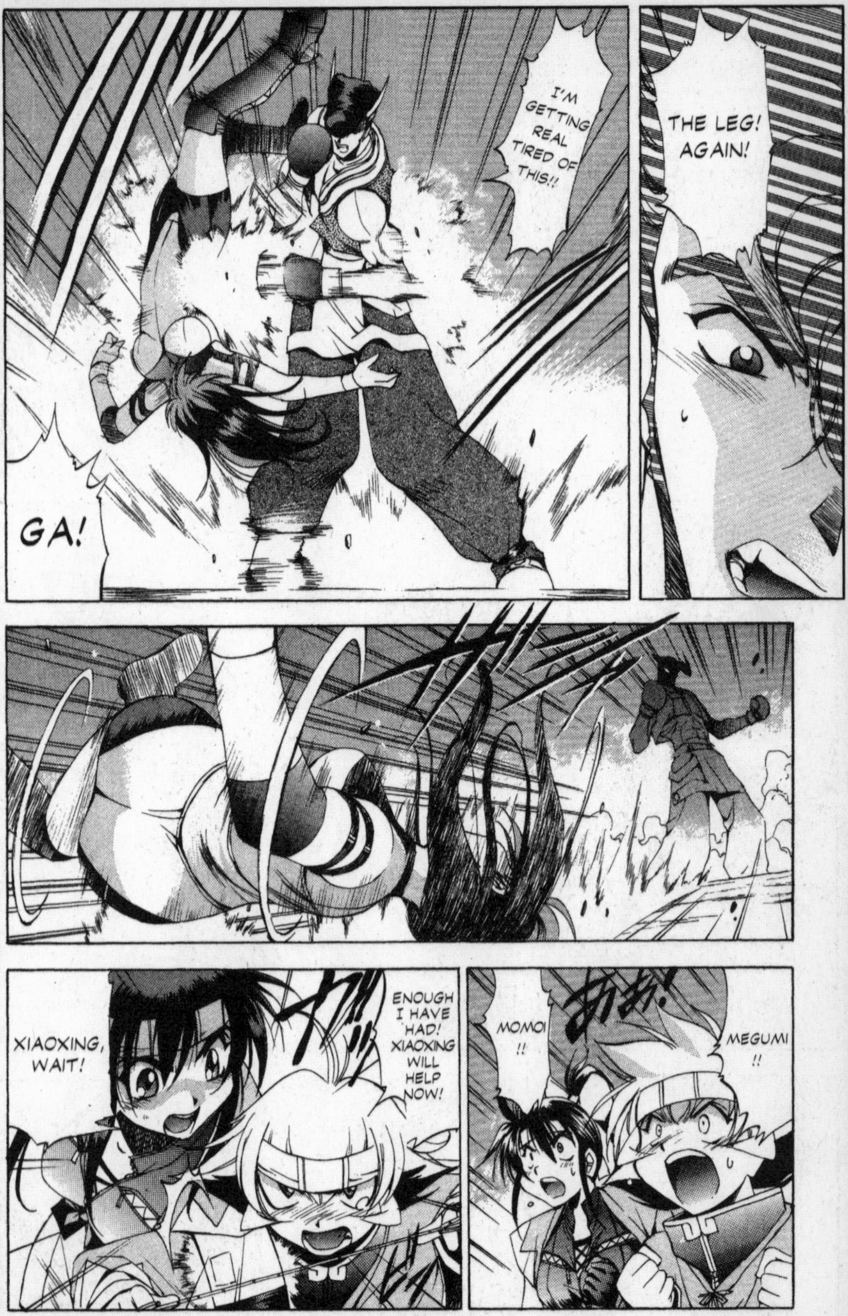
THE LEG! AGAIN!
I'M GETTING REAL TIRED OF THIS!!
GA!
MEGUMI !!
MOMOI !!
ENOUGH I HAVE HAD! XIAOXING WILL HELP NOW!
XIAOXING, WAIT!

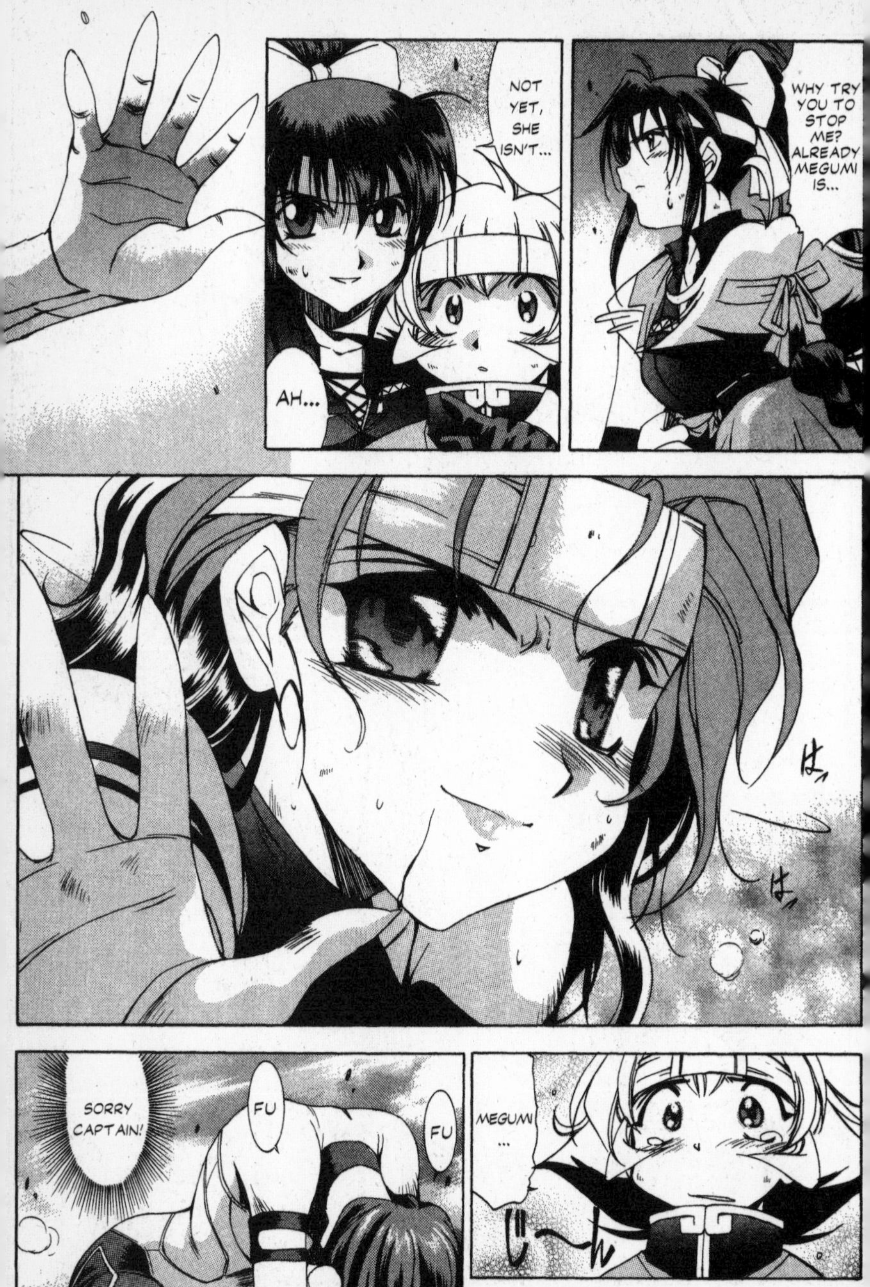

WHY TRY YOU TO STOP ME? ALREADY MEGUMI IS...
NOT YET, SHE ISN'T...
AH...
は、
は、
MEGUMI ...
じ~ん
FU
FU
SORRY CAPTAIN!

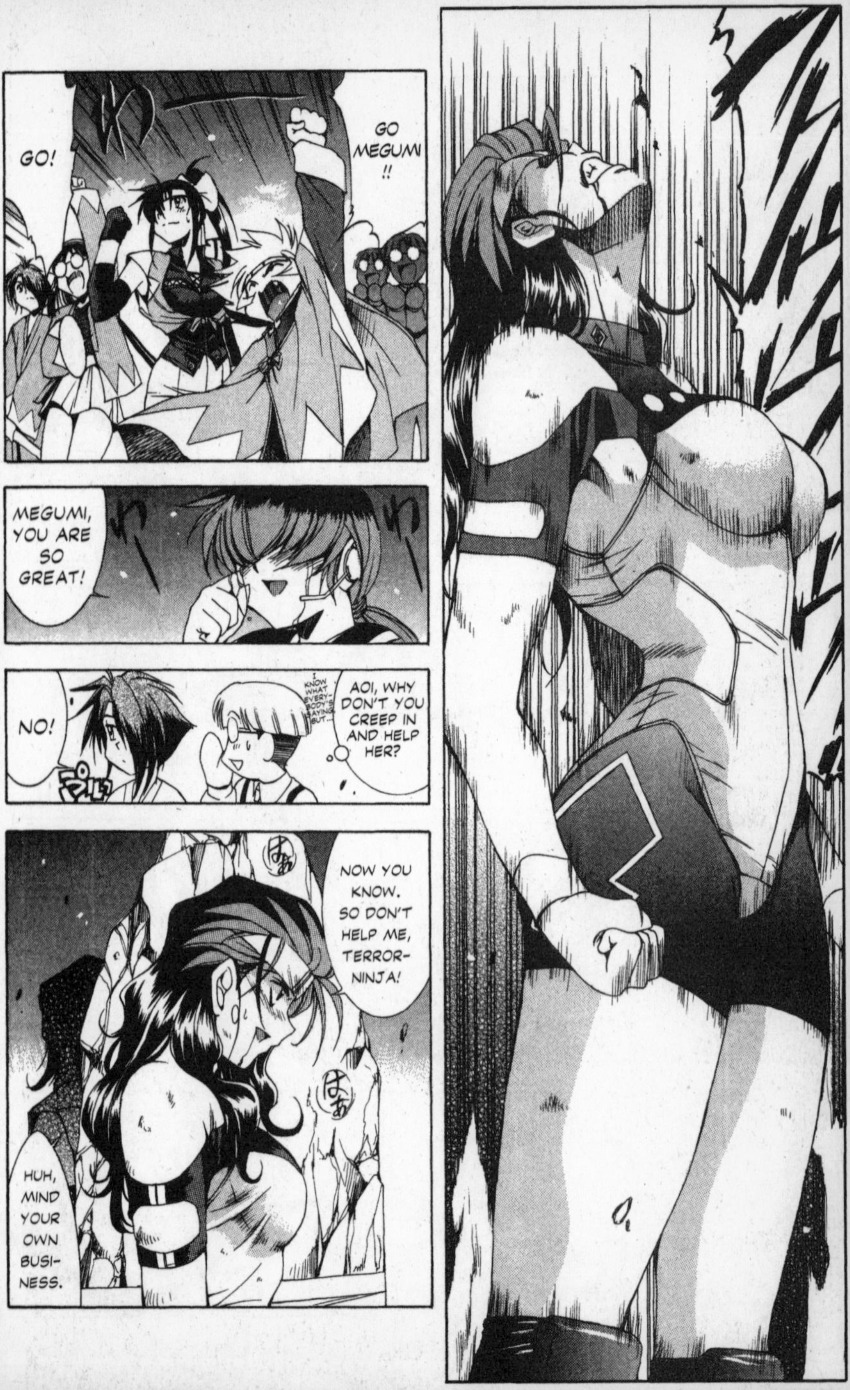
GO MEGUMI !!
GO!
MEGUMI, YOU ARE SO GREAT!
I KNOW WHAT EVERYBODY'S SAYING, BUT...
AOI, WHY DON'T YOU CREEP IN AND HELP HER?
NO!
NOW YOU KNOW. SO DON'T HELP ME, TERROR-NINJA!
HUH, MIND YOUR OWN BUSINESS.

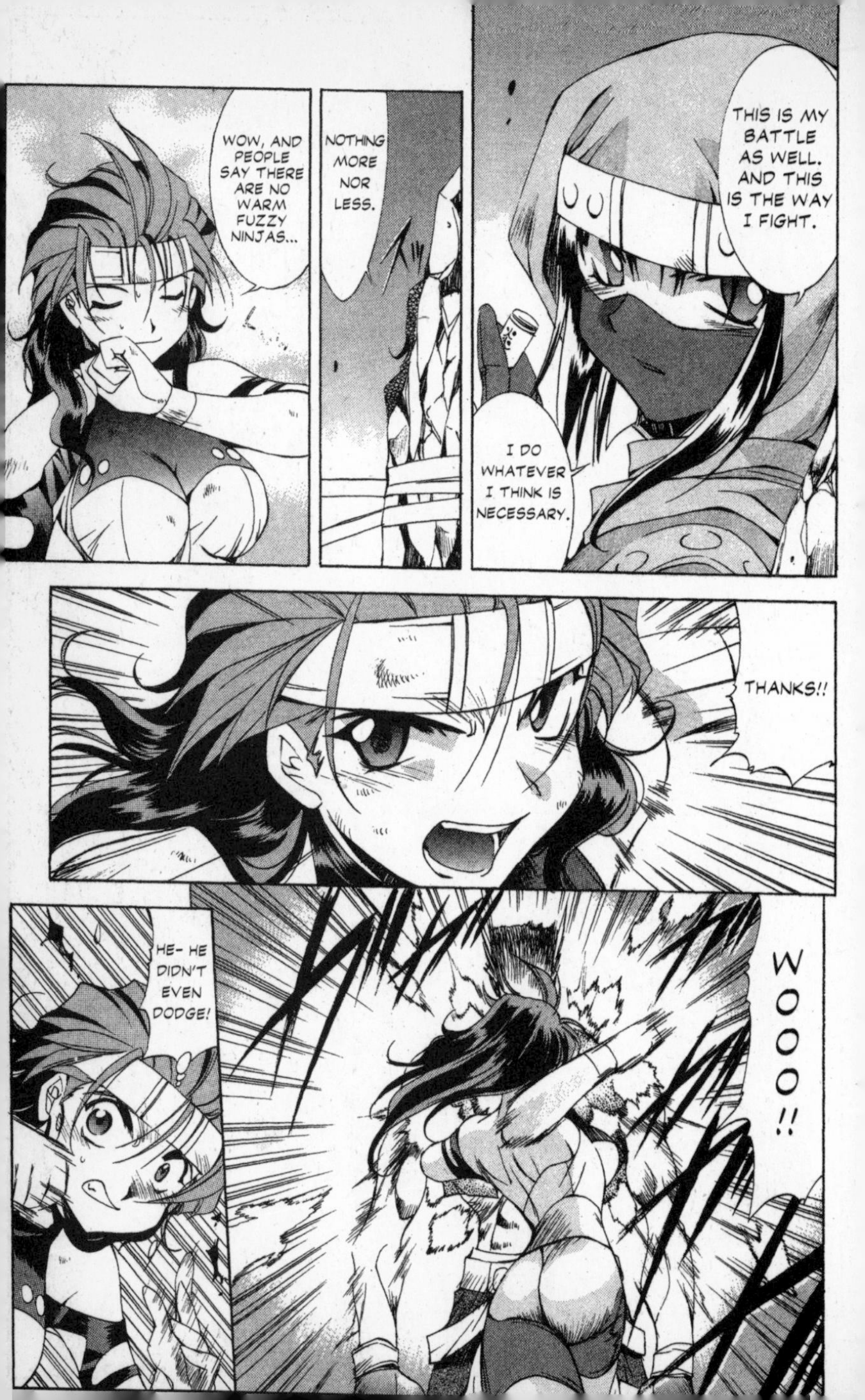
THIS IS MY BATTLE AS WELL. AND THIS IS THE WAY I FIGHT.
I DO WHATEVER I THINK IS NECESSARY.
NOTHING MORE NOR LESS.
WOW, AND PEOPLE SAY THERE ARE NO WARM FUZZY NINJAS...
THANKS!!
WOOOO!!
HE- HE DIDN'T EVEN DODGE!

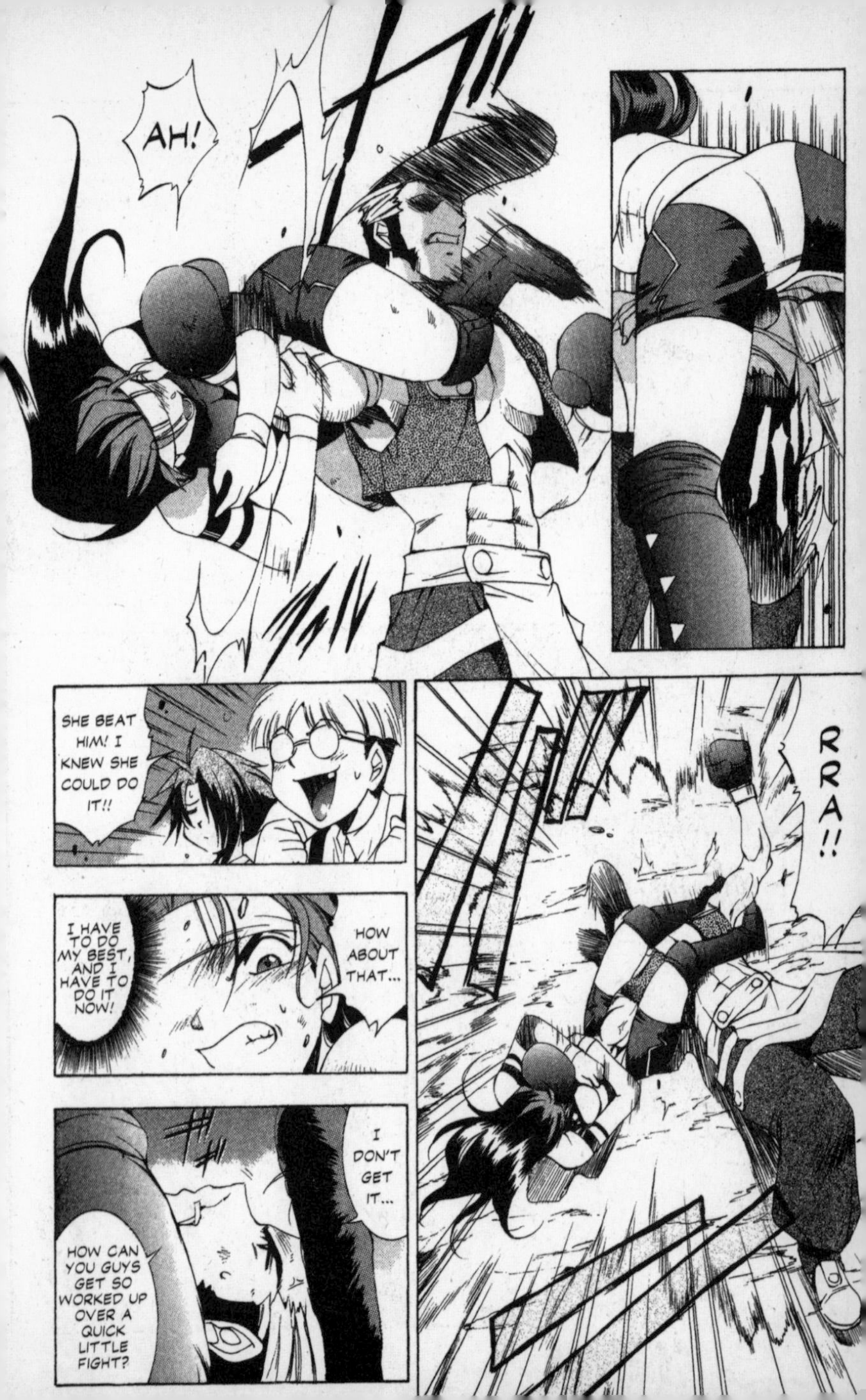
AH!
SHE BEAT HIM! I KNEW SHE COULD DO IT!!
HOW ABOUT THAT...
I HAVE TO DO MY BEST, AND I HAVE TO DO IT NOW!
I DON'T GET IT...
HOW CAN YOU GUYS GET SO WORKED UP OVER A QUICK LITTLE FIGHT?
RRA!!

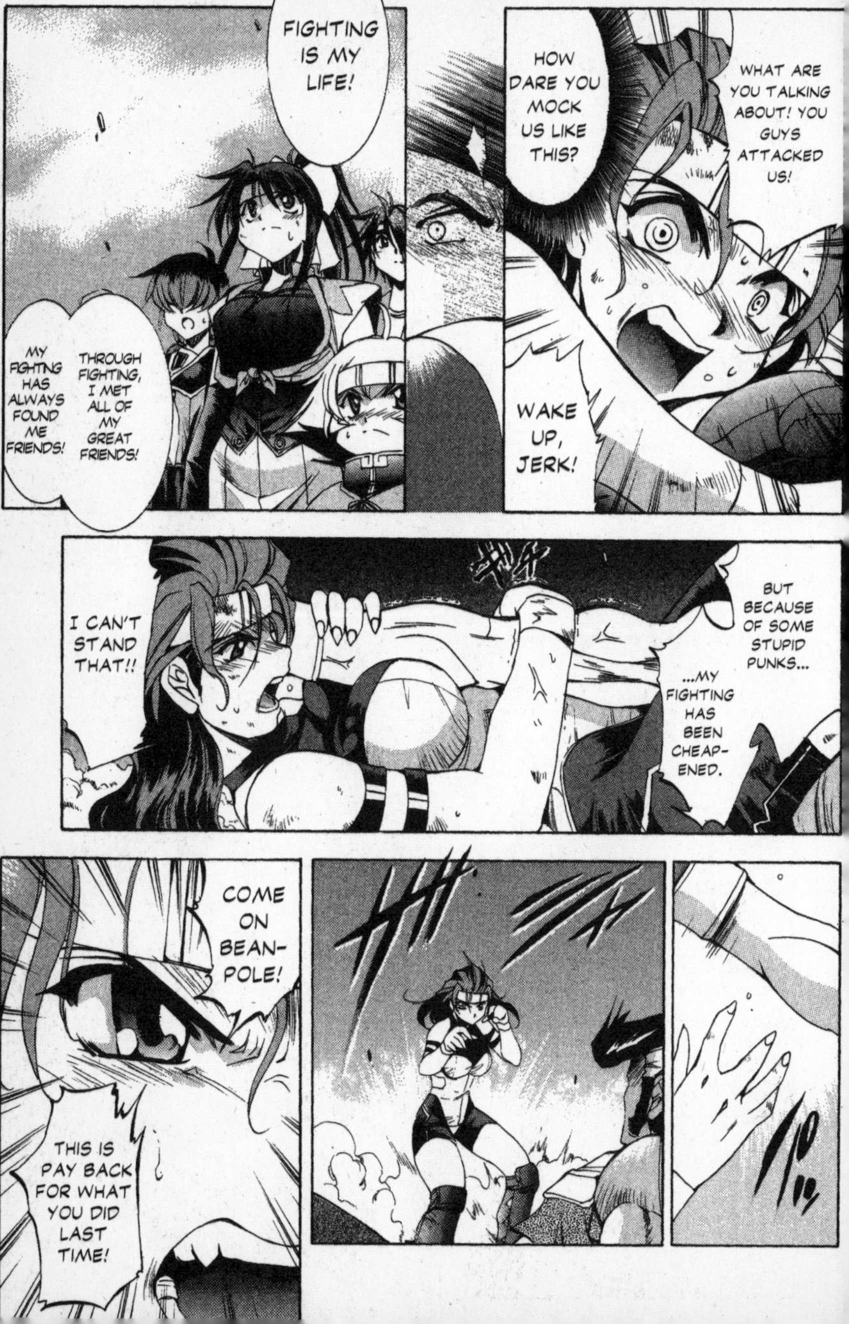
HOW DARE YOU MOCK US LIKE THIS?
WHAT ARE YOU TALKING ABOUT! YOU GUYS ATTACKED US!
WAKE UP, JERK!
FIGHTING IS MY LIFE!
THROUGH FIGHTING, I MET ALL OF MY GREAT FRIENDS!
MY FIGHTNG HAS ALWAYS FOUND ME FRIENDS!
BUT BECAUSE OF SOME STUPID PUNKS...
...MY FIGHTING HAS BEEN CHEAP-ENED.
I CAN'T STAND THAT!!
COME ON BEAN-POLE!
THIS IS PAY BACK FOR WHAT YOU DID LAST TIME!

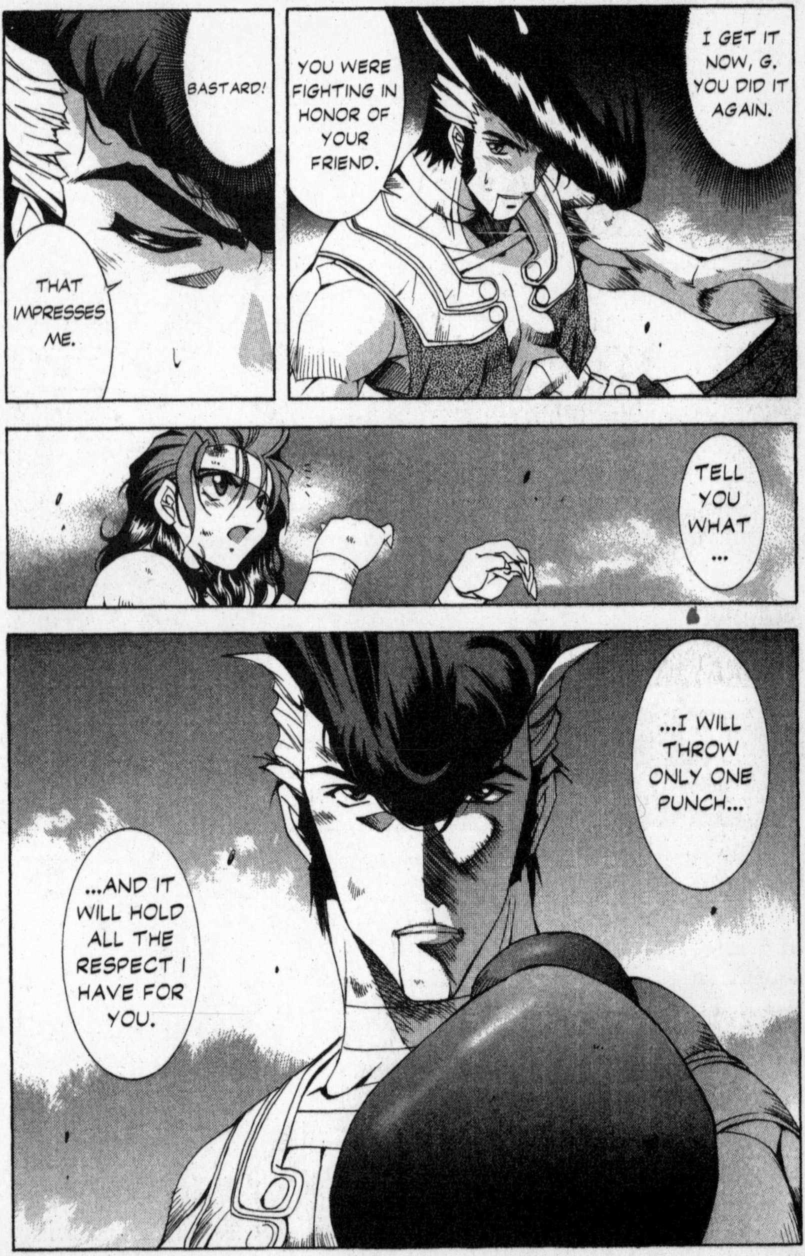
I GET IT NOW, G. YOU DID IT AGAIN.
YOU WERE FIGHTING IN HONOR OF YOUR FRIEND.
BASTARD!
THAT IMPRESSES ME.
TELL YOU WHAT...
...I WILL THROW ONLY ONE PUNCH...
...AND IT WILL HOLD ALL THE RESPECT I HAVE FOR YOU.

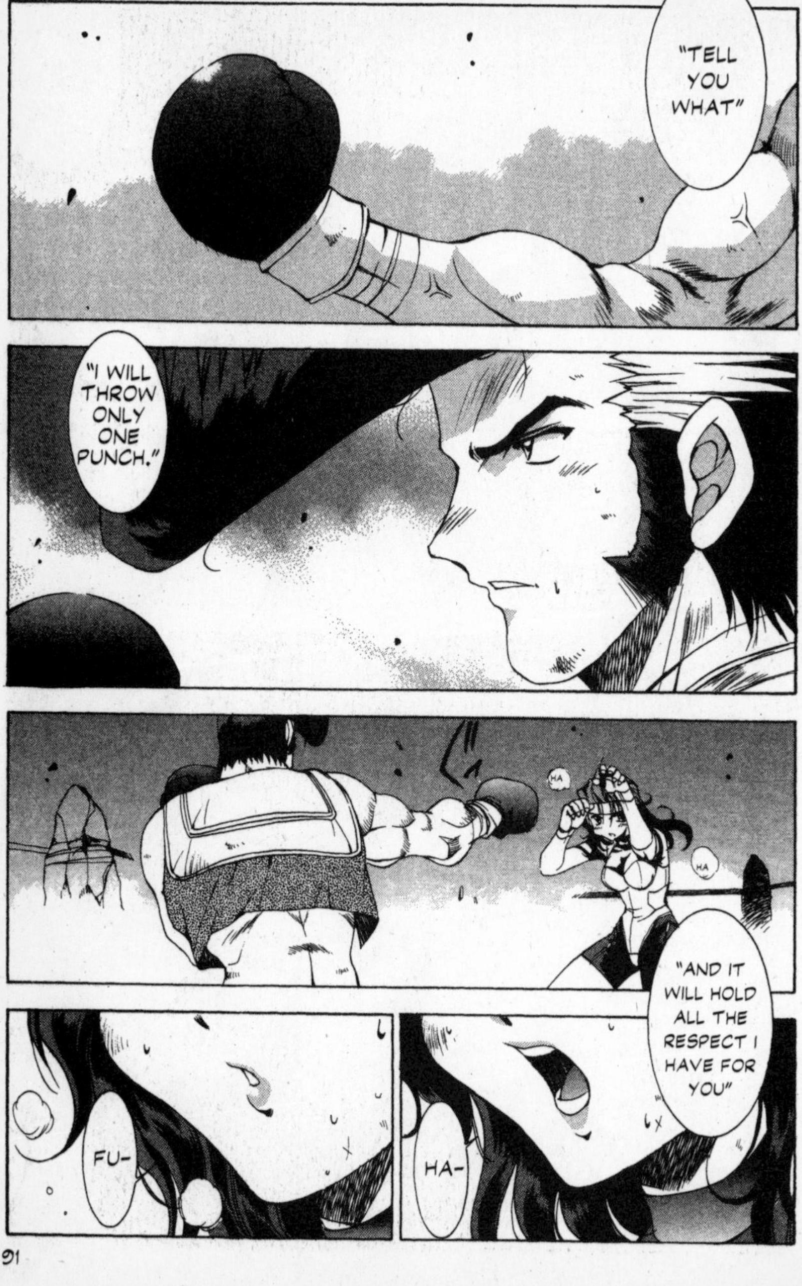
"TELL YOU WHAT"
"I WILL THROW ONLY ONE PUNCH."
HA
HA
"AND IT WILL HOLD ALL THE RESPECT I HAVE FOR YOU"
HA-
FU-

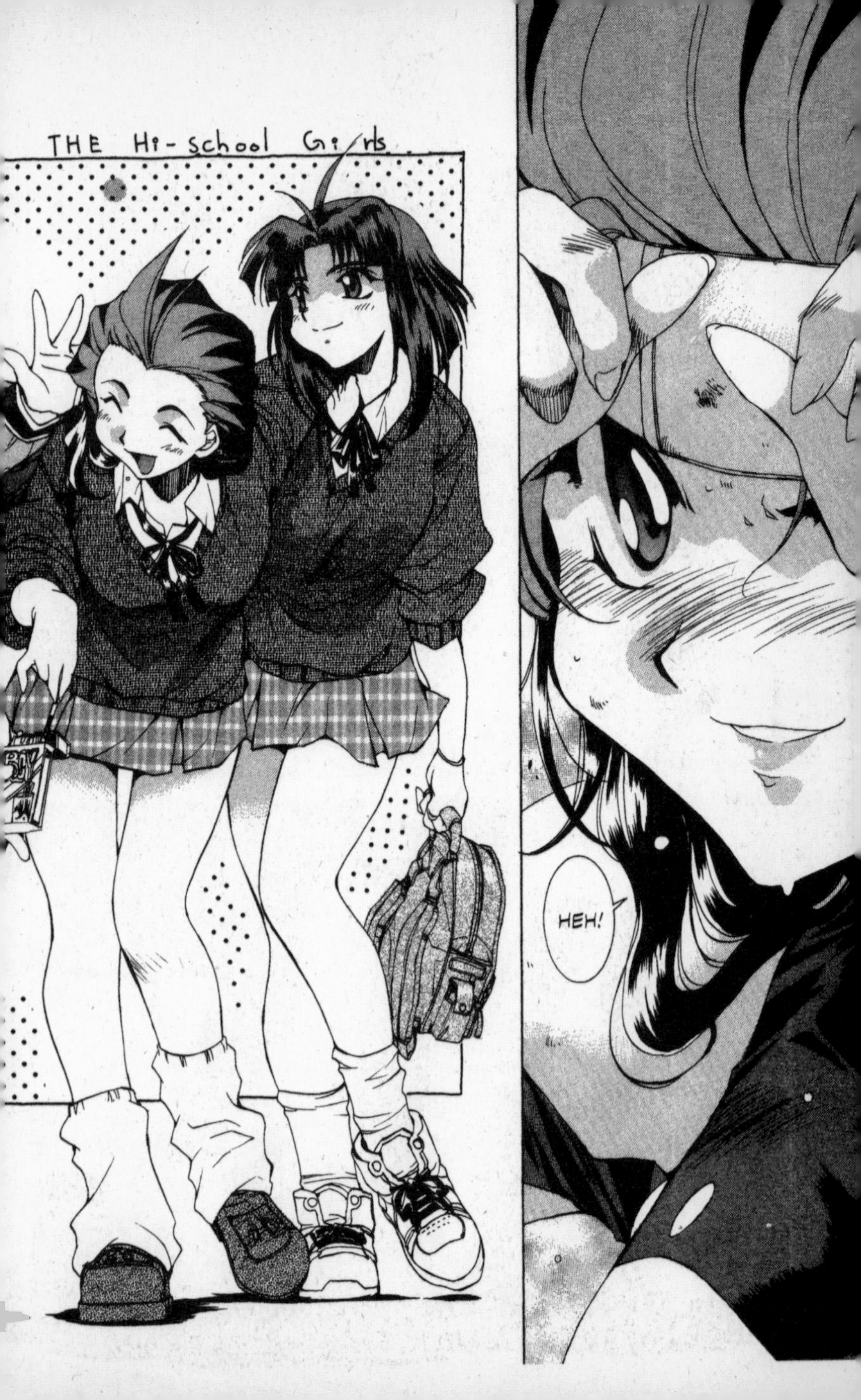
THE Hi-School Girls
HEH!

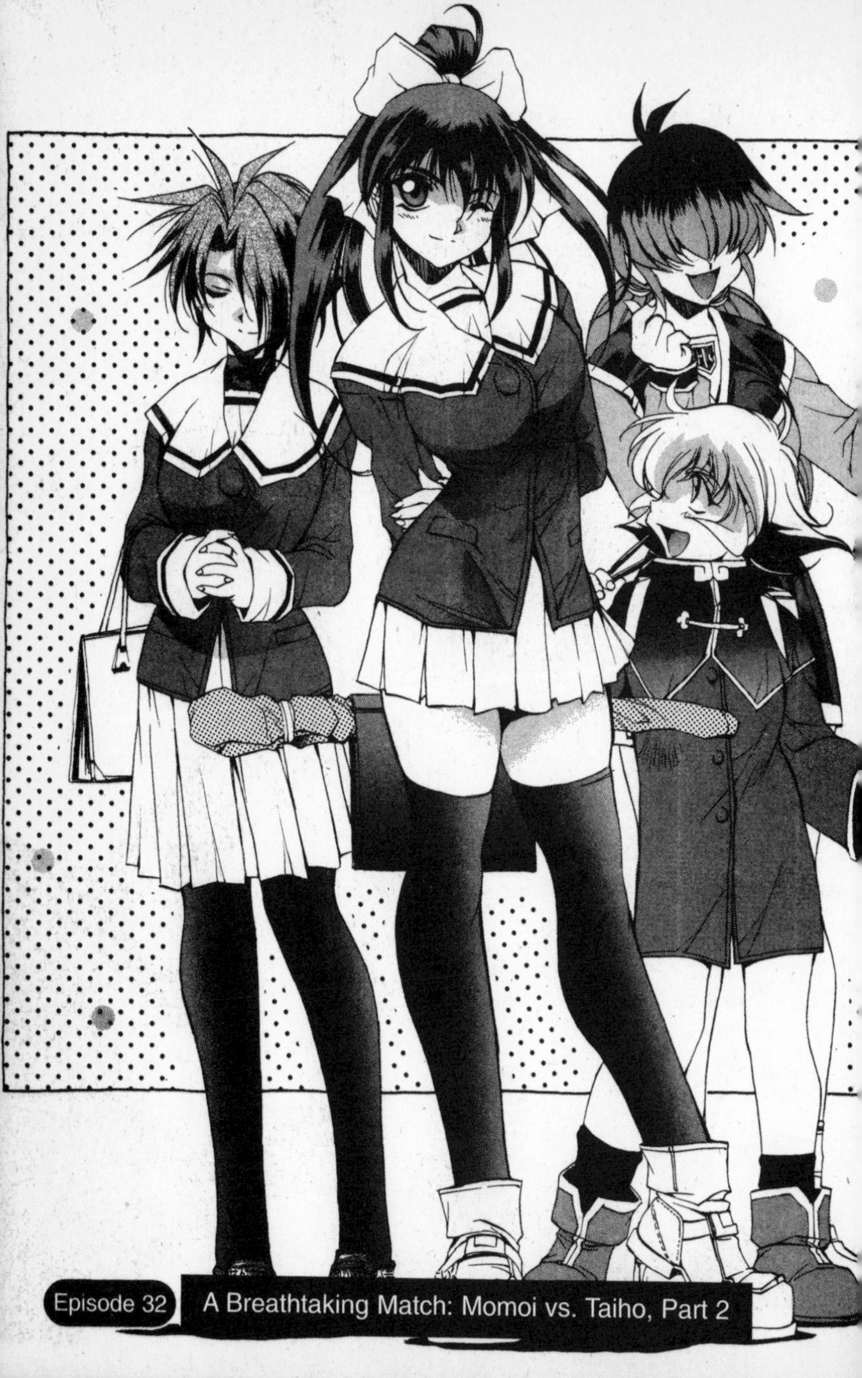

Episode 32 A Breathtaking Match: Momoi vs. Taiho, Part 2

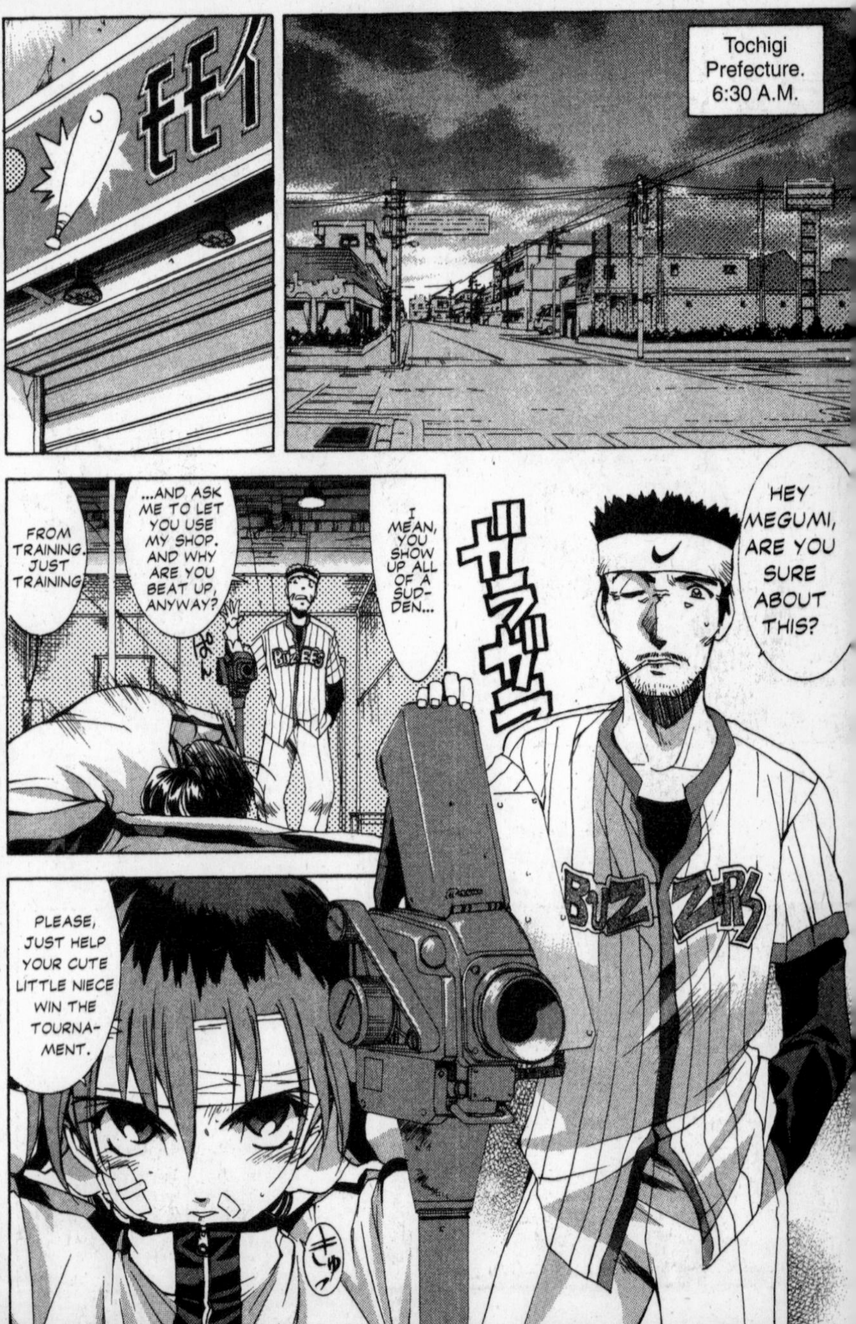

Tochigi Prefecture. 6:30 A.M.
HEY MEGUMI, ARE YOU SURE ABOUT THIS?
I MEAN, YOU SHOW UP ALL OF A SUD-DEN...
...AND ASK ME TO LET YOU USE MY SHOP. AND WHY ARE YOU BEAT UP, ANYWAY?
FROM TRAINING. JUST TRAINING.
PLEASE, JUST HELP YOUR CUTE LITTLE NIECE WIN THE TOURNA-MENT.

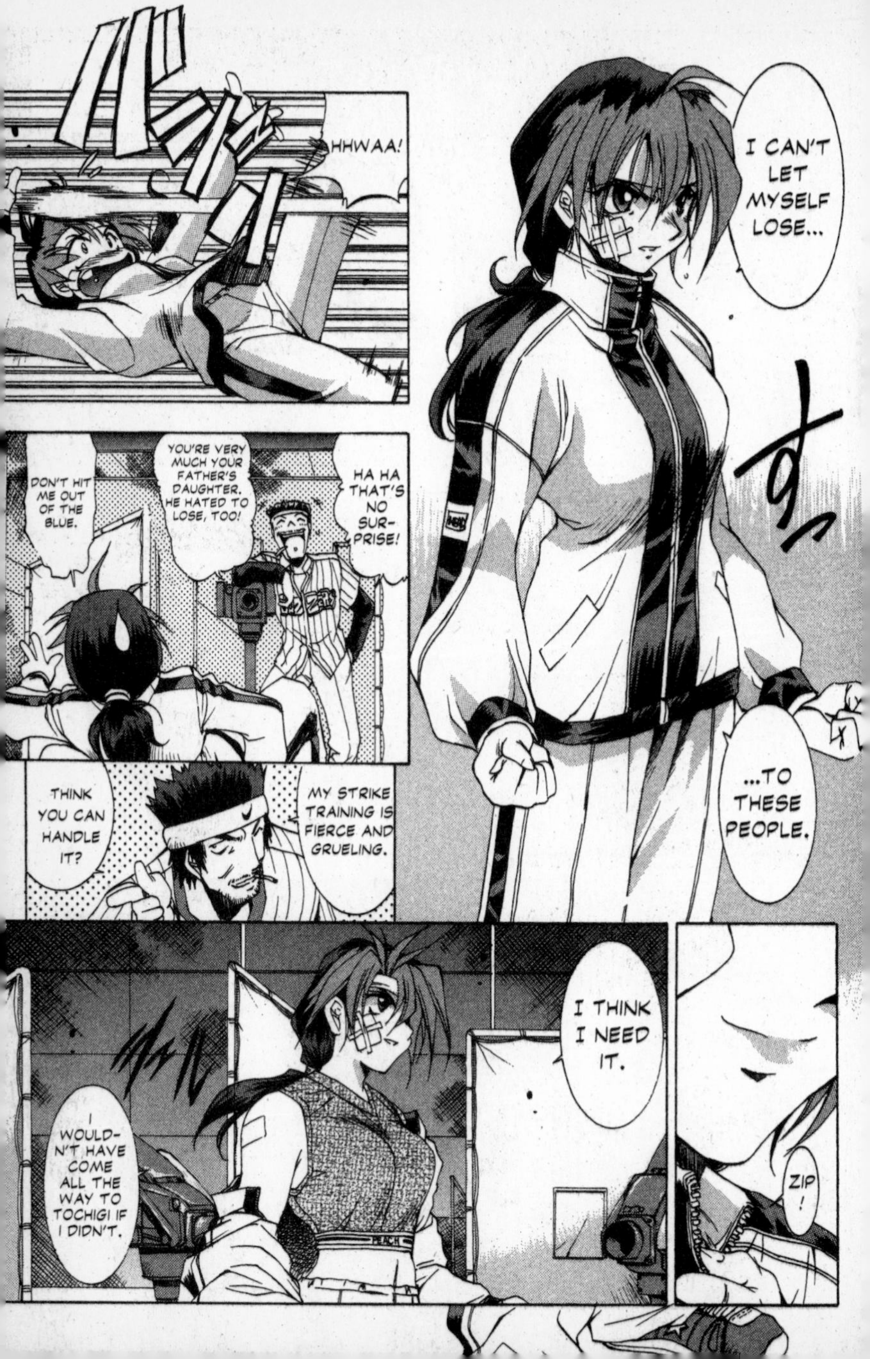
I CAN'T LET MYSELF LOSE...
...TO THESE PEOPLE.
すっ
HHWAA!
HA HA THAT'S NO SURPRISE!
YOU'RE VERY MUCH YOUR FATHER'S DAUGHTER. HE HATED TO LOSE, TOO!
DON'T HIT ME OUT OF THE BLUE.
MY STRIKE TRAINING IS FIERCE AND GRUELING.
THINK YOU CAN HANDLE IT?
ZIP!
I THINK I NEED IT.
I WOULDN'T HAVE COME ALL THE WAY TO TOCHIGI IF I DIDN'T.

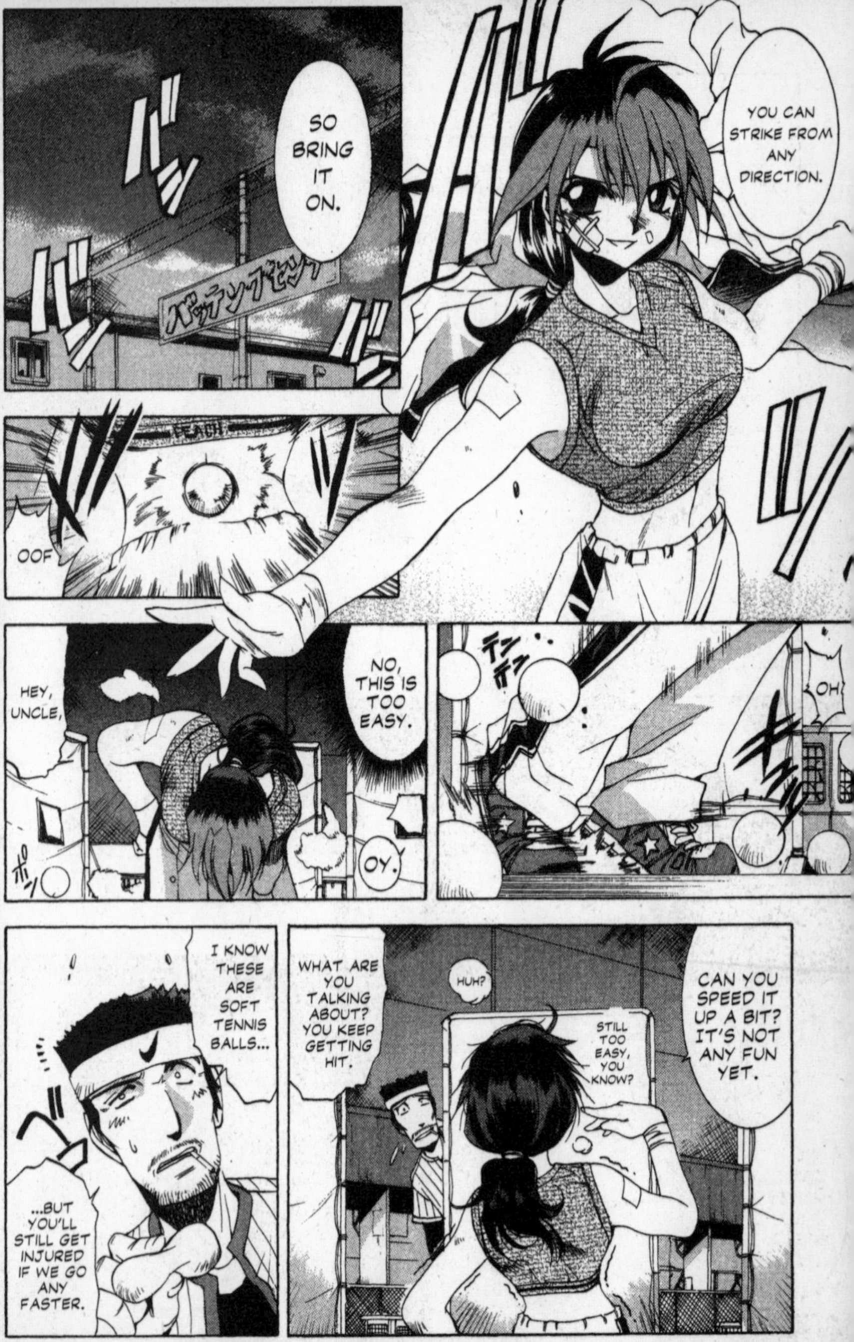
YOU CAN STRIKE FROM ANY DIRECTION.
SO BRING IT ON.
OOF
OH
NO, THIS IS TOO EASY.
HEY, UNCLE,
OY.
CAN YOU SPEED IT UP A BIT? IT'S NOT ANY FUN YET.
HUH?
STILL TOO EASY, YOU KNOW?
WHAT ARE YOU TALKING ABOUT? YOU KEEP GETTING HIT.
I KNOW THESE ARE SOFT TENNIS BALLS...
...BUT YOU'LL STILL GET INJURED IF WE GO ANY FASTER.

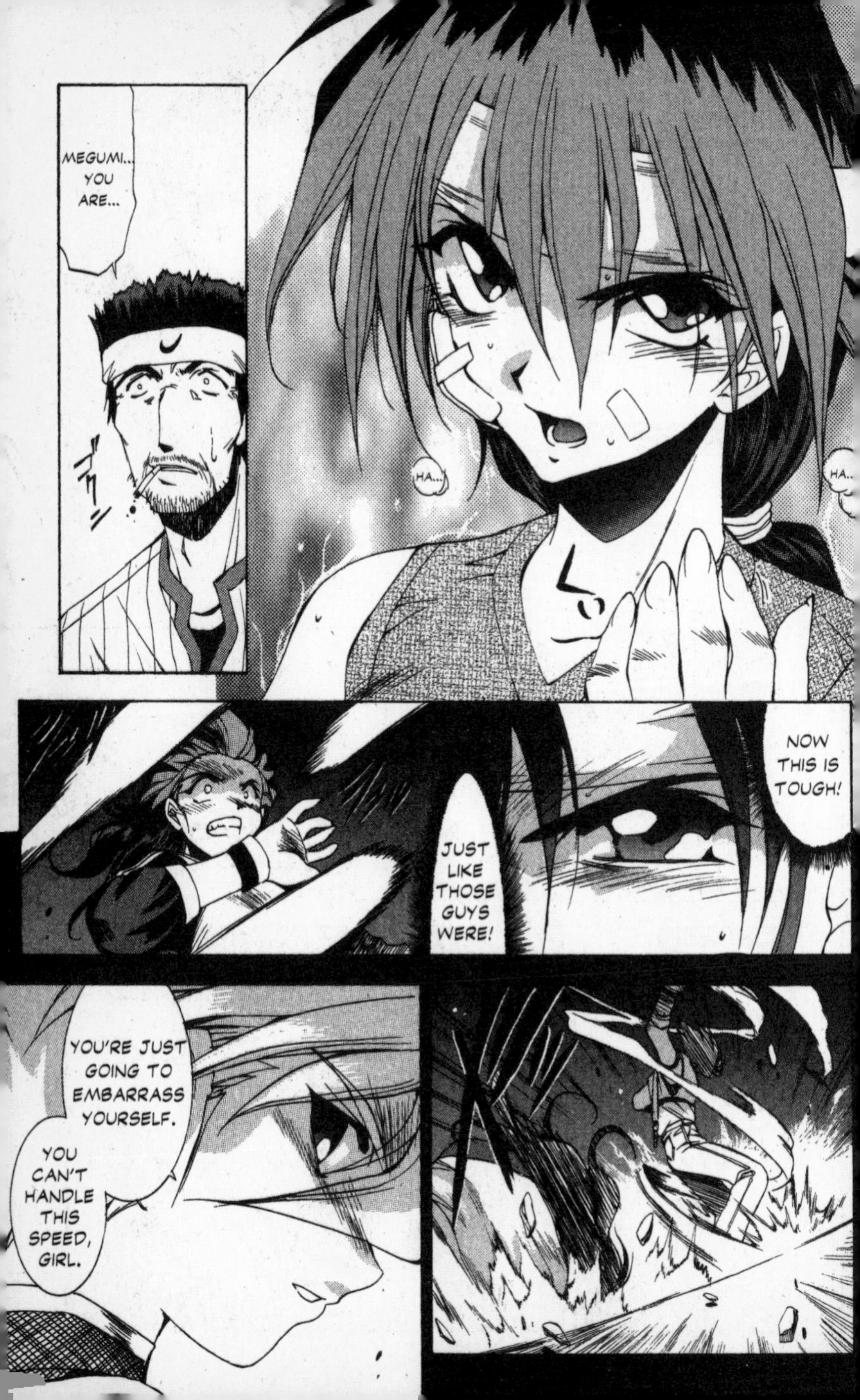
HA...
HA...
MEGUMI... YOU ARE...
NOW THIS IS TOUGH!
JUST LIKE THOSE GUYS WERE!
YOU'RE JUST GOING TO EMBARRASS YOURSELF.
YOU CAN'T HANDLE THIS SPEED, GIRL.

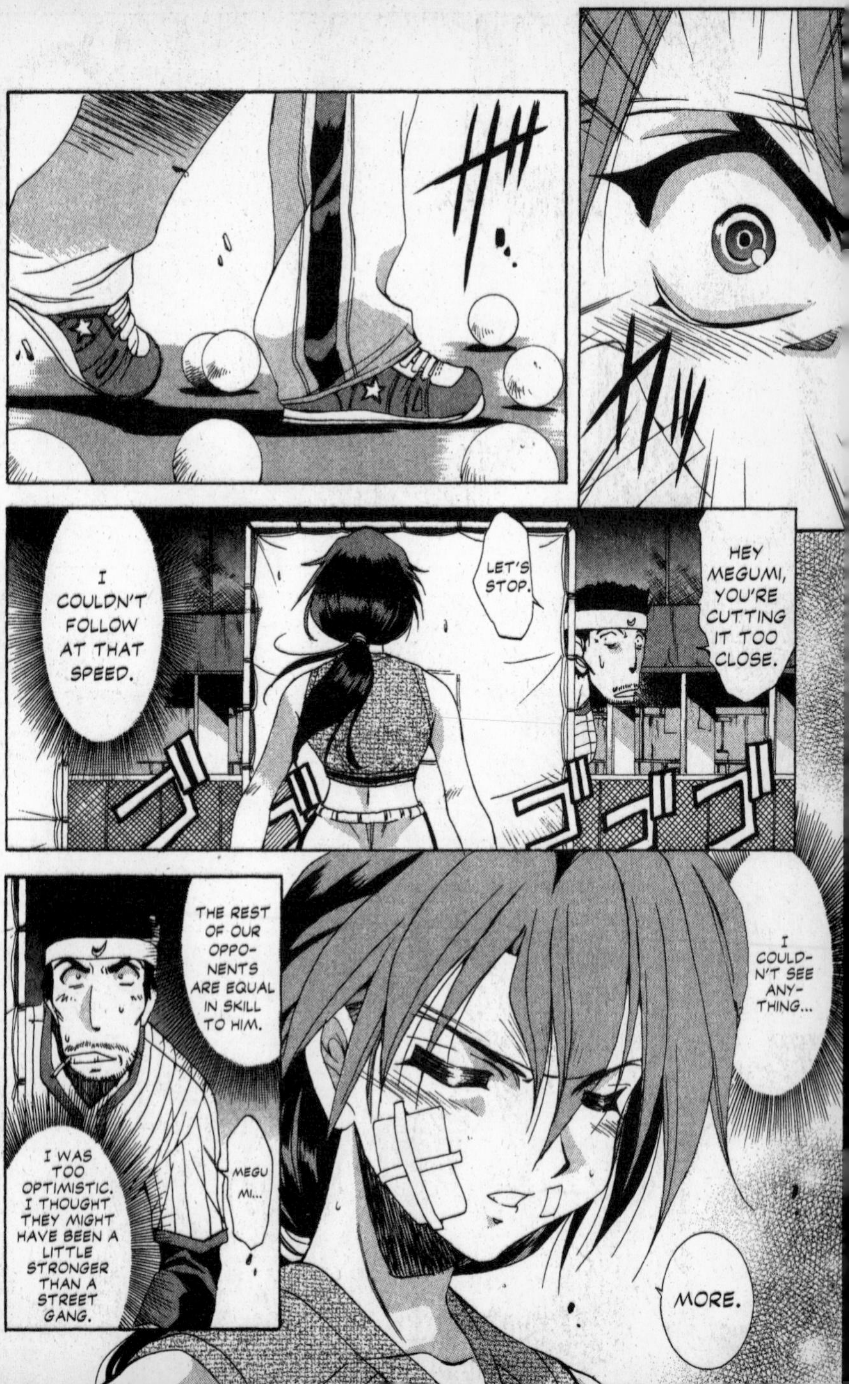
HEY MEGUMI, YOU'RE CUTTING IT TOO CLOSE.
LET'S STOP.
I COULDN'T FOLLOW AT THAT SPEED.
I COULDN'T SEE ANYTHING...
THE REST OF OUR OPPONENTS ARE EQUAL IN SKILL TO HIM.
MEGUMI...
I WAS TOO OPTIMISTIC. I THOUGHT THEY MIGHT HAVE BEEN A LITTLE STRONGER THAN A STREET GANG.
MORE.

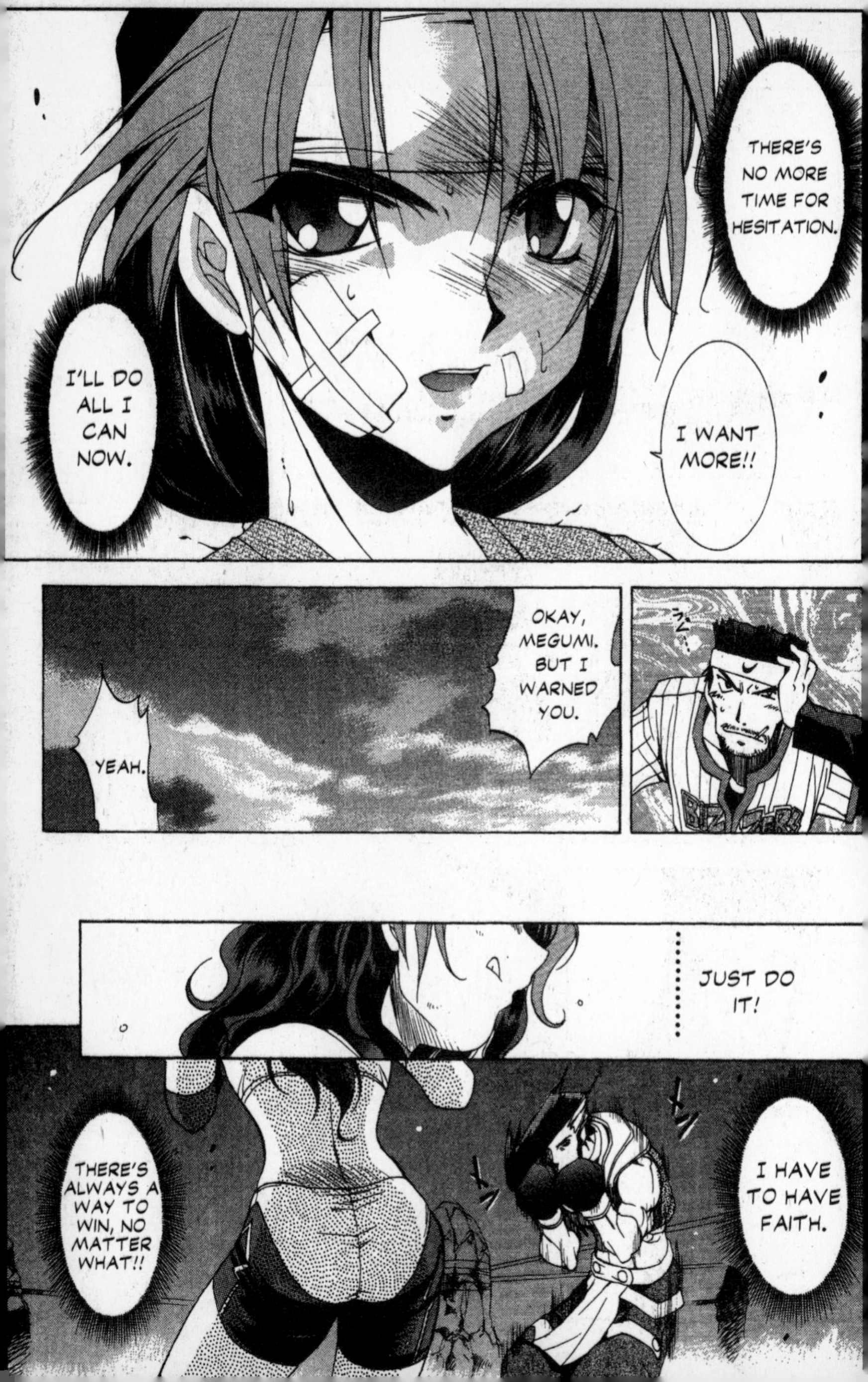
THERE'S NO MORE TIME FOR HESITATION.
I WANT MORE!!
I'LL DO ALL I CAN NOW.
OKAY, MEGUMI. BUT I WARNED YOU.
YEAH.
JUST DO IT!
I HAVE TO HAVE FAITH.
THERE'S ALWAYS A WAY TO WIN, NO MATTER WHAT!!

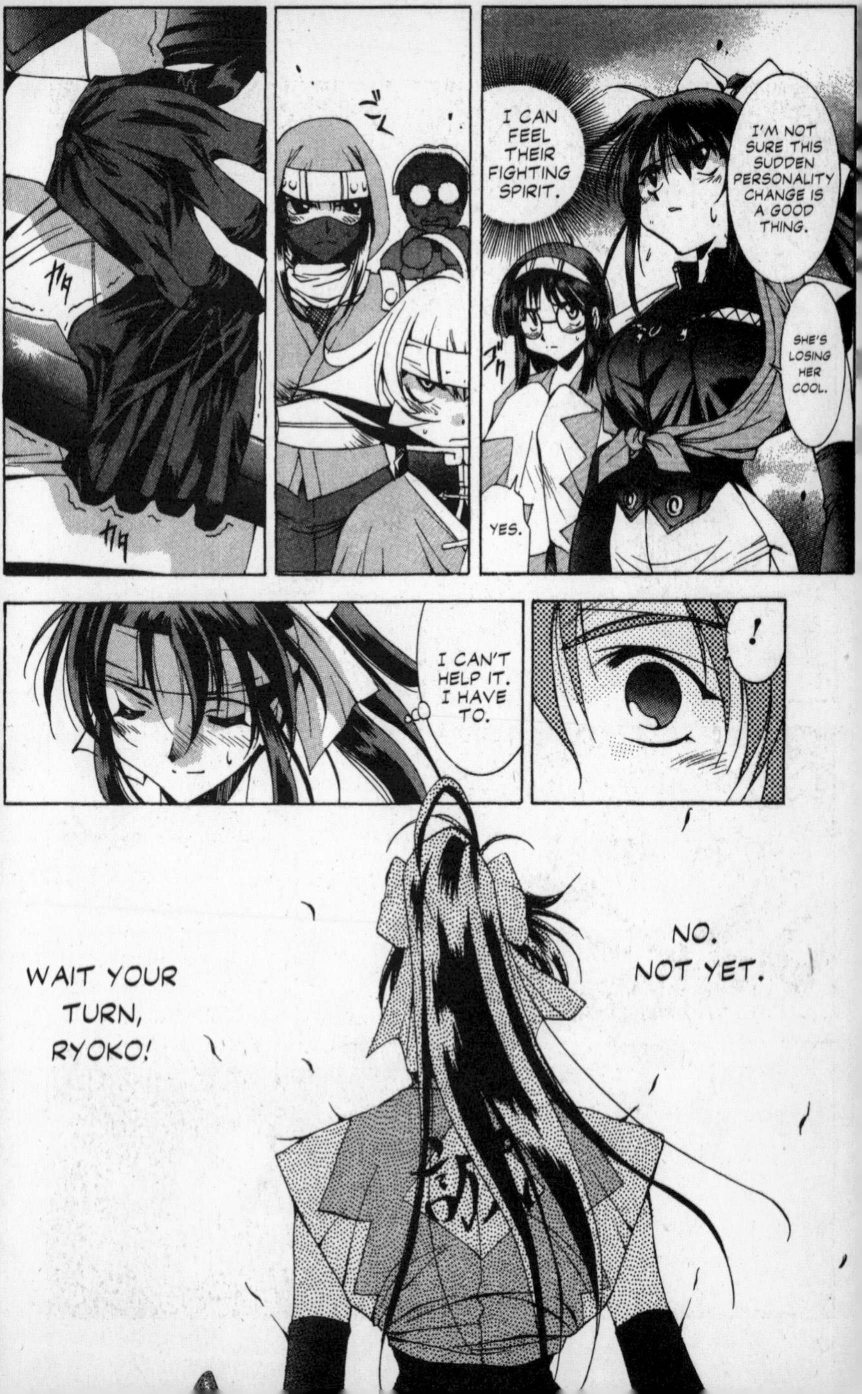
I'M NOT SURE THIS SUDDEN PERSONALITY CHANGE IS A GOOD THING.
SHE'S LOSING HER COOL.
I CAN FEEL THEIR FIGHTING SPIRIT.
YES.
!
I CAN'T HELP IT. I HAVE TO.
NO. NOT YET.
WAIT YOUR TURN, RYOKO!

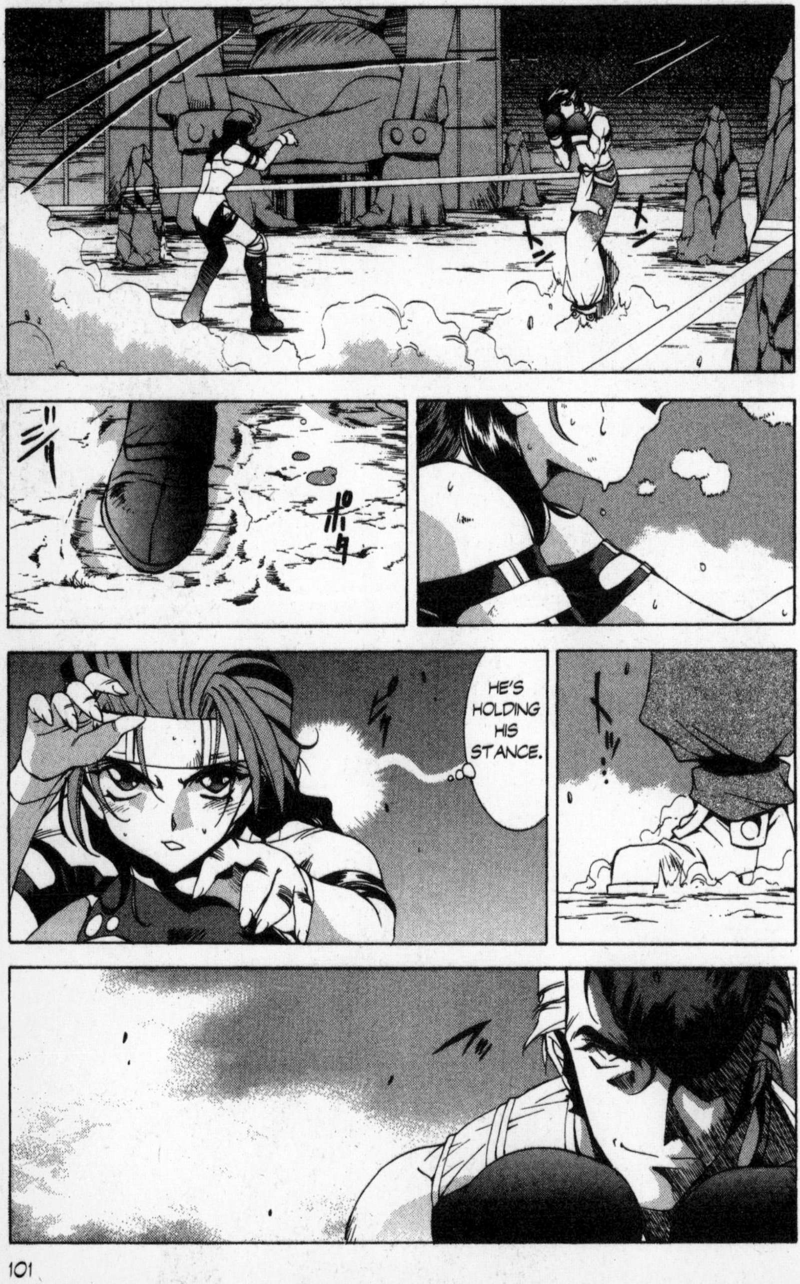
HE'S HOLDING HIS STANCE.

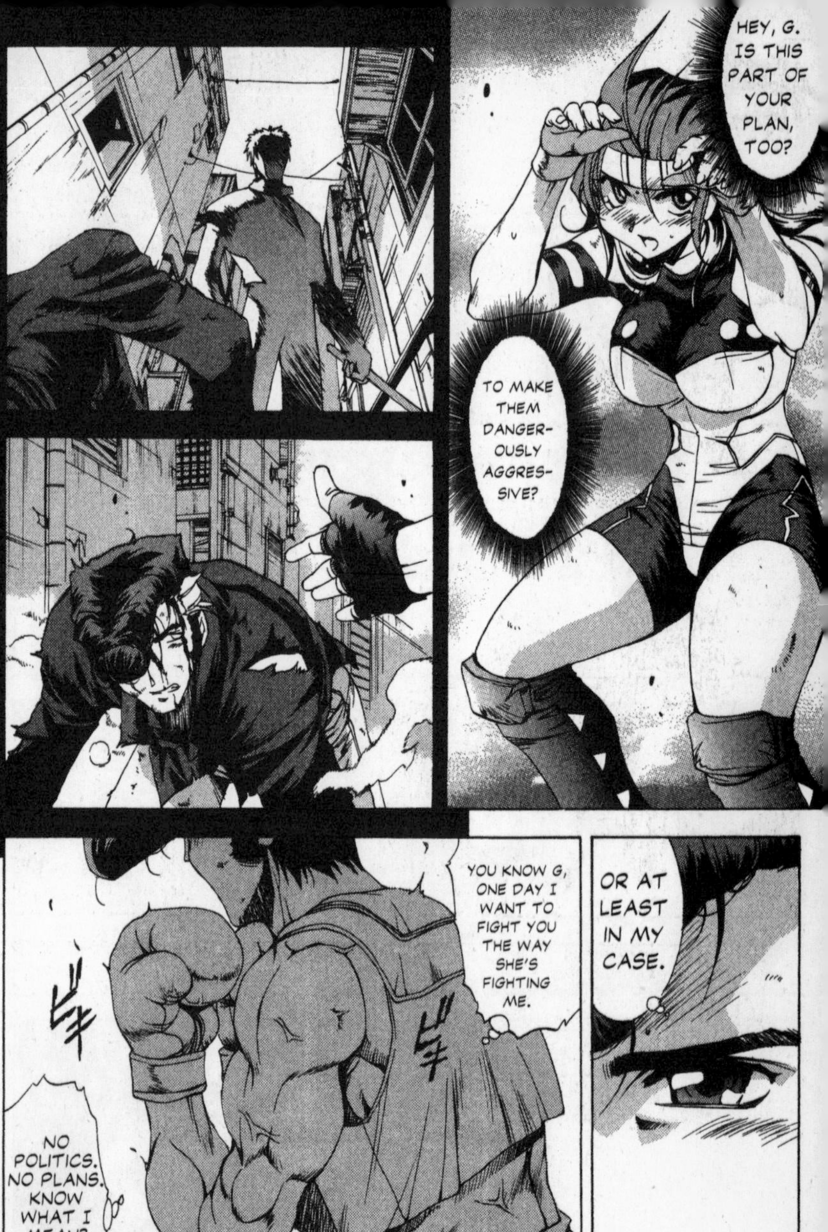
HEY, G. IS THIS PART OF YOUR PLAN, TOO?
TO MAKE THEM DANGER-OUSLY AGGRES-SIVE?
OR AT LEAST IN MY CASE.
YOU KNOW G, ONE DAY I WANT TO FIGHT YOU THE WAY SHE'S FIGHTING ME.
NO POLITICS. NO PLANS. KNOW WHAT I MEAN?

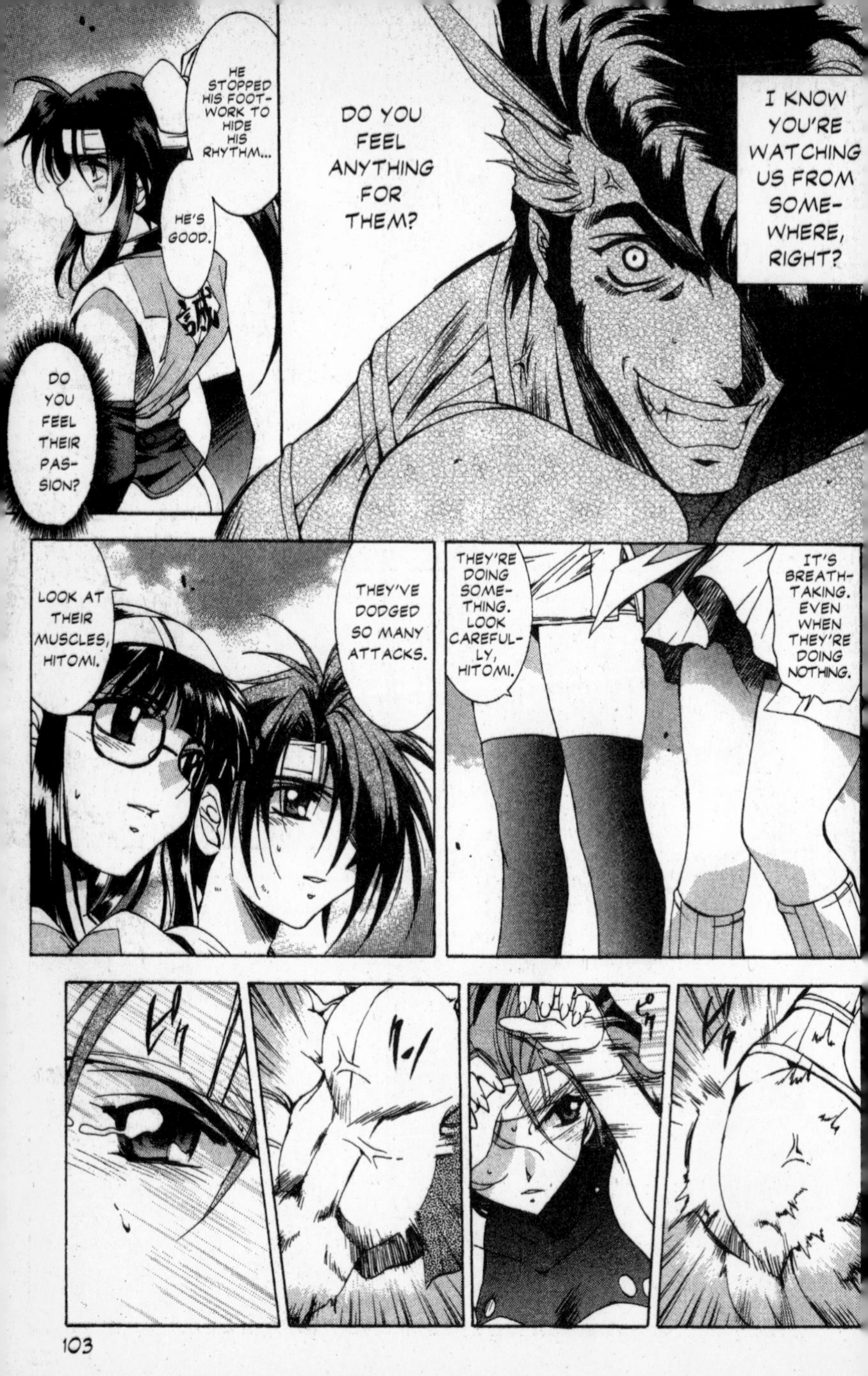
I KNOW YOU'RE WATCHING US FROM SOMEWHERE, RIGHT?
DO YOU FEEL ANYTHING FOR THEM?
HE STOPPED HIS FOOTWORK TO HIDE HIS RHYTHM...
HE'S GOOD.
DO YOU FEEL THEIR PASSION?
IT'S BREATHTAKING. EVEN WHEN THEY'RE DOING NOTHING.
THEY'RE DOING SOMETHING. LOOK CAREFULLY, HITOMI.
THEY'VE DODGED SO MANY ATTACKS.
LOOK AT THEIR MUSCLES, HITOMI.

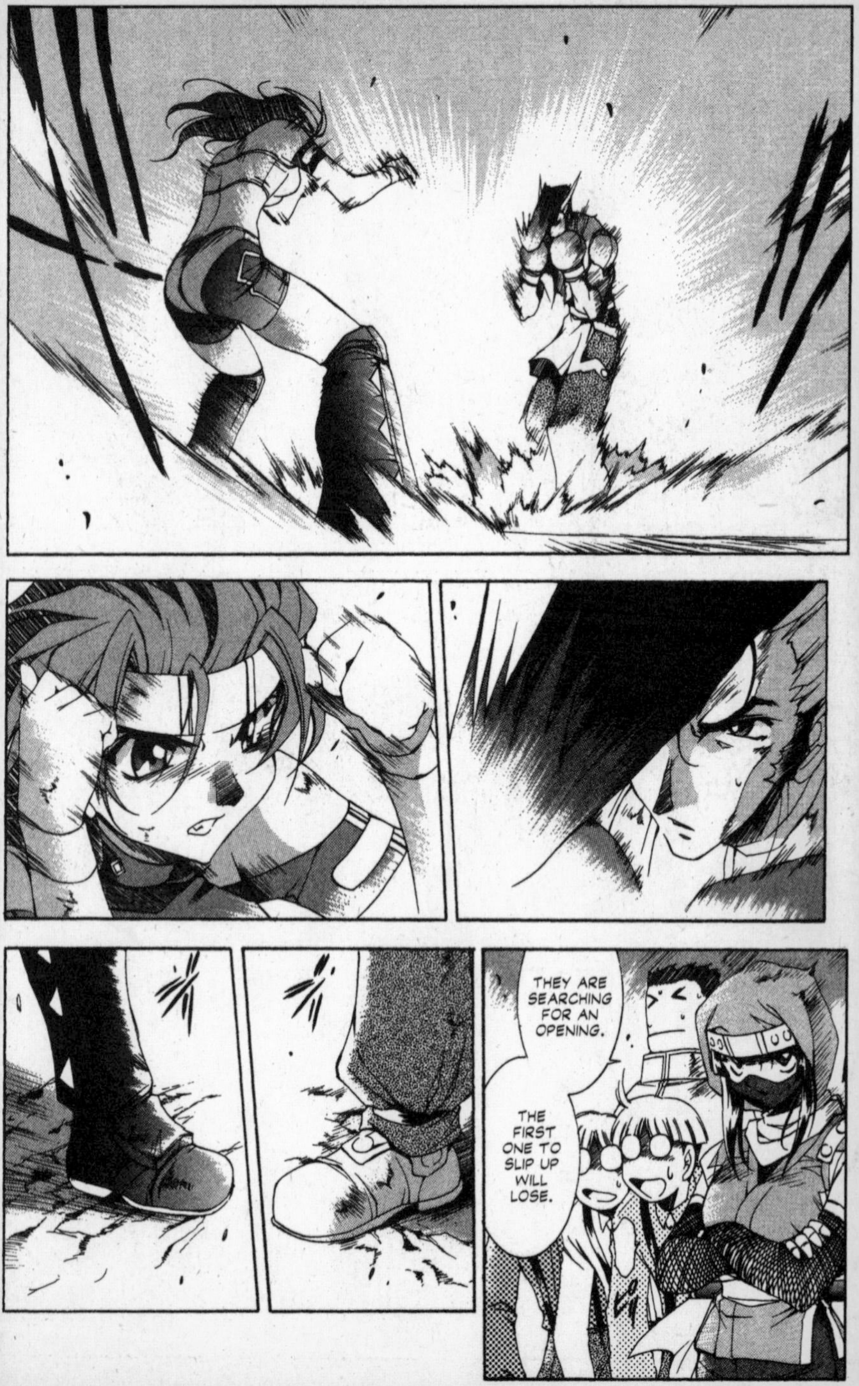
THEY ARE SEARCHING FOR AN OPENING.
THE FIRST ONE TO SLIP UP WILL LOSE.

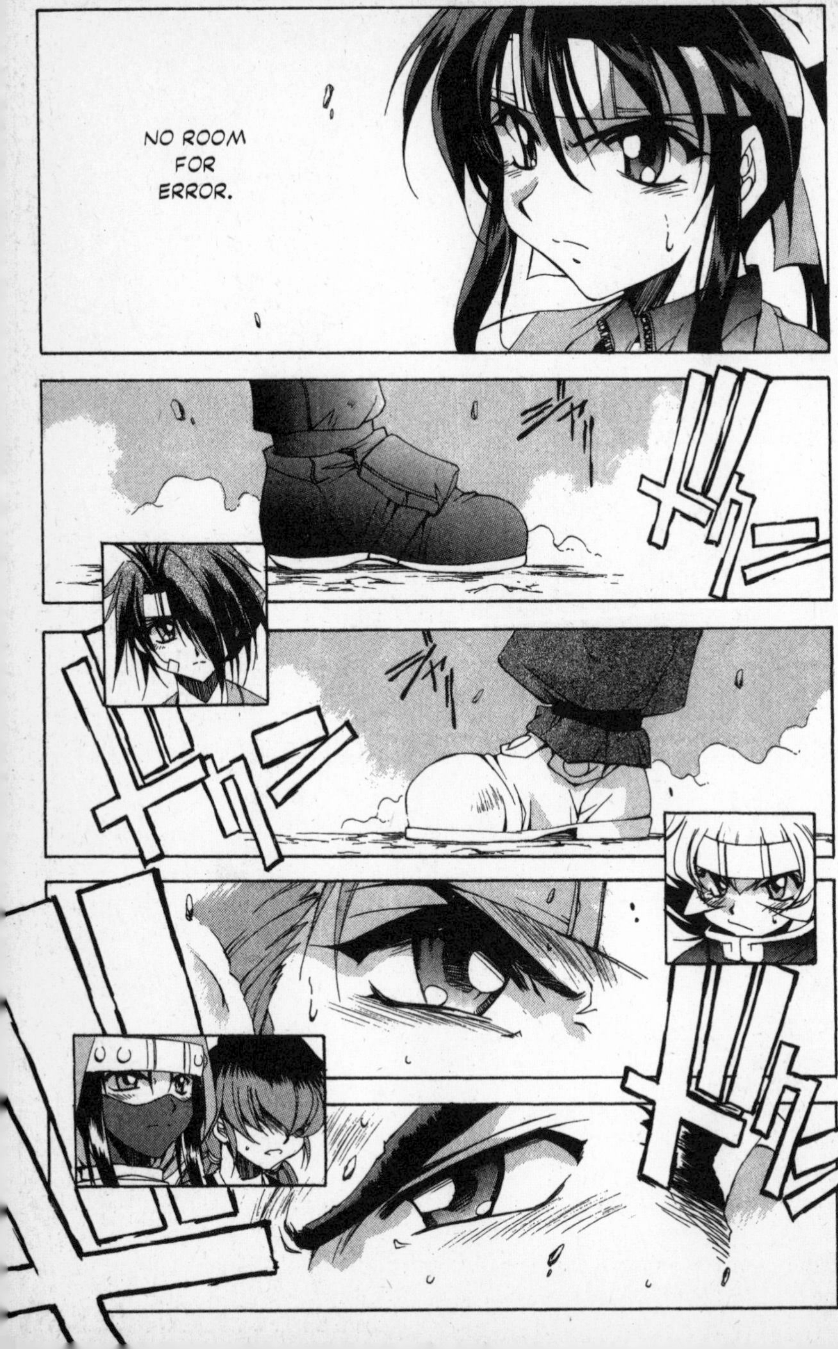
NO ROOM FOR ERROR.

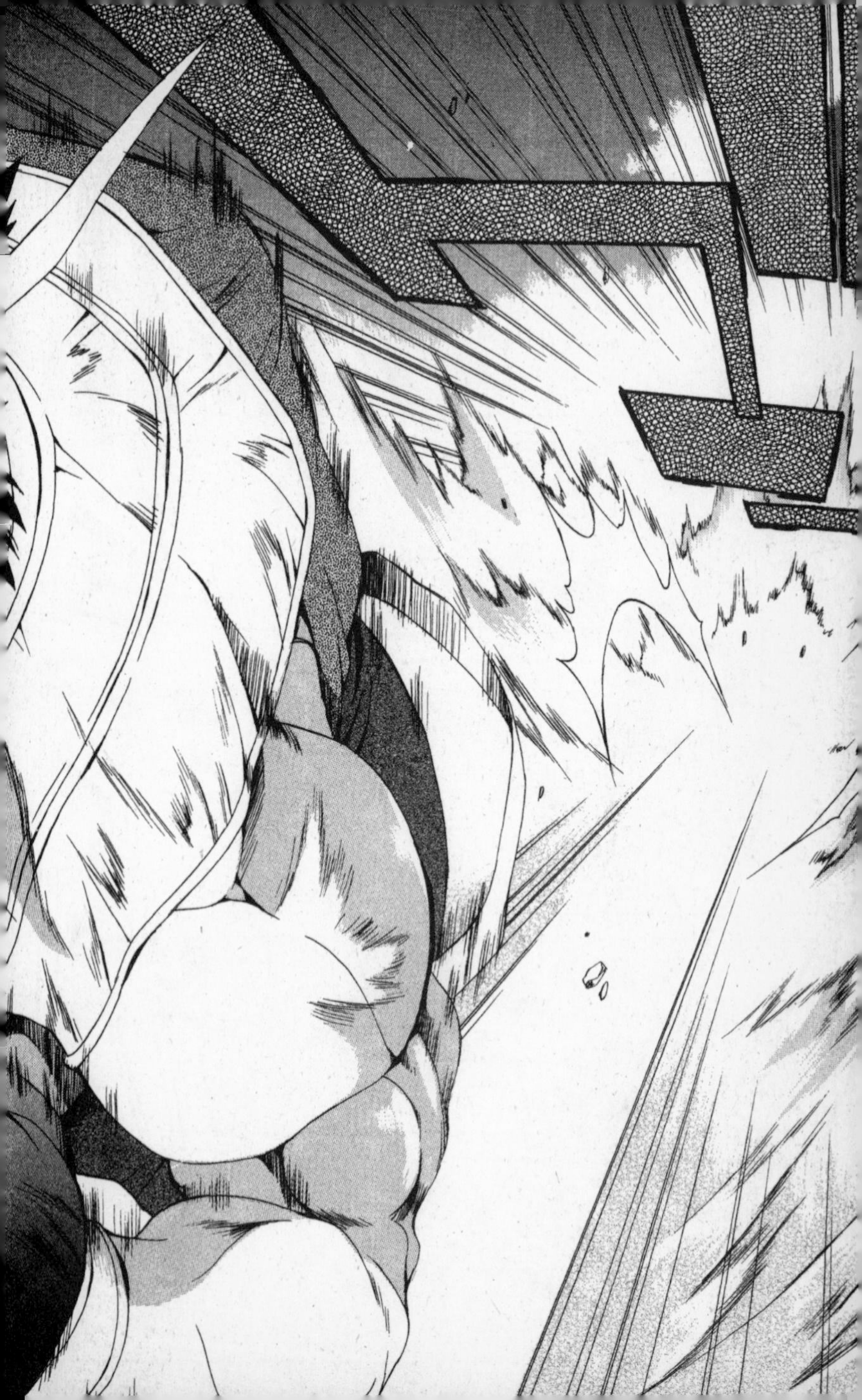

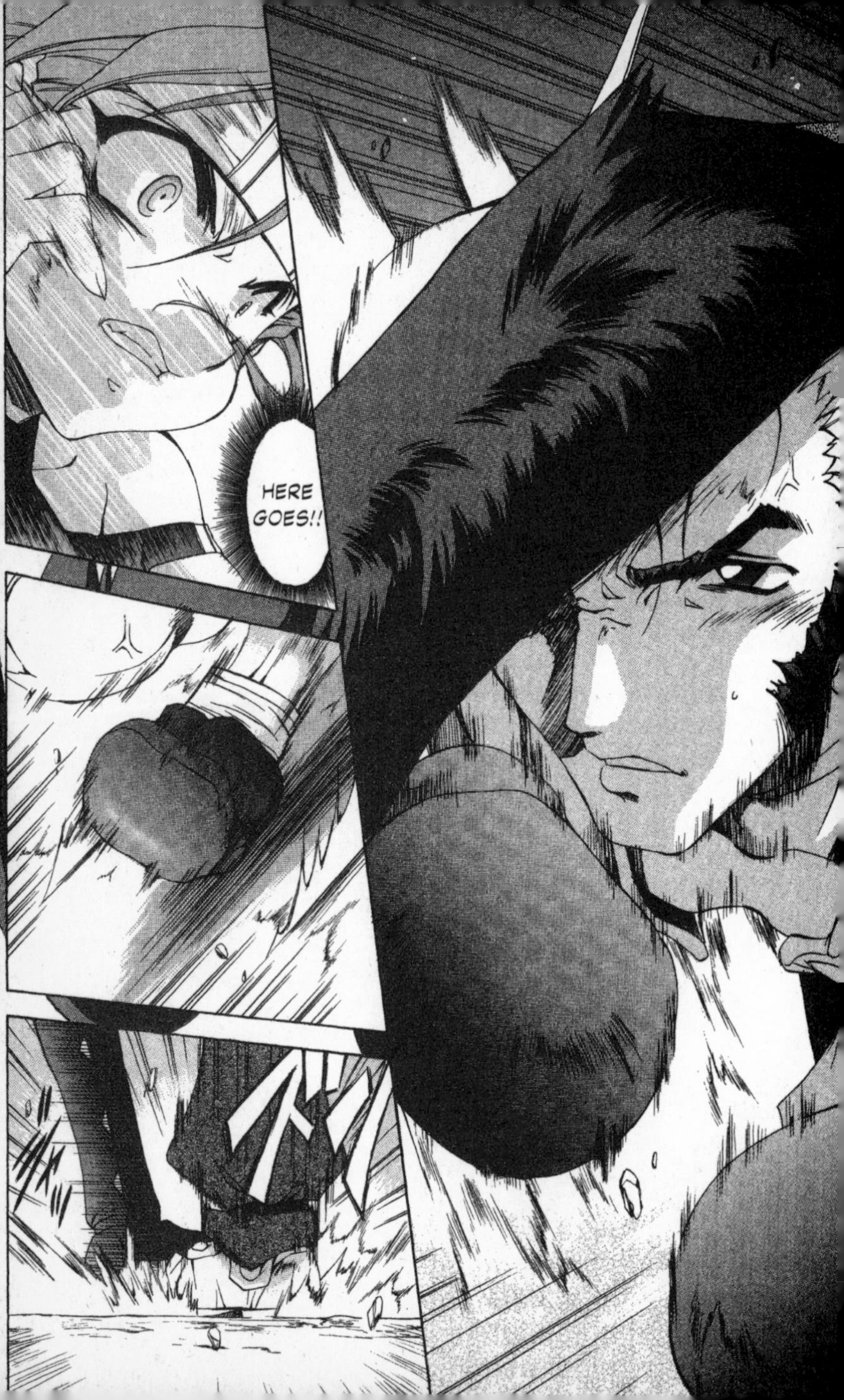
HERE GOES!!

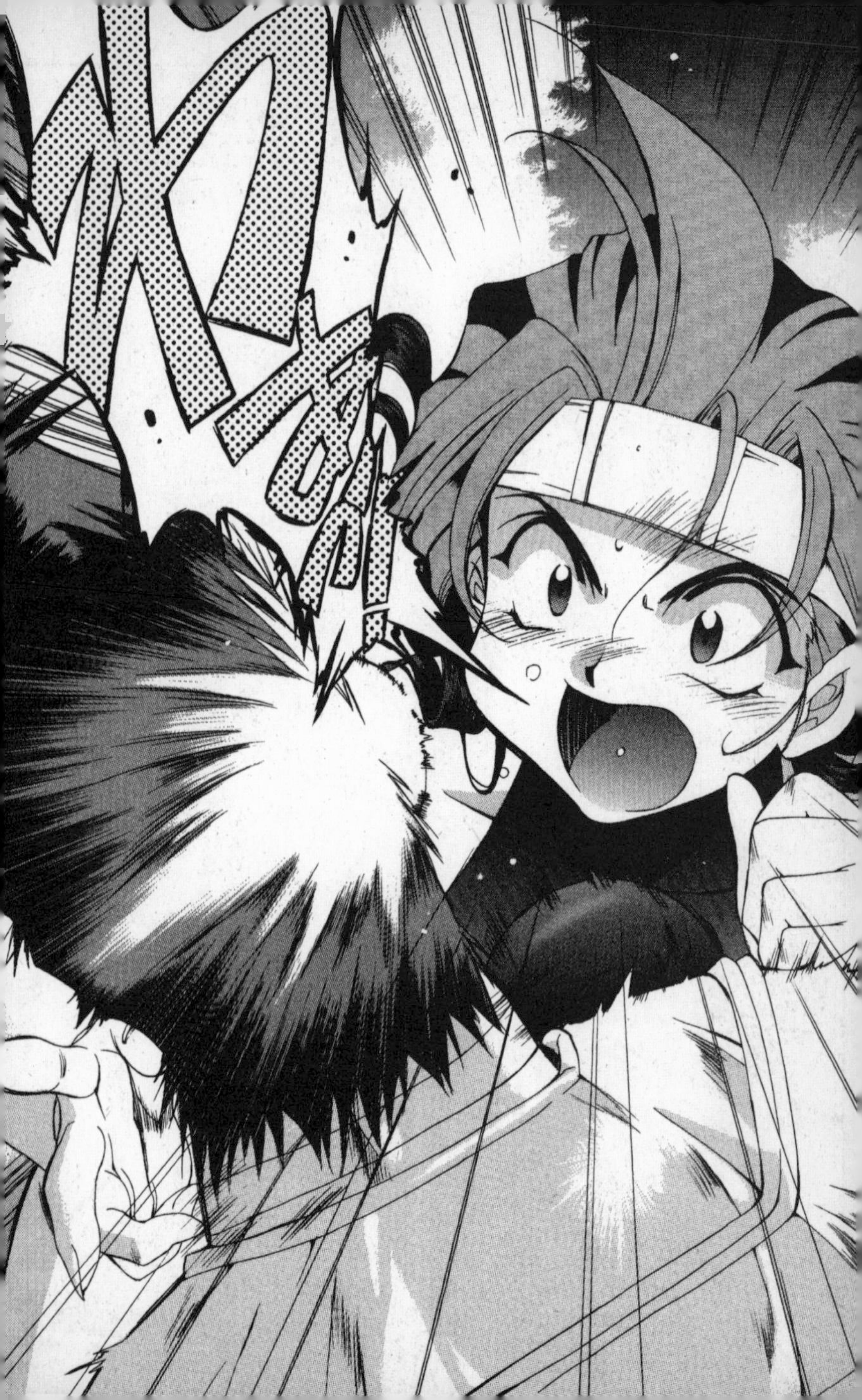

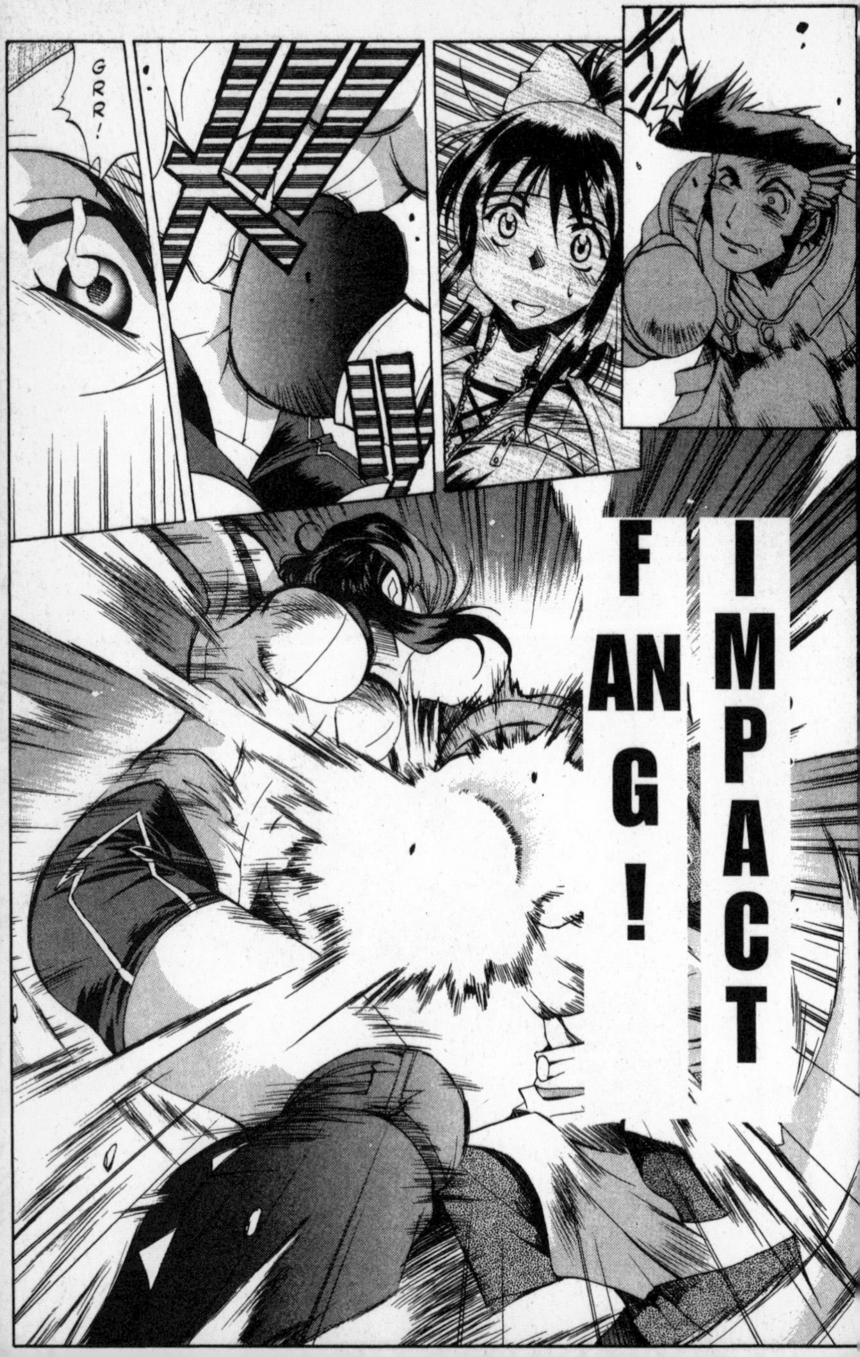
GRR!
IMPACT
FANG!

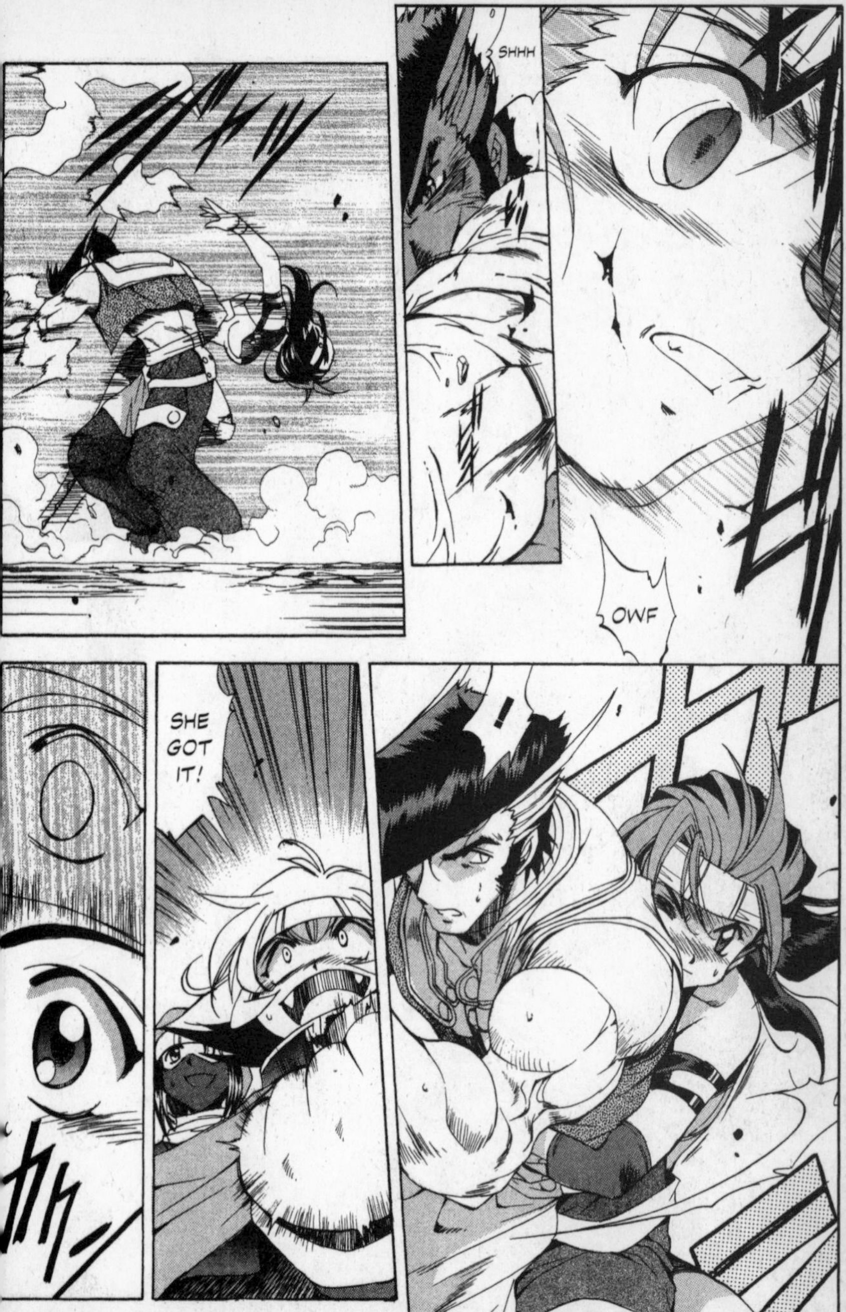
SHHH
OWF
!
SHE GOT IT!

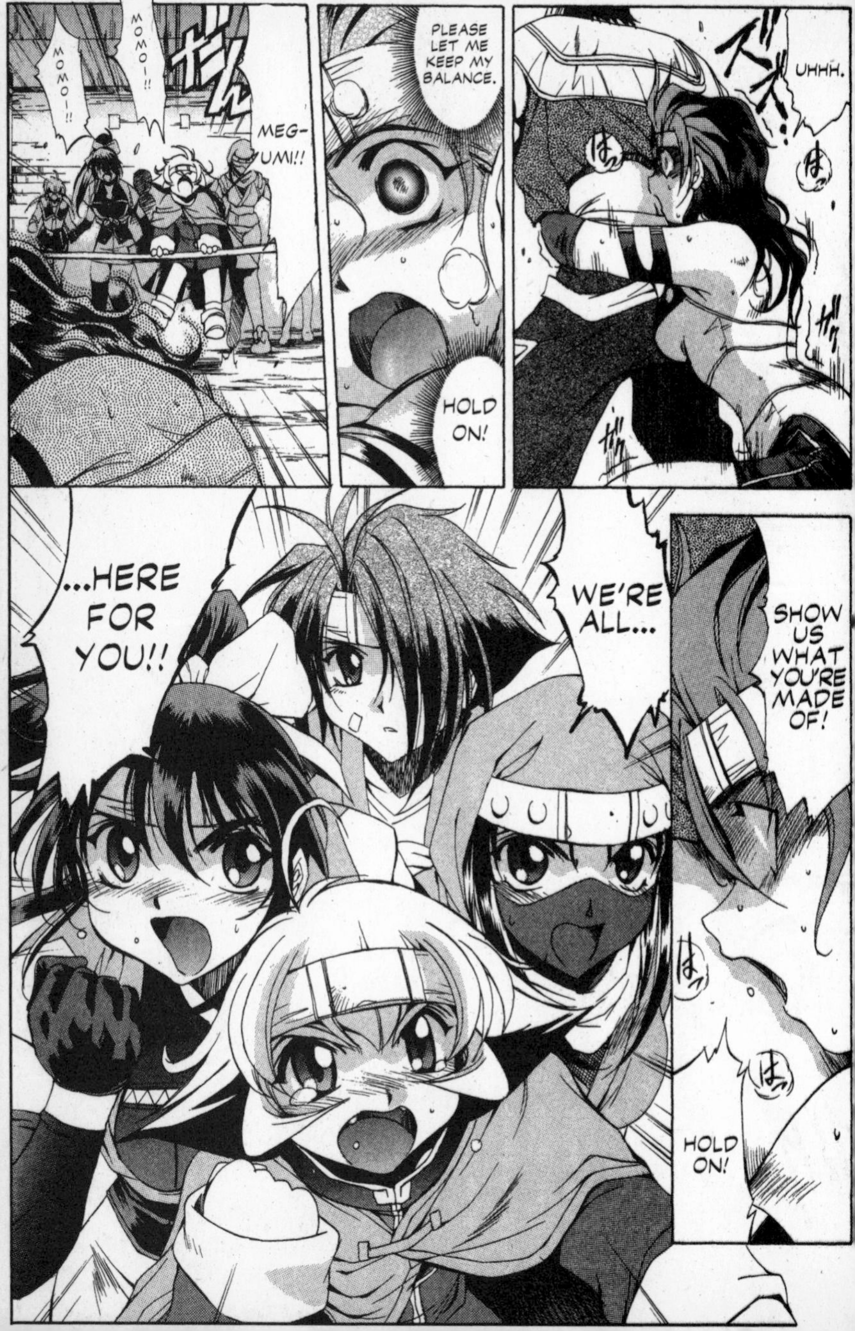

UHHH.
PLEASE LET ME KEEP MY BALANCE.
HOLD ON!
MOMO-I!!
MOMO-I!!
MEG-UMI!!
SHOW US WHAT YOU'RE MADE OF!
HOLD ON!
WE'RE ALL...
...HERE FOR YOU!!

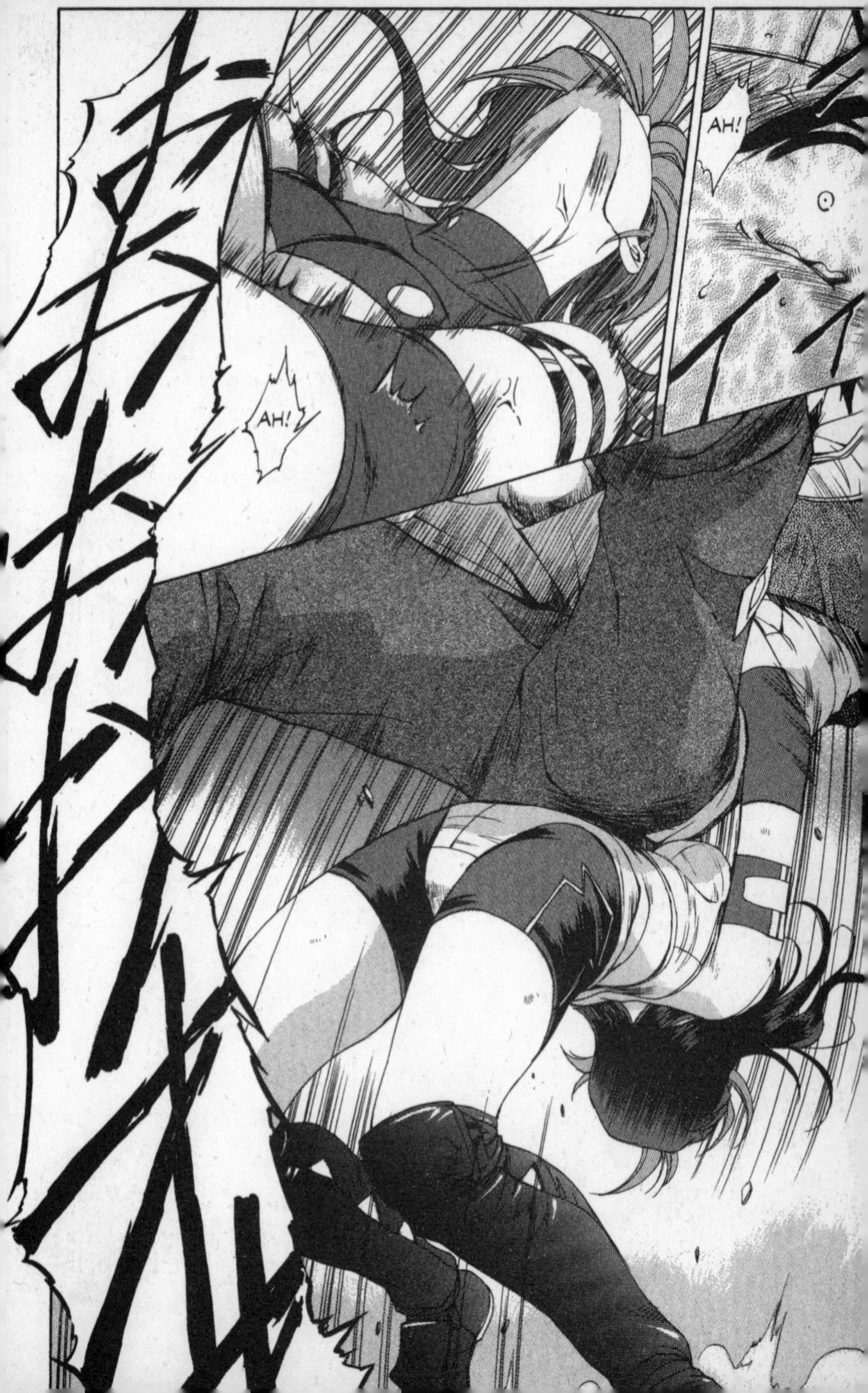
AH!
AH!

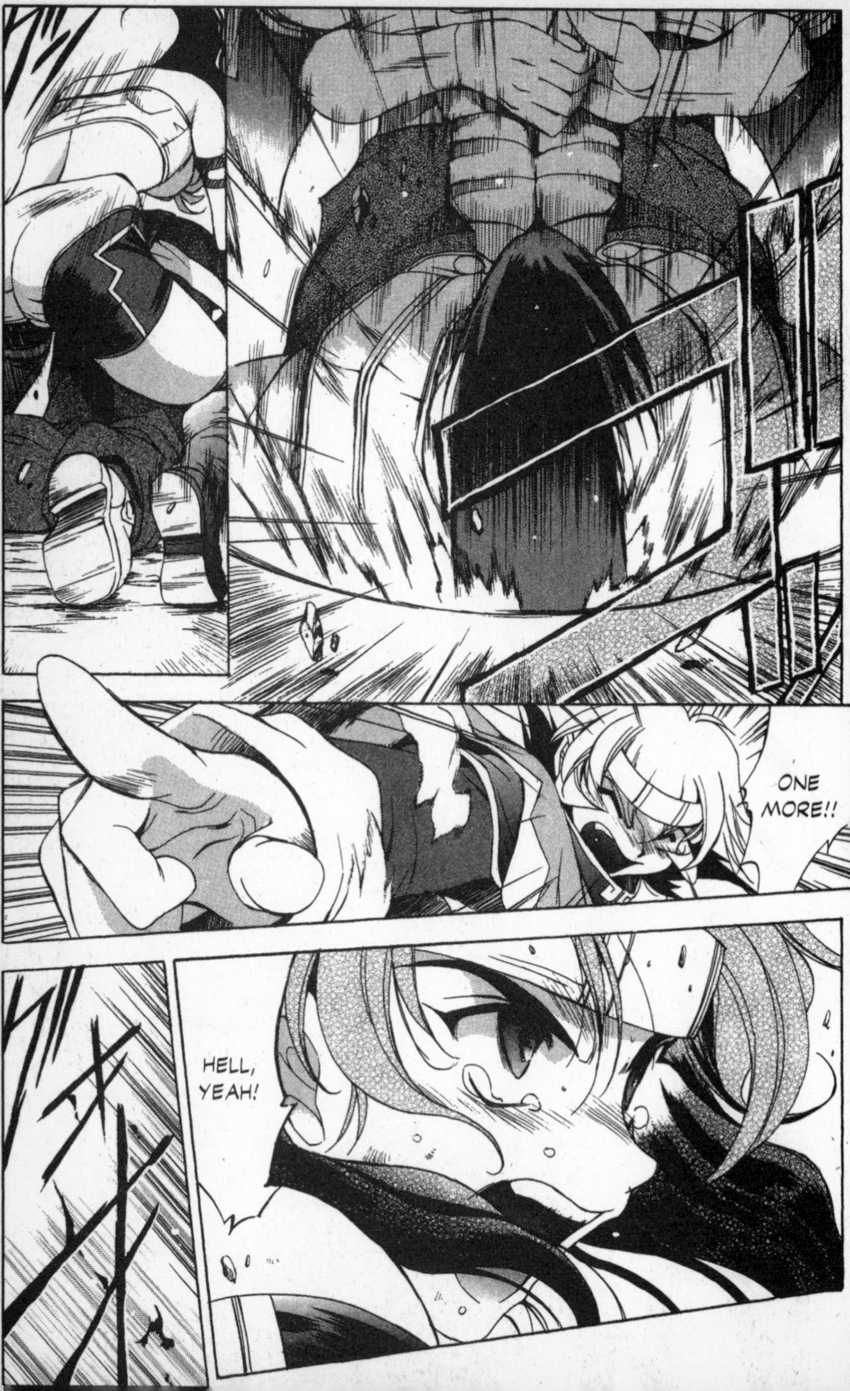
ONE MORE!!
HELL, YEAH!

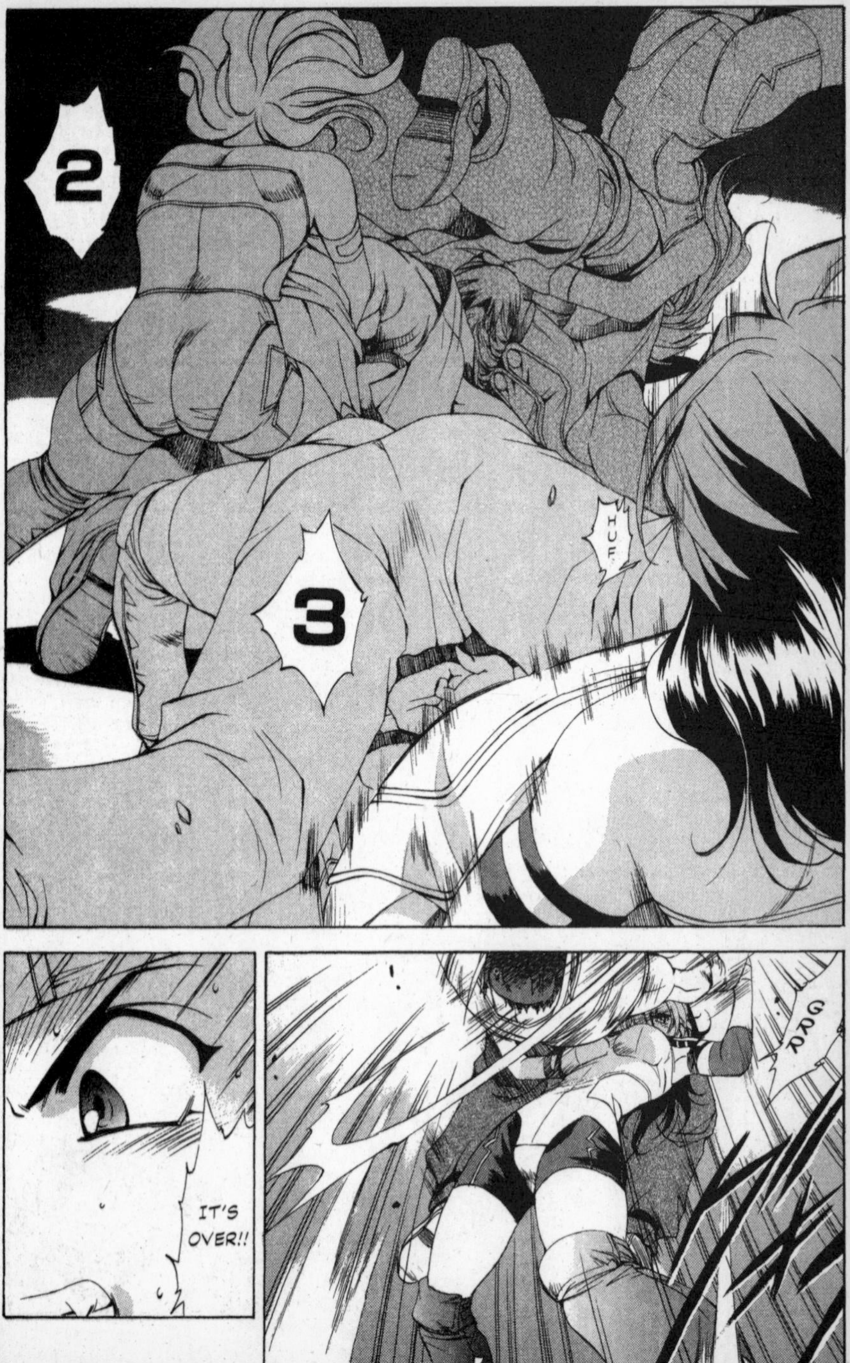
2
HUF
3
GRR
IT'S OVER!!

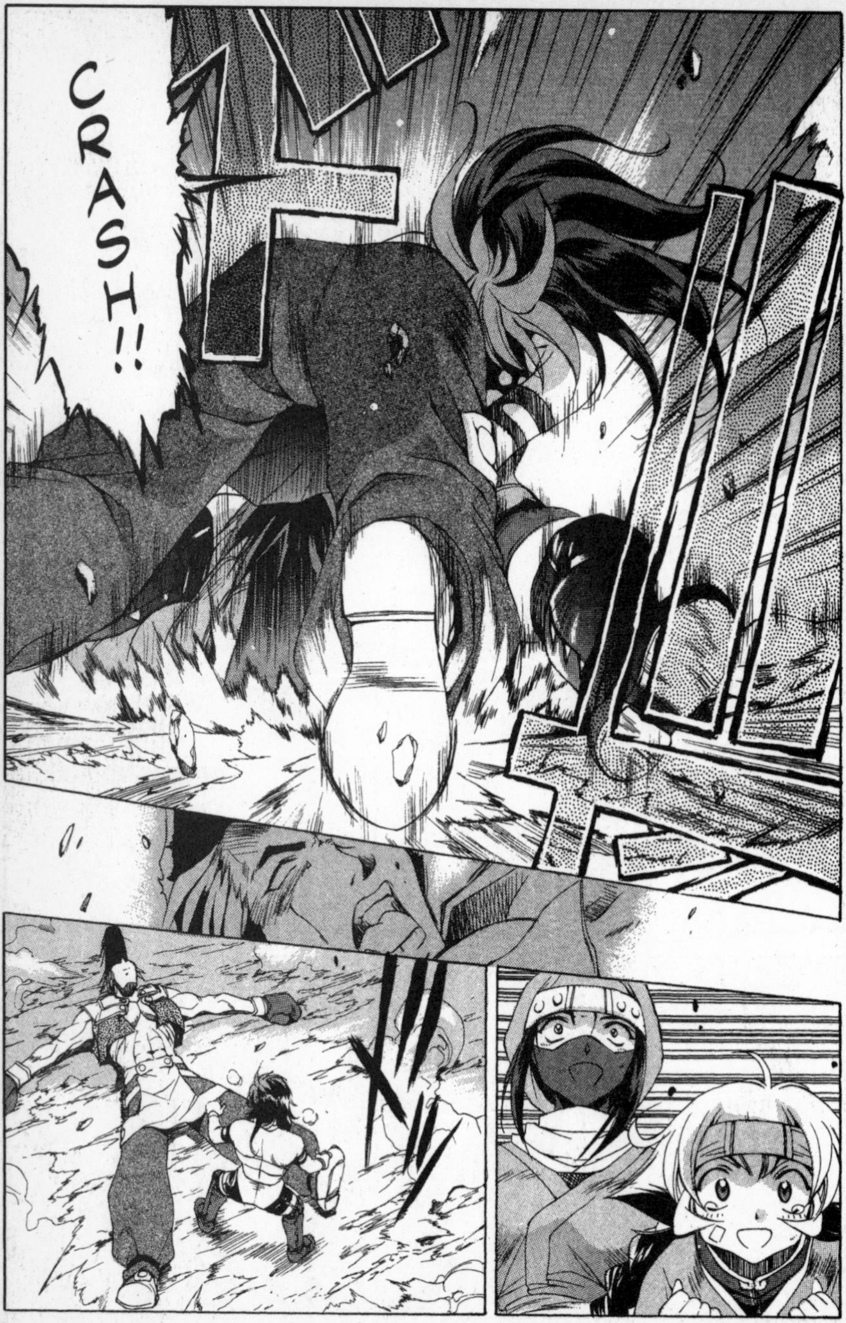
CRASH!!

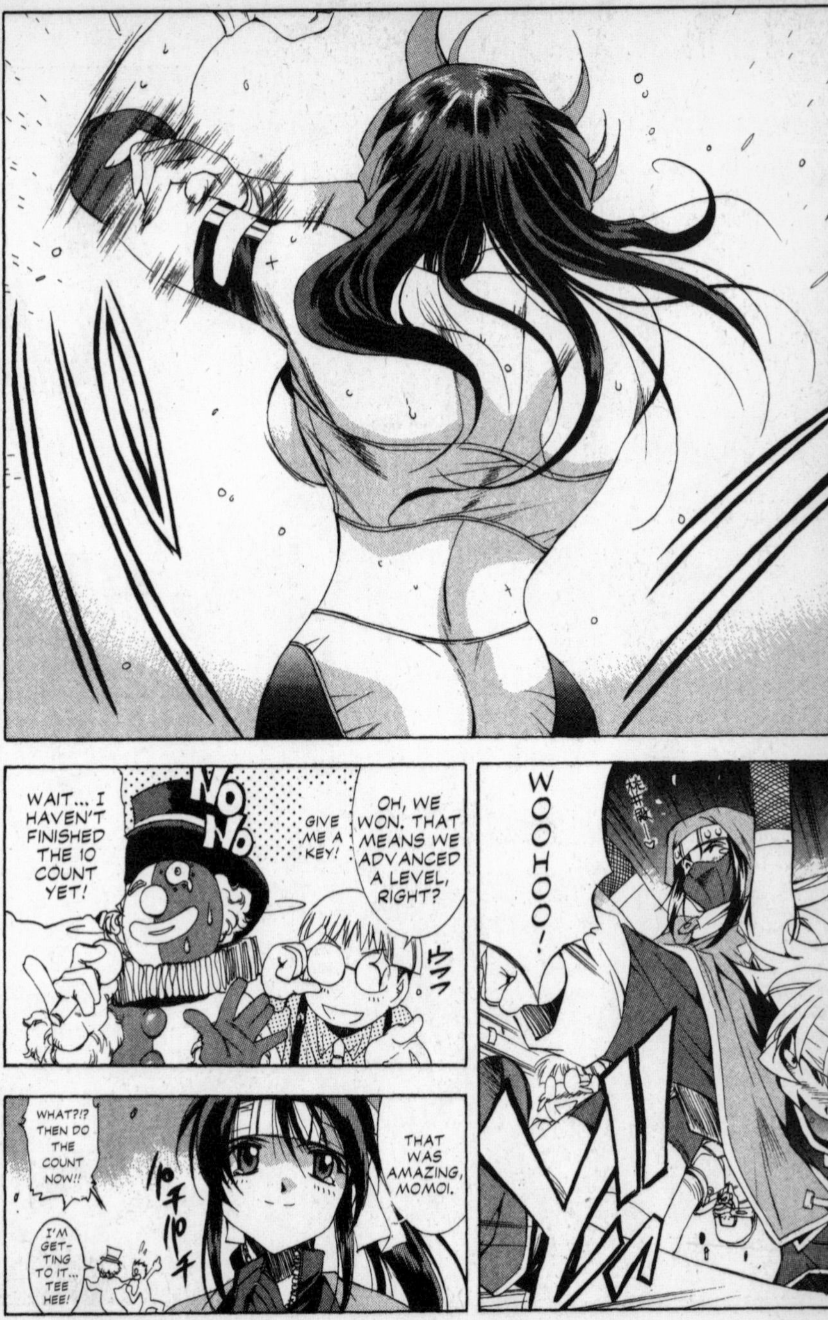
WOOHOO!
OH, WE WON. THAT MEANS WE ADVANCED A LEVEL, RIGHT?
GIVE ME A KEY!
NO NO
WAIT... I HAVEN'T FINISHED THE 10 COUNT YET!
THAT WAS AMAZING, MOMOI.
パチパチ
WHAT?!? THEN DO THE COUNT NOW!!
I'M GETTING TO IT... TEE HEE!

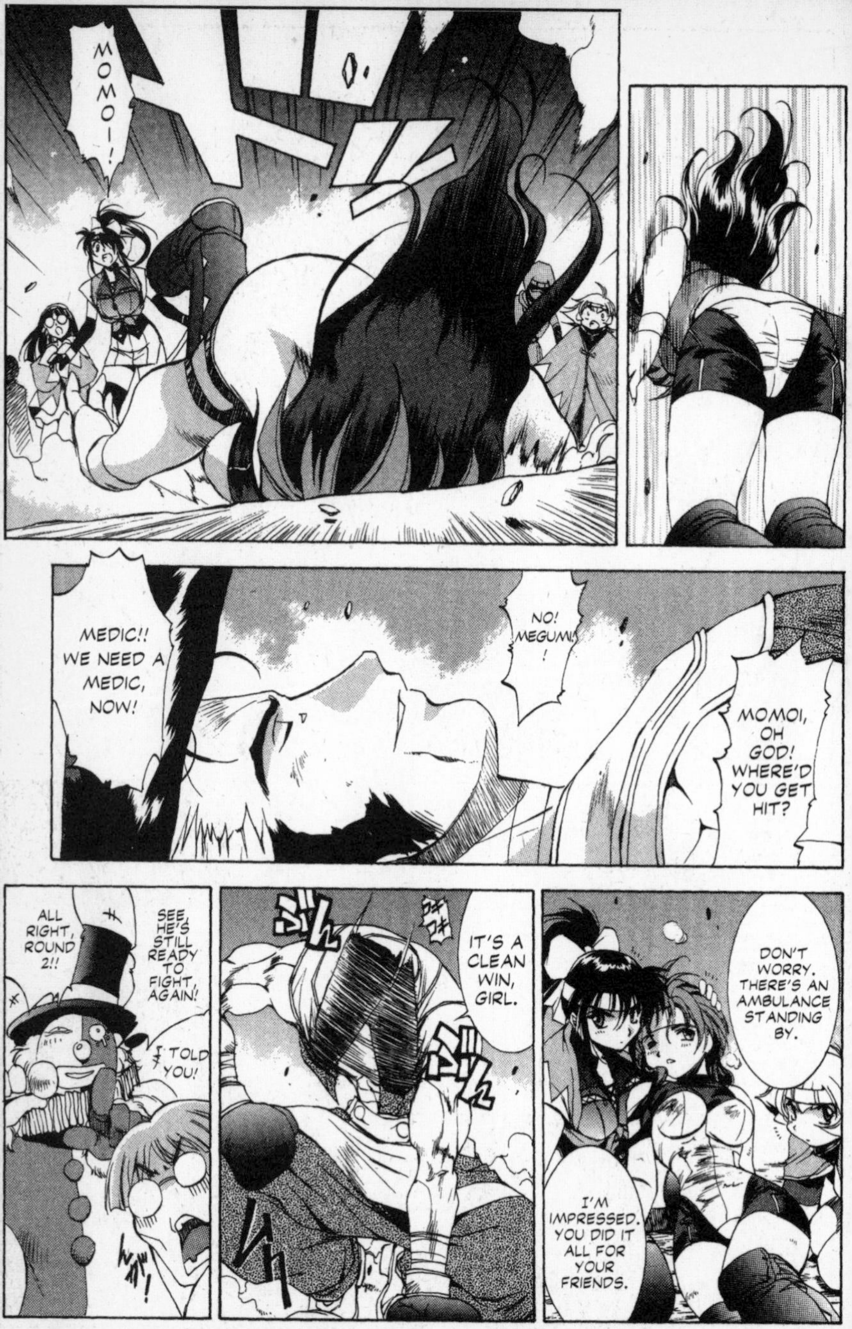
MOMOI!!
MOMOI, OH GOD! WHERE'D YOU GET HIT?
NO! MEGUMI!!
MEDIC!! WE NEED A MEDIC, NOW!
DON'T WORRY. THERE'S AN AMBULANCE STANDING BY.
I'M IMPRESSED. YOU DID IT ALL FOR YOUR FRIENDS.
IT'S A CLEAN WIN, GIRL.
SEE, HE'S STILL READY TO FIGHT, AGAIN!
ALL RIGHT, ROUND 2!!
I TOLD YOU!

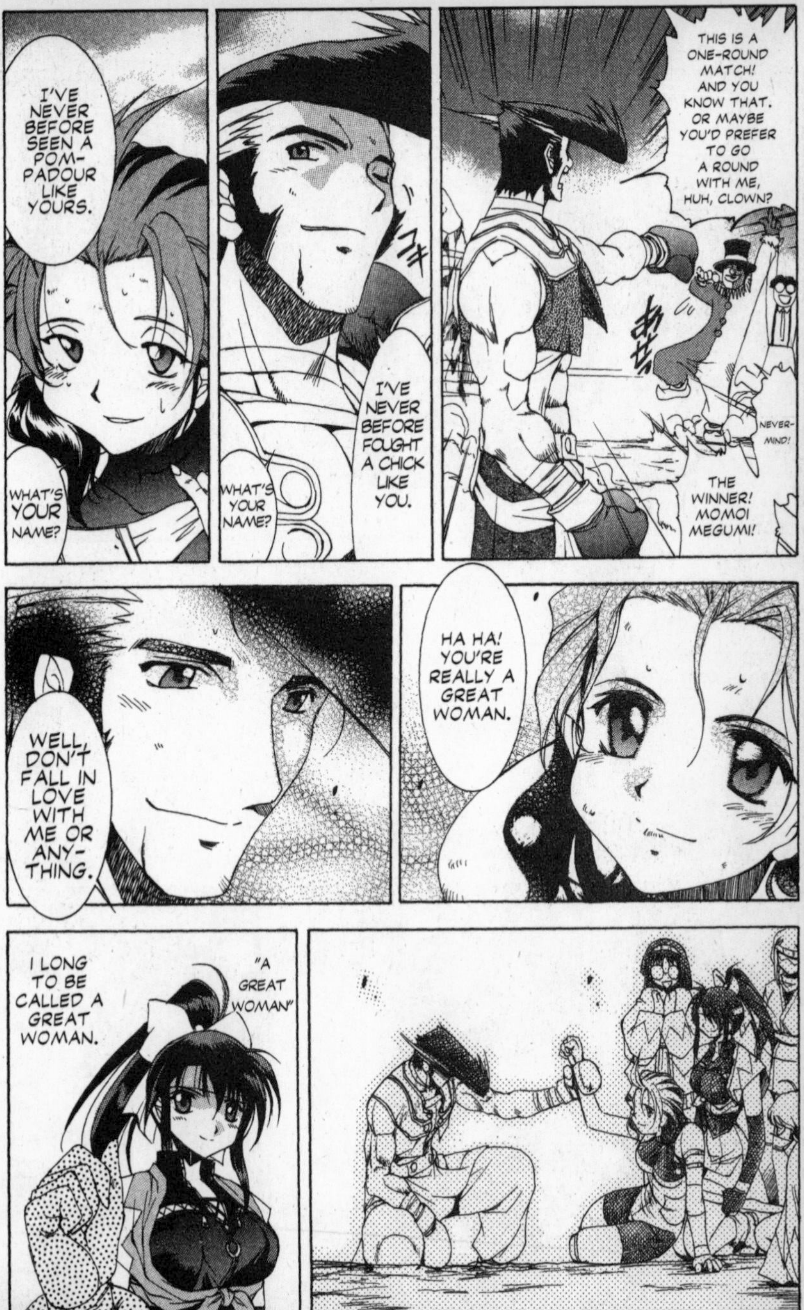

THIS IS A ONE-ROUND MATCH! AND YOU KNOW THAT. OR MAYBE YOU'D PREFER TO GO A ROUND WITH ME, HUH, CLOWN?
NEVER-MIND!
THE WINNER! MOMOI MEGUMI!
I'VE NEVER BEFORE FOUGHT A CHICK LIKE YOU.
WHAT'S YOUR NAME?
I'VE NEVER BEFORE SEEN A POM-PADOUR LIKE YOURS.
WHAT'S YOUR NAME?
HA HA! YOU'RE REALLY A GREAT WOMAN.
WELL, DON'T FALL IN LOVE WITH ME OR ANY-THING.
"A GREAT WOMAN"
I LONG TO BE CALLED A GREAT WOMAN.

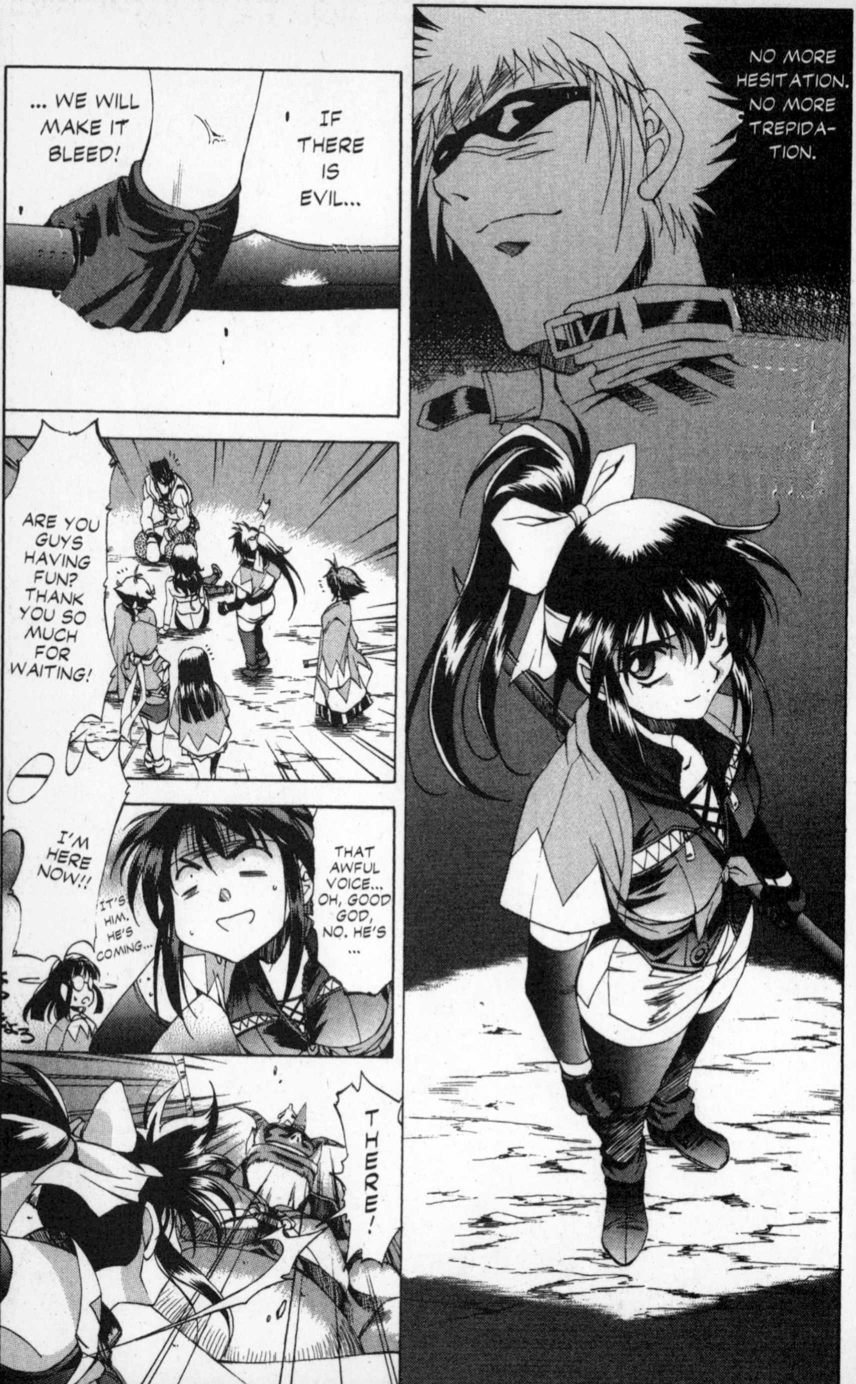
NO MORE HESITATION. NO MORE TREPIDATION.
IF THERE IS EVIL...
... WE WILL MAKE IT BLEED!
ARE YOU GUYS HAVING FUN? THANK YOU SO MUCH FOR WAITING!
I'M HERE NOW!!
THAT AWFUL VOICE... OH, GOOD GOD, NO. HE'S ...
IT'S HIM. HE'S COMING...
THERE!

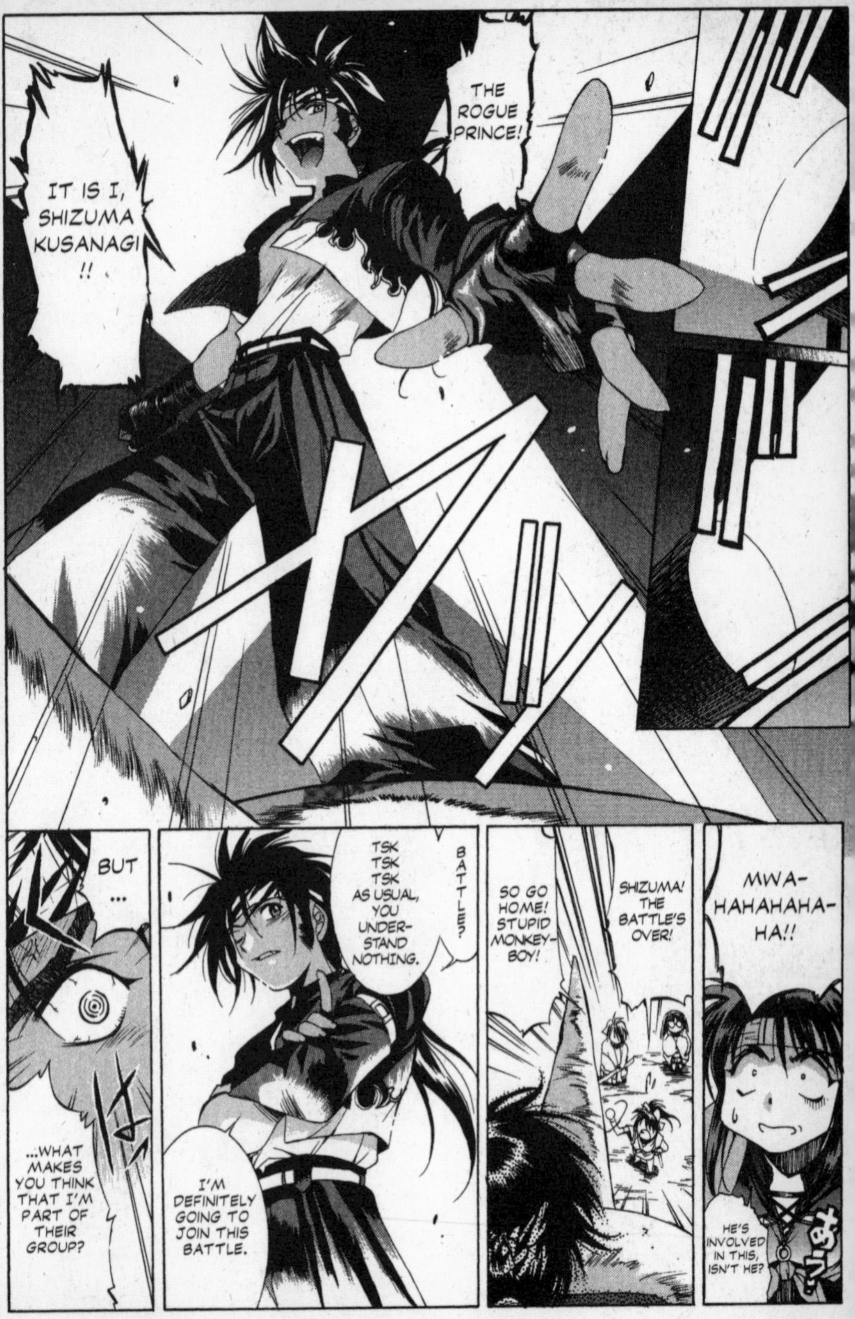
THE ROGUE PRINCE!
IT IS I, SHIZUMA KUSANAGI !!
MWA-HAHAHAHA-HA!!
HE'S INVOLVED IN THIS, ISN'T HE?
SHIZUMA! THE BATTLE'S OVER!
SO GO HOME! STUPID MONKEY-BOY!
BATTLE?
TSK TSK TSK AS USUAL, YOU UNDER-STAND NOTHING.
I'M DEFINITELY GOING TO JOIN THIS BATTLE.
BUT ...
...WHAT MAKES YOU THINK THAT I'M PART OF THEIR GROUP?

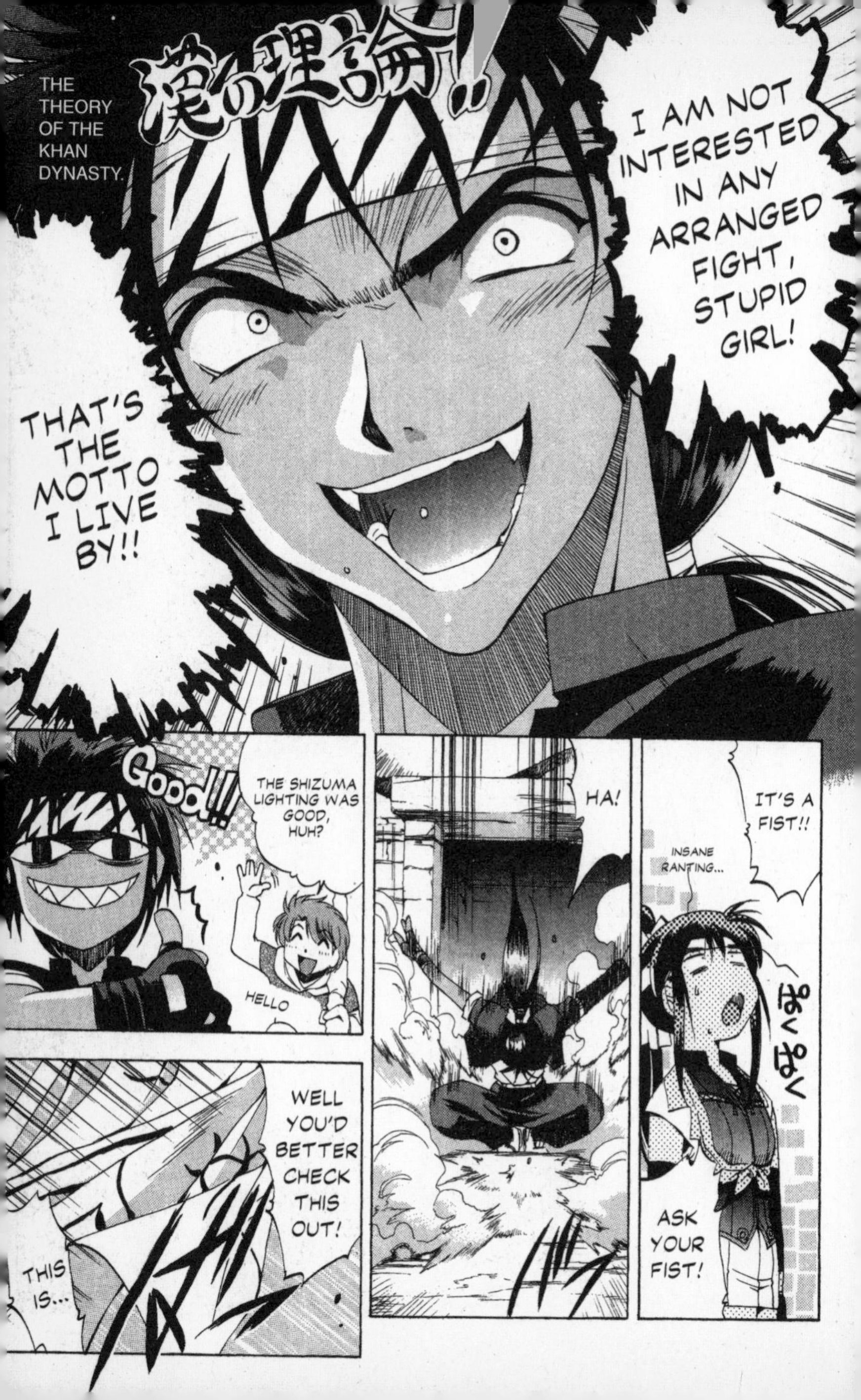
漢の理論!!
THE THEORY OF THE KHAN DYNASTY.
I AM NOT INTERESTED IN ANY ARRANGED FIGHT, STUPID GIRL!
THAT'S THE MOTTO I LIVE BY!!
IT'S A FIST!!
INSANE RANTING...
ぱくぱく
ASK YOUR FIST!
HA!
THE SHIZUMA LIGHTING WAS GOOD, HUH?
GOOD!!
HELLO
WELL YOU'D BETTER CHECK THIS OUT!
THIS IS...

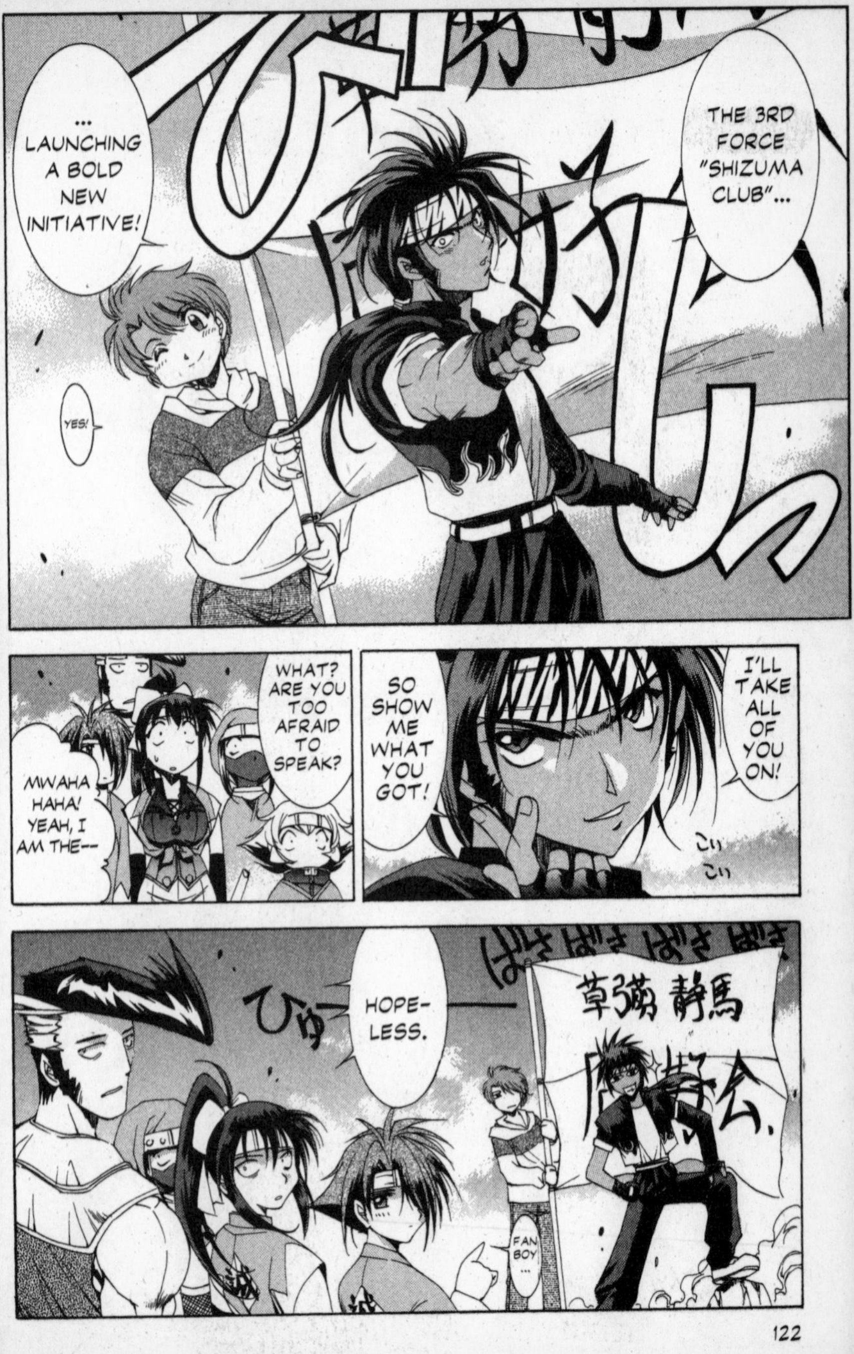
THE 3RD FORCE "SHIZUMA CLUB"...
... LAUNCHING A BOLD NEW INITIATIVE!
YES!
I'LL TAKE ALL OF YOU ON!
SO SHOW ME WHAT YOU GOT!
こい こい
WHAT? ARE YOU TOO AFRAID TO SPEAK?
MWAHA HAHA! YEAH, I AM THE--
ばさ ばさ ばさ ばさ
静馬
HOPE-LESS.
ひゅー
FAN BOY ...

Chapter 33 The Gimmick Castle and the Shadow Castle, Part 1

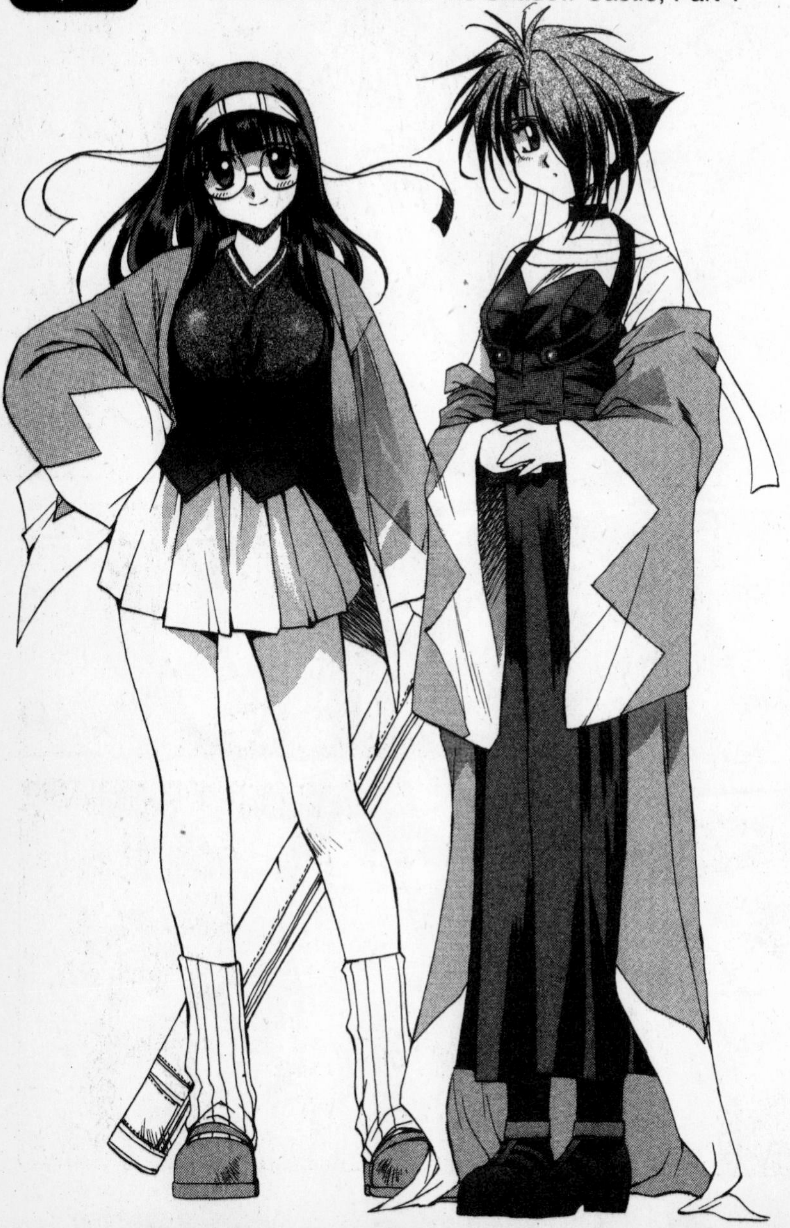

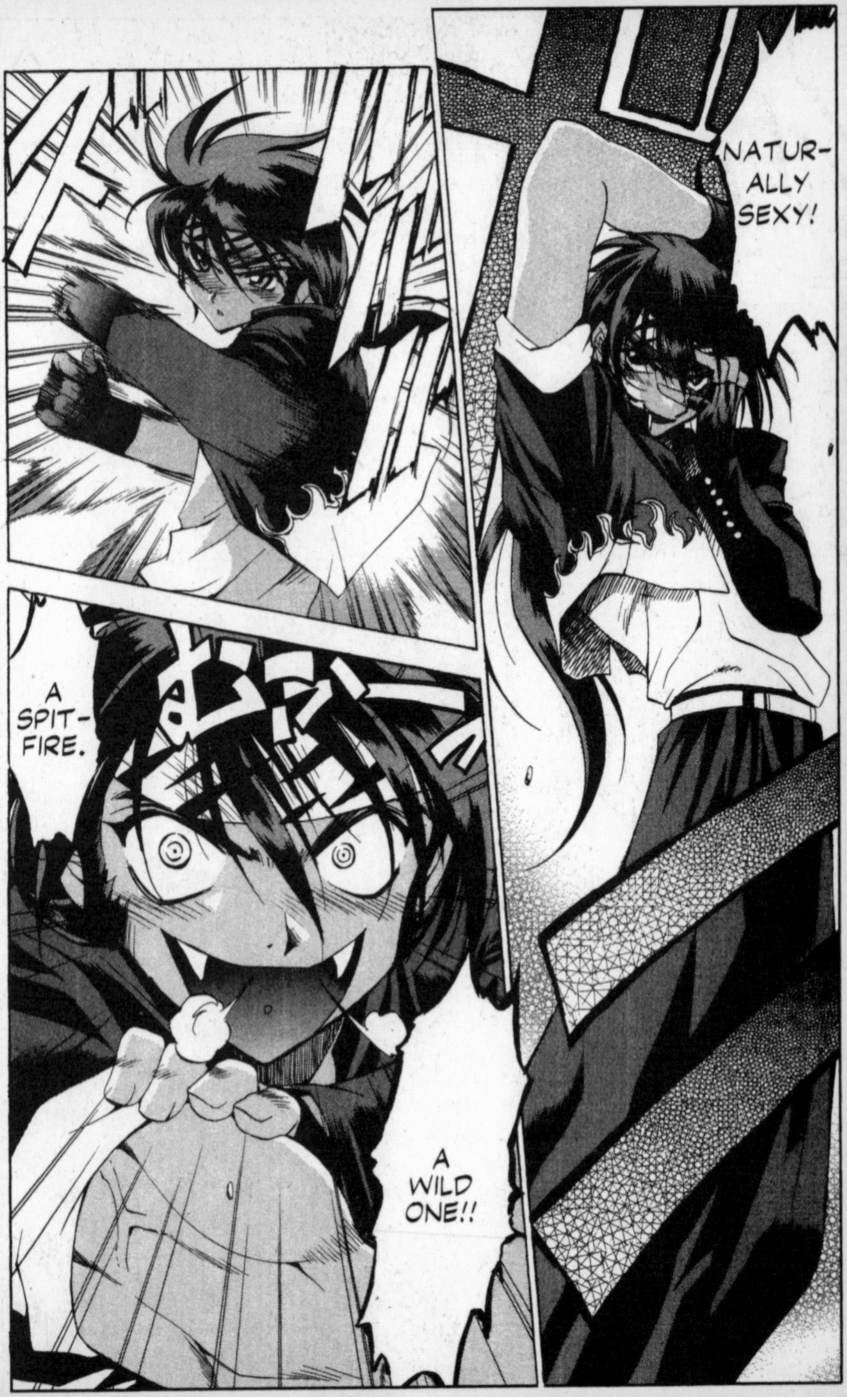
NATUR-ALLY SEXY!
A SPIT-FIRE.
A WILD ONE!!

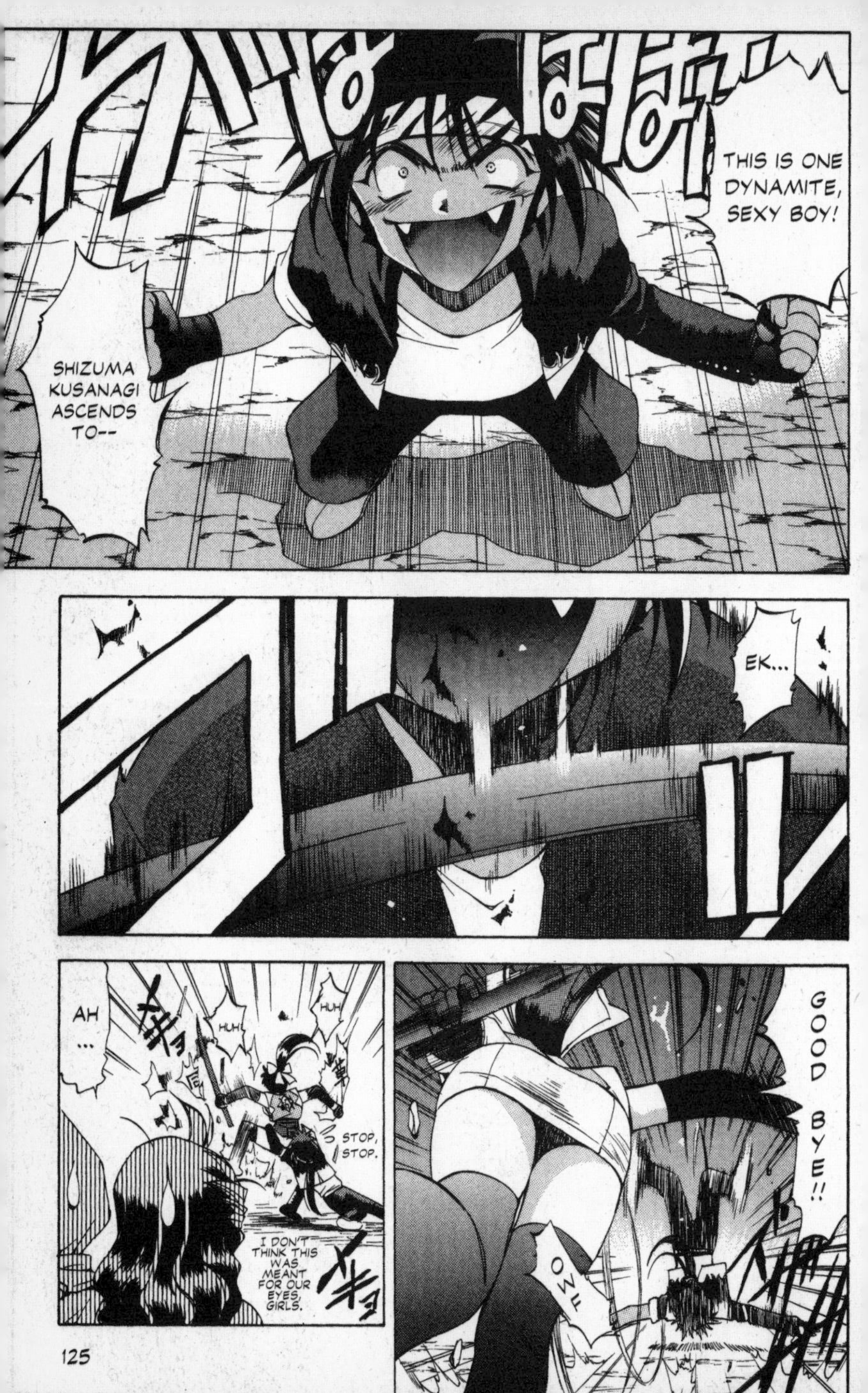
THIS IS ONE DYNAMITE, SEXY BOY!
SHIZUMA KUSANAGI ASCENDS TO--
EK...
GOOD BYE!!
OW!
HUH
HUH
STOP, STOP.
AH ...
I DON'T THINK THIS WAS MEANT FOR OUR EYES, GIRLS.

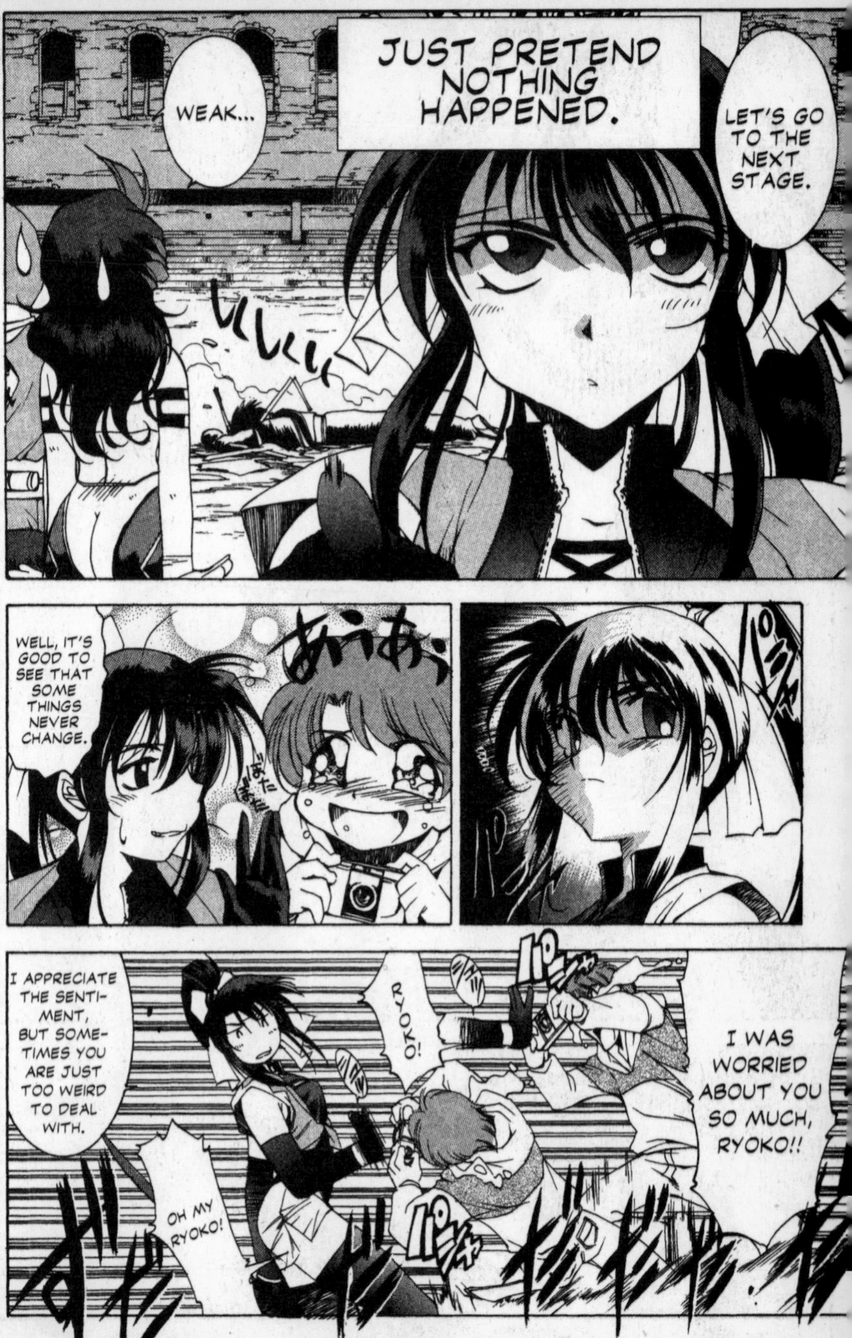

LET'S GO TO THE NEXT STAGE.
JUST PRETEND NOTHING HAPPENED.
WEAK...
WELL, IT'S GOOD TO SEE THAT SOME THINGS NEVER CHANGE.
I WAS WORRIED ABOUT YOU SO MUCH, RYOKO!!
RYOKO!
OH MY RYOKO!
I APPRECIATE THE SENTI-MENT, BUT SOME-TIMES YOU ARE JUST TOO WEIRD TO DEAL WITH.

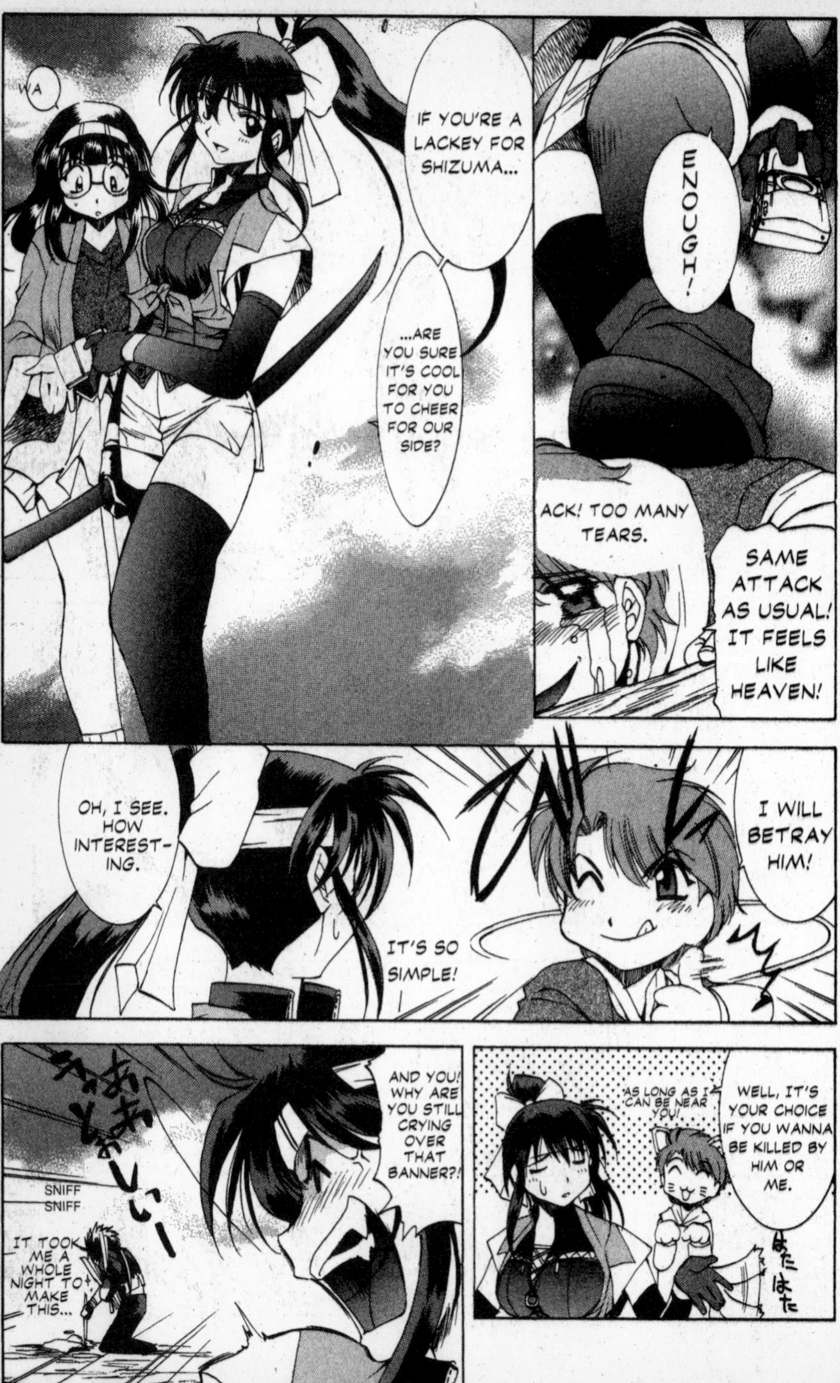
ENOUGH!
SAME ATTACK AS USUAL! IT FEELS LIKE HEAVEN!
ACK! TOO MANY TEARS.
IF YOU'RE A LACKEY FOR SHIZUMA...
...ARE YOU SURE IT'S COOL FOR YOU TO CHEER FOR OUR SIDE?
WA
I WILL BETRAY HIM!
IT'S SO SIMPLE!
OH, I SEE. HOW INTERESTING.
WELL, IT'S YOUR CHOICE IF YOU WANNA BE KILLED BY HIM OR ME.
AS LONG AS I CAN BE NEAR YOU!
はたはた
AND YOU! WHY ARE YOU STILL CRYING OVER THAT BANNER?!
SNIFF SNIFF
IT TOOK ME A WHOLE NIGHT TO MAKE THIS...

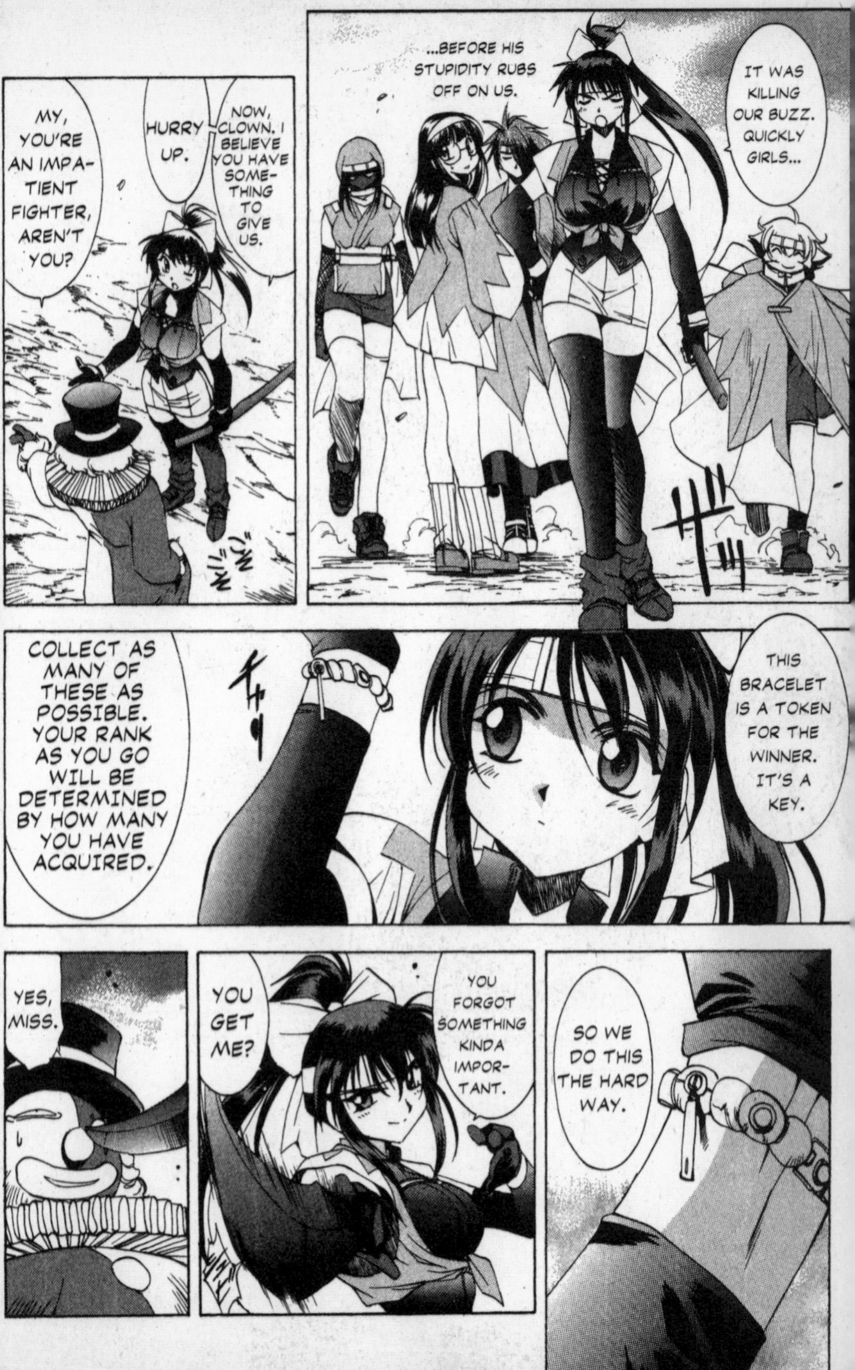
IT WAS KILLING OUR BUZZ. QUICKLY GIRLS...
...BEFORE HIS STUPIDITY RUBS OFF ON US.
NOW, CLOWN. I BELIEVE YOU HAVE SOME-THING TO GIVE US.
HURRY UP.
MY, YOU'RE AN IMPA-TIENT FIGHTER, AREN'T YOU?
THIS BRACELET IS A TOKEN FOR THE WINNER. IT'S A KEY.
COLLECT AS MANY OF THESE AS POSSIBLE. YOUR RANK AS YOU GO WILL BE DETERMINED BY HOW MANY YOU HAVE ACQUIRED.
SO WE DO THIS THE HARD WAY.
YOU FORGOT SOMETHING KINDA IMPOR-TANT.
YOU GET ME?
YES, MISS.

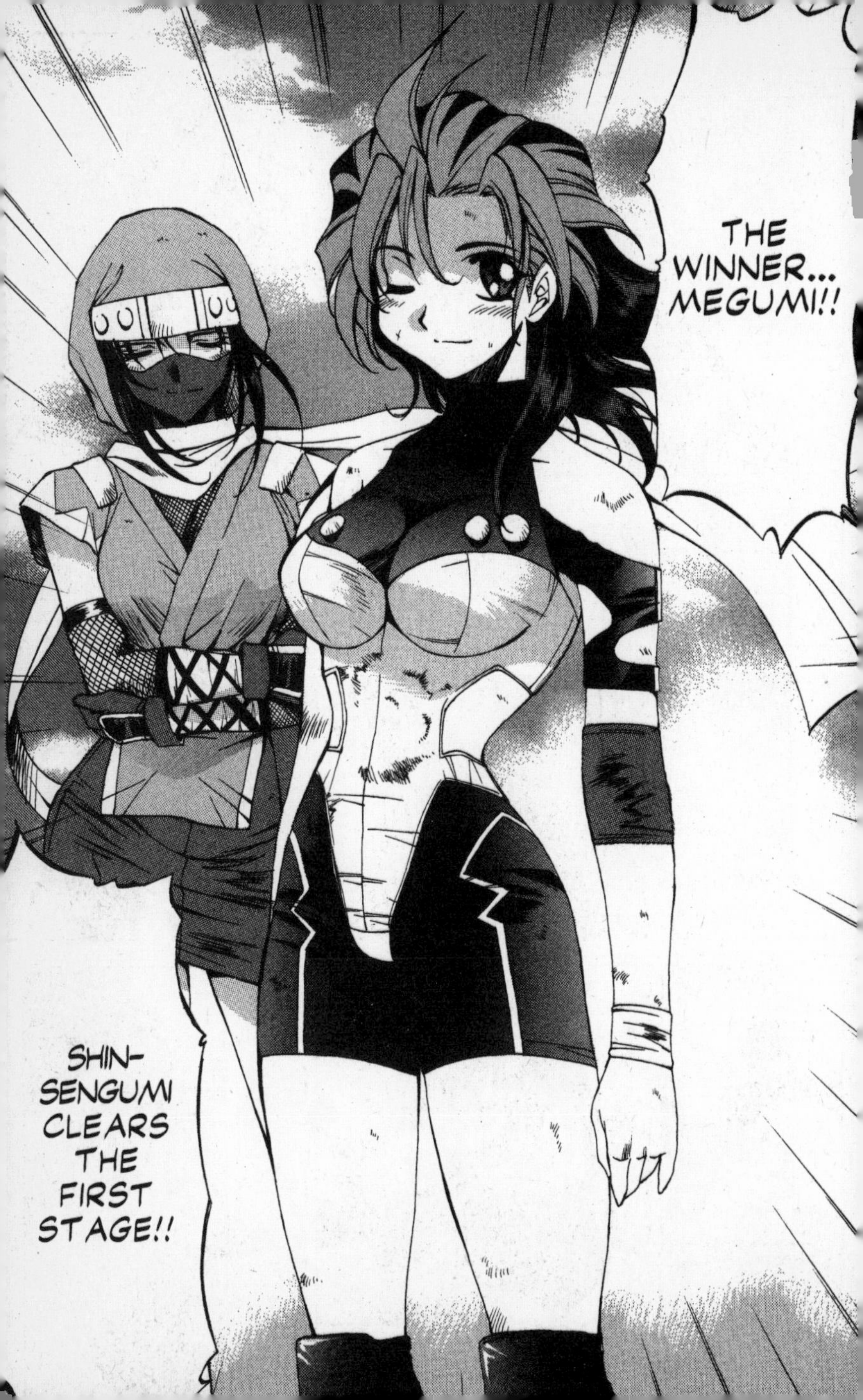
THE WINNER... MEGUMI!!
SHIN-SENGUMI CLEARS THE FIRST STAGE!!

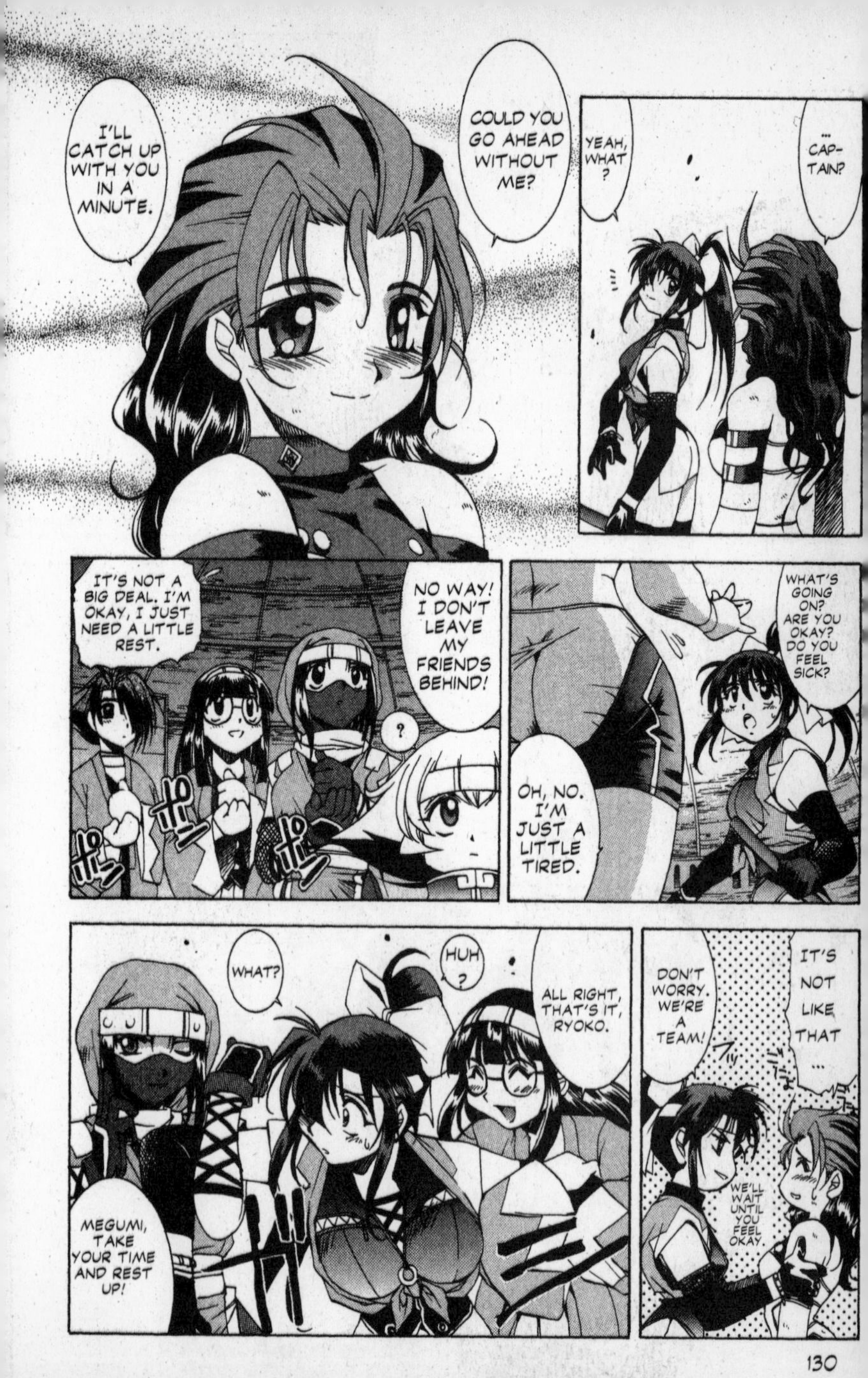

...CAP-TAIN?
YEAH, WHAT?
COULD YOU GO AHEAD WITHOUT ME?
I'LL CATCH UP WITH YOU IN A MINUTE.
WHAT'S GOING ON? ARE YOU OKAY? DO YOU FEEL SICK?
OH, NO. I'M JUST A LITTLE TIRED.
NO WAY! I DON'T LEAVE MY FRIENDS BEHIND!
?
IT'S NOT A BIG DEAL. I'M OKAY, I JUST NEED A LITTLE REST.
IT'S NOT LIKE THAT ...
DON'T WORRY. WE'RE A TEAM!
WE'LL WAIT UNTIL YOU FEEL OKAY.
ALL RIGHT, THAT'S IT, RYOKO.
HUH?
WHAT?
MEGUMI, TAKE YOUR TIME AND REST UP!

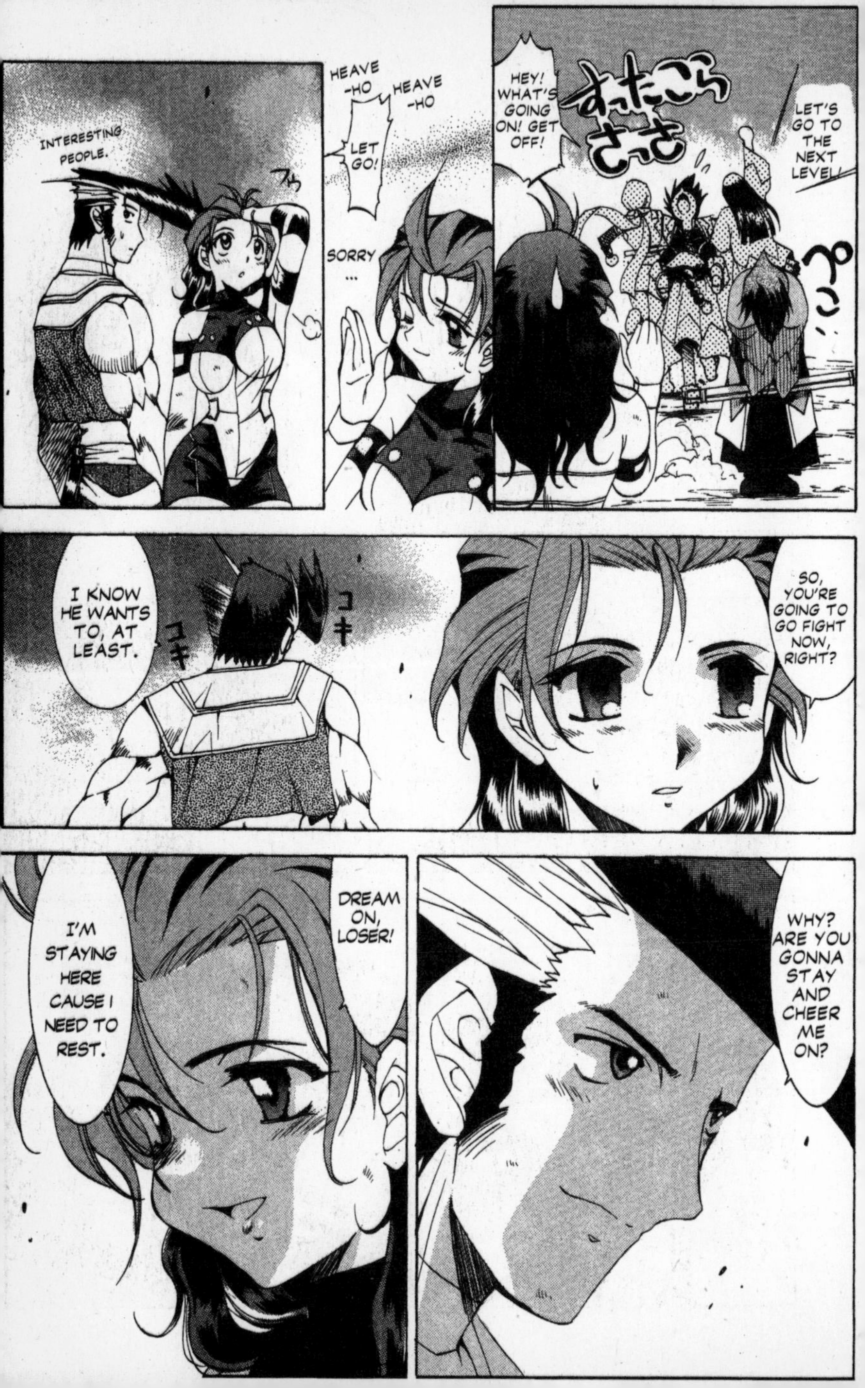
LET'S GO TO THE NEXT LEVEL!
すったこら さっさ
HEY! WHAT'S GOING ON! GET OFF!
ぺこ
HEAVE-HO HEAVE-HO
LET GO!
SORRY...
INTERESTING PEOPLE.
SO, YOU'RE GOING TO GO FIGHT NOW, RIGHT?
コキ
コキ
I KNOW HE WANTS TO, AT LEAST.
WHY? ARE YOU GONNA STAY AND CHEER ME ON?
DREAM ON, LOSER!
I'M STAYING HERE CAUSE I NEED TO REST.

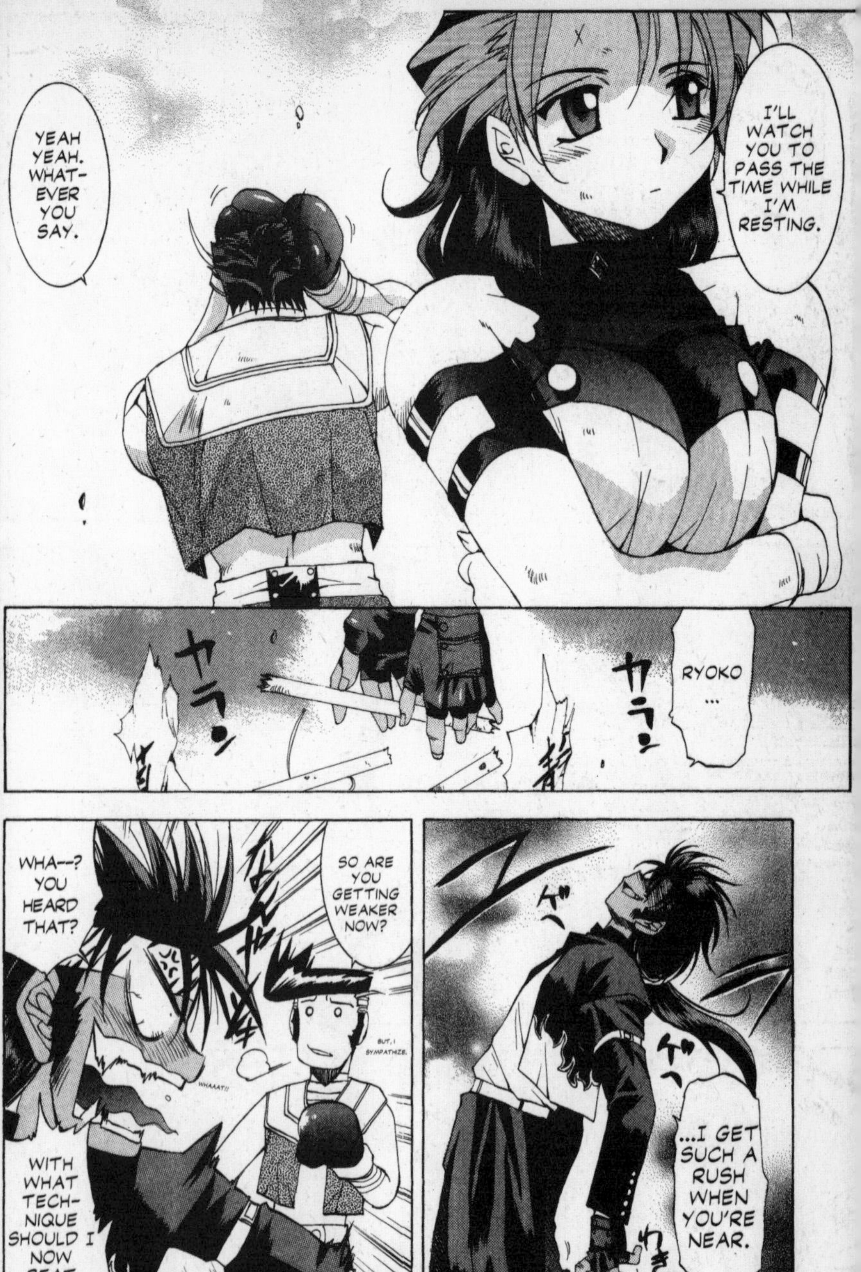
I'LL WATCH YOU TO PASS THE TIME WHILE I'M RESTING.
YEAH YEAH. WHATEVER YOU SAY.
RYOKO ...
...I GET SUCH A RUSH WHEN YOU'RE NEAR.
わきわき
SO ARE YOU GETTING WEAKER NOW?
WHA--? YOU HEARD THAT?
BUT, I SYMPATHIZE.
WHAAAT!!
WITH WHAT TECHNIQUE SHOULD I NOW BEAT YOU!?!

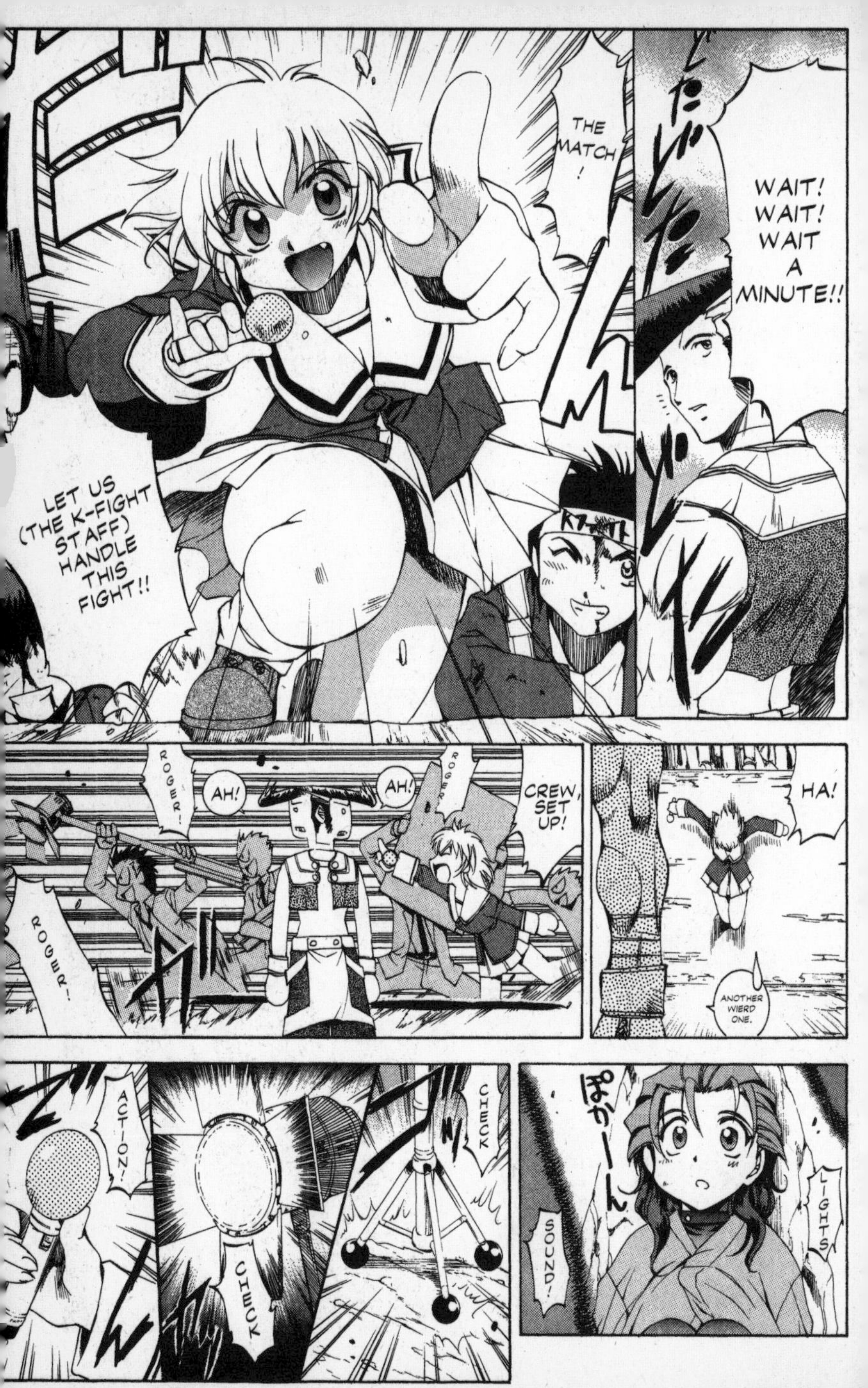
WAIT! WAIT! WAIT A MINUTE!!
THE MATCH!
LET US (THE K-FIGHT STAFF) HANDLE THIS FIGHT!!
HA!
ANOTHER WIERD ONE.
CREW, SET UP!
ROGER!
AH!
AH!
ROGER!
ROGER!
ぽかーん
LIGHTS
SOUND!
CHECK
CHECK
ACTION!

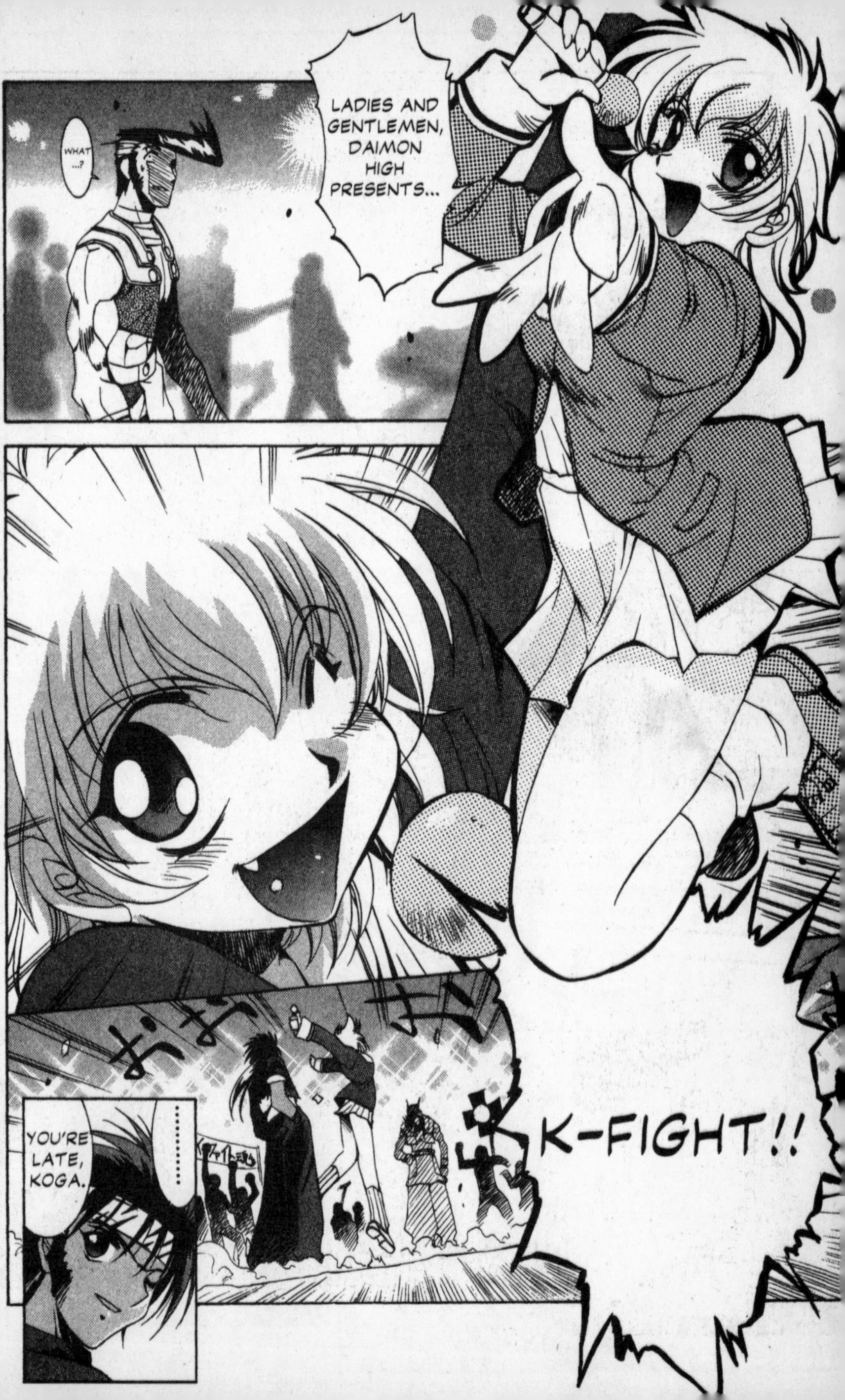
WHAT ...?
LADIES AND GENTLEMEN, DAIMON HIGH PRESENTS...
K-FIGHT!!
......
YOU'RE LATE, KOGA.

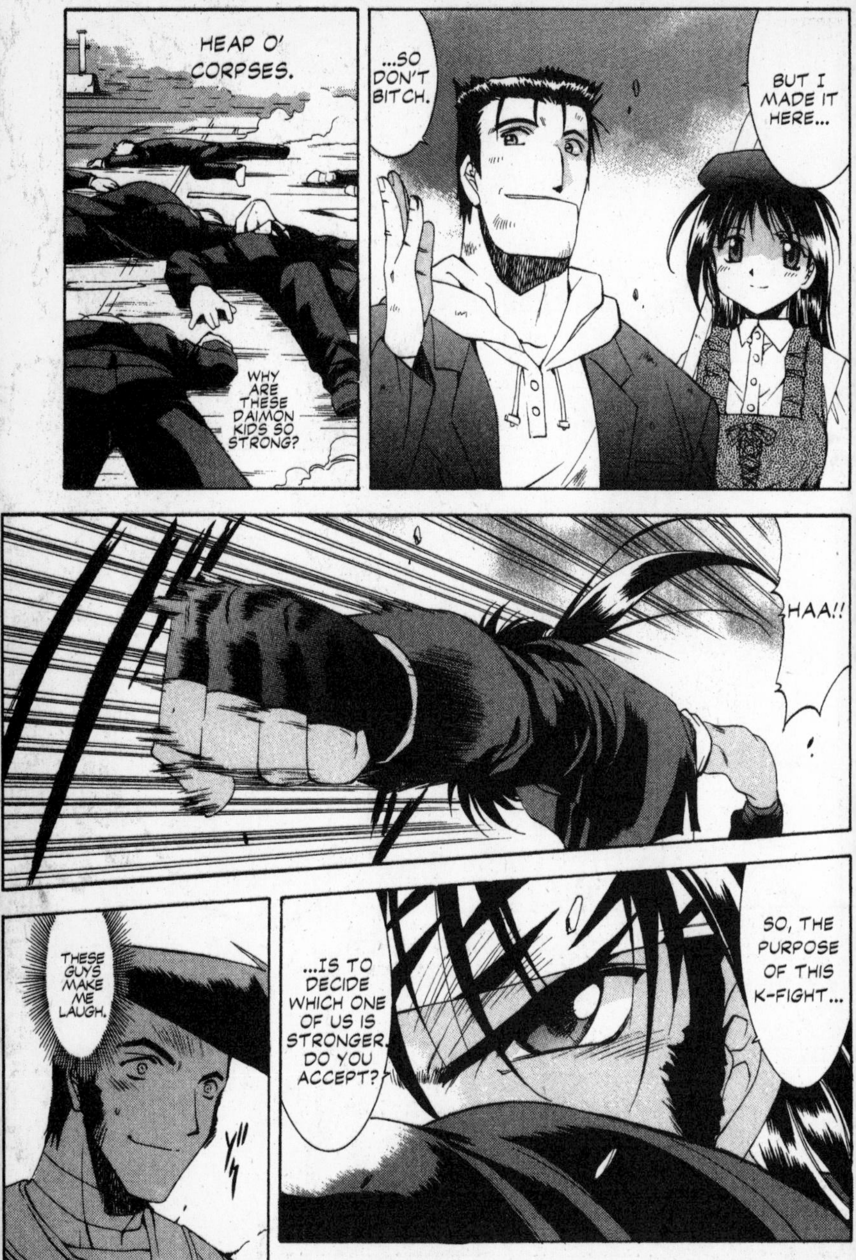
BUT I MADE IT HERE...
...SO DON'T BITCH.
HEAP O' CORPSES.
WHY ARE THESE DAIMON KIDS SO STRONG?
HAA!!
SO, THE PURPOSE OF THIS K-FIGHT...
...IS TO DECIDE WHICH ONE OF US IS STRONGER. DO YOU ACCEPT?
THESE GUYS MAKE ME LAUGH.

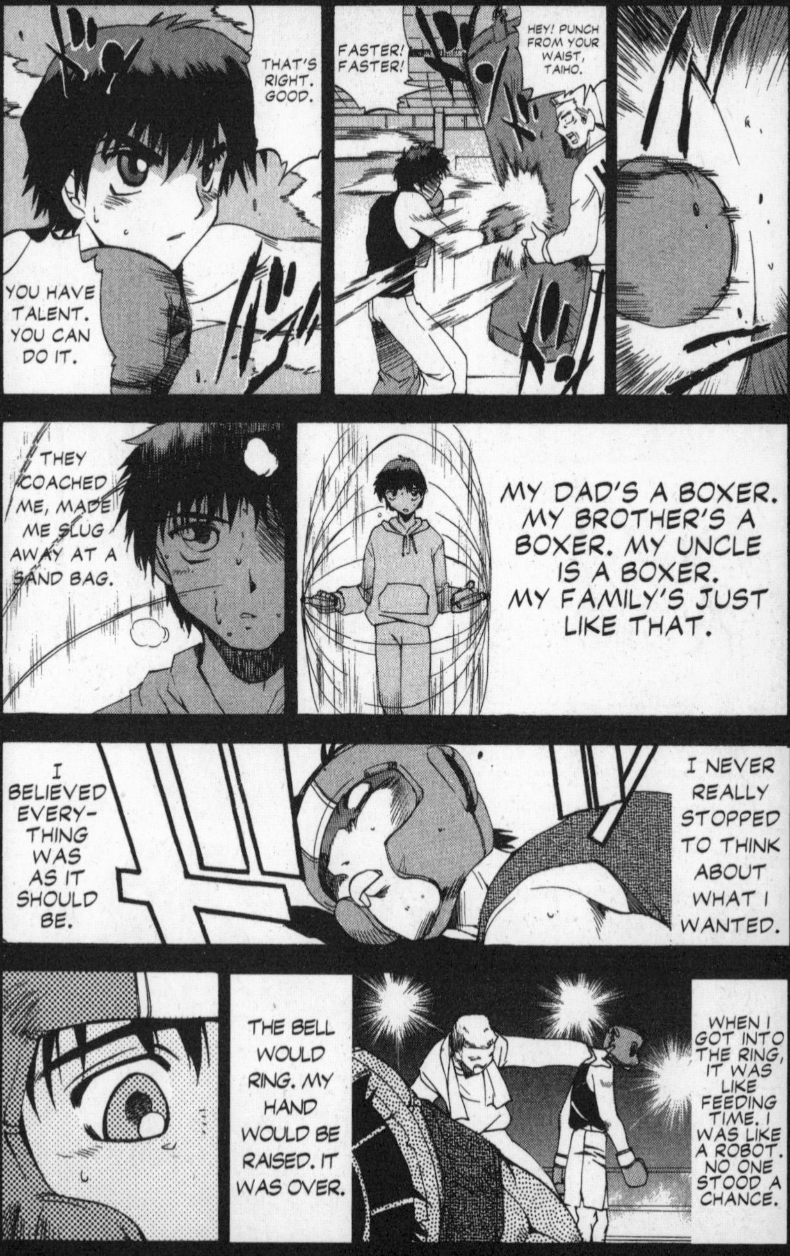
HEY! PUNCH FROM YOUR WAIST, TAIHO.
FASTER! FASTER!
THAT'S RIGHT. GOOD.
YOU HAVE TALENT. YOU CAN DO IT.
MY DAD'S A BOXER. MY BROTHER'S A BOXER. MY UNCLE IS A BOXER. MY FAMILY'S JUST LIKE THAT.
THEY COACHED ME, MADE ME SLUG AWAY AT A SAND BAG.
I NEVER REALLY STOPPED TO THINK ABOUT WHAT I WANTED.
I BELIEVED EVERY-THING WAS AS IT SHOULD BE.
WHEN I GOT INTO THE RING, IT WAS LIKE FEEDING TIME. I WAS LIKE A ROBOT. NO ONE STOOD A CHANCE.
THE BELL WOULD RING. MY HAND WOULD BE RAISED. IT WAS OVER.

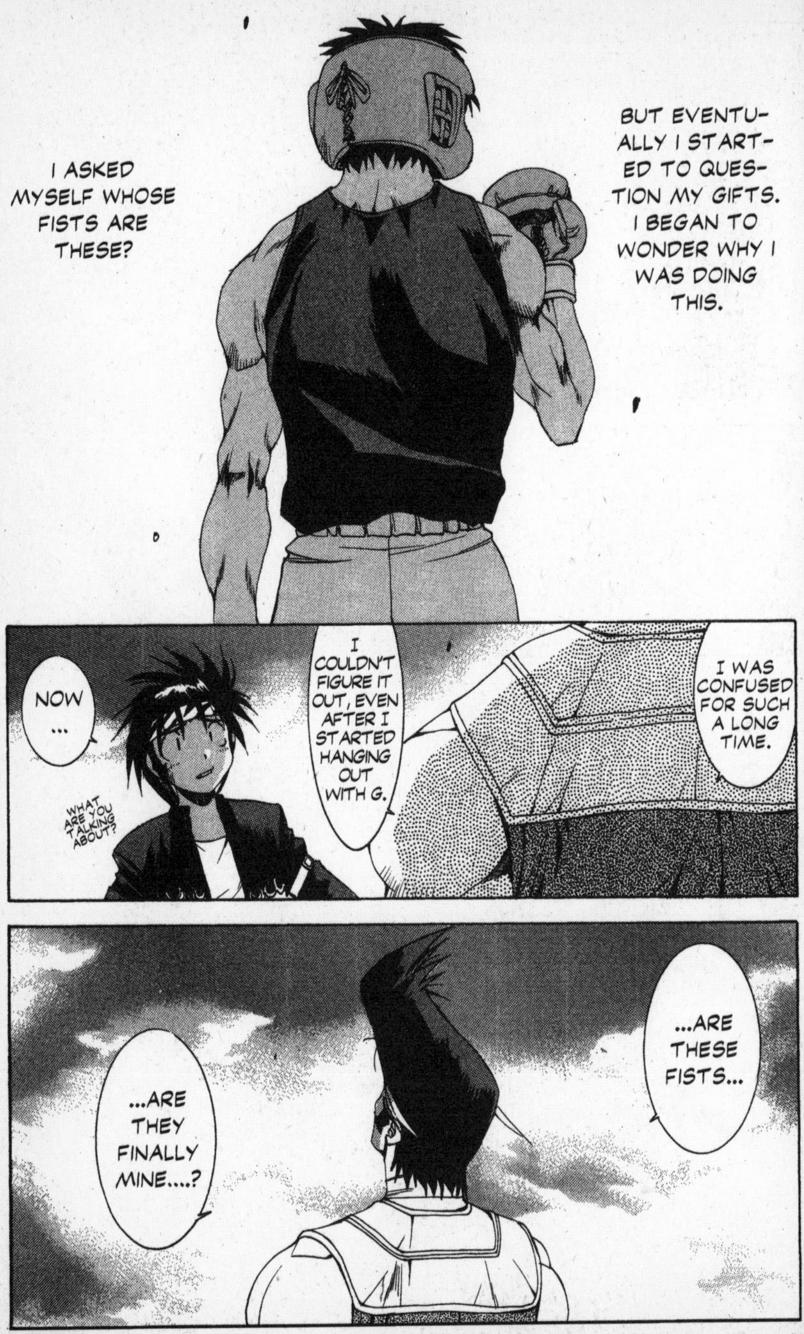
BUT EVENTU-ALLY I START-ED TO QUES-TION MY GIFTS. I BEGAN TO WONDER WHY I WAS DOING THIS.
I ASKED MYSELF WHOSE FISTS ARE THESE?
I WAS CONFUSED FOR SUCH A LONG TIME.
I COULDN'T FIGURE IT OUT, EVEN AFTER I STARTED HANGING OUT WITH G.
NOW ...
WHAT ARE YOU TALKING ABOUT?
...ARE THESE FISTS...
...ARE THEY FINALLY MINE....?

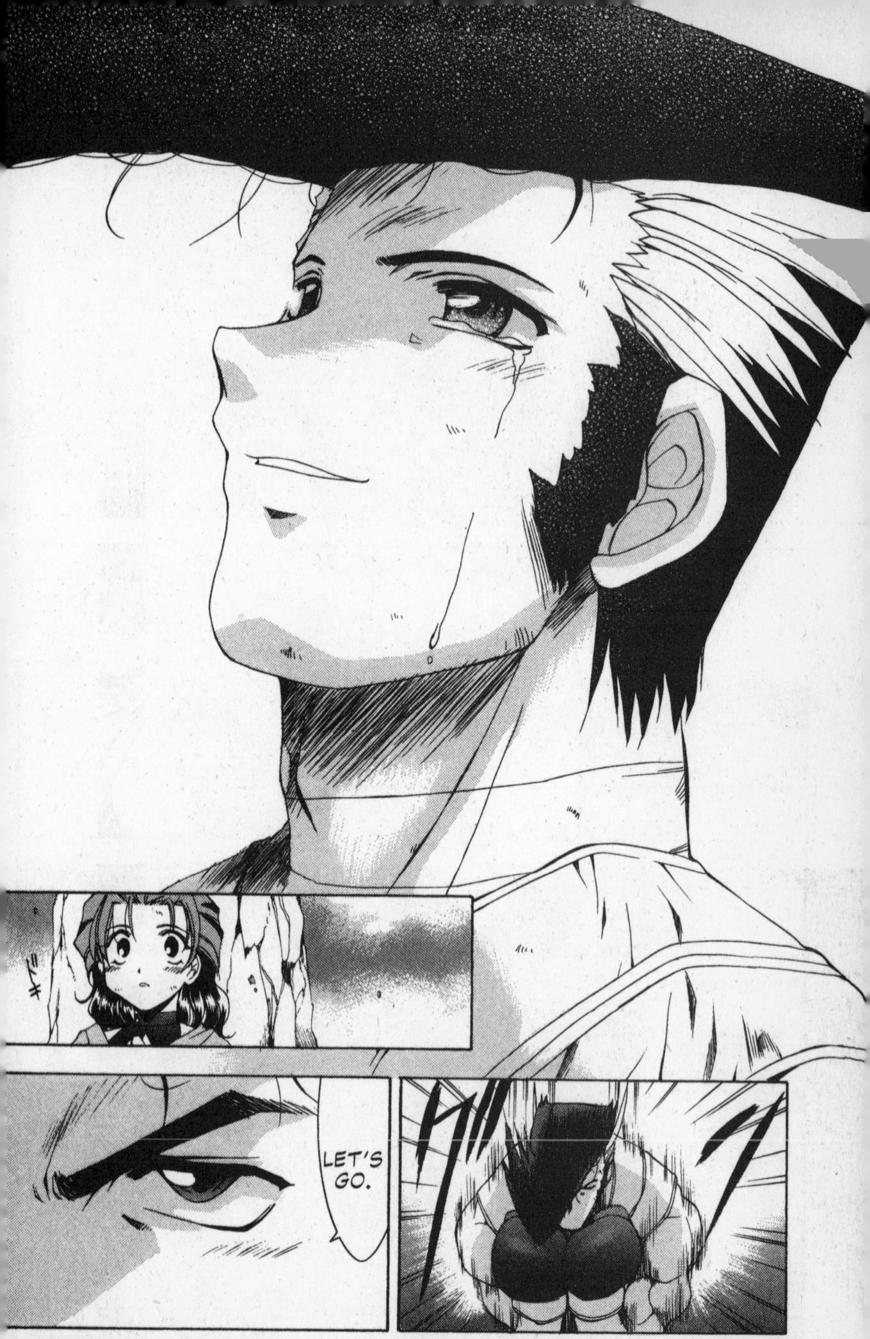
LET'S GO.

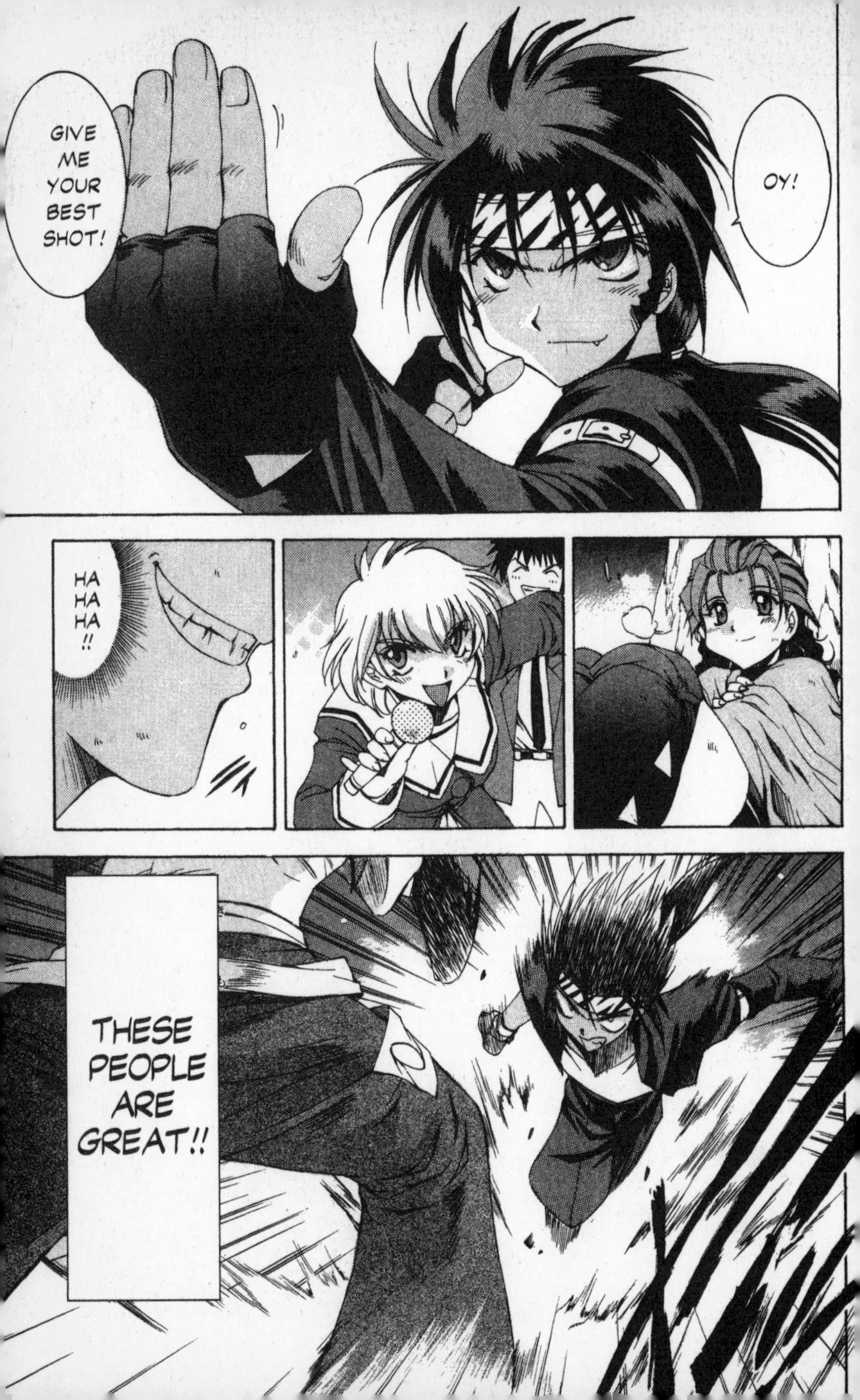
OY!
GIVE ME YOUR BEST SHOT!
HA HA HA!!
THESE PEOPLE ARE GREAT!!

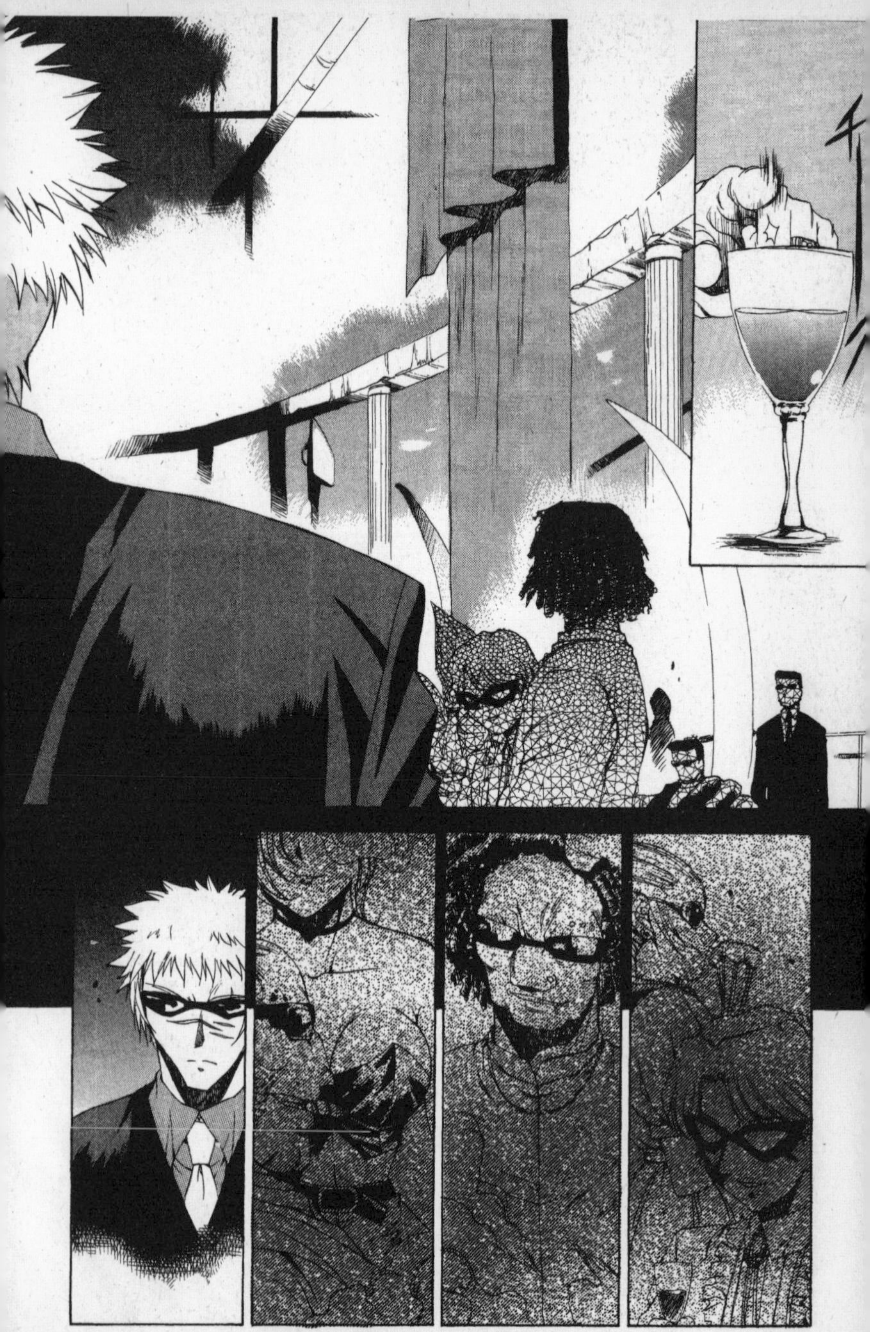
チ

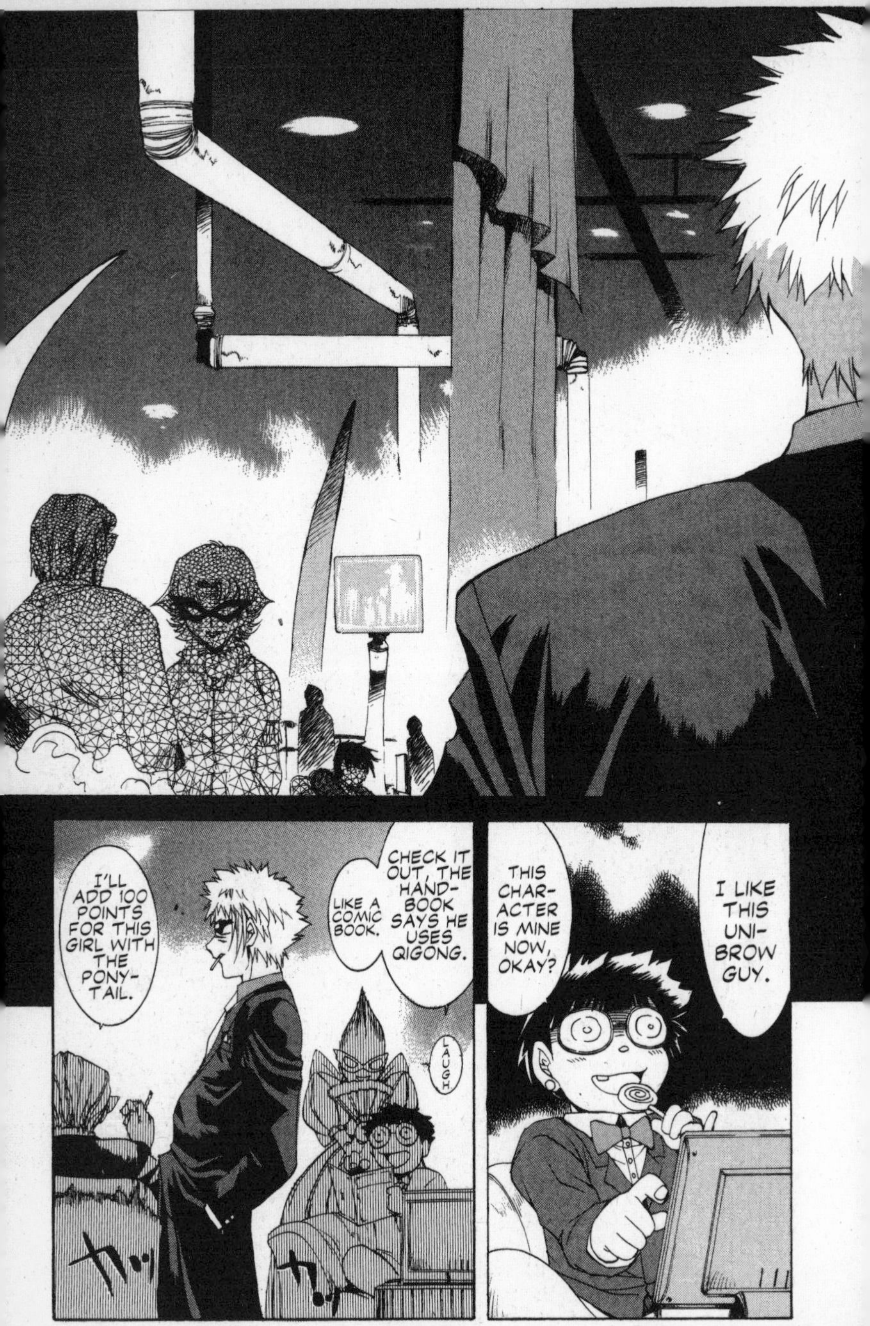
I LIKE THIS UNI-BROW GUY.
THIS CHAR-ACTER IS MINE NOW, OKAY?
CHECK IT OUT, THE HAND-BOOK SAYS HE USES QIGONG.
LIKE A COMIC BOOK.
LAUGH
I'LL ADD 100 POINTS FOR THIS GIRL WITH THE PONY-TAIL.

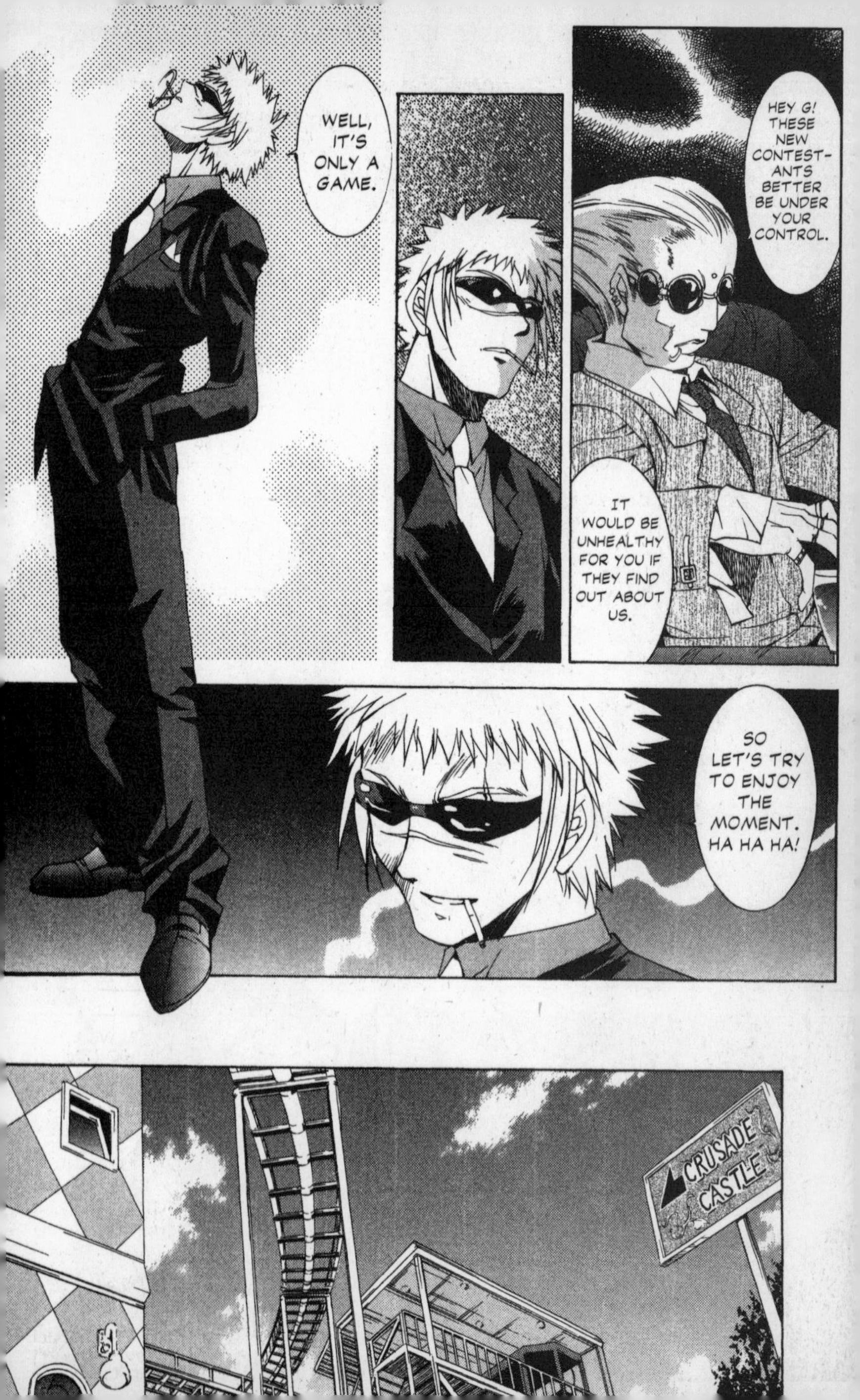
HEY G! THESE NEW CONTEST-ANTS BETTER BE UNDER YOUR CONTROL.
IT WOULD BE UNHEALTHY FOR YOU IF THEY FIND OUT ABOUT US.
WELL, IT'S ONLY A GAME.
SO LET'S TRY TO ENJOY THE MOMENT. HA HA HA!
CRUSADE CASTLE

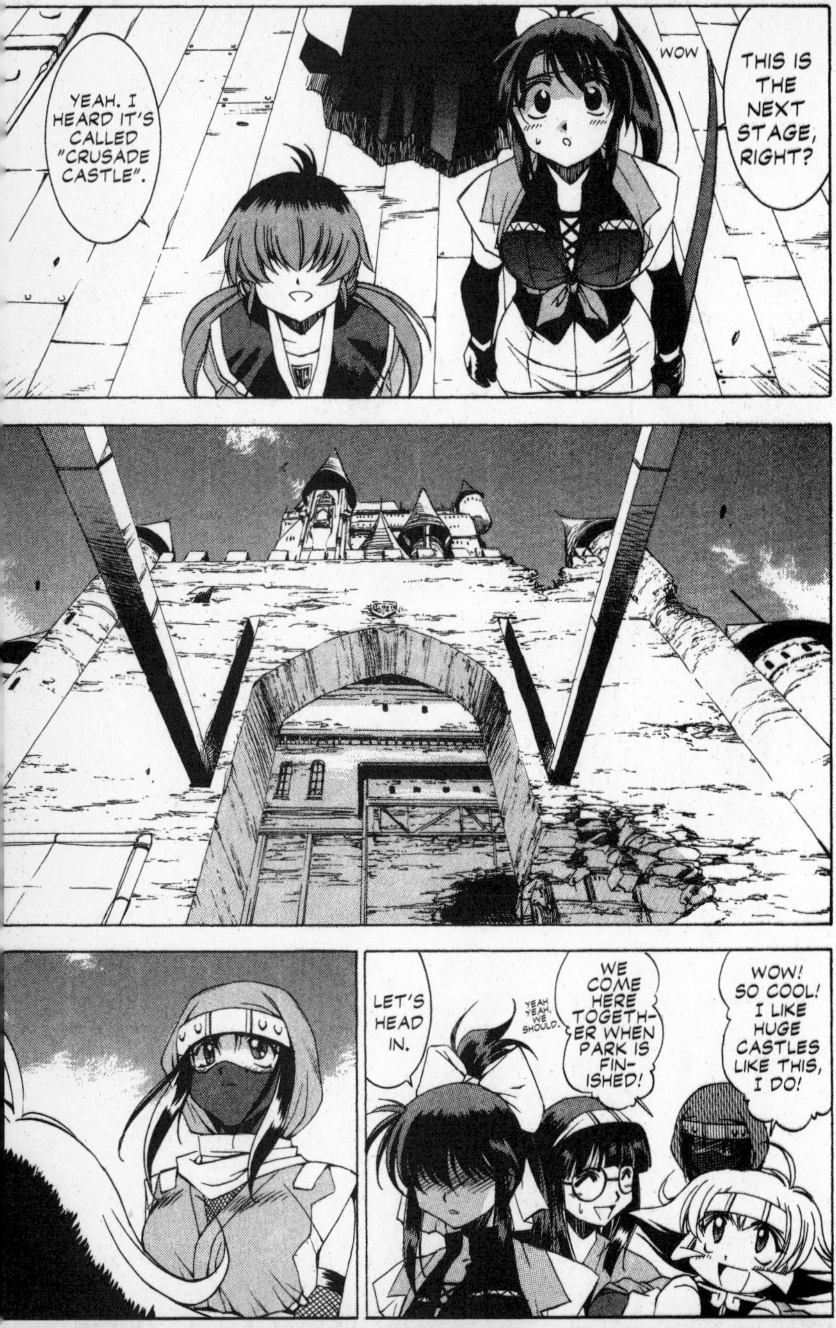
WOW
THIS IS THE NEXT STAGE, RIGHT?
YEAH. I HEARD IT'S CALLED "CRUSADE CASTLE".
WOW! SO COOL! I LIKE HUGE CASTLES LIKE THIS, I DO!
WE COME HERE TOGETH-ER WHEN PARK IS FIN-ISHED!
YEAH YEAH, WE SHOULD.
LET'S HEAD IN.

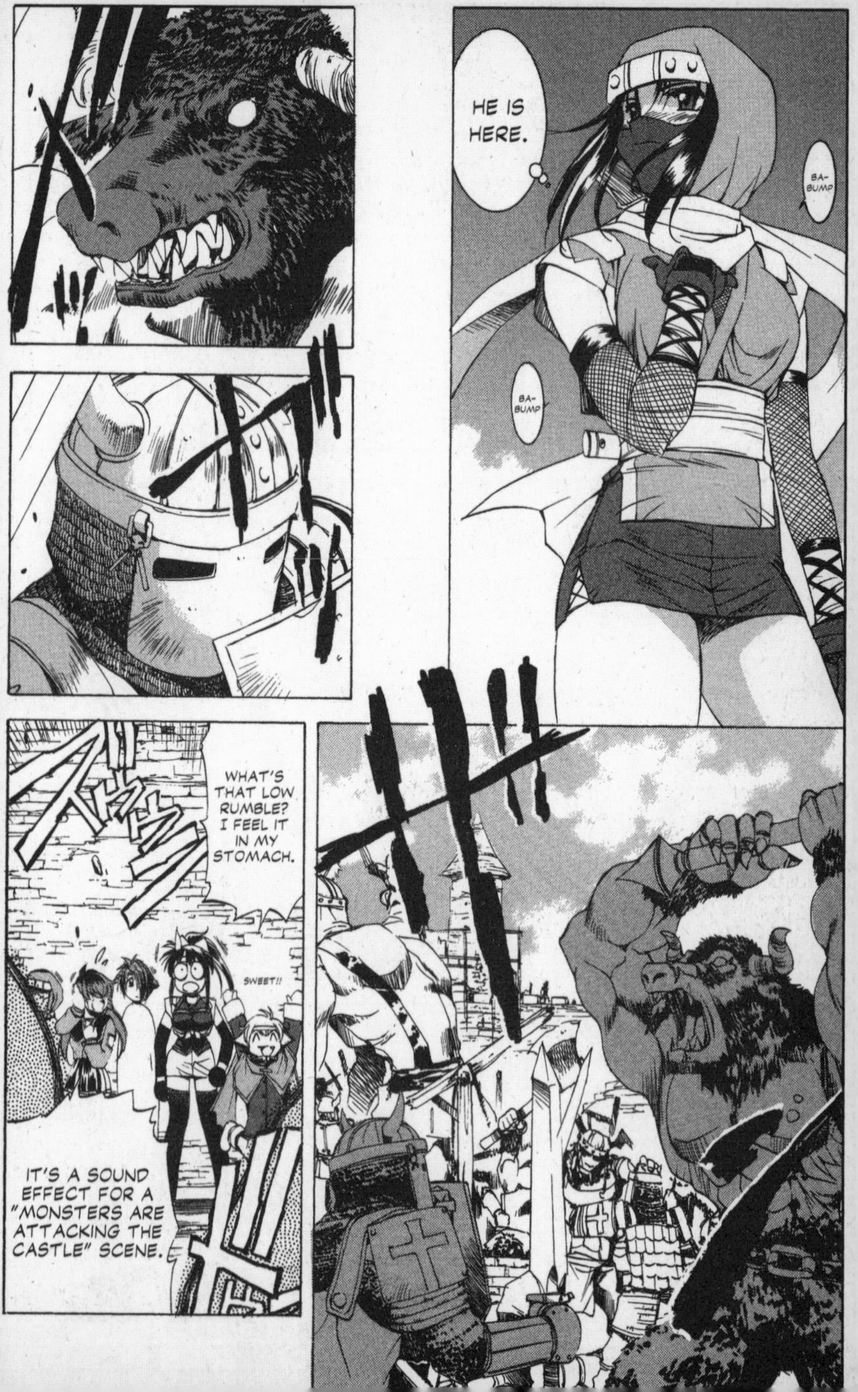
HE IS HERE.
BA-BUMP
BA-BUMP
WHAT'S THAT LOW RUMBLE? I FEEL IT IN MY STOMACH.
SWEET!!
IT'S A SOUND EFFECT FOR A "MONSTERS ARE ATTACKING THE CASTLE" SCENE.

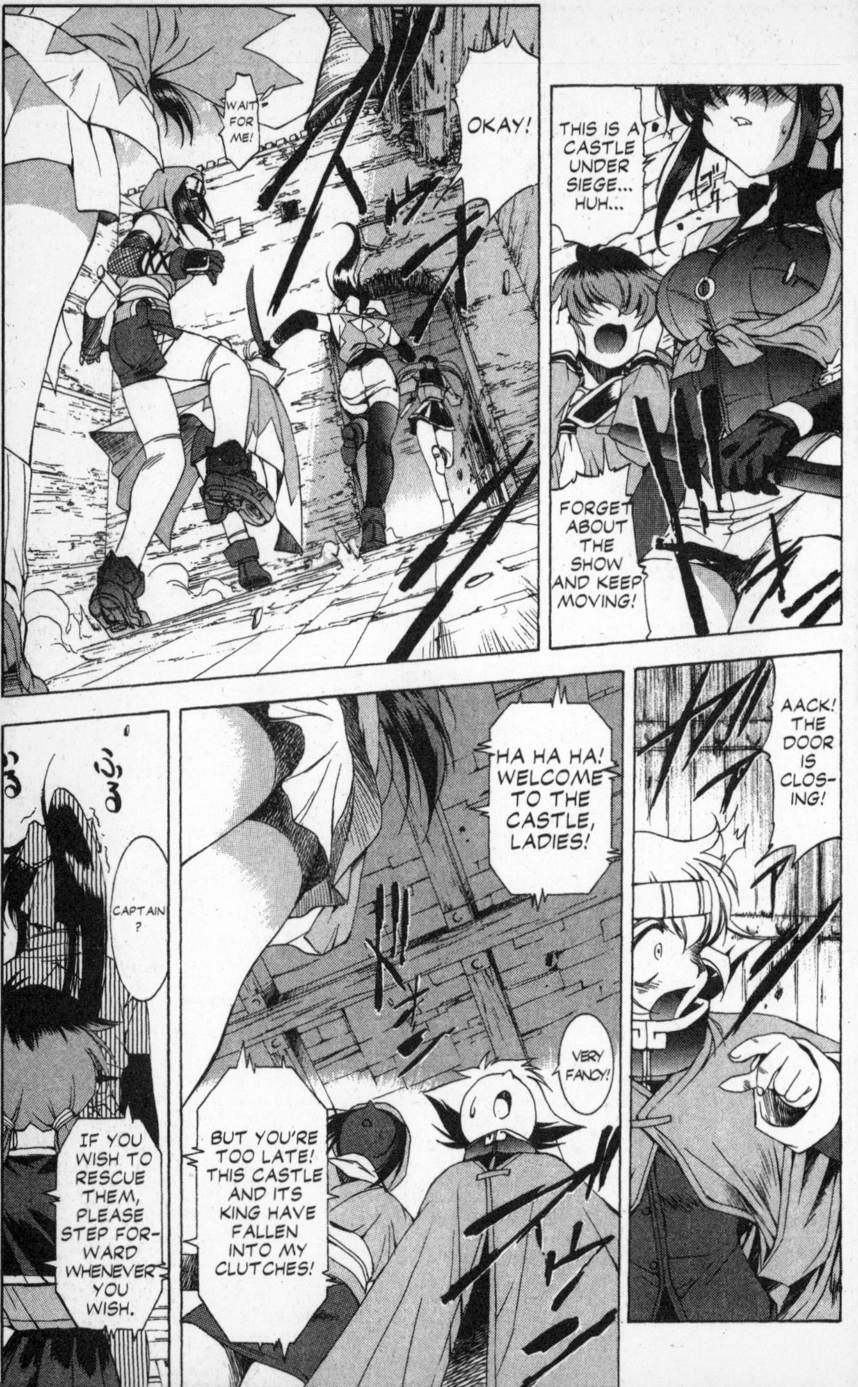
THIS IS A CASTLE UNDER SIEGE... HUH...
FORGET ABOUT THE SHOW AND KEEP MOVING!
OKAY!
WAIT FOR ME!
AACK! THE DOOR IS CLOS-ING!
HA HA HA! WELCOME TO THE CASTLE, LADIES!
VERY FANCY!
BUT YOU'RE TOO LATE! THIS CASTLE AND ITS KING HAVE FALLEN INTO MY CLUTCHES!
CAPTAIN?
IF YOU WISH TO RESCUE THEM, PLEASE STEP FOR-WARD WHENEVER YOU WISH.

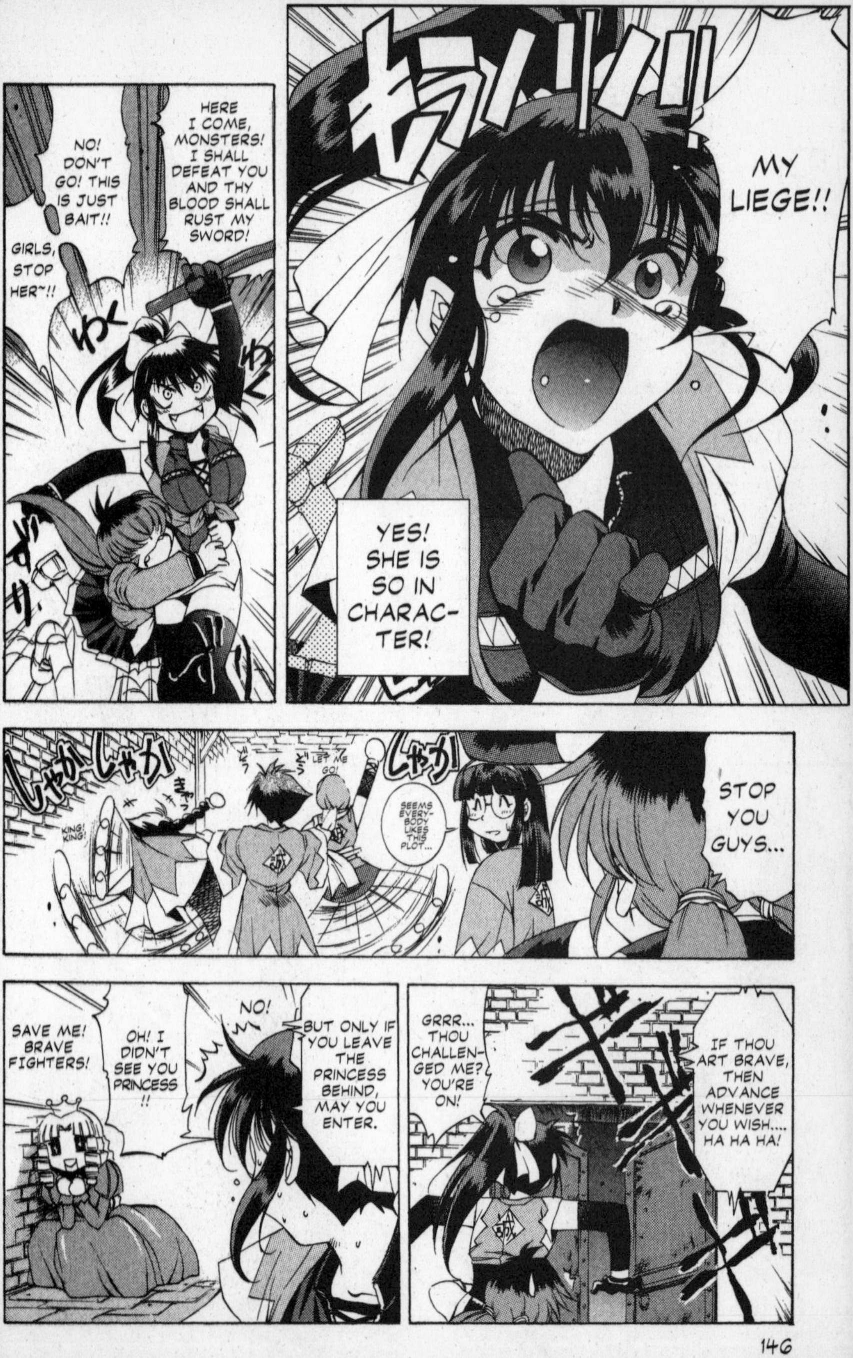
MY LIEGE!!
YES! SHE IS SO IN CHARACTER!
HERE I COME, MONSTERS! I SHALL DEFEAT YOU AND THY BLOOD SHALL RUST MY SWORD!
NO! DON'T GO! THIS IS JUST BAIT!!
GIRLS, STOP HER~!!
STOP YOU GUYS...
SEEMS EVERYBODY LIKES THIS PLOT...
LET ME GO!
KING! KING!
IF THOU ART BRAVE, THEN ADVANCE WHENEVER YOU WISH.... HA HA HA!
GRRR... THOU CHALLENGED ME? YOU'RE ON!
BUT ONLY IF YOU LEAVE THE PRINCESS BEHIND, MAY YOU ENTER.
NO!
OH! I DIDN'T SEE YOU PRINCESS !!
SAVE ME! BRAVE FIGHTERS!

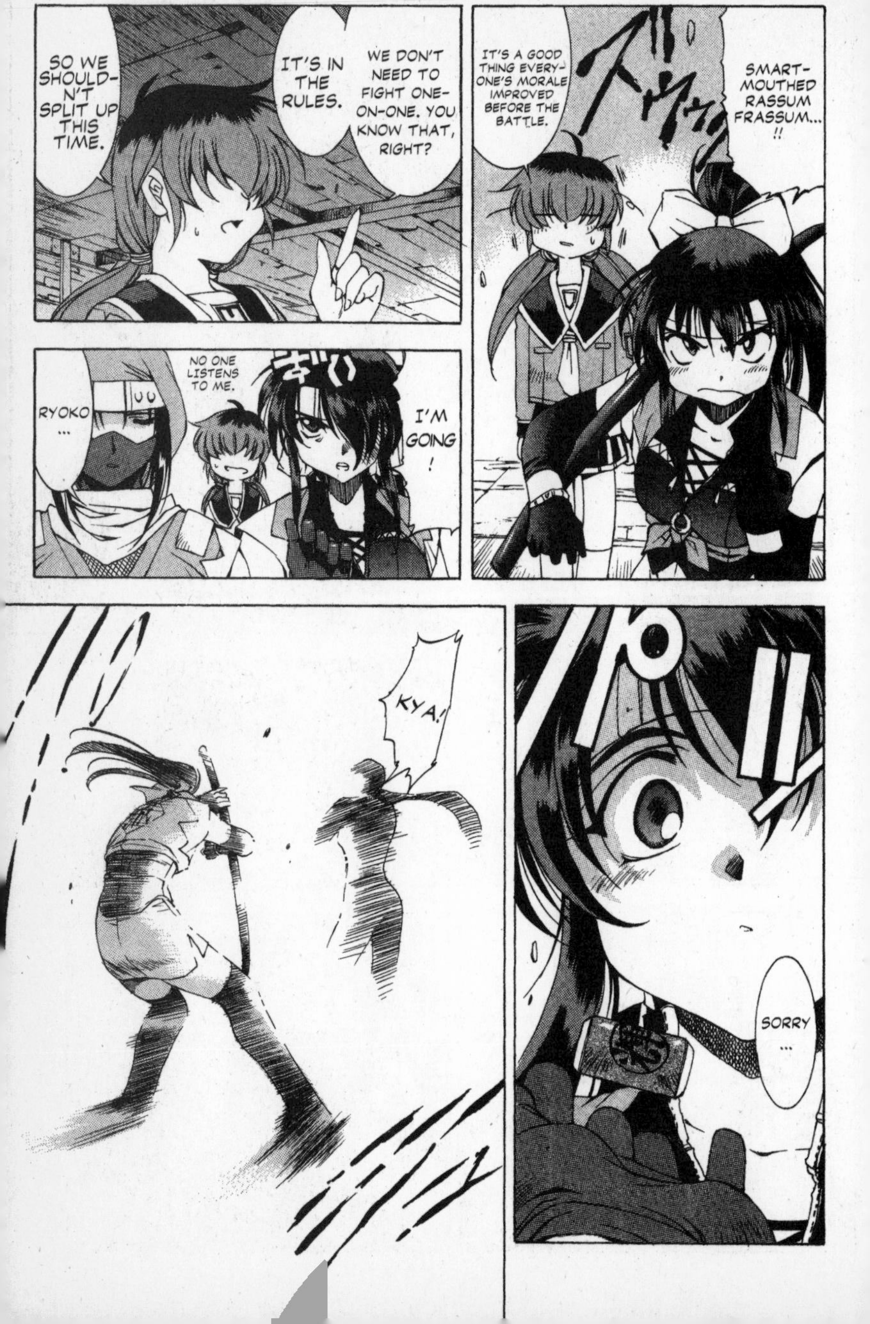
SMART-MOUTHED RASSUM FRASSUM...!!
IT'S A GOOD THING EVERYONE'S MORALE IMPROVED BEFORE THE BATTLE.
WE DON'T NEED TO FIGHT ONE-ON-ONE. YOU KNOW THAT, RIGHT?
IT'S IN THE RULES.
SO WE SHOULDN'T SPLIT UP THIS TIME.
I'M GOING!
NO ONE LISTENS TO ME.
RYOKO...
SORRY...
KYA!

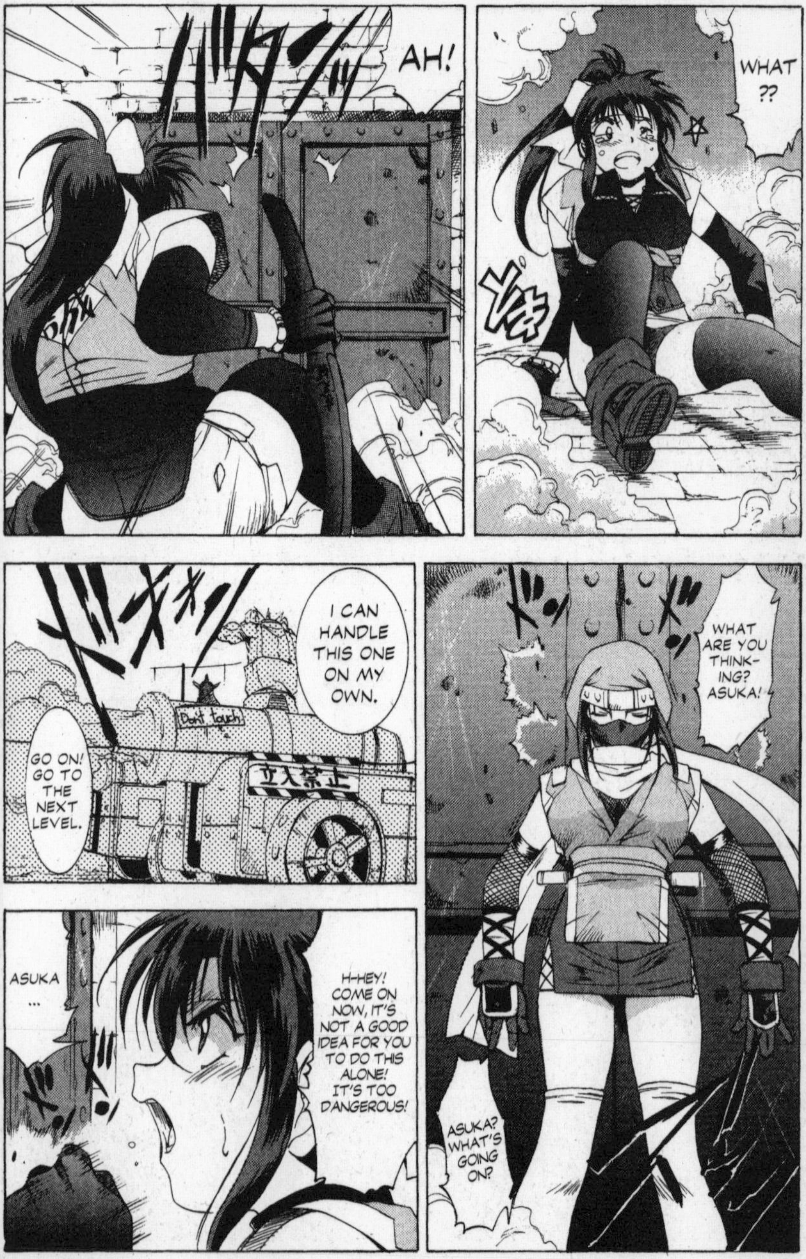
WHAT ??
AH!
I CAN HANDLE THIS ONE ON MY OWN.
GO ON! GO TO THE NEXT LEVEL.
WHAT ARE YOU THINK-ING? ASUKA!
H-HEY! COME ON NOW, IT'S NOT A GOOD IDEA FOR YOU TO DO THIS ALONE! IT'S TOO DANGEROUS!
ASUKA ...
ASUKA? WHAT'S GOING ON?
Don't touch
立入禁止

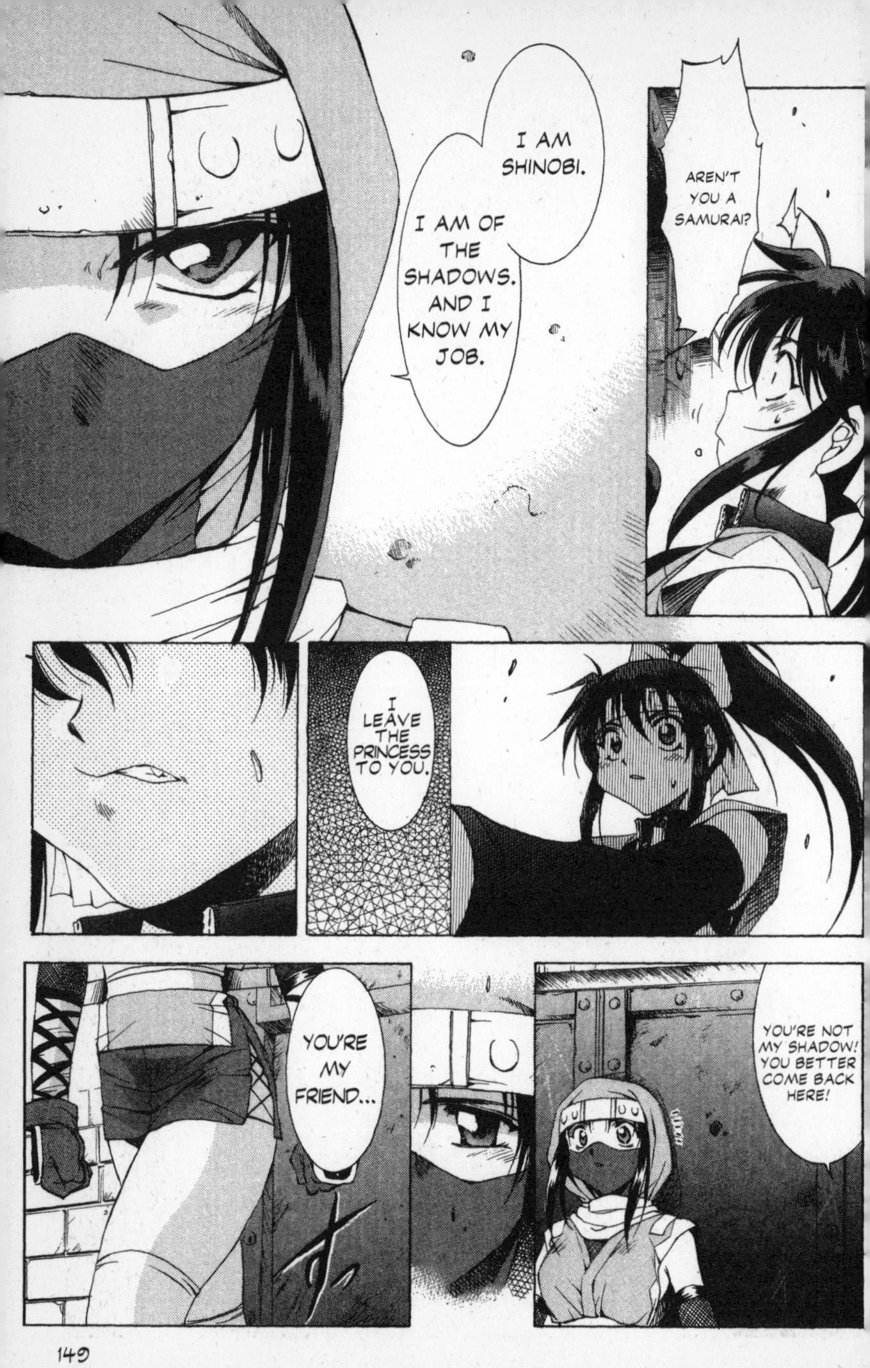

AREN'T YOU A SAMURAI?
I AM SHINOBI.
I AM OF THE SHADOWS. AND I KNOW MY JOB.
I LEAVE THE PRINCESS TO YOU.
YOU'RE NOT MY SHADOW! YOU BETTER COME BACK HERE!
YOU'RE MY FRIEND...

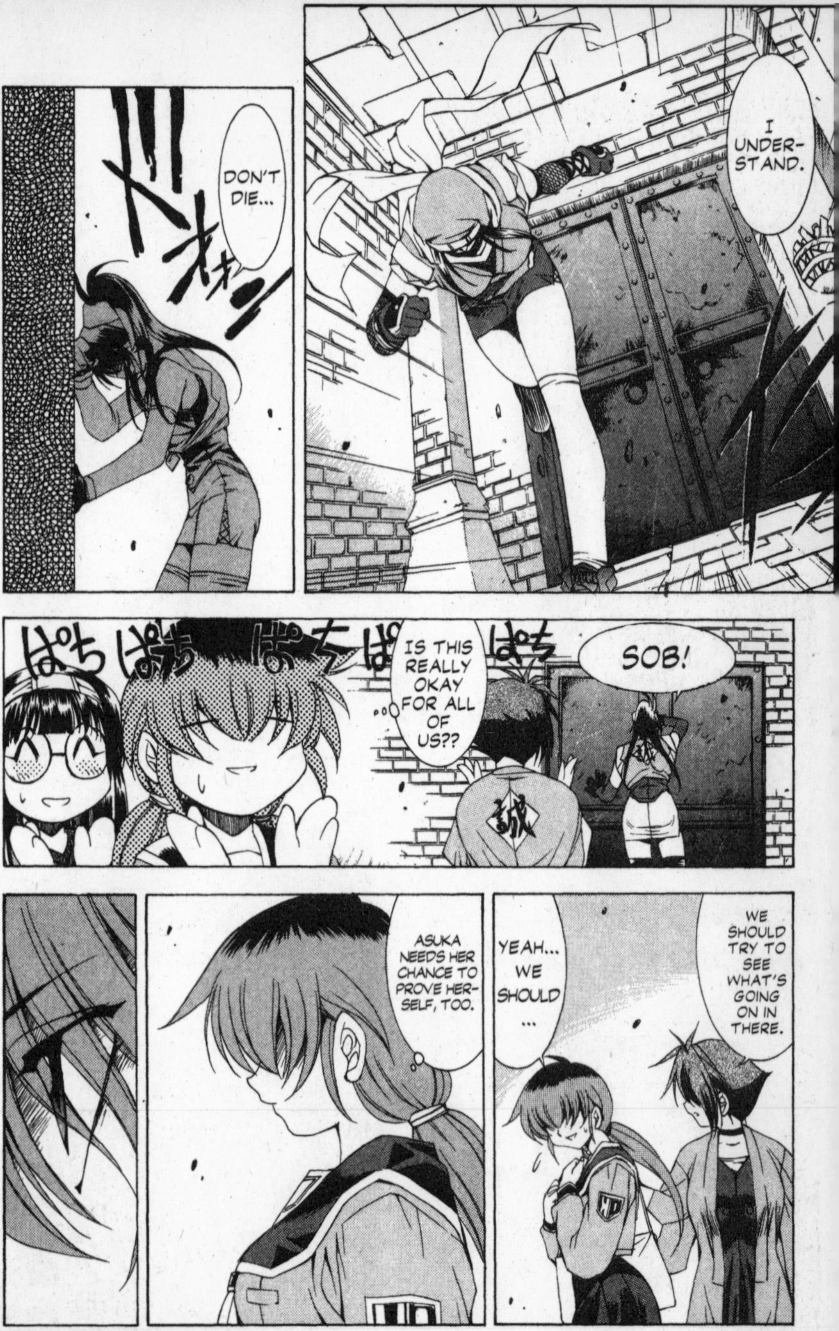

I UNDER-STAND.
DON'T DIE...
SOB!
IS THIS REALLY OKAY FOR ALL OF US??
WE SHOULD TRY TO SEE WHAT'S GOING ON IN THERE.
YEAH... WE SHOULD ...
ASUKA NEEDS HER CHANCE TO PROVE HER-SELF, TOO.

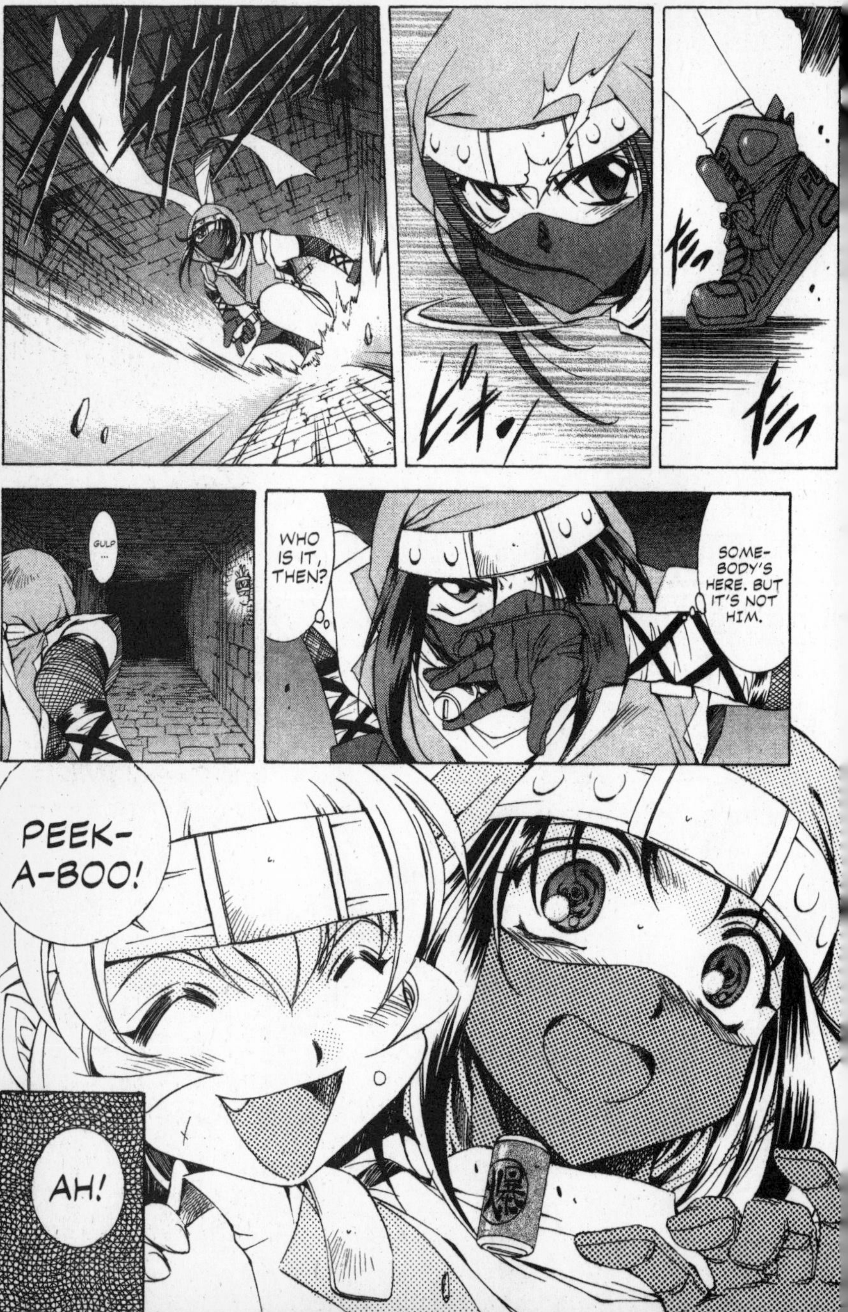
SOME-BODY'S HERE. BUT IT'S NOT HIM.
WHO IS IT, THEN?
GULP ...
PEEK-A-BOO!
AH!
爆

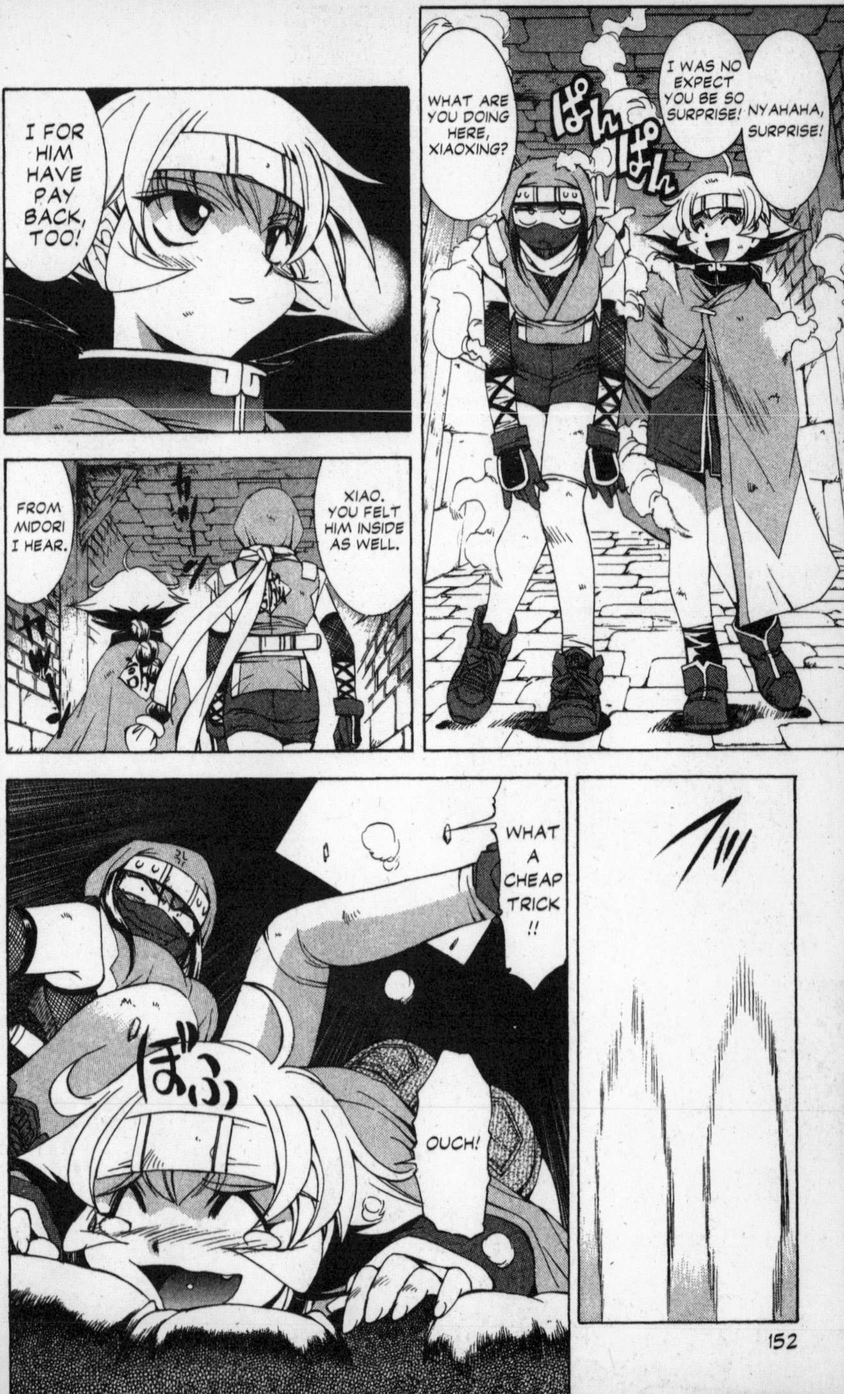
NYAHAHA, SURPRISE!
I WAS NO EXPECT YOU BE SO SURPRISE!
ぱんぱん
WHAT ARE YOU DOING HERE, XIAOXING?
I FOR HIM HAVE PAY BACK, TOO!
XIAO. YOU FELT HIM INSIDE AS WELL.
FROM MIDORI I HEAR.
ぼふ
WHAT A CHEAP TRICK !!
OUCH!

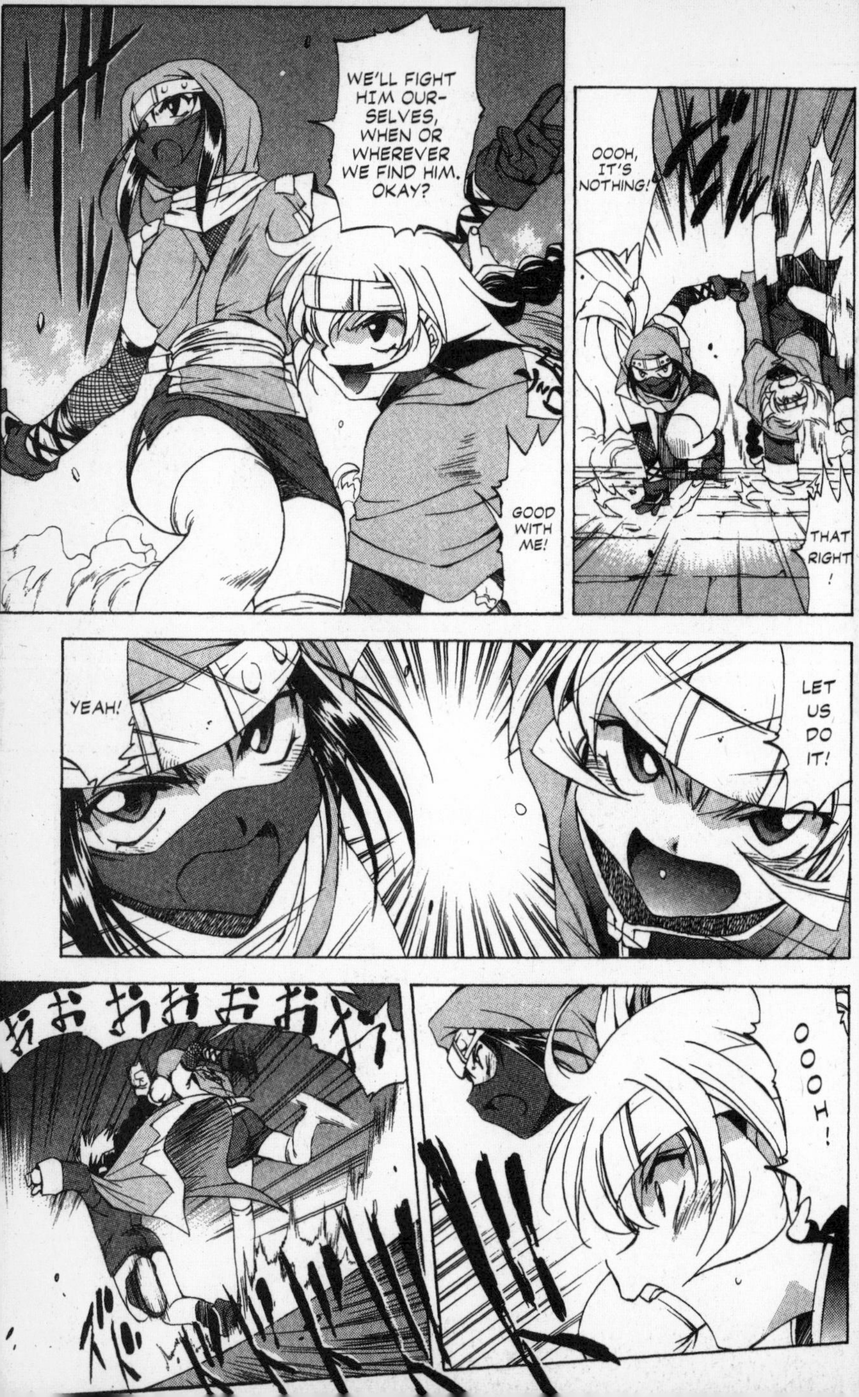

WE'LL FIGHT HIM OUR-SELVES, WHEN OR WHEREVER WE FIND HIM. OKAY?
GOOD WITH ME!
OOOH, IT'S NOTHING!
THAT RIGHT!
LET US DO IT!
YEAH!
OOOOH!

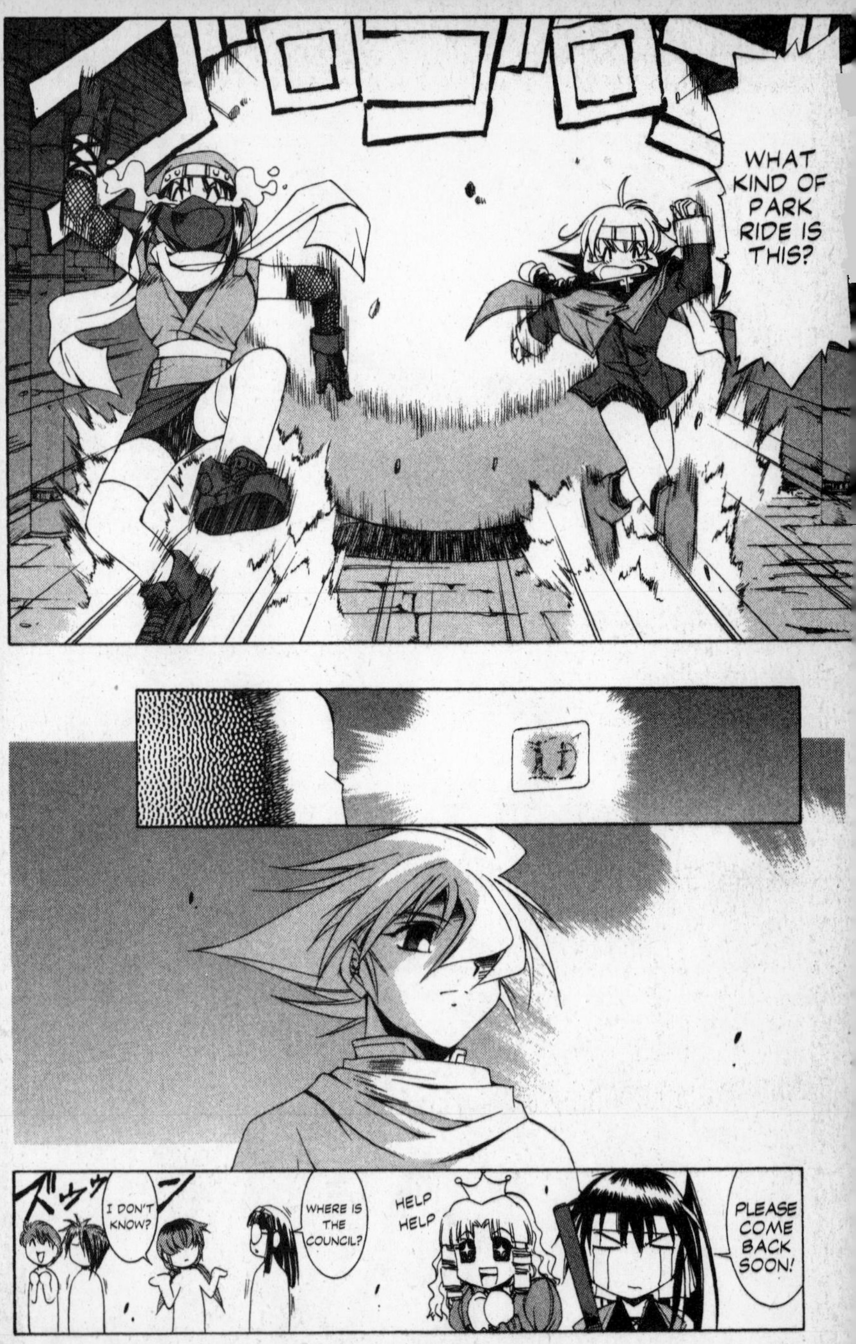
WHAT KIND OF PARK RIDE IS THIS?
PLEASE COME BACK SOON!
HELP HELP
WHERE IS THE COUNCIL?
I DON'T KNOW?

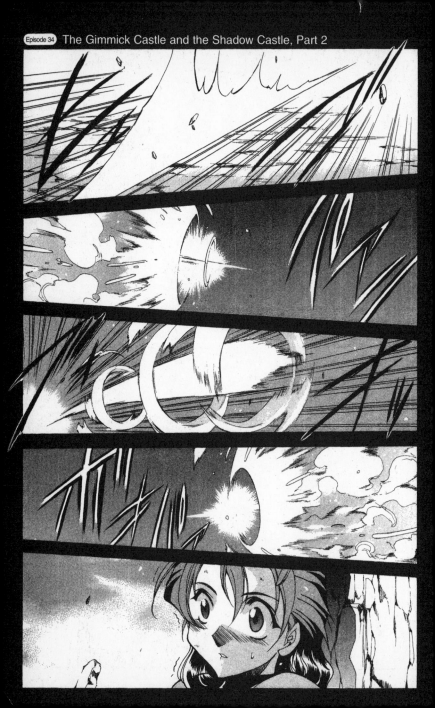

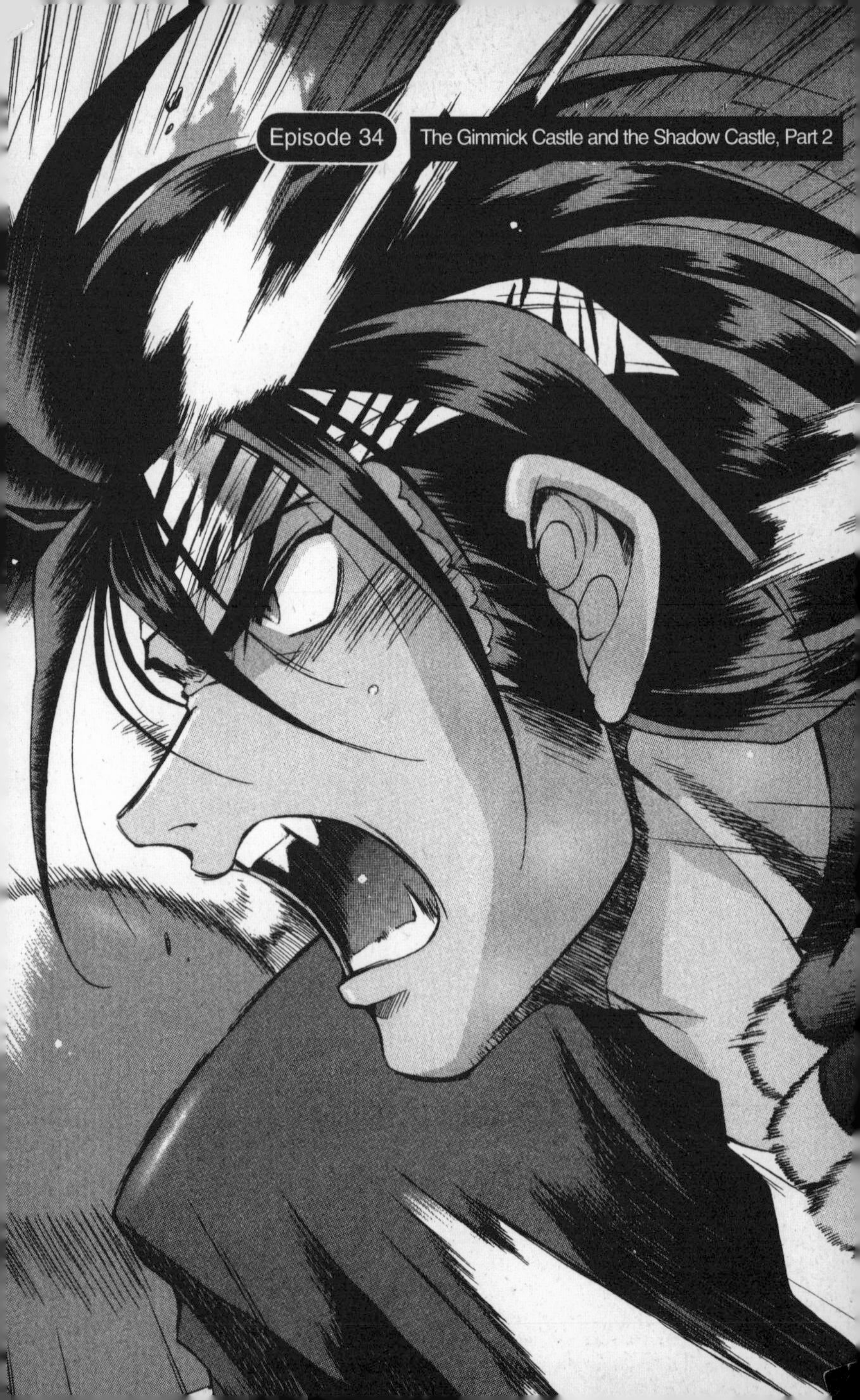
Episode 34
The Gimmick Castle and the Shadow Castle, Part 2

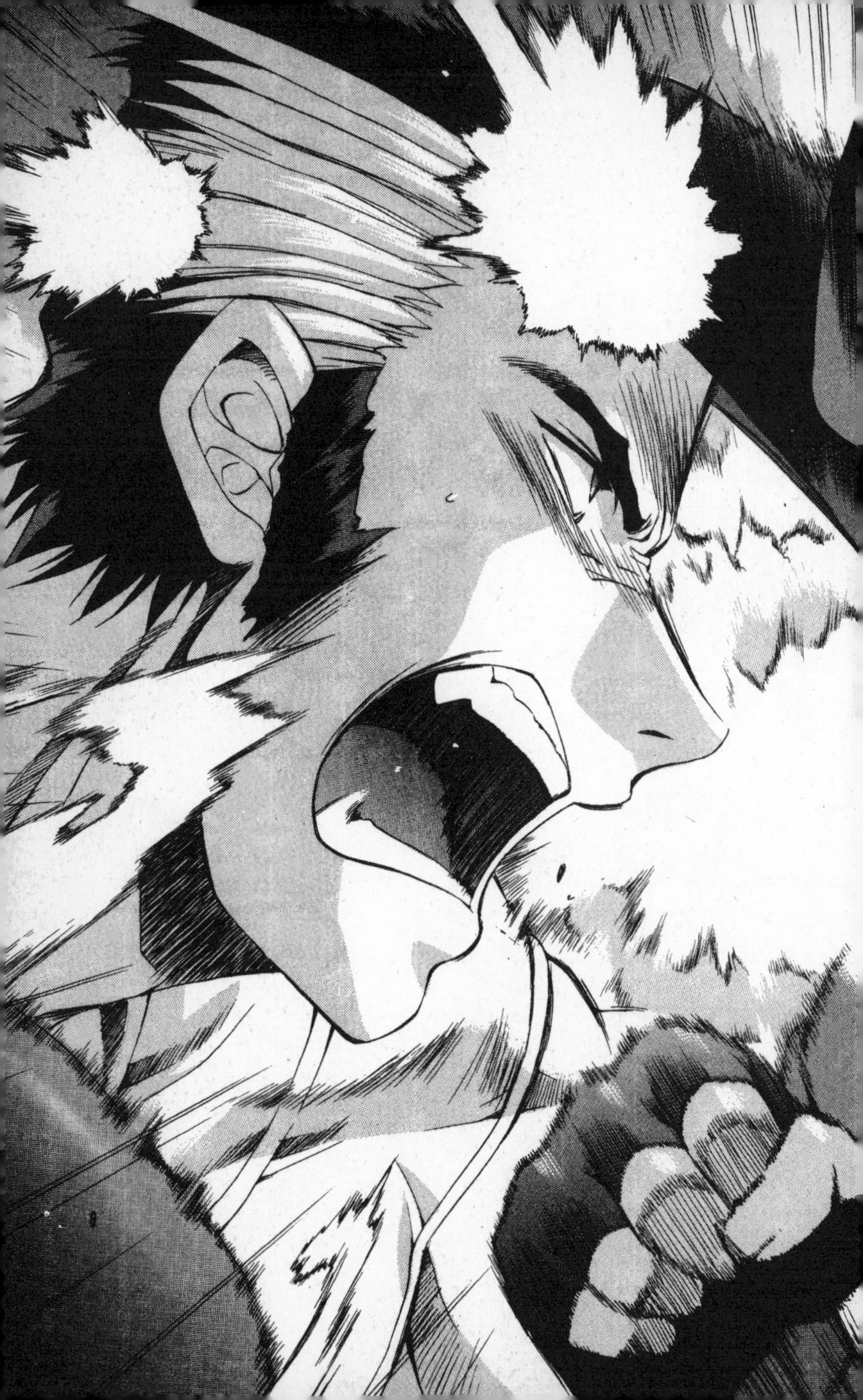

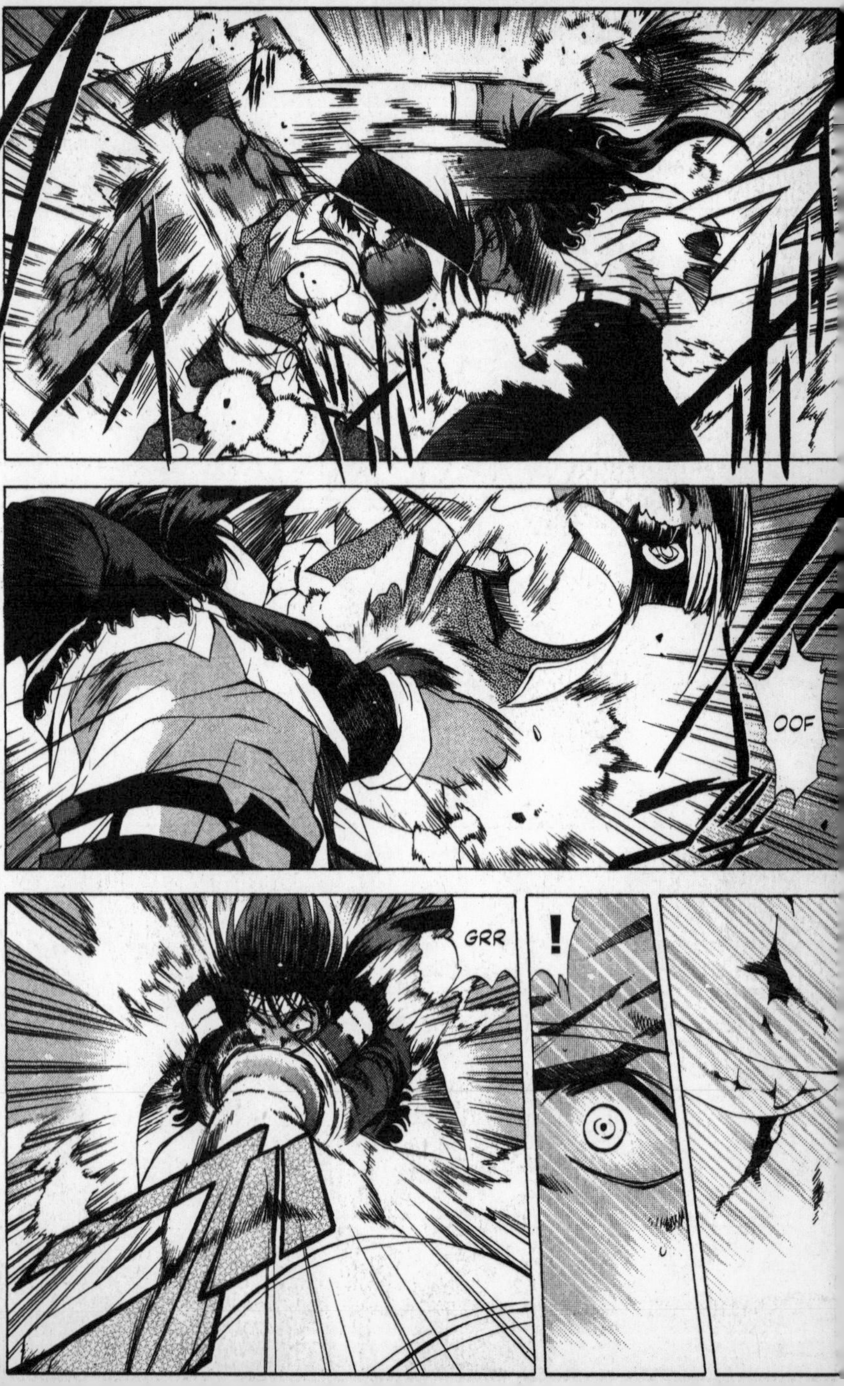
OOF
GRR
!

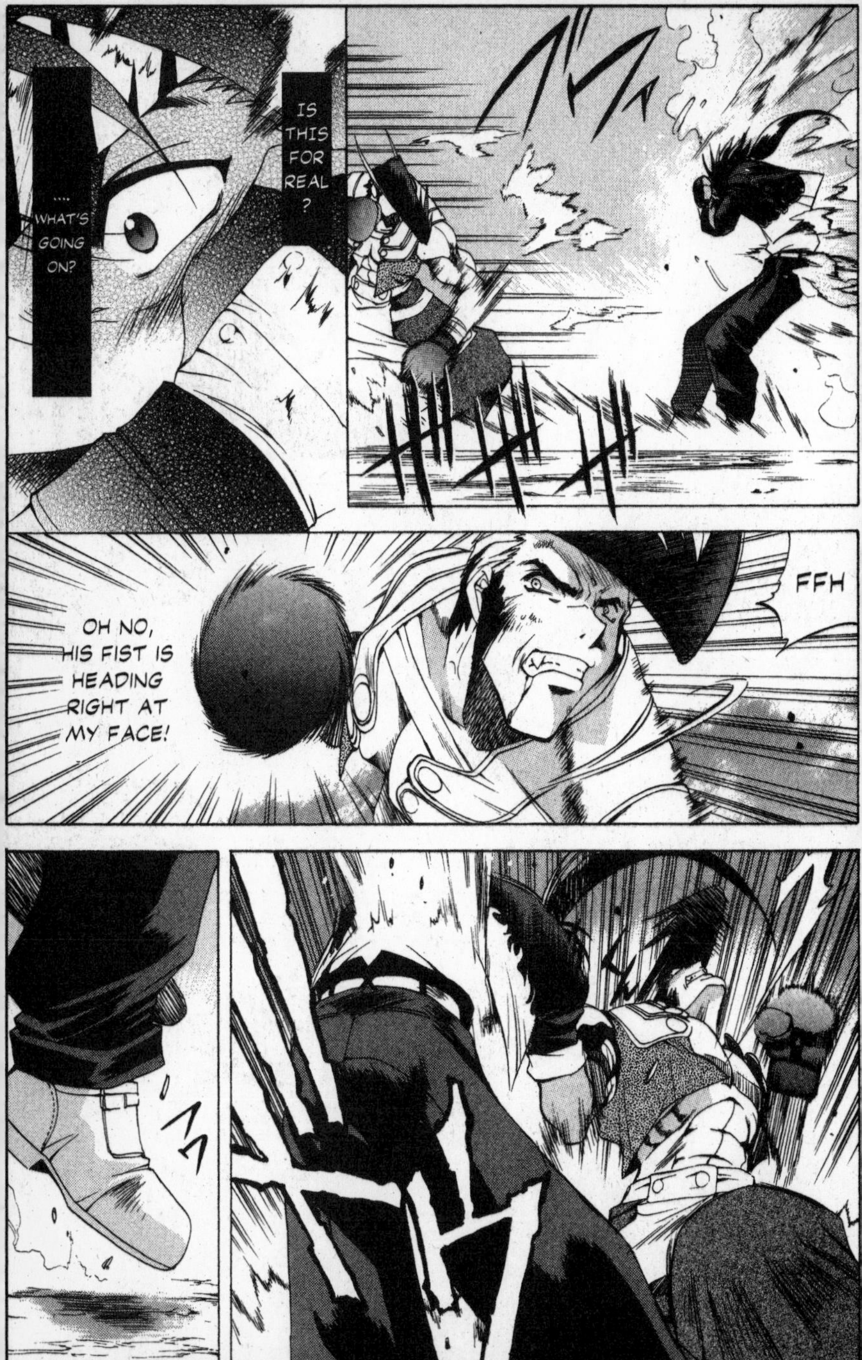
IS THIS FOR REAL?
.... WHAT'S GOING ON?
FFH
OH NO, HIS FIST IS HEADING RIGHT AT MY FACE!

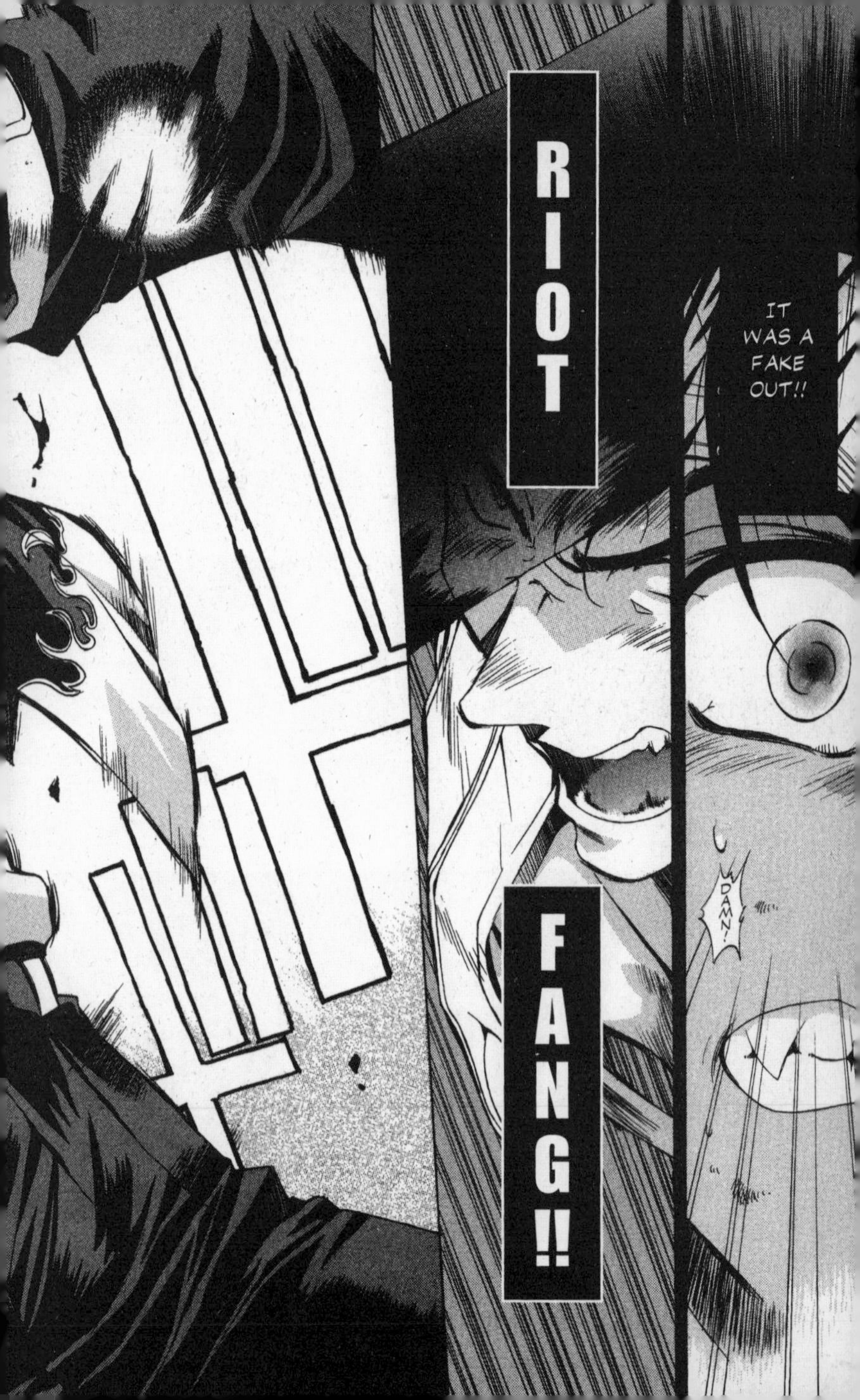
IT WAS A FAKE OUT!!
DAMN!
RIOT
FANG!!

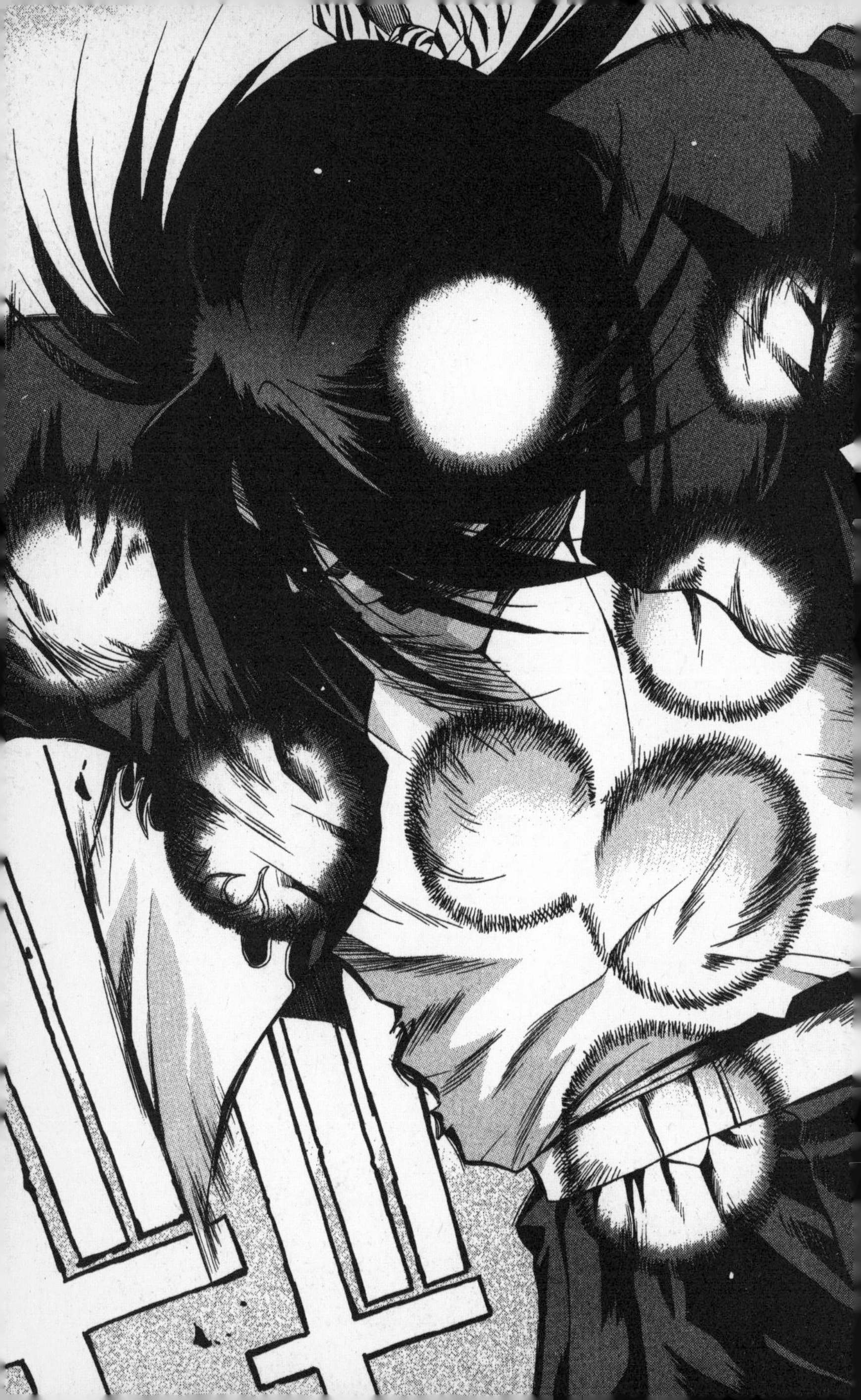

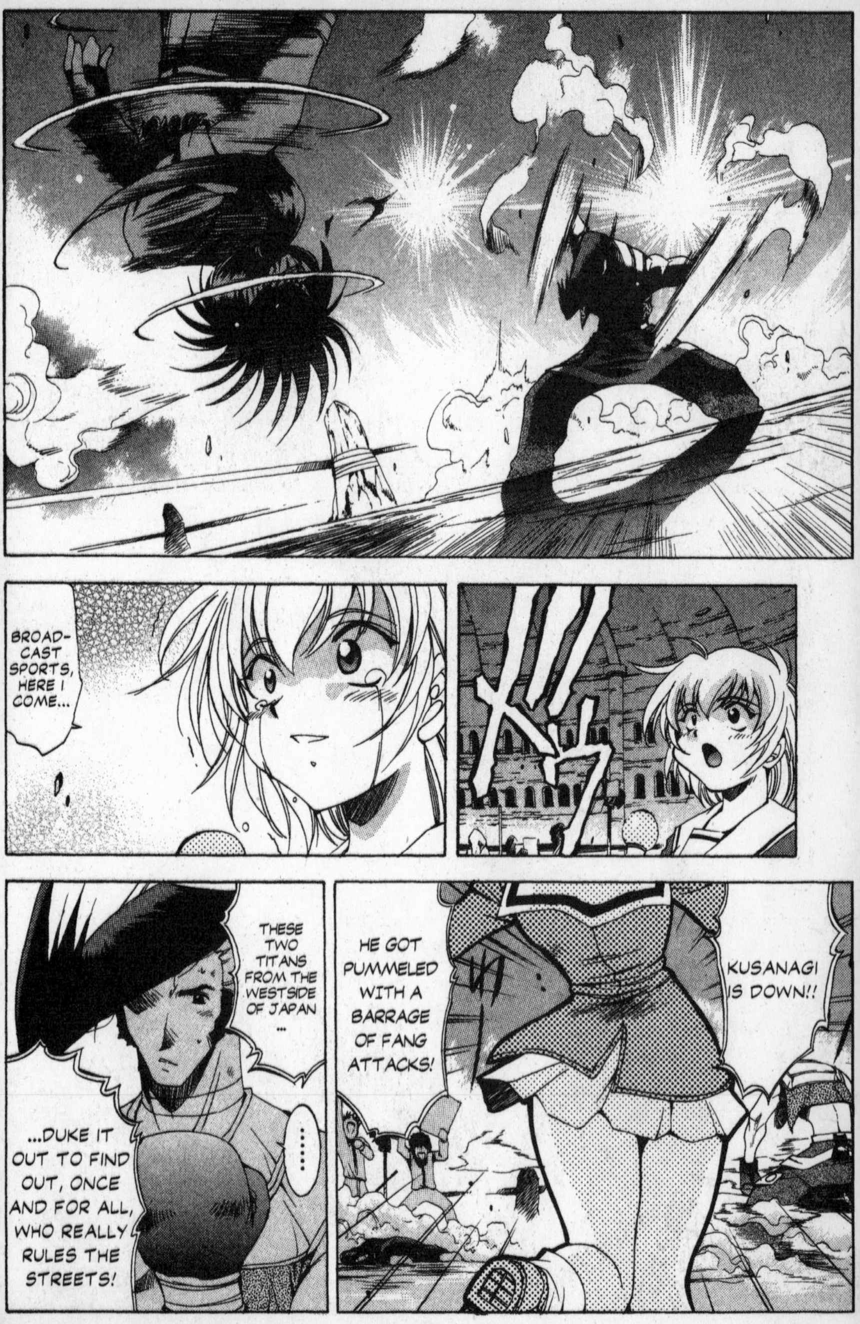
BROAD-CAST SPORTS, HERE I COME...
KUSANAGI IS DOWN!!
HE GOT PUMMELED WITH A BARRAGE OF FANG ATTACKS!
THESE TWO TITANS FROM THE WESTSIDE OF JAPAN ...
......
...DUKE IT OUT TO FIND OUT, ONCE AND FOR ALL, WHO REALLY RULES THE STREETS!

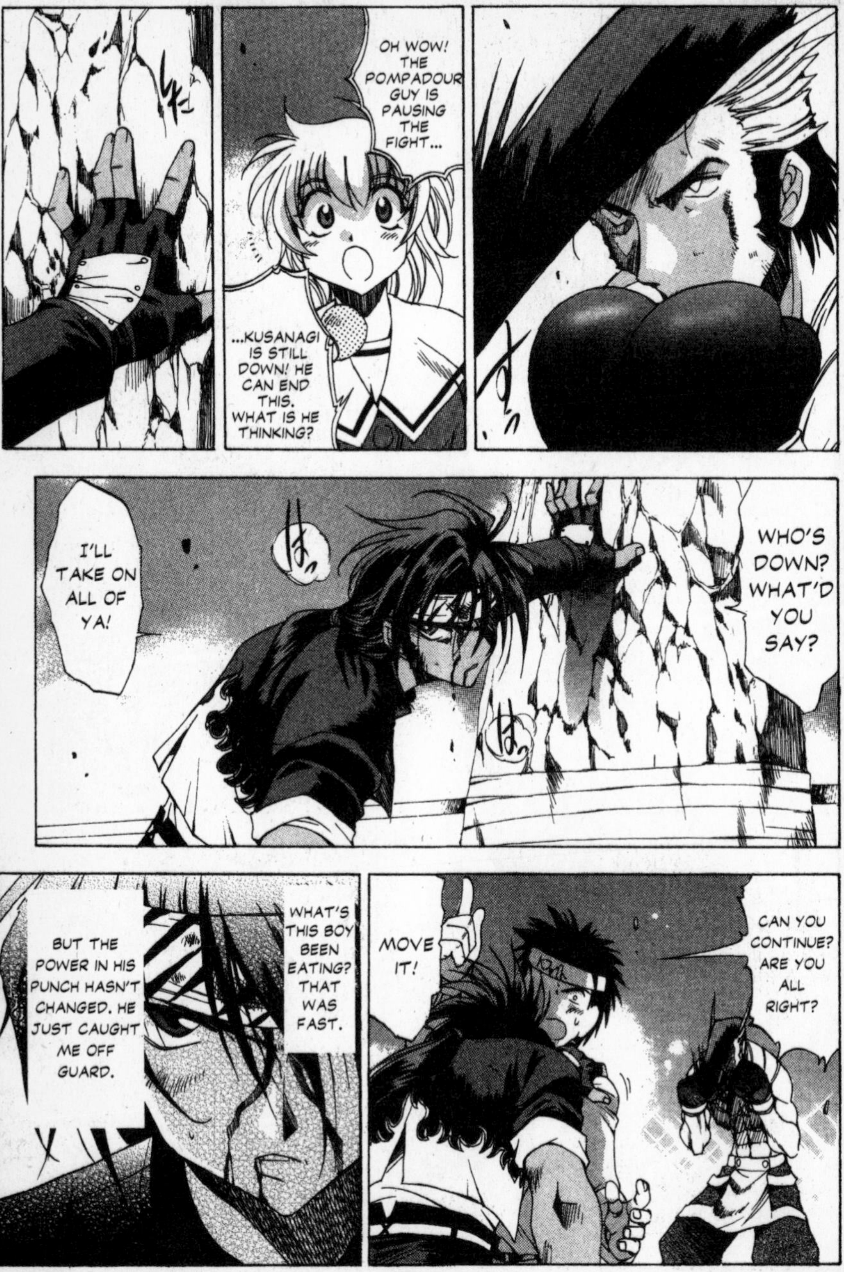
OH WOW! THE POMPADOUR GUY IS PAUSING THE FIGHT...
...KUSANAGI IS STILL DOWN! HE CAN END THIS. WHAT IS HE THINKING?
WHO'S DOWN? WHAT'D YOU SAY?
I'LL TAKE ON ALL OF YA!
CAN YOU CONTINUE? ARE YOU ALL RIGHT?
MOVE IT!
WHAT'S THIS BOY BEEN EATING? THAT WAS FAST.
BUT THE POWER IN HIS PUNCH HASN'T CHANGED. HE JUST CAUGHT ME OFF GUARD.

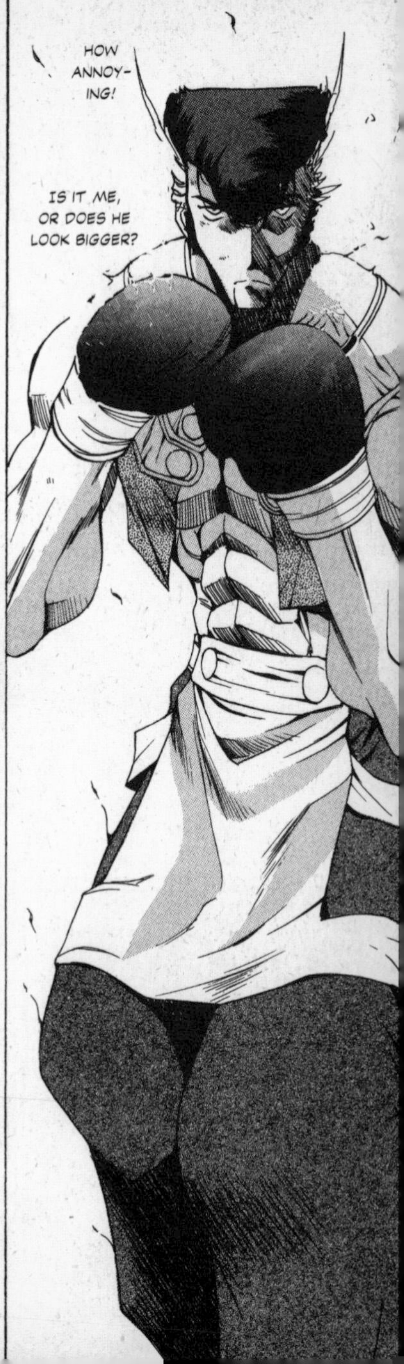
HOW ANNOYING!
IS IT ME, OR DOES HE LOOK BIGGER?

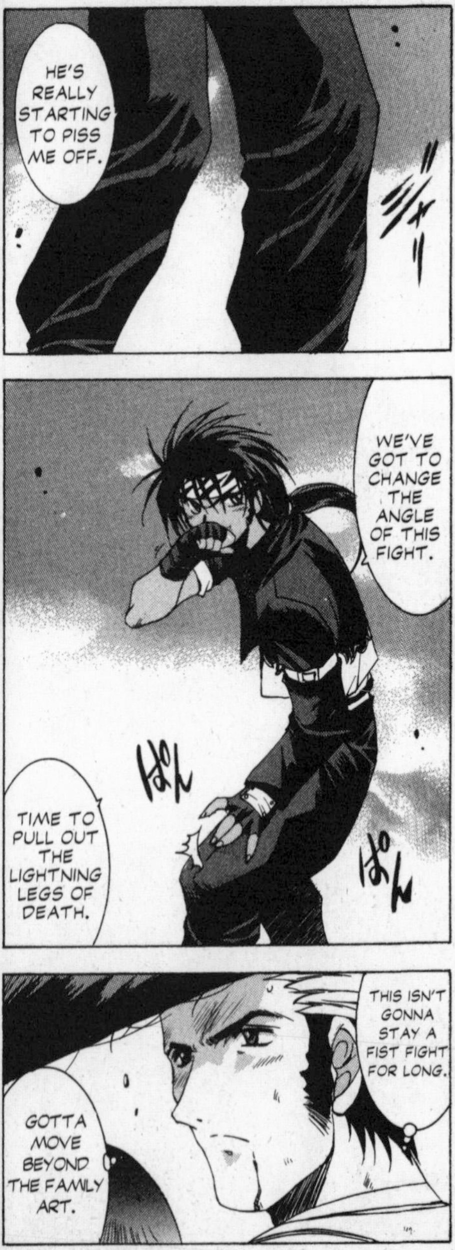
HE'S REALLY STARTING TO PISS ME OFF.
ジャリ
WE'VE GOT TO CHANGE THE ANGLE OF THIS FIGHT.
ぱん
ぱん
TIME TO PULL OUT THE LIGHTNING LEGS OF DEATH.
THIS ISN'T GONNA STAY A FIST FIGHT FOR LONG.
GOTTA MOVE BEYOND THE FAMILY ART.

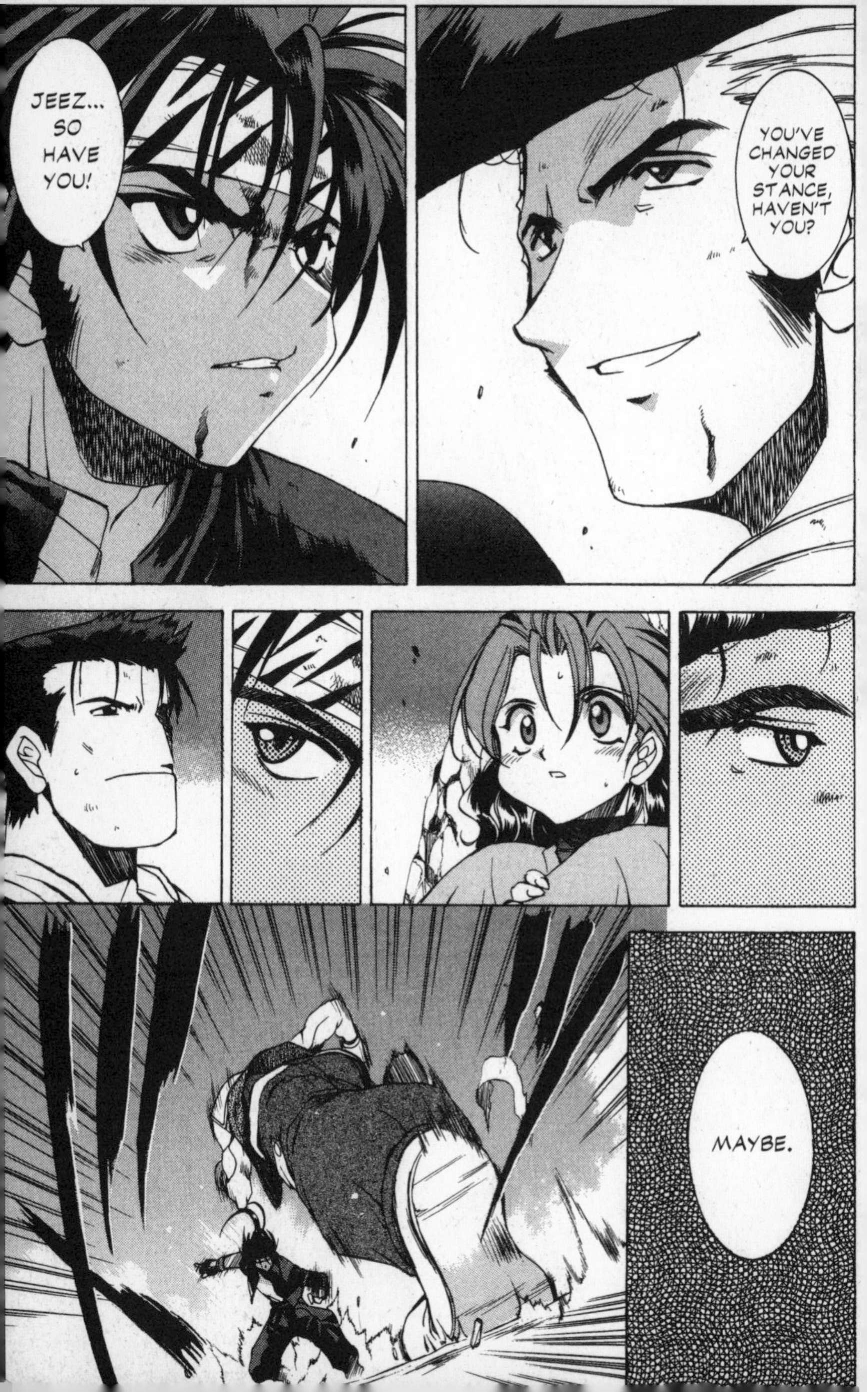
YOU'VE CHANGED YOUR STANCE, HAVEN'T YOU?
JEEZ... SO HAVE YOU!
MAYBE.

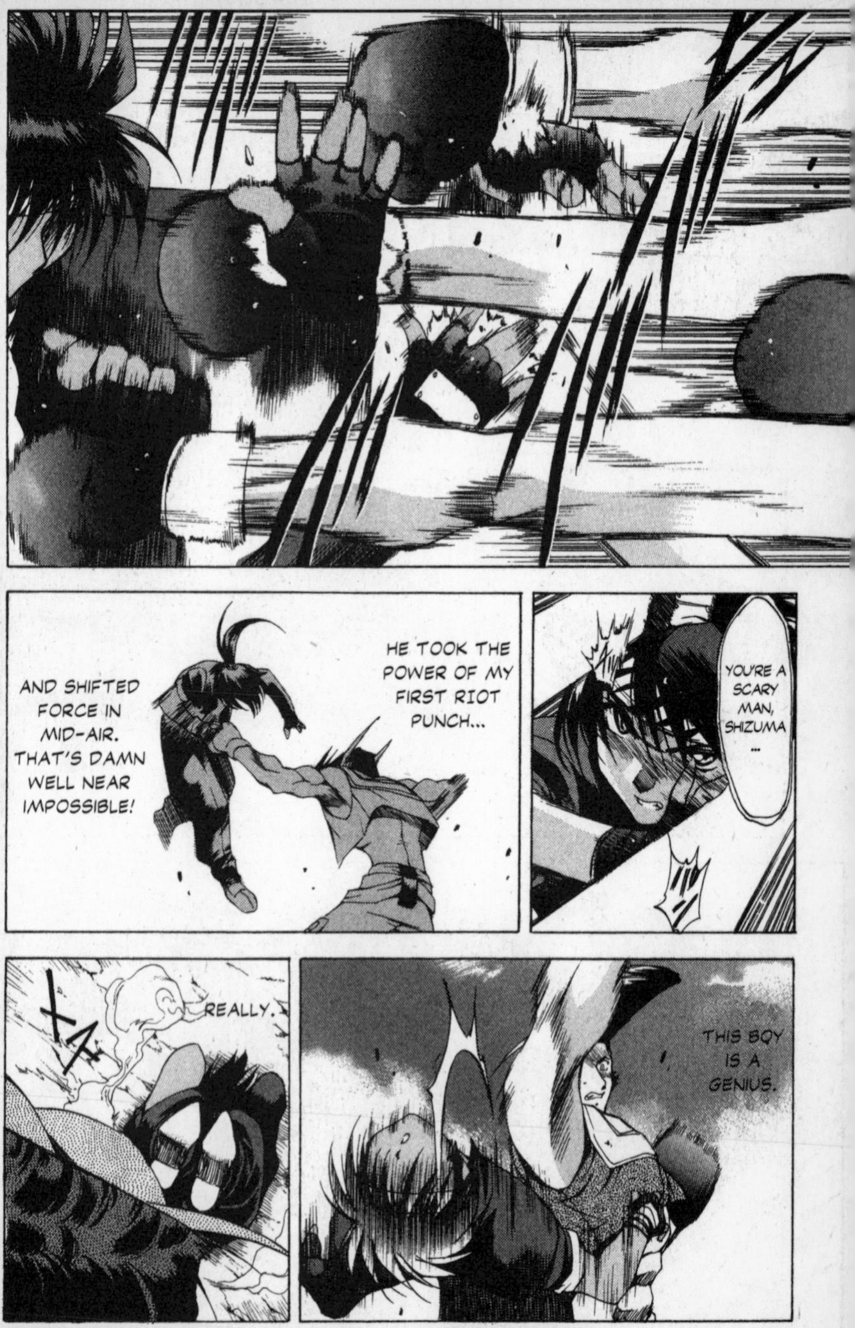
YOU'RE A SCARY MAN, SHIZUMA...
HE TOOK THE POWER OF MY FIRST RIOT PUNCH...
AND SHIFTED FORCE IN MID-AIR. THAT'S DAMN WELL NEAR IMPOSSIBLE!
THIS BOY IS A GENIUS.
REALLY.

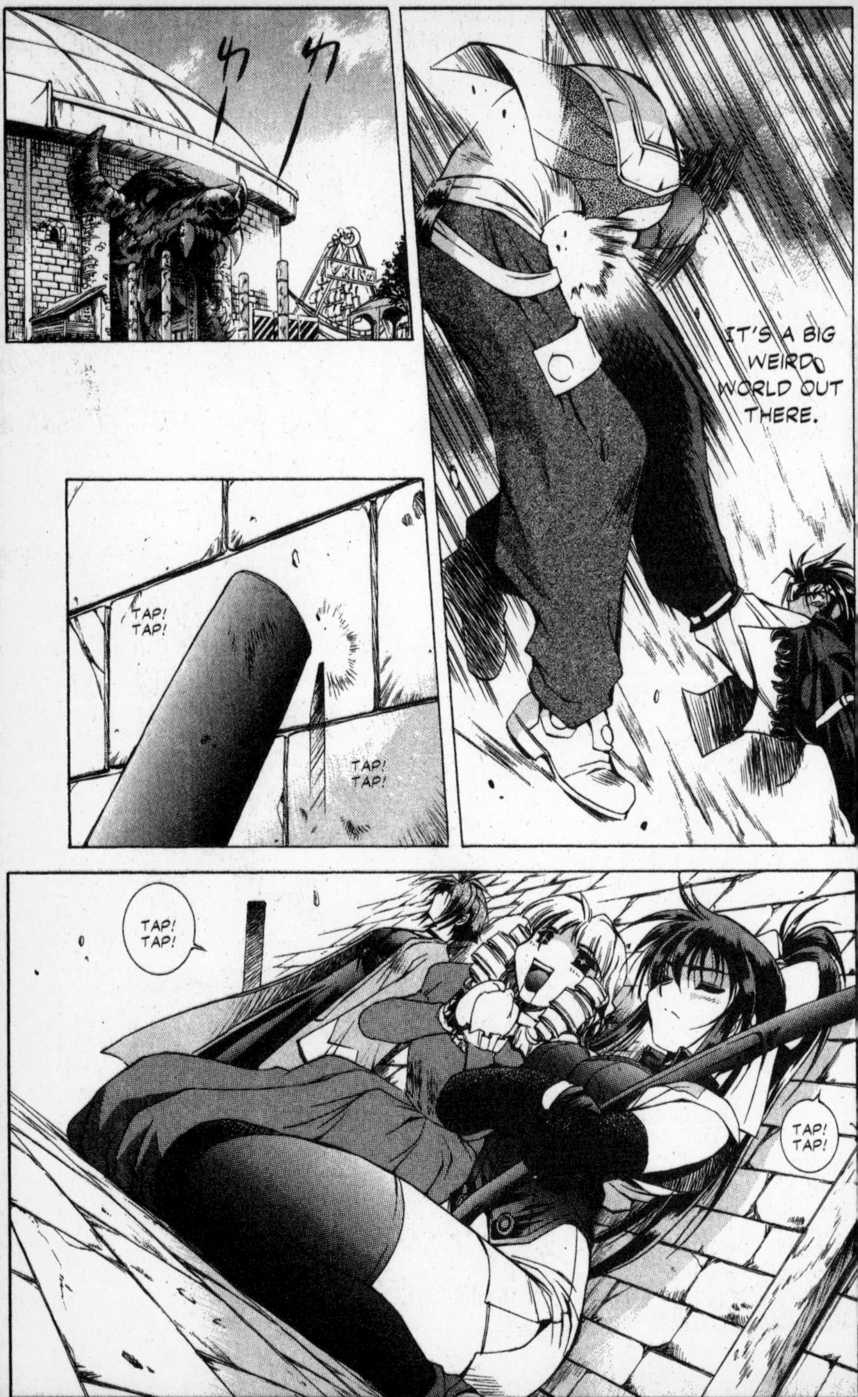
IT'S A BIG WEIRD WORLD OUT THERE.
TAP! TAP!
TAP! TAP!
TAP! TAP!
TAP! TAP!

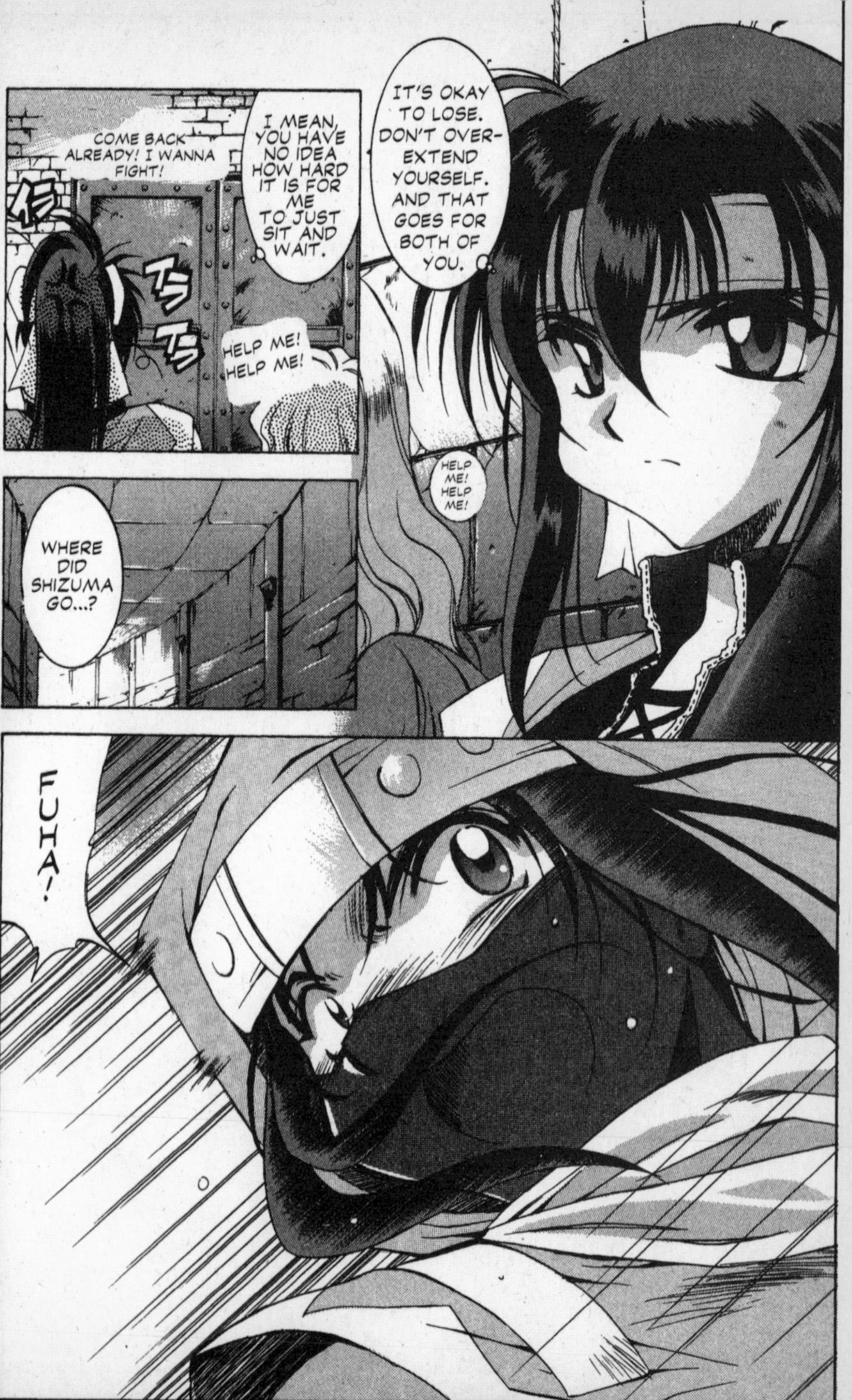
IT'S OKAY TO LOSE. DON'T OVER-EXTEND YOURSELF. AND THAT GOES FOR BOTH OF YOU.
I MEAN, YOU HAVE NO IDEA HOW HARD IT IS FOR ME TO JUST SIT AND WAIT.
COME BACK ALREADY! I WANNA FIGHT!
HELP ME! HELP ME!
HELP ME! HELP ME!
WHERE DID SHIZUMA GO...?
FUHA!

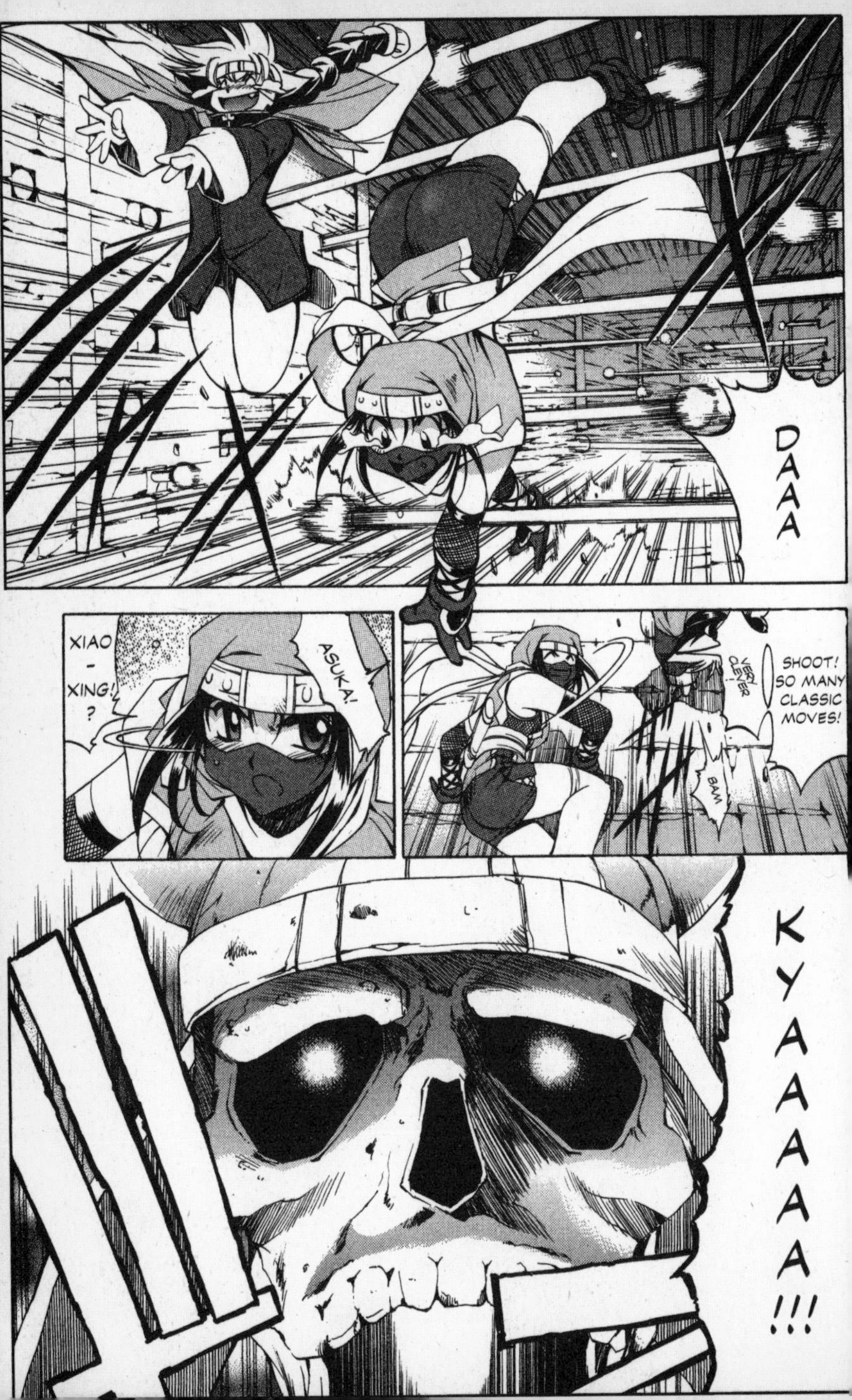
DAAAA
SHOOT! SO MANY CLASSIC MOVES!
VERY CLEVER...!
BAM
ASUKA!
XIAO-XING!?
KYAAAAAA!!!

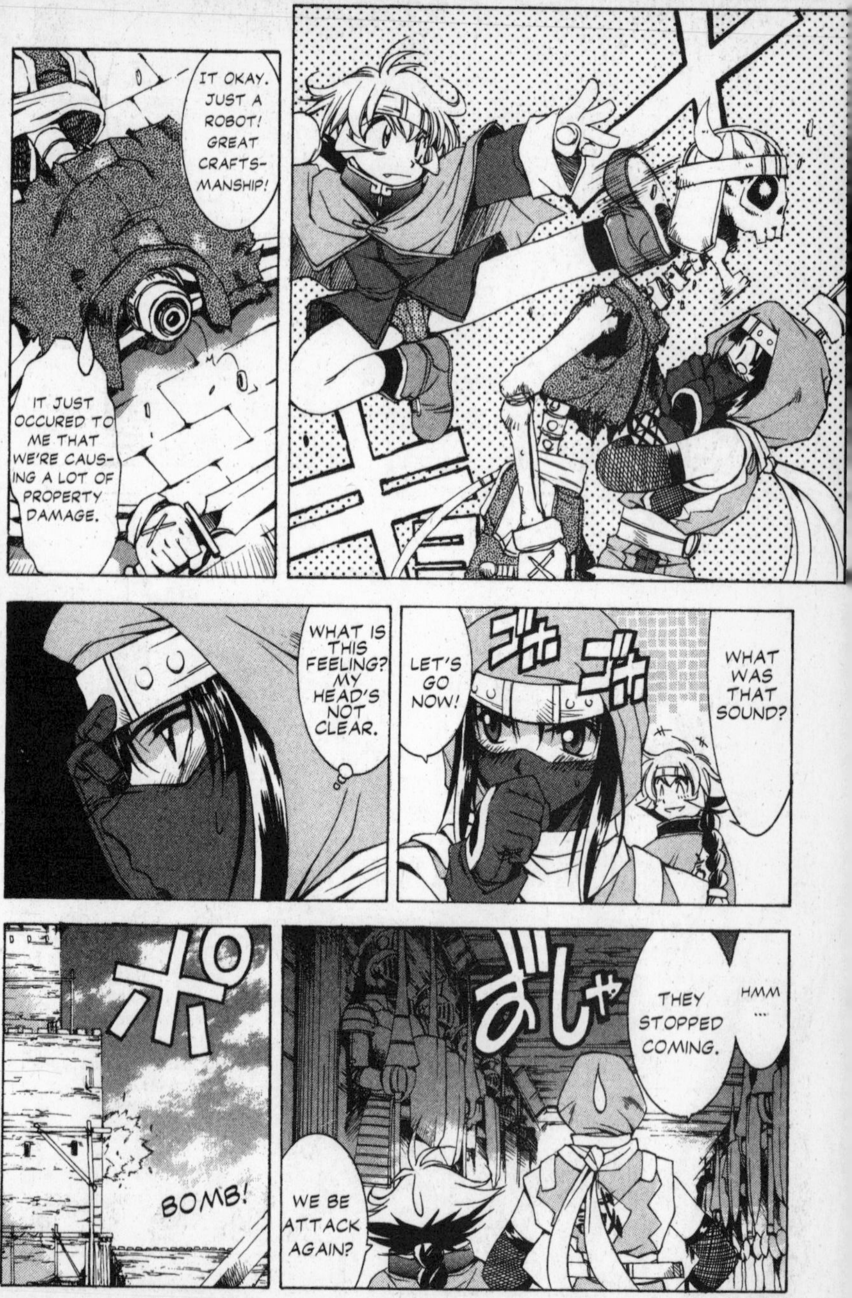
IT OKAY. JUST A ROBOT! GREAT CRAFTS-MANSHIP!
IT JUST OCCURED TO ME THAT WE'RE CAUSING A LOT OF PROPERTY DAMAGE.
WHAT WAS THAT SOUND?
LET'S GO NOW!
WHAT IS THIS FEELING? MY HEAD'S NOT CLEAR.
HMM ...
THEY STOPPED COMING.
WE BE ATTACK AGAIN?
BOMB!

THAT WAS LUCK.

WE MUST HAVE TRIG-GERED THEIR SELF-DESTRUCT.

FORCED TERMINA-TION! EXCELLENT, IT'S FINISHED!

NHM?

LET'S KEEP MOVING.

UH... OH...

CAUTION!
We are currently in the middle of some delicate construction!
Please refrain from using any large explosive devices.
We apologize for the inconvenience.
The Mgt.

CAUTION!
We are currently in the middle of some delicate construction!
Please refrain from using any large explosive devices.
We apologize for the inconvenience.
The Mgt.

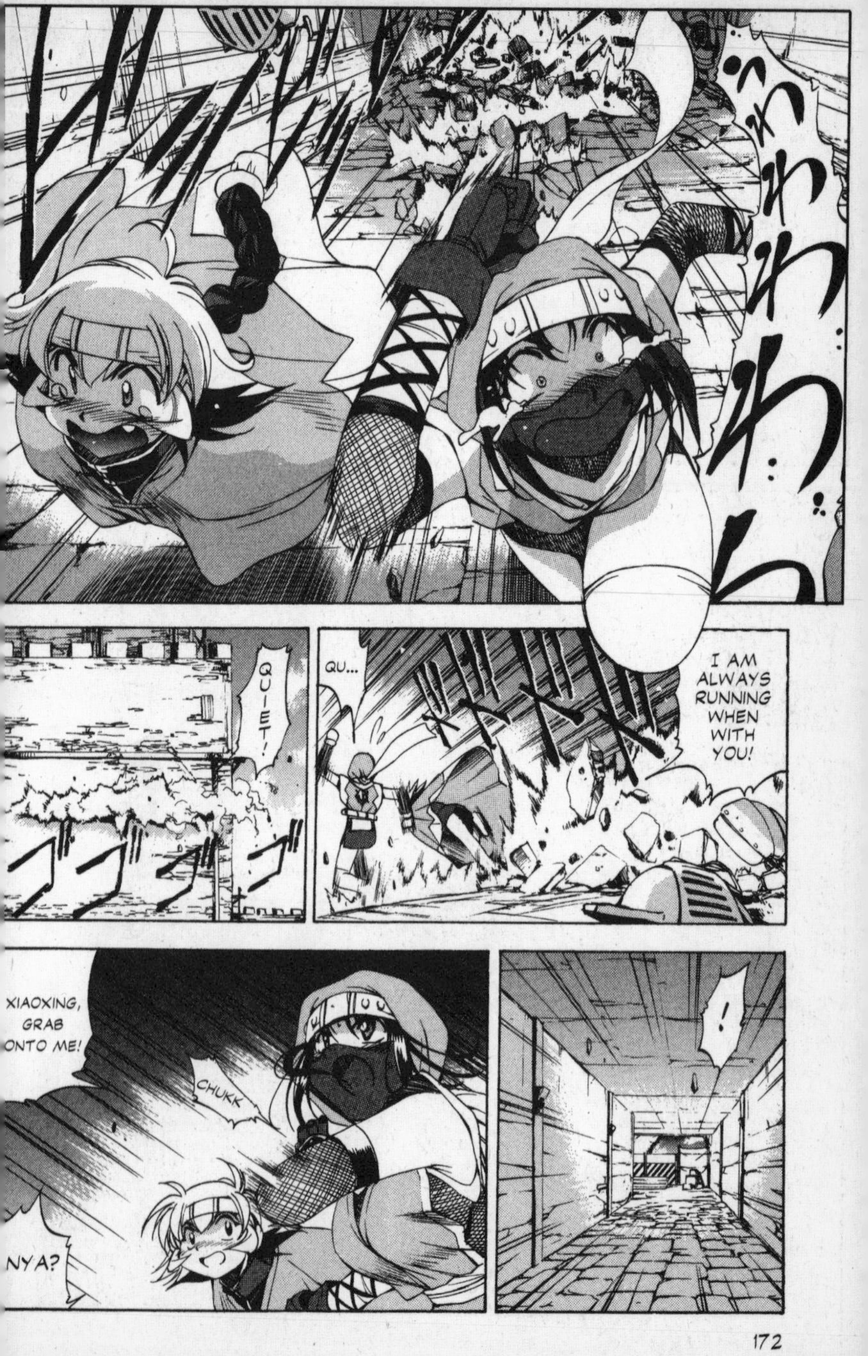
へわわわわわ
I AM ALWAYS RUNNING WHEN WITH YOU!
QU...
QUIET!
!
XIAOXING, GRAB ONTO ME!
CHUKK
NYA?

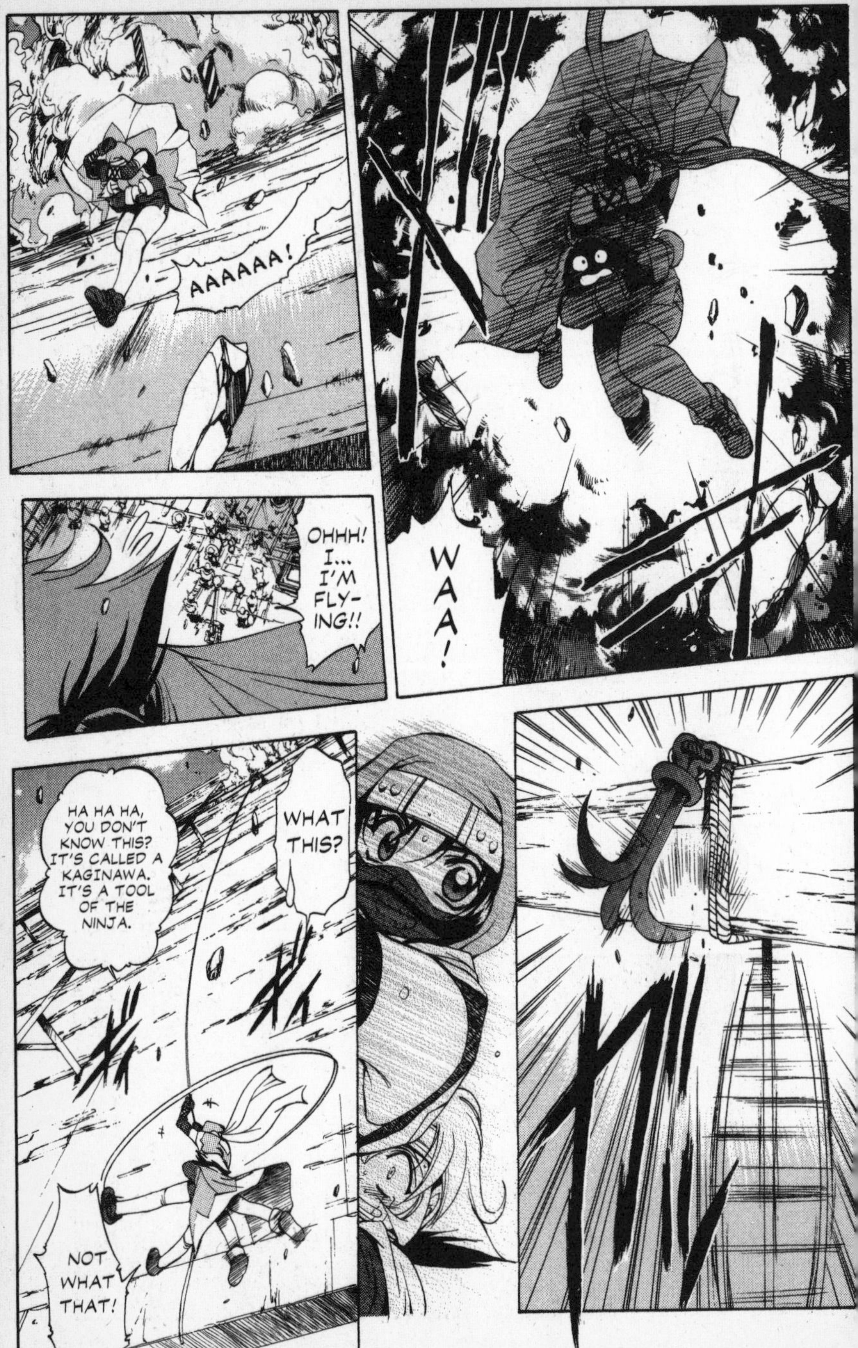

WAAA!
AAAAAA!
OHHH! I... I'M FLY-ING!!
WHAT THIS?
HA HA HA, YOU DON'T KNOW THIS? IT'S CALLED A KAGINAWA. IT'S A TOOL OF THE NINJA.
NOT WHAT THAT!

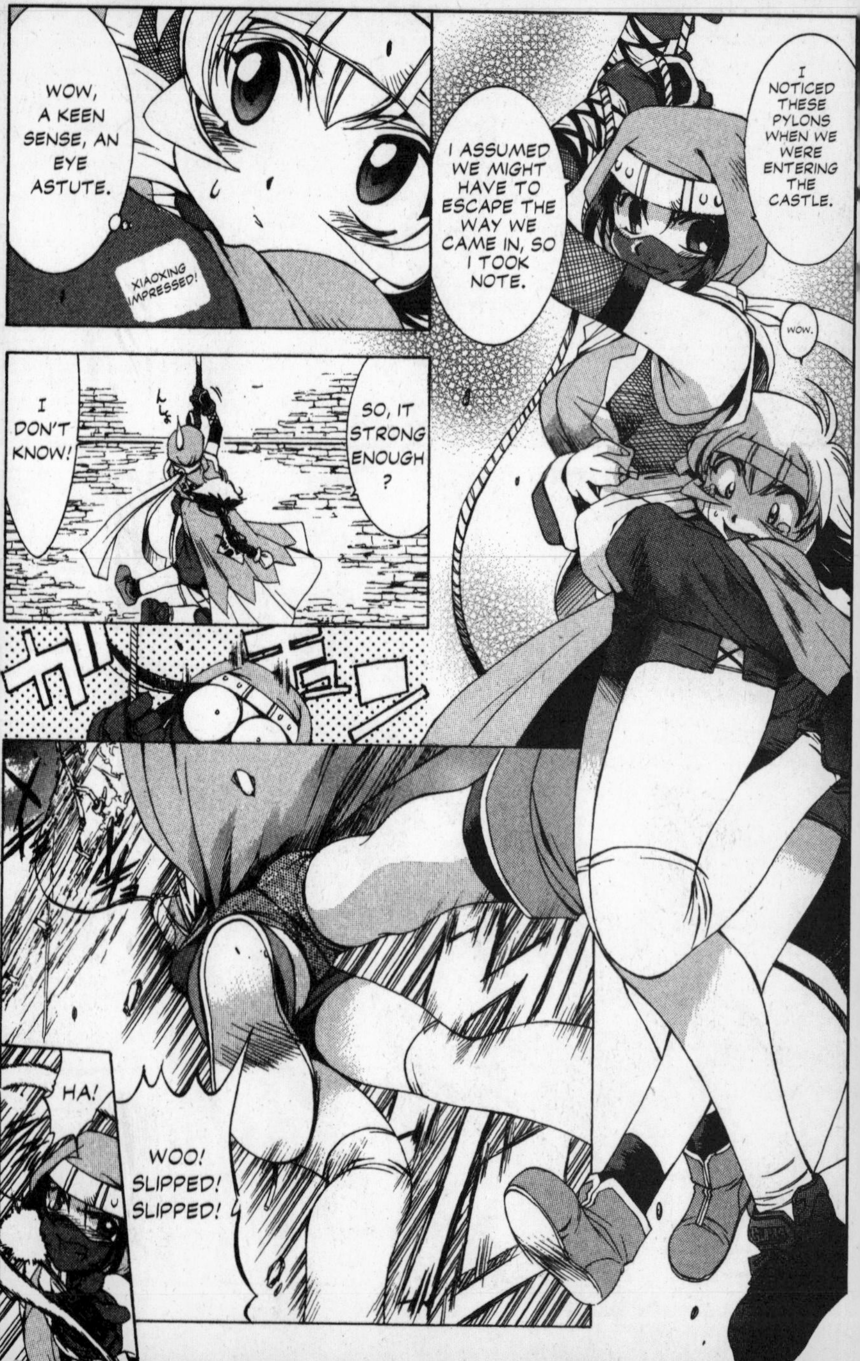
I NOTICED THESE PYLONS WHEN WE WERE ENTERING THE CASTLE.
I ASSUMED WE MIGHT HAVE TO ESCAPE THE WAY WE CAME IN, SO I TOOK NOTE.
WOW.
WOW, A KEEN SENSE, AN EYE ASTUTE.
XIAOXING IMPRESSED!
SO, IT STRONG ENOUGH?
I DON'T KNOW!
HA!
WOO! SLIPPED! SLIPPED!

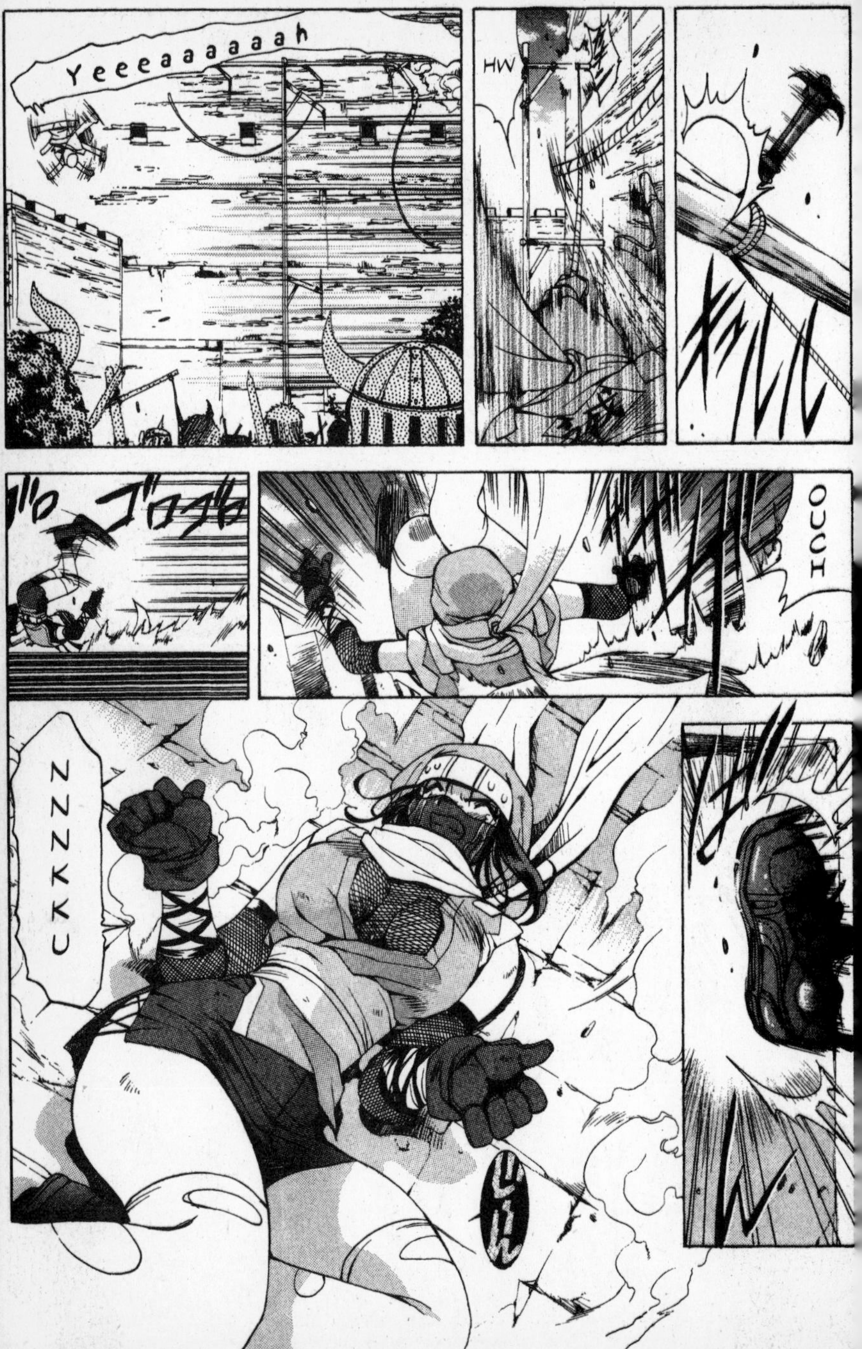
Yeeeaaaaaaah
HW
OUCH
NNNKKU

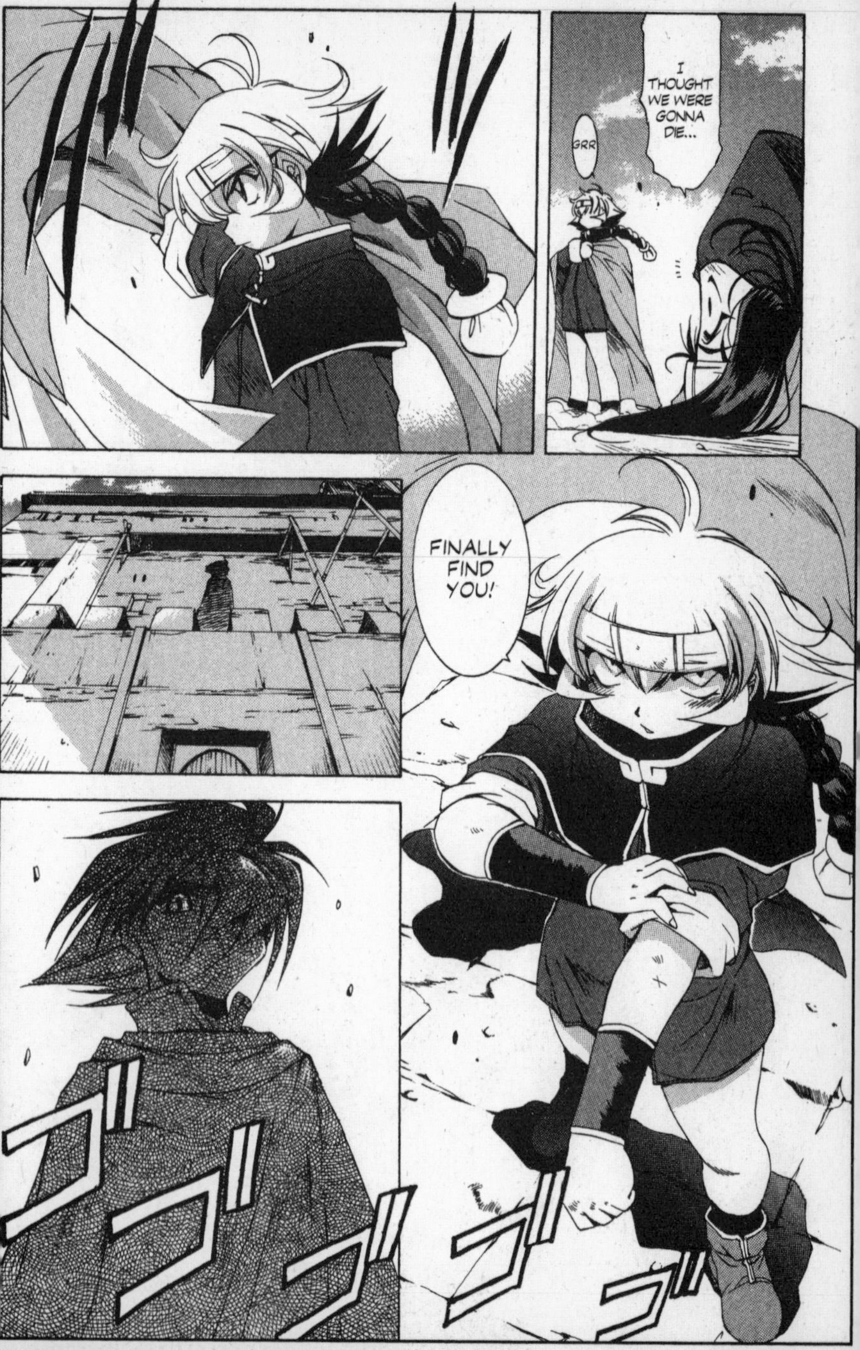
I THOUGHT WE WERE GONNA DIE...
GRR
FINALLY FIND YOU!

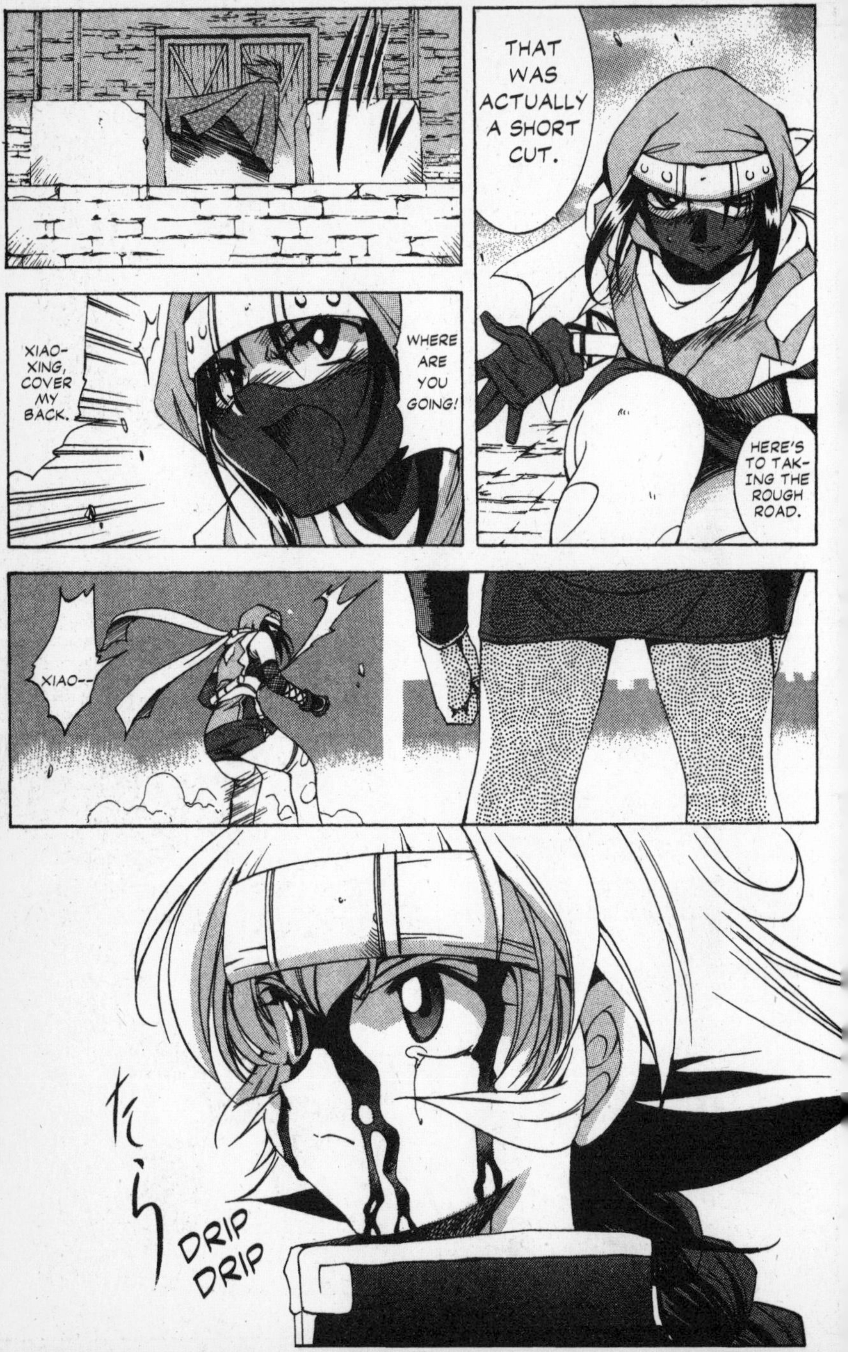
THAT WAS ACTUALLY A SHORT CUT.
HERE'S TO TAKING THE ROUGH ROAD.
WHERE ARE YOU GOING!
XIAO-XING, COVER MY BACK.
XIAO--
たら
DRIP DRIP

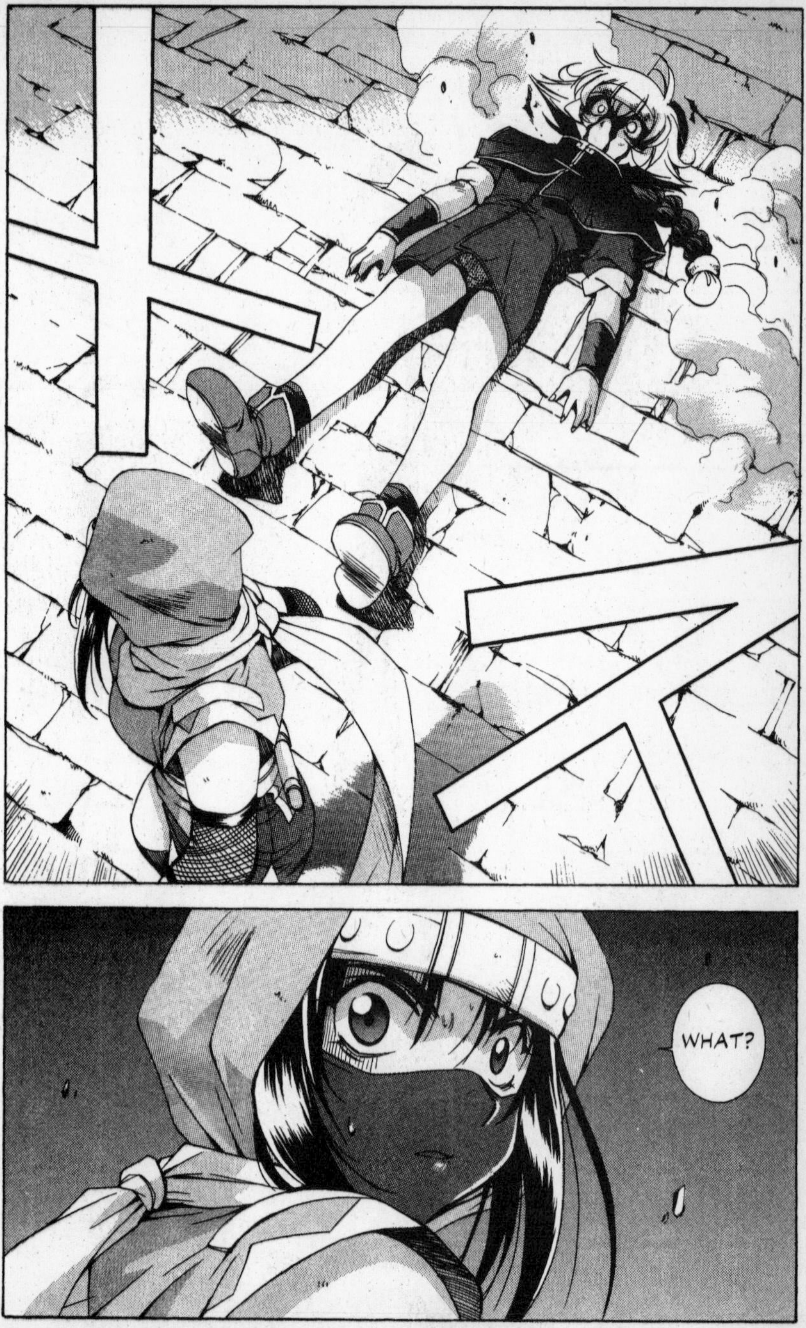
WHAT?

Episode 35 The Gimmick Castle and the Shadow Castle, Part 3

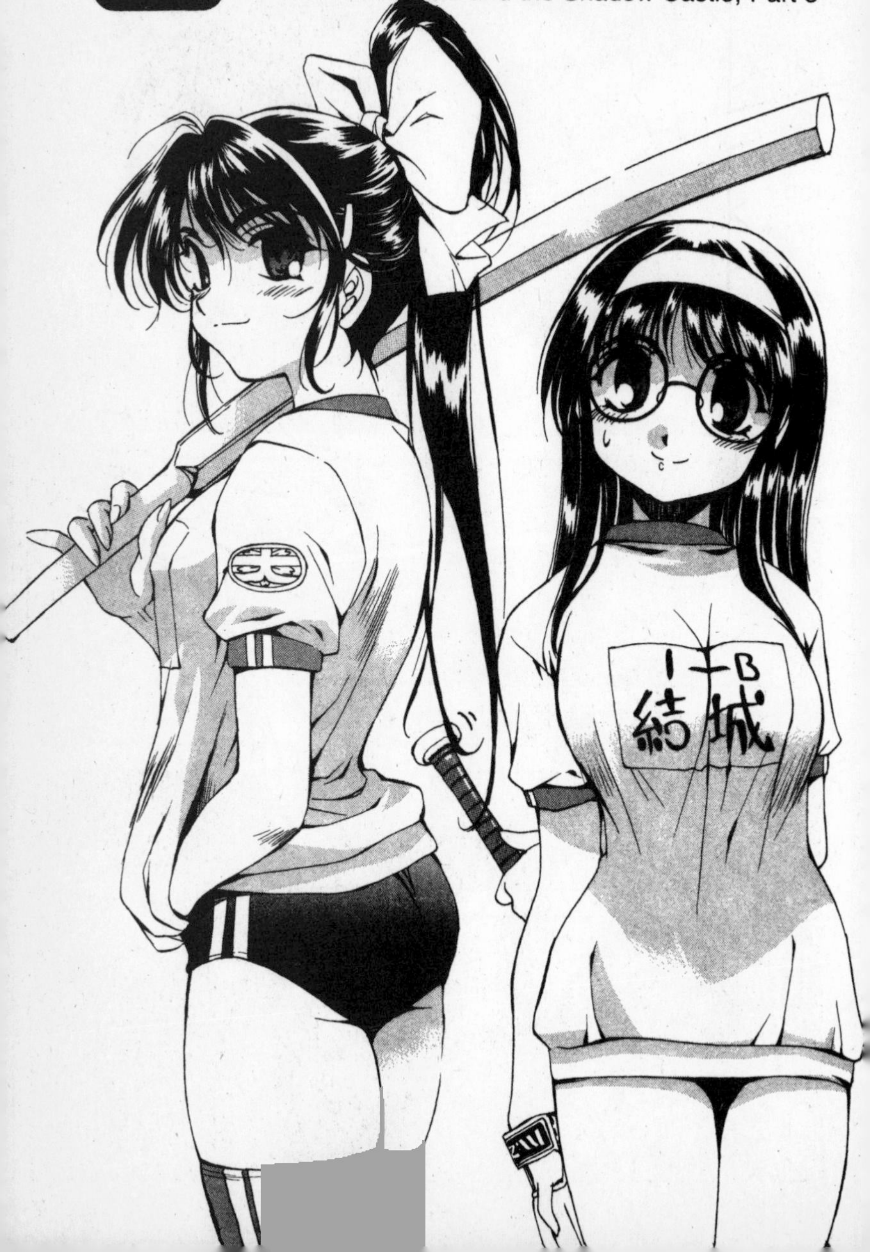
1-B
結城

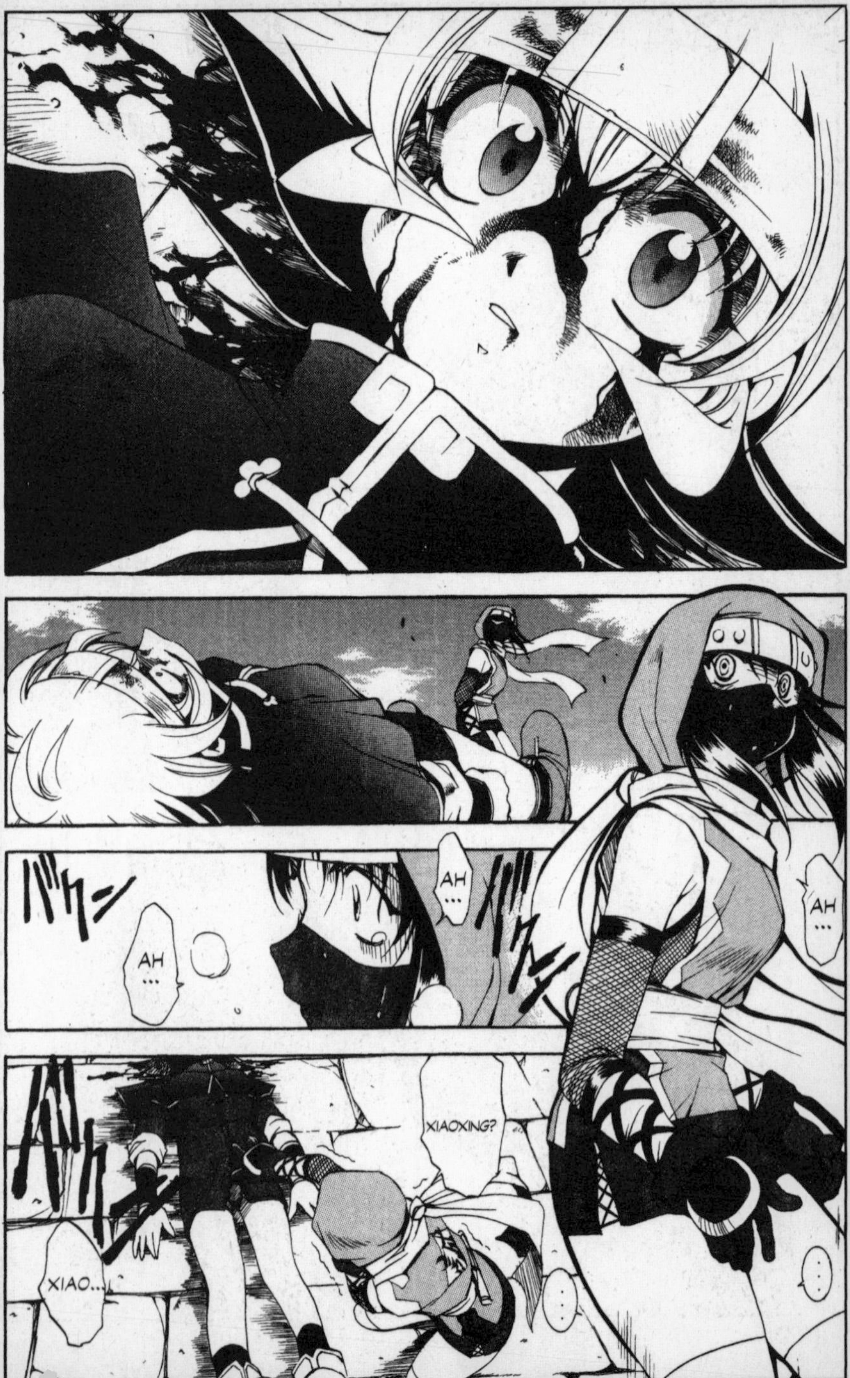

AH ...
AH ...
AH ...
...
XIAOXING?
...
XIAO...

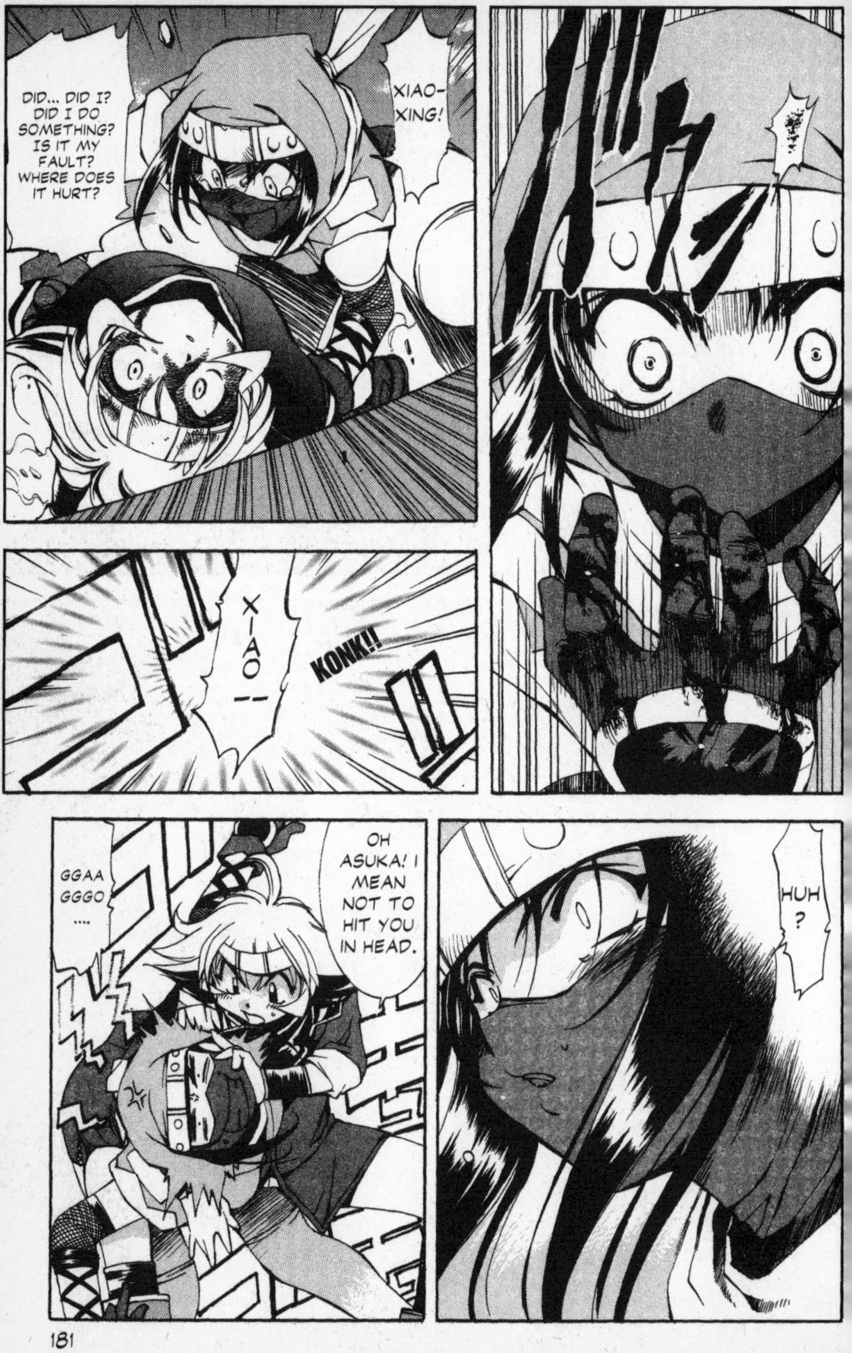
XIAO-XING!
DID... DID I? DID I DO SOMETHING? IS IT MY FAULT? WHERE DOES IT HURT?
XIAO--
KONK!!
HUH?
OH ASUKA! I MEAN NOT TO HIT YOU IN HEAD.
GGAA GGGO ....

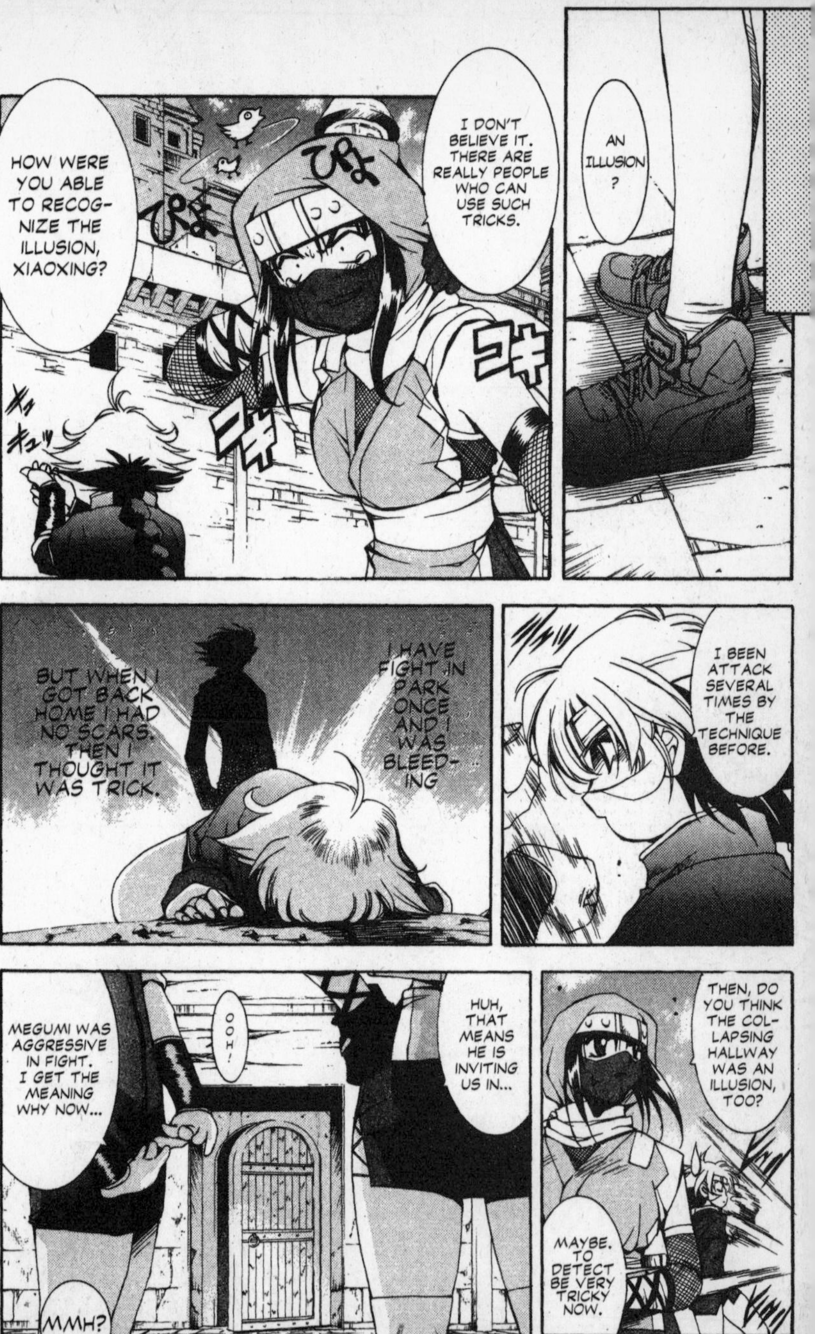
AN ILLUSION ?
I DON'T BELIEVE IT. THERE ARE REALLY PEOPLE WHO CAN USE SUCH TRICKS.
ぴよ
ぴよ
コキ
コキ
HOW WERE YOU ABLE TO RECOG-NIZE THE ILLUSION, XIAOXING?
I BEEN ATTACK SEVERAL TIMES BY THE TECHNIQUE BEFORE.
I HAVE FIGHT IN PARK ONCE AND I WAS BLEED-ING
BUT WHEN I GOT BACK HOME I HAD NO SCARS. THEN I THOUGHT IT WAS TRICK.
THEN, DO YOU THINK THE COL-LAPSING HALLWAY WAS AN ILLUSION, TOO?
MAYBE. TO DETECT BE VERY TRICKY NOW.
HUH, THAT MEANS HE IS INVITING US IN...
OOH!
MEGUMI WAS AGGRESSIVE IN FIGHT. I GET THE MEANING WHY NOW...
MMH?

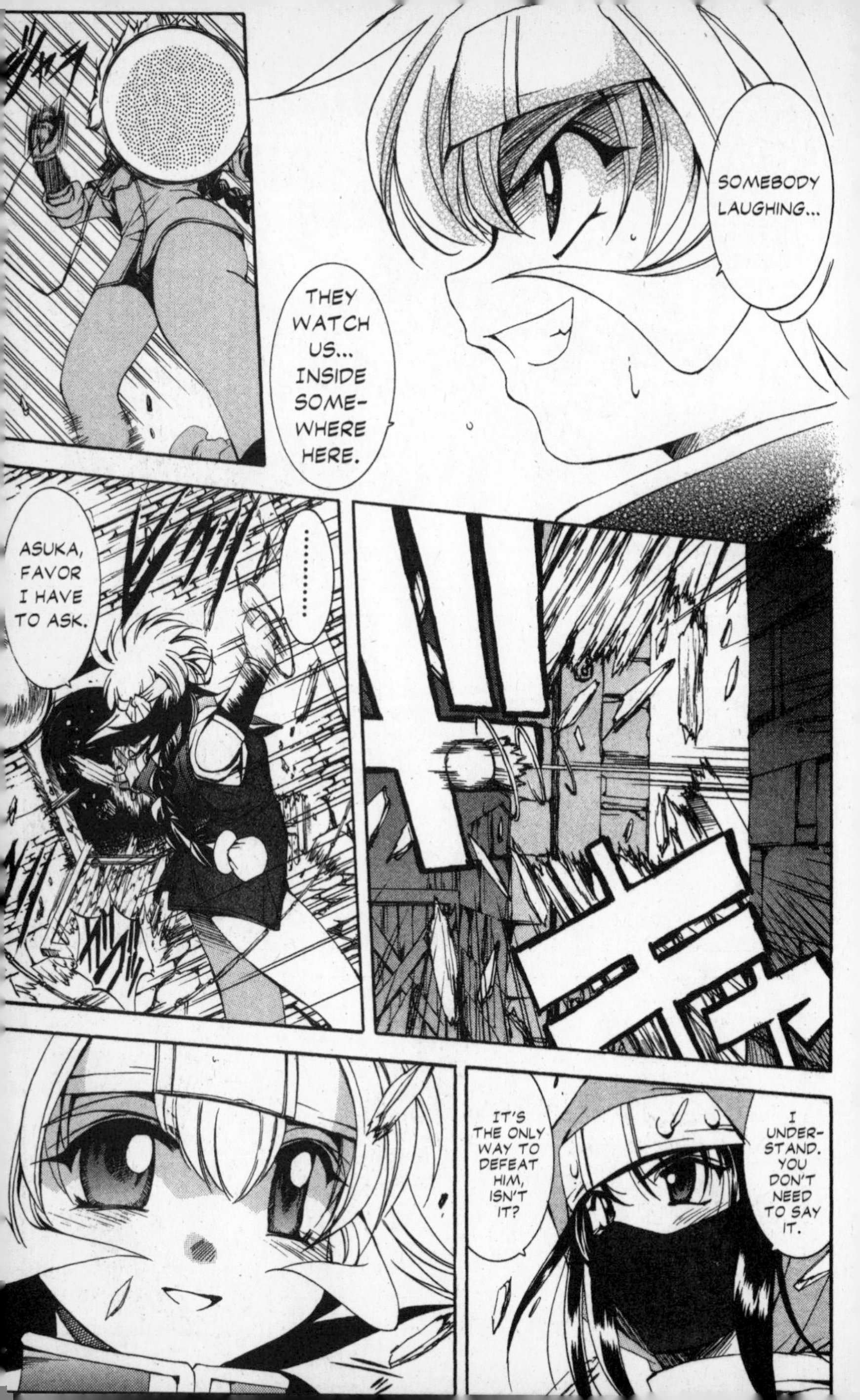

SOMEBODY LAUGHING...
THEY WATCH US... INSIDE SOME-WHERE HERE.
......
ASUKA, FAVOR I HAVE TO ASK.
I UNDER-STAND. YOU DON'T NEED TO SAY IT.
IT'S THE ONLY WAY TO DEFEAT HIM, ISN'T IT?

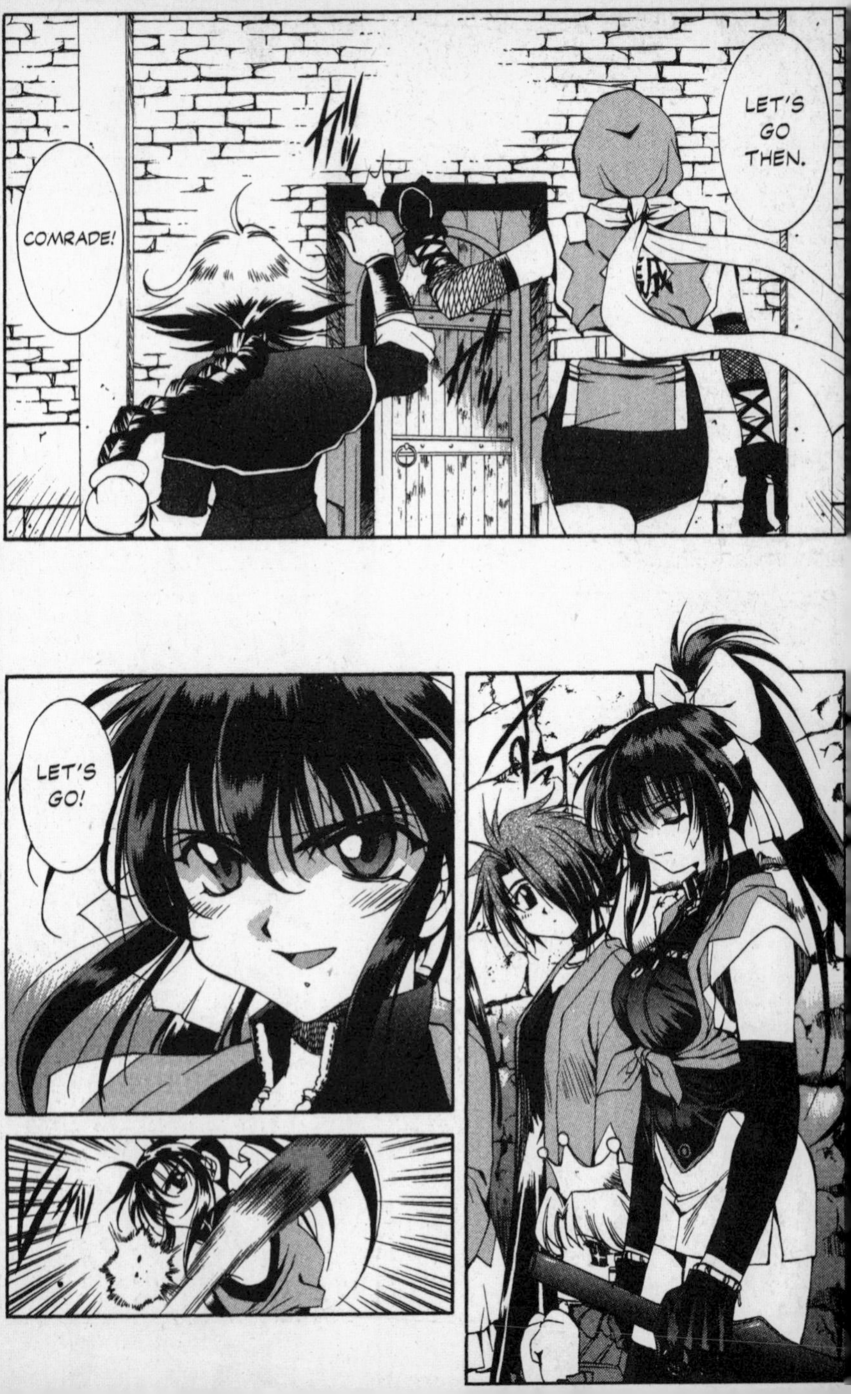
LET'S GO THEN.
COMRADE!
LET'S GO!

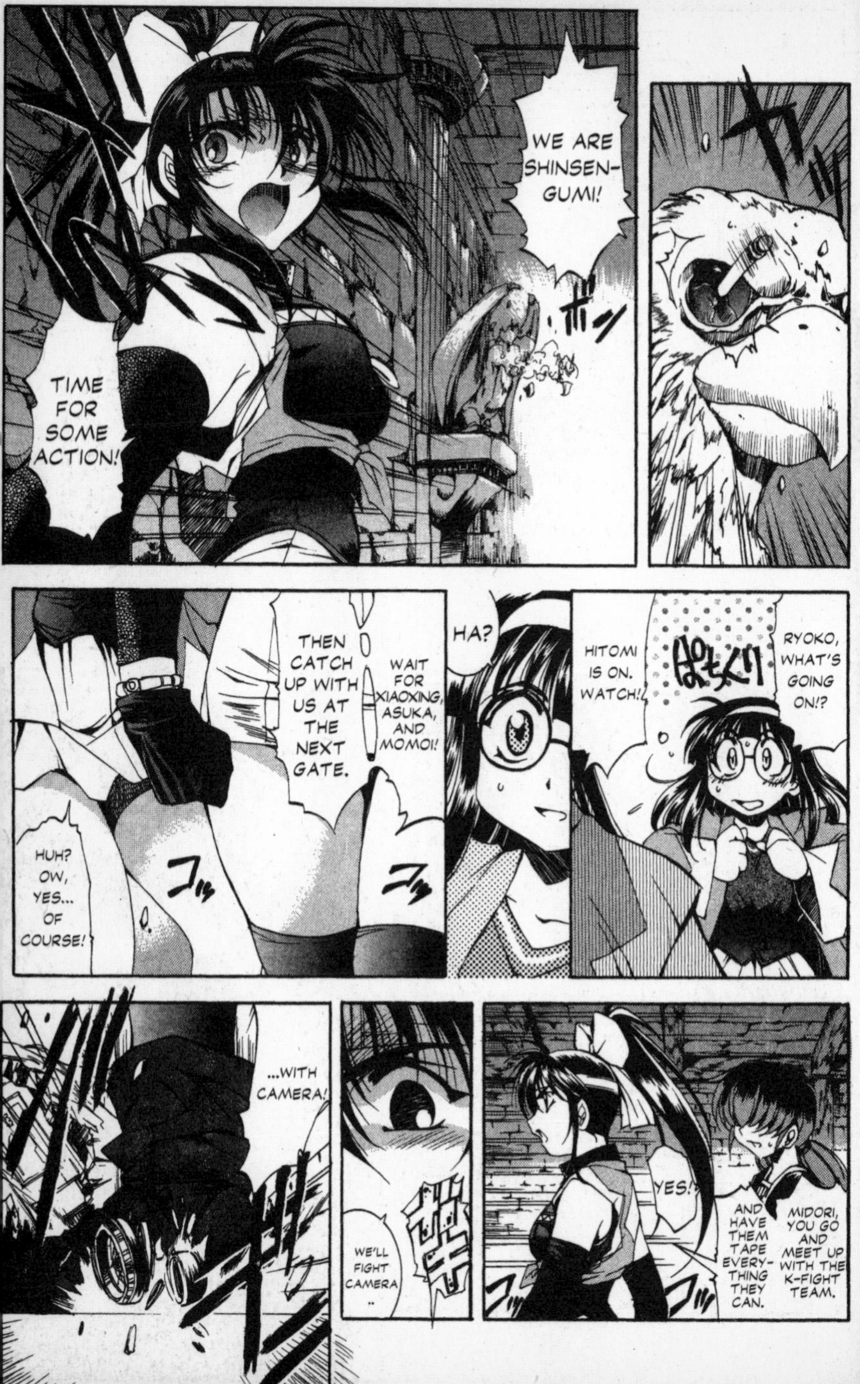
WE ARE SHINSEN-GUMI!
TIME FOR SOME ACTION!
RYOKO, WHAT'S GOING ON!?
ぱちくり
HITOMI IS ON. WATCH!
HA?
WAIT FOR XIAOXING, ASUKA, AND MOMOI!
THEN CATCH UP WITH US AT THE NEXT GATE.
HUH? OW, YES... OF COURSE!
MIDORI, YOU GO AND MEET UP WITH THE K-FIGHT TEAM.
AND HAVE THEM TAPE EVERYTHING THEY CAN.
YES!
WE'LL FIGHT CAMERA ..
...WITH CAMERA!

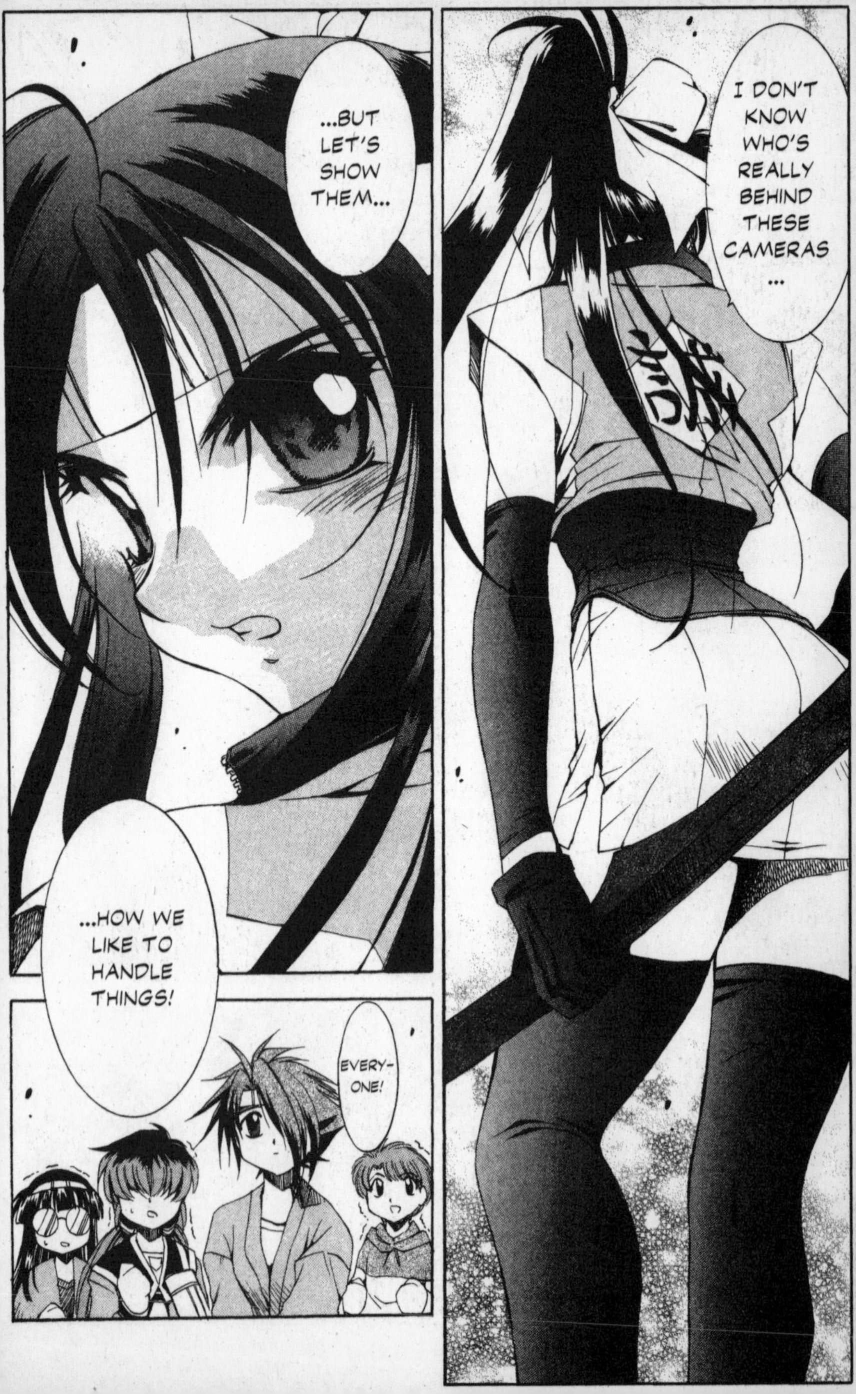
I DON'T KNOW WHO'S REALLY BEHIND THESE CAMERAS ...
...BUT LET'S SHOW THEM...
...HOW WE LIKE TO HANDLE THINGS!
EVERY-ONE!

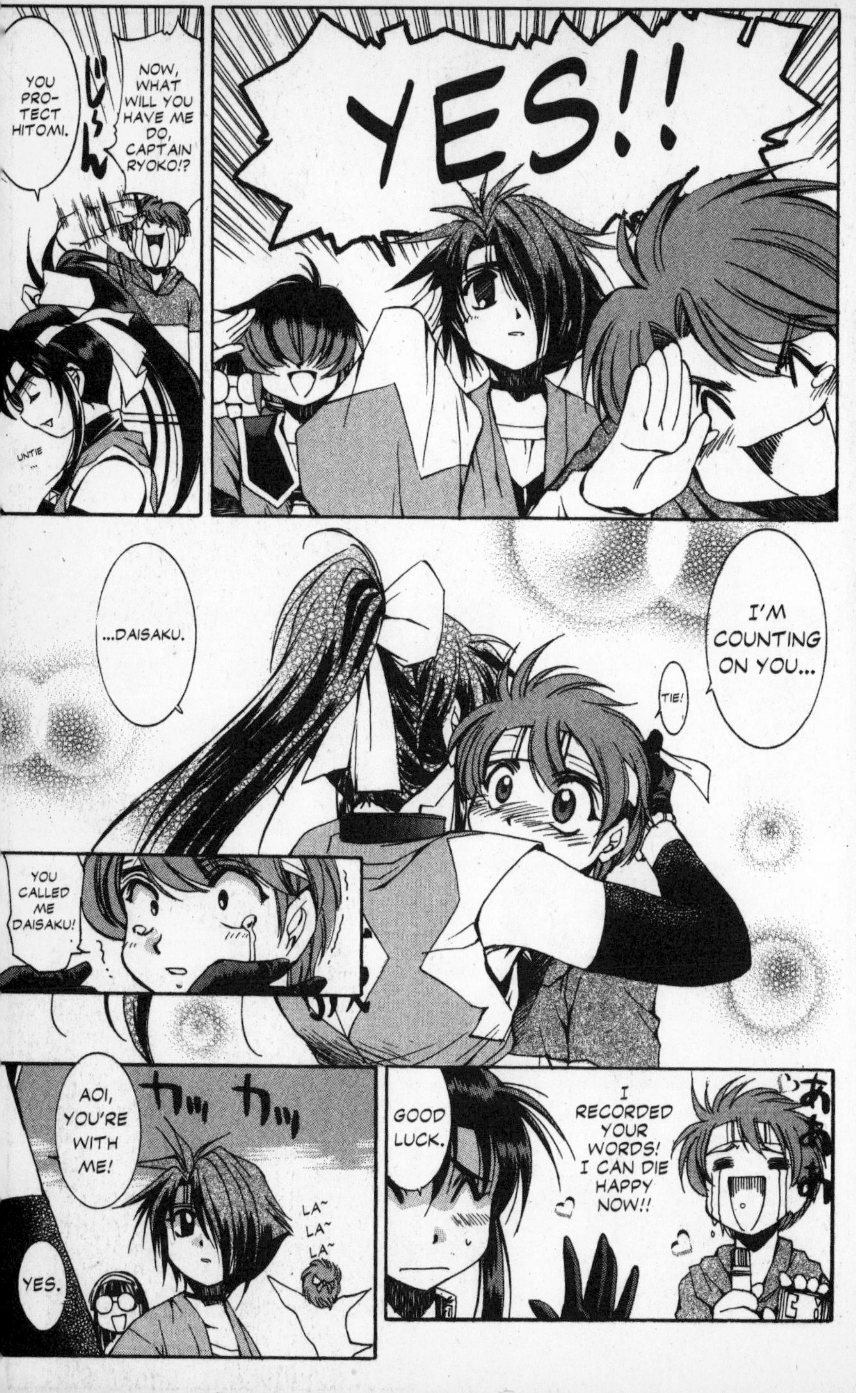
YES!!
NOW, WHAT WILL YOU HAVE ME DO, CAPTAIN RYOKO!?
YOU PROTECT HITOMI.
UNTIE ...
I'M COUNTING ON YOU...
TIE!
...DAISAKU.
YOU CALLED ME DAISAKU!
I RECORDED YOUR WORDS! I CAN DIE HAPPY NOW!!
GOOD LUCK.
AOI, YOU'RE WITH ME!
カッ カッ
LA~ LA~ LA~
YES.

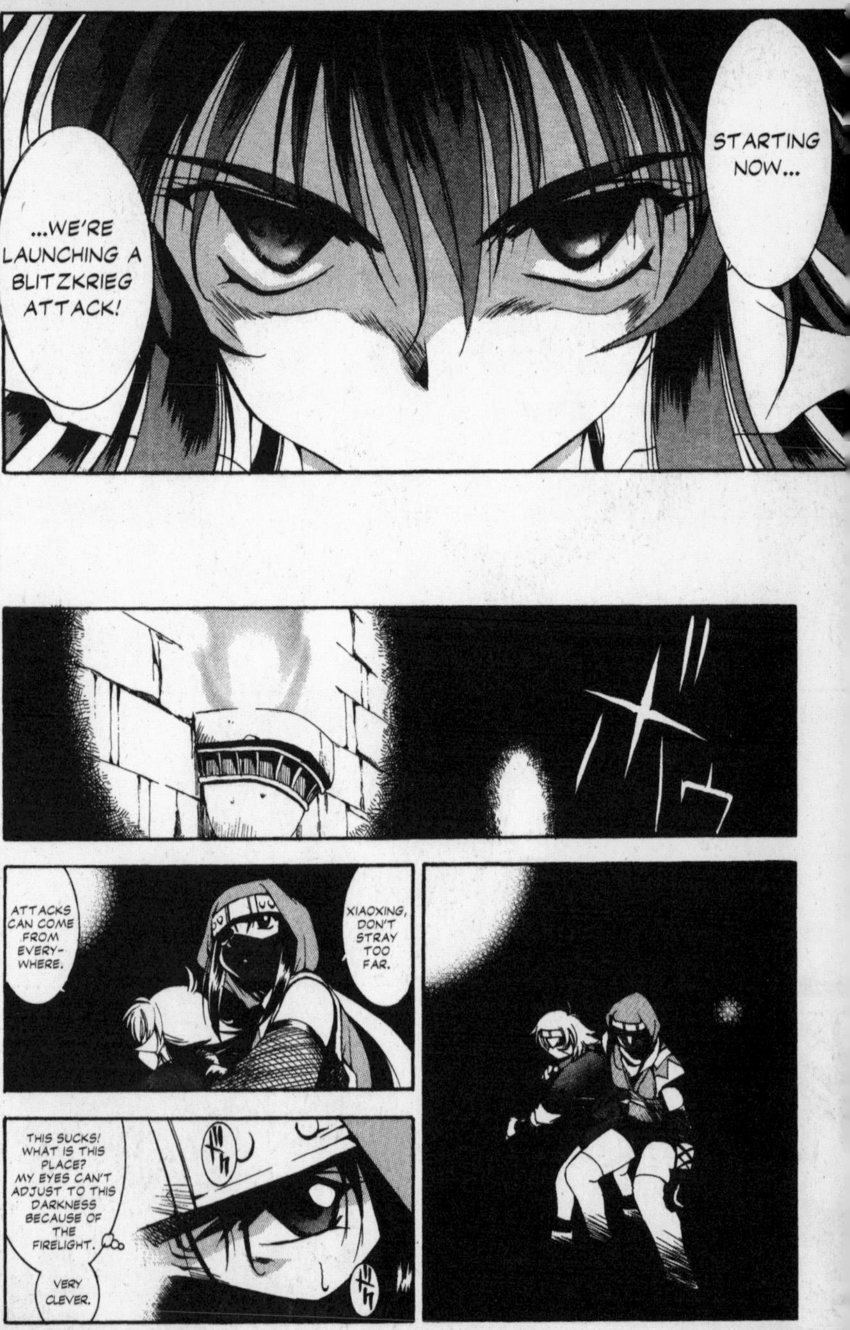
STARTING NOW...
...WE'RE LAUNCHING A BLITZKRIEG ATTACK!
XIAOXING, DON'T STRAY TOO FAR.
ATTACKS CAN COME FROM EVERY-WHERE.
THIS SUCKS! WHAT IS THIS PLACE? MY EYES CAN'T ADJUST TO THIS DARKNESS BECAUSE OF THE FIRELIGHT.
VERY CLEVER.

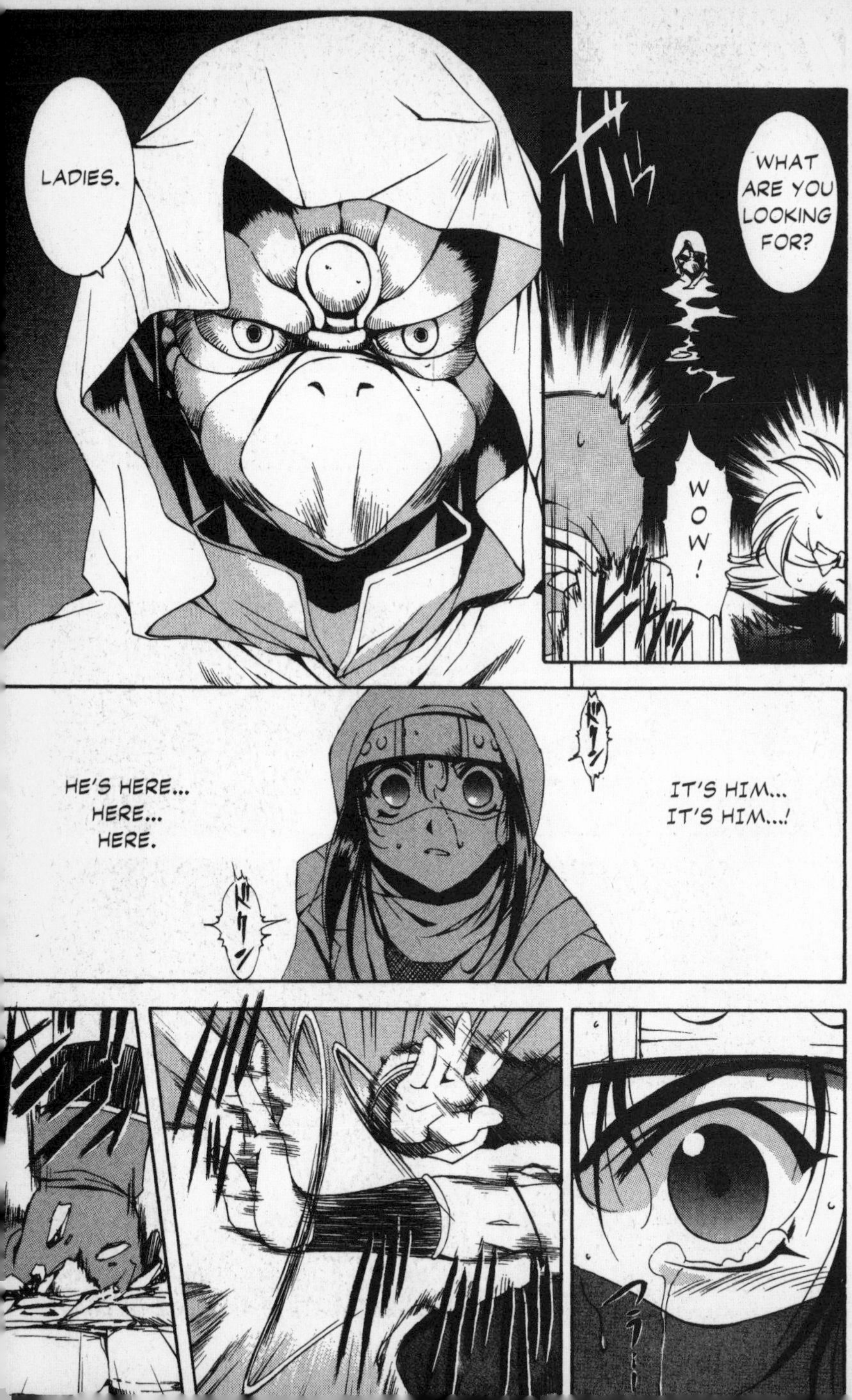
WHAT ARE YOU LOOKING FOR?
WOW!
LADIES.
IT'S HIM... IT'S HIM...!
HE'S HERE... HERE... HERE.

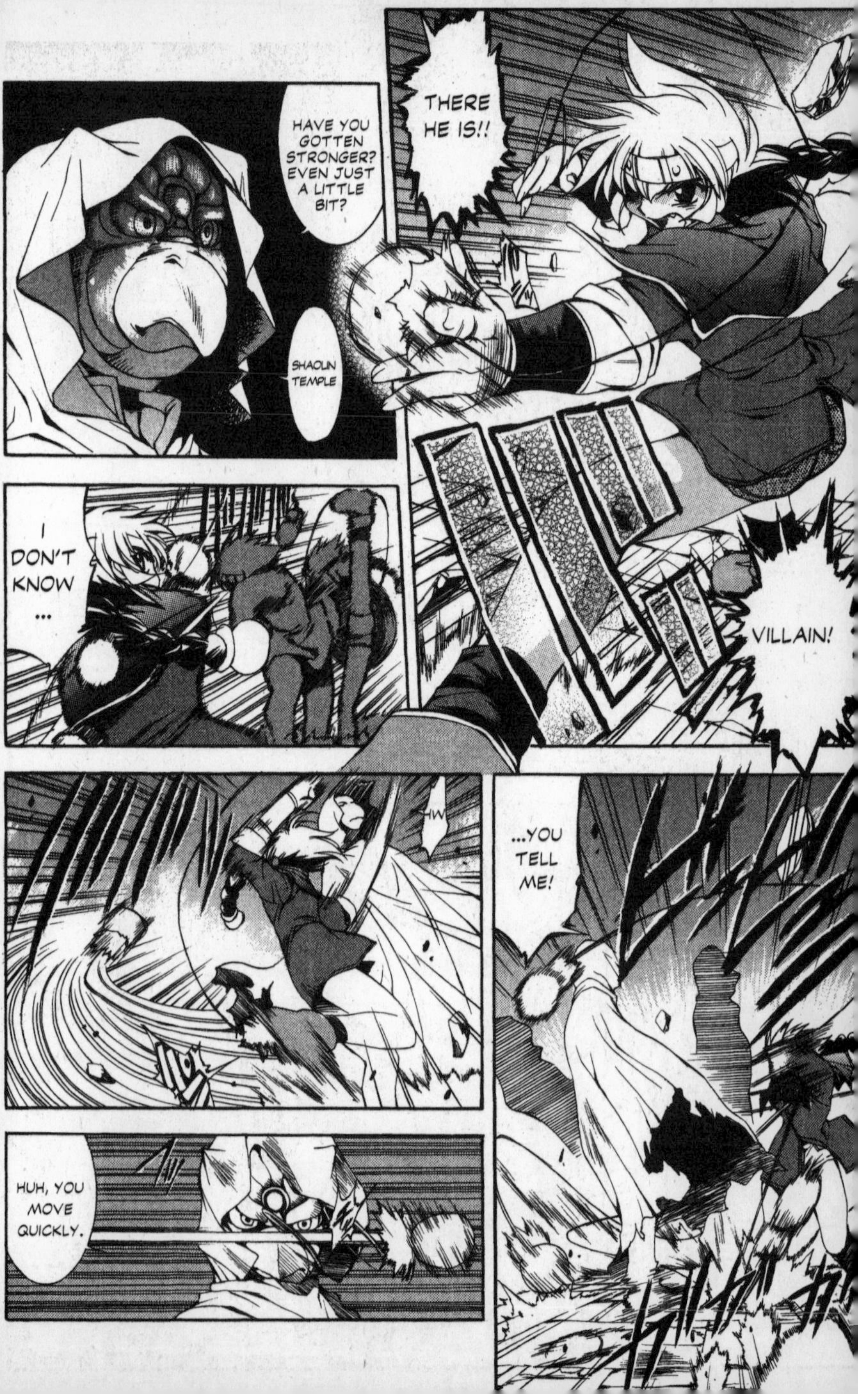
THERE HE IS!!
HAVE YOU GOTTEN STRONGER? EVEN JUST A LITTLE BIT?
SHAOLIN TEMPLE
VILLAIN!
I DON'T KNOW ...
...YOU TELL ME!
HUH, YOU MOVE QUICKLY.

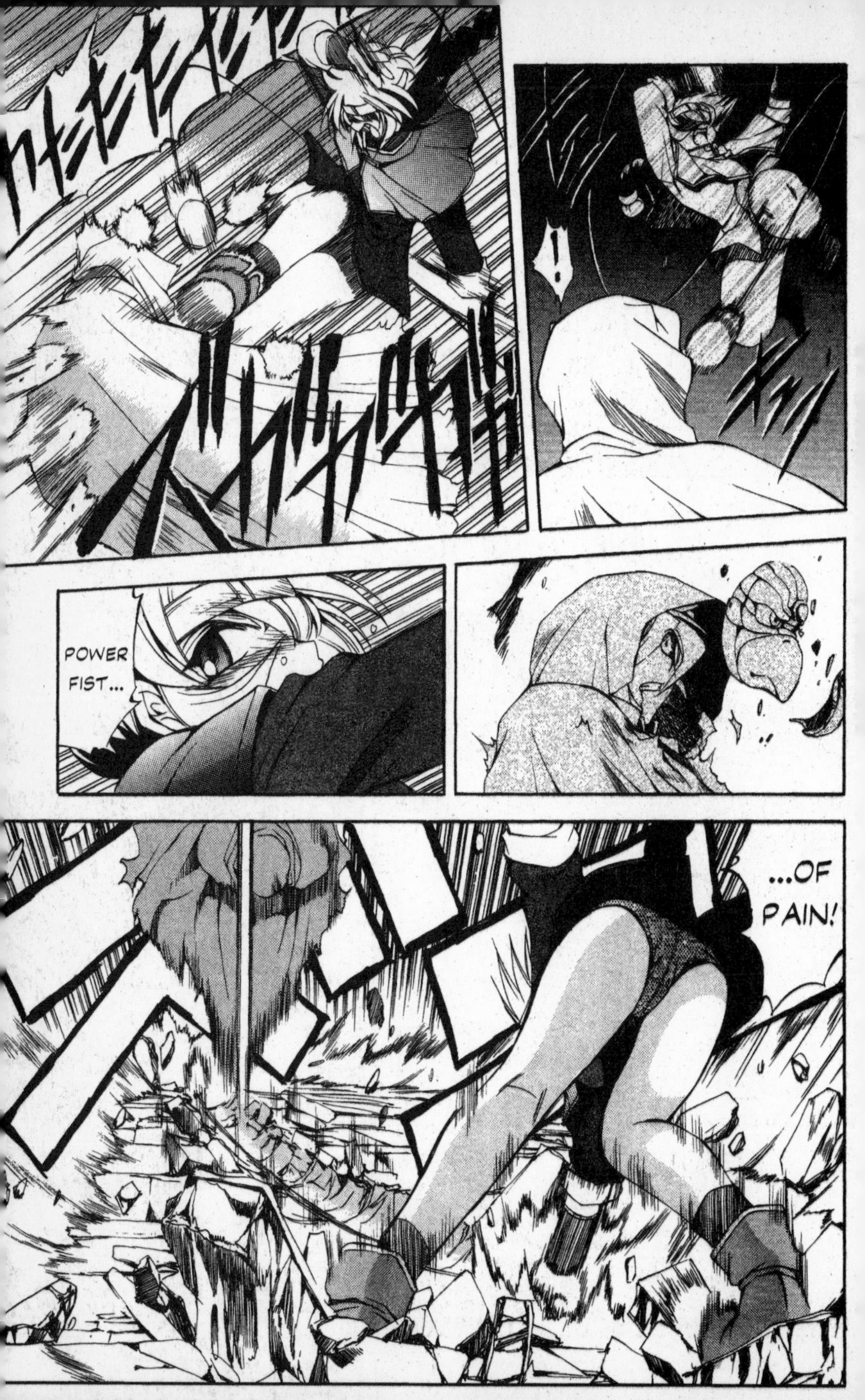
!
POWER FIST...
...OF PAIN!

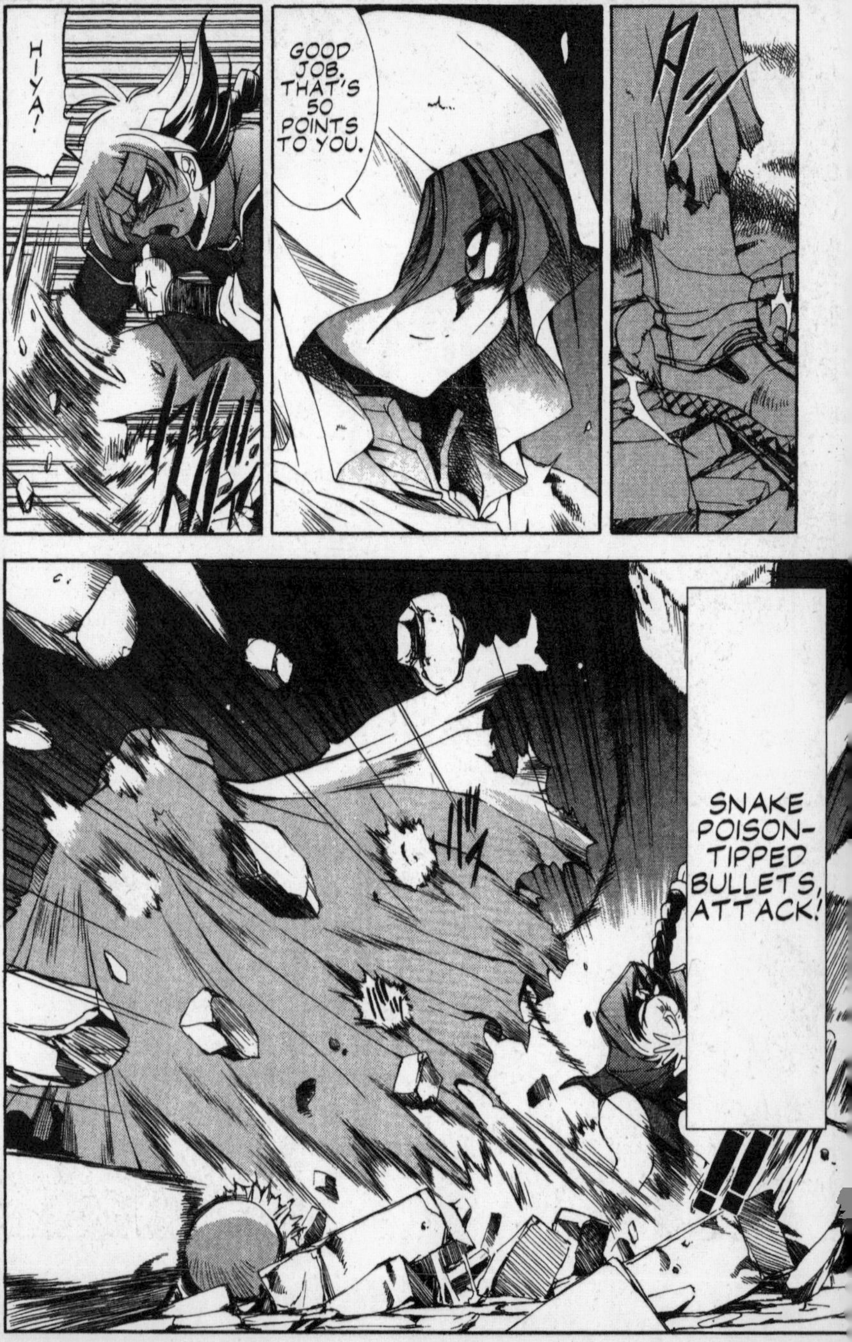
HIYA!
GOOD JOB. THAT'S 50 POINTS TO YOU.
SNAKE POISON-TIPPED BULLETS, ATTACK!

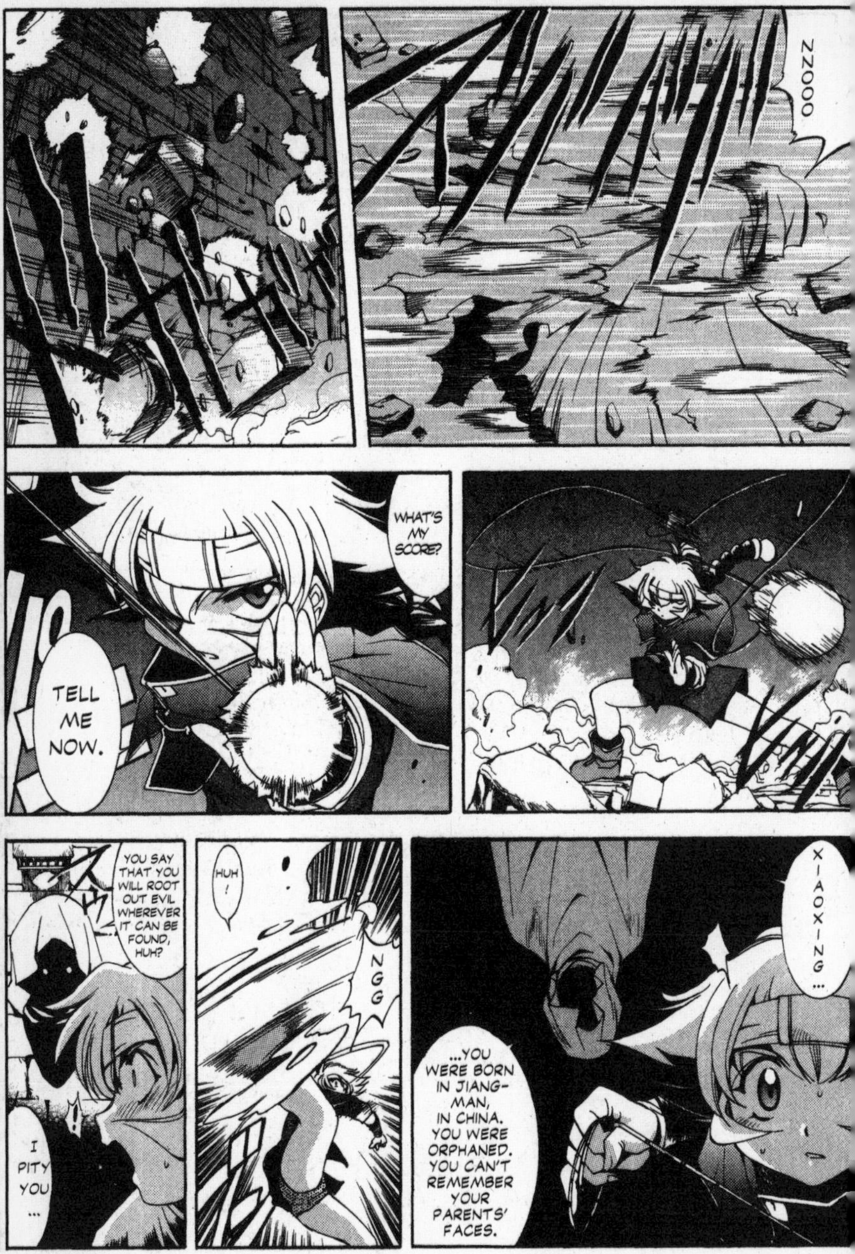
NZOOO
WHAT'S MY SCORE?
TELL ME NOW.
XIAOXING...
...YOU WERE BORN IN JIANG-MAN, IN CHINA. YOU WERE ORPHANED. YOU CAN'T REMEMBER YOUR PARENTS' FACES.
HUH!
NGG
YOU SAY THAT YOU WILL ROOT OUT EVIL WHEREVER IT CAN BE FOUND, HUH?
I PITY YOU...

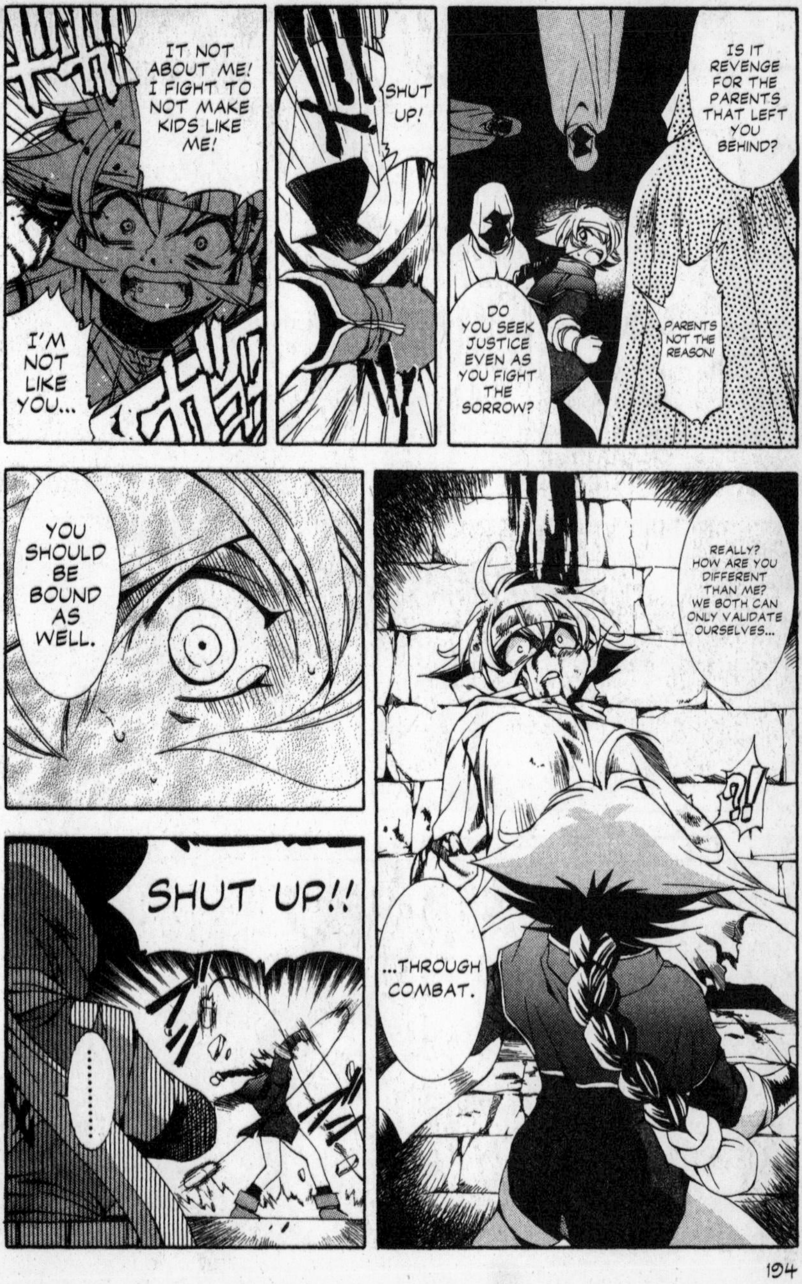
IS IT REVENGE FOR THE PARENTS THAT LEFT YOU BEHIND?
PARENTS NOT THE REASON!
DO YOU SEEK JUSTICE EVEN AS YOU FIGHT THE SORROW?
SHUT UP!
IT NOT ABOUT ME! I FIGHT TO NOT MAKE KIDS LIKE ME!
I'M NOT LIKE YOU...
REALLY? HOW ARE YOU DIFFERENT THAN ME? WE BOTH CAN ONLY VALIDATE OURSELVES...
...THROUGH COMBAT.
YOU SHOULD BE BOUND AS WELL.
SHUT UP!!
......

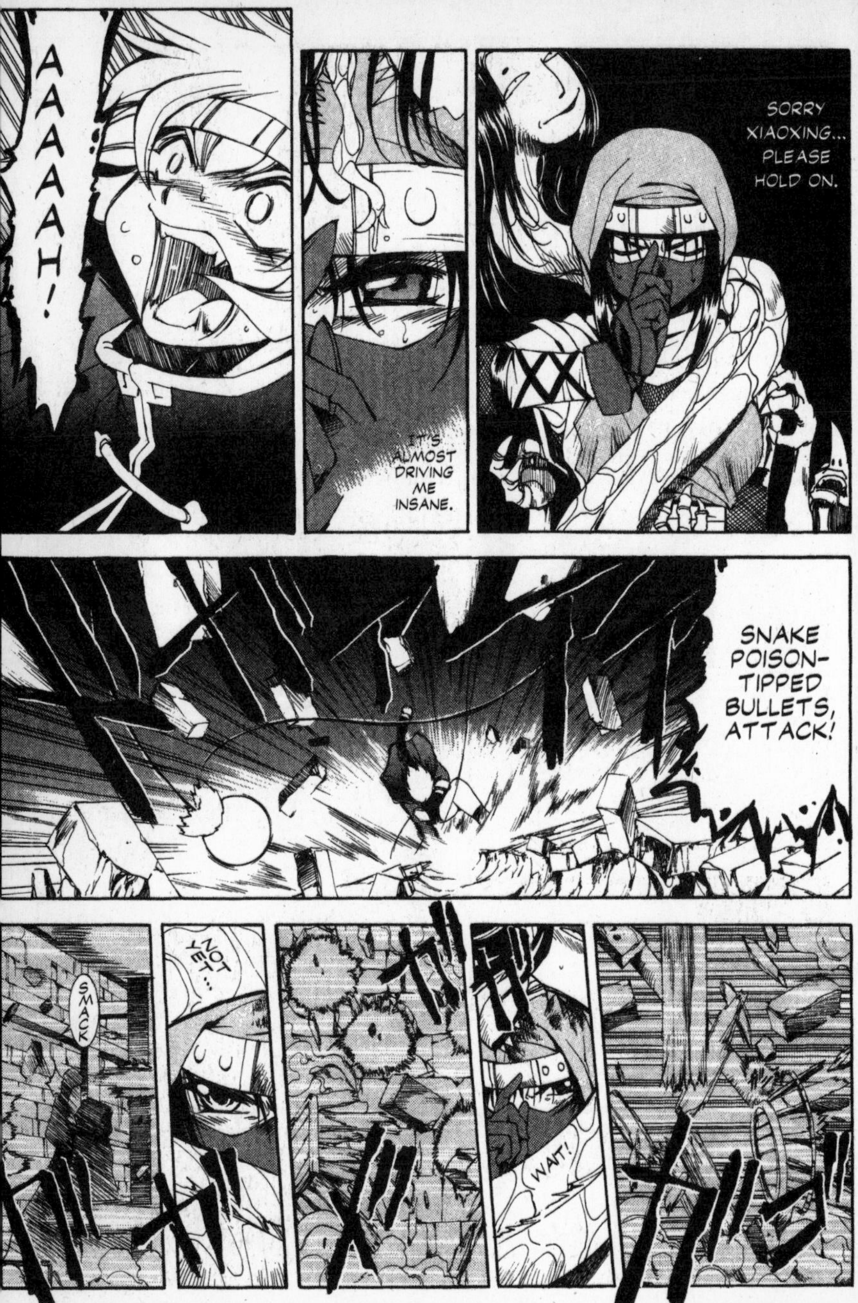
SORRY XIAOXING... PLEASE HOLD ON.
IT'S ALMOST DRIVING ME INSANE.
AAAAAAH!
SNAKE POISON-TIPPED BULLETS, ATTACK!
WAIT!
NOT YET...
SMACK

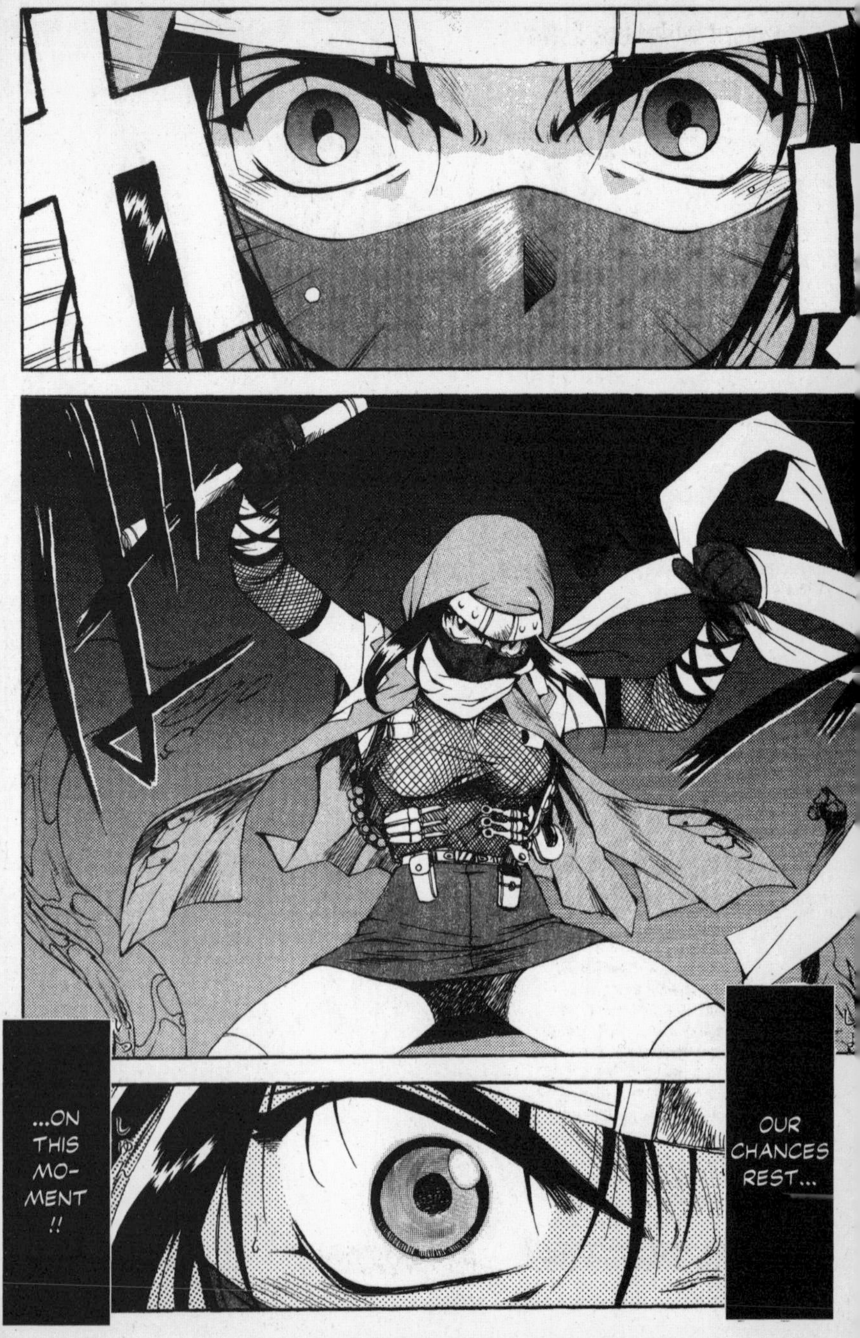
OUR CHANCES REST...
...ON THIS MOMENT!!

A Moment with Sora Inoue:

EVERY DAY IS A REAL BOUT DAY!!

REAL BOUT HIGHSCHOOL

WE'VE PASSED THE MIDDLE OF THE "SHINSENGUMI" STORY LINE! ARE YOU GUYS ENJOYING THE MANGA? I'VE BEEN SO STRESSED WRITING THIS MANGA, AGONIZING PHRASES SUCH AS "WOO" AND "GUGAA" HAVE BEEN SPILLING FROM MY MOUTH.

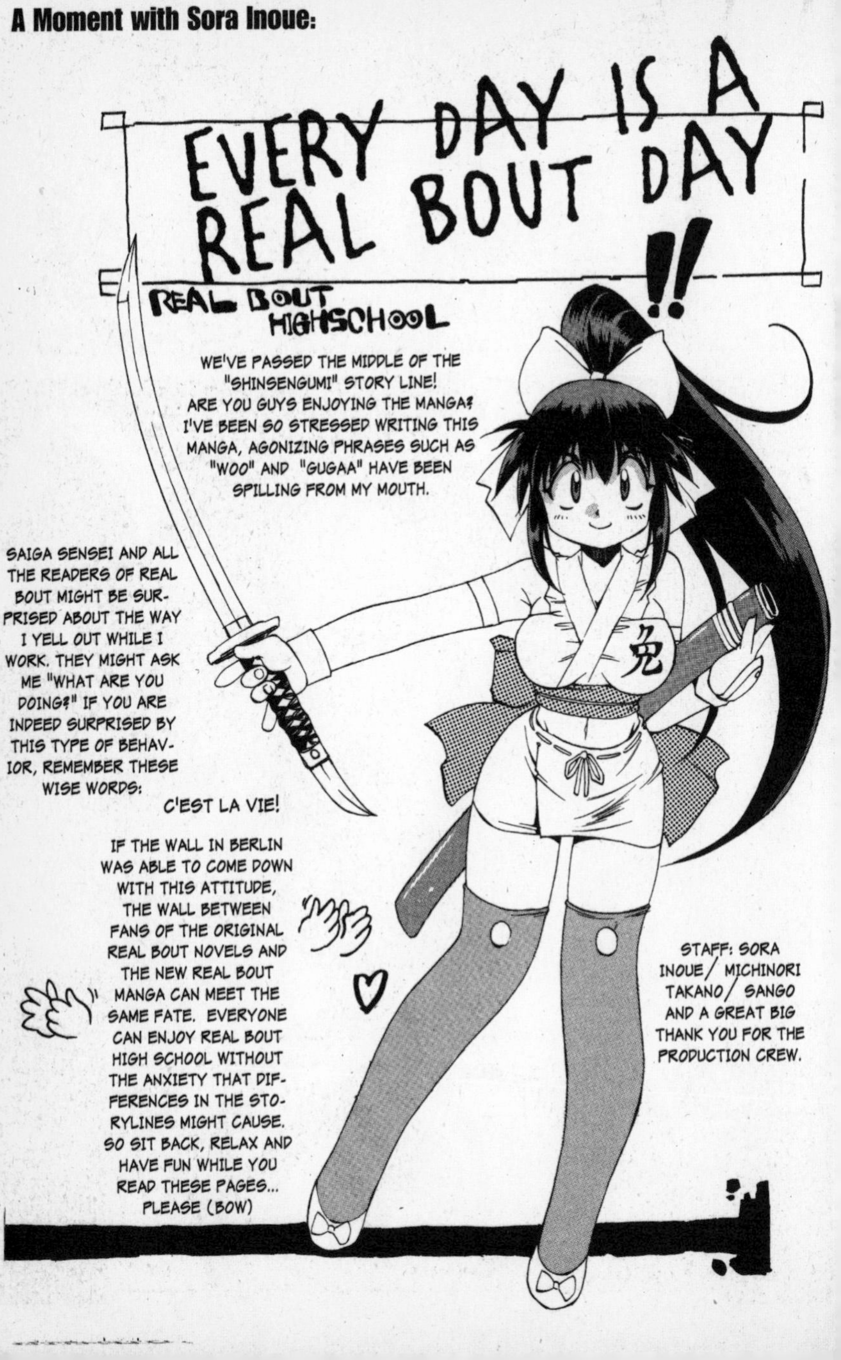

兎

SAIGA SENSEI AND ALL THE READERS OF REAL BOUT MIGHT BE SURPRISED ABOUT THE WAY I YELL OUT WHILE I WORK. THEY MIGHT ASK ME "WHAT ARE YOU DOING?" IF YOU ARE INDEED SURPRISED BY THIS TYPE OF BEHAVIOR, REMEMBER THESE WISE WORDS:

C'EST LA VIE!

IF THE WALL IN BERLIN WAS ABLE TO COME DOWN WITH THIS ATTITUDE, THE WALL BETWEEN FANS OF THE ORIGINAL REAL BOUT NOVELS AND THE NEW REAL BOUT MANGA CAN MEET THE SAME FATE. EVERYONE CAN ENJOY REAL BOUT HIGH SCHOOL WITHOUT THE ANXIETY THAT DIFFERENCES IN THE STORYLINES MIGHT CAUSE. SO SIT BACK, RELAX AND HAVE FUN WHILE YOU READ THESE PAGES... PLEASE (BOW)

STAFF: SORA INOUE / MICHINORI TAKANO / SANGO AND A GREAT BIG THANK YOU FOR THE PRODUCTION CREW.

SAN PABLO

STOP!

This is the back of the book. You wouldn't want to spoil a great ending!

This book is printed "manga-style," in the authentic Japanese right-to-left format. Since none of the artwork has been flipped or altered, readers get to experience the story just as the creator intended. You've been asking for it, so TOKYOPOP® delivered: authentic, hot-off-the-press, and far more fun!

DIRECTIONS

1
2
3
4
5
6
7
8
9
10

If this is your first time reading manga-style, here's a quick guide to help you understand how it works.

It's easy... just start in the top right panel and follow the numbers. Have fun, and look for more 100% authentic manga from TOKYOPOP®!

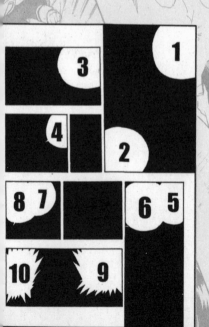

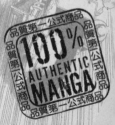